2019 10-8
Mike Hill

Custer's Gray Rival:

The Life of Confederate Major General Thomas Lafayette Rosser

Also by Sheridan R. Barringer:

Fighting for General Lee:
Confederate General Rufus Barringer
and the North Carolina Cavalry Brigade

Winner of:

2016 Douglas Southall Freeman History Book Award.

2016 North Carolina Society of Historians History Book Award.

Custer's Gray Rival:

The Life of Confederate Major General Thomas Lafayette Rosser

Sheridan **R.** Barringer

FOX RUN
PUBLISHING
QUALITY PUBLISHING ONE BOOK AT A TIME

Publisher's Cataloging-in-Publication Data
provided by Five Rainbows Cataloging Services

Names: Barringer, Sheridan Reid, 1943- author. | Wittenberg, Eric J., 1961- writer of introduction.
Title: Custer's gray rival : the life of Confederate Major General Thomas Lafayette Rosser / Sheridan Reid Barringer ; [introduction by] Eric J. Wittenberg.
Description: Burlington, NC : Fox Run Publishers, 2019. | Includes bibliographical references and index.
Identifiers: LCCN 2019938476 | ISBN 978-1-945602-08-5 (hardcover) | ISBN 978-1-945602-09-2 (paperback)
Subjects: LCSH: Rosser, Thomas Lafayette, 1836-1910. | Generals--Confederate States of America--Biography. | Confederate States of America. Army--Biography. | United States--History--Civil War, 1861-1865--Biography. | United States--History--Civil War, 1861-1865--Cavalry operations. | BISAC: BIOGRAPHY & AUTOBIOGRAPHY / Military. | BIOGRAPHY & AUTOBIOGRAPHY / Historical. | HISTORY / United States / Civil War Period (1850-1877)
Classification: LCC E467.1.R76 B37 2019 (print) | LCC E467.1.R76 (ebook) | DDC 973.7/42--dc23.

Cover design by Sandra Miller Linhart

Published by
Fox Run Publishing LLC
2966 South Church Street, #305
Burlington, NC 27215
http://www.foxrunpub.com/

For Shannon and Michael

Table of Contents

List of Maps

List of Images

Preface

Even before I had finished writing about the life of Brig. Gen. Rufus Barringer, the final commander of the North Carolina Cavalry Brigade, I knew I wanted to write another biography about one of Maj. Gen. James Ewell Brown (J. E. B.) Stuart's intrepid cavalry commanders. Of all the men I considered, Maj. Gen. Thomas Lafayette Rosser intrigued me the most. On the surface, Rosser was a charmer, and J. E. B. Stuart, his commanding officer, liked him. He became Stuart's friend and protégé, and Stuart helped advance Rosser's career, supporting him for promotion several times.

To undertake the task, I first had to convince myself that another biography was warranted. To date, the only thorough narrative about Rosser's life is the 1983 biography *Fightin' Tom Rosser, C.S.A.* by Millard K. and Dean M. Bushong. Another book, *Riding with Rosser* by S. Roger Keller, contains Rosser's account regarding parts of the Civil War, which were taken largely from newspaper descriptions. While both books served their purpose for the time in which they were written, I noted areas of Rosser's life that had not been explored and required more explanation. A matter needing further attention involves Rosser's extreme reluctance to accept Stuart's transfer to his cavalry command. Rosser's resistance nearly resulted in his dismissal from the service—only Stuart's intervention saved his military career. Other topics requiring more context include: the complex relationship between Rosser and Stuart; the controversies surrounding Rosser taking command of the 5th Virginia Cavalry Regiment and his subsequent troubles with Lt. Col. Henry Clay Pate; the relationship between Rosser and Col. Thomas T. Munford; the relationship between Rosser and Maj. Gen. Jubal A. Early; the shad bake incident at the battle of Five Forks; Rosser's postwar years; and, finally, chronicling Rosser's life in a more balanced timeline.

In short, my digging revealed a great amount of additional information pertaining to Rosser's life, and, indeed, I found a new chronicling of his life justified. I have undertaken the task, and it is my fervent hope that I have in some measure succeeded. It certainly has been an interesting journey through the life of a controversial and enigmatic Southern cavalry commander.

Sheridan R. Barringer

Acknowledgments

I wish to express my sincere thanks to the following individuals and institutions for their contributions in the creation of this book:

To Rob Maurer and Walter Beam for helping me with the historical details and perspective on the original Rosser family homestead. Walter Beam and his family actually lived in the home from 1936 to 1942. Thanks to Douglass Cochran and Eleanor Cochran, descendants of Maj. Gen. Thomas L. Rosser, for providing some fine photographs of their ancestor and of the final family home, Rugby Hall. To Eric J. Wittenberg for his suggestions and for writing the Introduction to this book. To Edward G. Longacre for his review and comments. Special thanks to my friend and mentor Dr. James M. Morris who reviewed the entire manuscript. To Clark B. Hall, Robert Trout, Robert O'Neil, Dr. James Jewell, Jeffrey Hunt, Michael McCarthy, J. Michael Moore, Tom Schott, Juliane Murphy, and Bryce Suderow for their individual contributions in reviewing chapters and making suggestions for improvements. To cartographer Hal Jespersen for the fine maps. Also, thanks to Tonia J. Smith for her suggestions and encouragement.

To my wife, Pam, for her encouragement and for putting up with all the time I was away from her while doing research or at the computer updating the manuscript.

Thanks to the staffs at the following institutions: Albert and Shirley Small Special Collections Library at the University of Virginia; Virginia State Library; Perkins Library at Duke University; Virginia Historical Society; Southern Historical Collection at the University of North Carolina; Reynolds Library at Wake Forest University; Minnesota Historical Society; National Archives; Library of Congress; Penn State Library; West Virginia Division of Culture and History; Virginia Military Institute; United States Army History Center at Carlisle, Pennsylvania; United States Cavalry Association at Fort Riley, Kansas; Pearce Museum at Navarro College; National Park Service; Fluvanna Historical Society at Palmyra, Virginia; and the United States Military Academy at West Point, New York.

Thanks to my publisher, Fox Run Publishers, and Keith Jones in particular for managing the process of getting this book released. Thanks to a fine editor, Heather Ammel, for her diligent work.

Sheridan R. Barringer

Foreword

Thomas Rosser was a complicated man, and historians' treatment of the general shifted throughout the years. Millard K. and Dean M. Bushong, early biographers, recorded his life in glowing terms, characterizing him as a gallant cavalryman, dashing and brave in the mold of Maj. Gen. J. E. B. Stuart. A subsequent author, S. Roger Keller, presented Rosser's own words of the war from 1863 to 1865 (taken largely from newspaper clippings), and held Rosser in high regard in the book's introduction. In truth, letters and diaries from soldiers who served with Rosser run the gamut, from enthusiastic admiration to downright loathing. Initially, many accounts revealed a positive assessment of Rosser; over time, though, opinions soured as the fortunes of the Confederacy declined and as Rosser hunted for scapegoats to blame for disastrous defeats, such as at the battle of Tom's Brook. Some of the commissioned officers under Rosser's command, including Richard H. Dulany, Mottrom D. Ball, and his good friend James Dearing, consistently retained a favorable opinion of him.

In recent years, Civil War historians and authors have treated Rosser with declining respect for his ability as a commander— many see him a less positive light, who at times was reckless (a behavior that actually helped him succeed during some famous raids), disloyal, and complaining. He was an able regimental commander and an adequate brigade commander, but his leadership of a division was less effective, with the exception of his memorable hit-and-run raids. His preparation and organizational skills appeared modest at best, as he further demonstrated with his postwar northwest railroad career and his political quests. Rosser lacked the larger vision required of a successful division commander.

I am hopeful that this biography shows a more balanced assessment of Rosser than earlier biographical writings depict. He was an important military figure. His self-image was that of an extremely capable leader—more so than in actuality. During his post war career, he was an important contributor to the expansion of the Northwest Railroad.

Sheridan R. Barringer

Introduction

A big, bluff Virginian who grew up in the wilds of Texas, Maj. Gen. Thomas Lafayette Rosser looms large over the landscape of the American Civil War. In many ways, Thomas Rosser was a walking contradiction in terms. He was the primary beneficiary of the largesse of his patron, Maj. Gen. J. E. B. Stuart, who advanced Rosser beyond his abilities, along the way incurring the wrath of an ungrateful officer who was livid that Stuart took so long to promote him to brigadier general. An ungrateful Rosser stabbed Stuart in the back, even though Stuart harbored nothing but the greatest respect for him, and despite the fact that Rosser owed his high rank to Stuart.

Rosser was trained at West Point where he became close friends with another tall, lanky cadet who was bound for future service in the cavalry—George A. Custer. Rosser resigned from West Point a few weeks from graduation in order to accept a commission with a Confederate artillery unit. Rosser and Custer met again and again on the field of battle, with mixed results. At the battle of Tom's Brook, on October 9, 1864, Custer rode out between the lines to bow to his old friend before leading a decisive charge that routed Rosser's horse soldiers. The two resumed their friendship in the years after the Civil War, and Rosser became one of Custer's strongest defenders after his longtime friend met his untimely end at the Little Big Horn in 1876.

Rosser started out in the artillery, performing well at the first battle of Bull Run in July 1861. He later became colonel of the 5th Virginia Cavalry. In the fall of 1863, after Brig. Gen. William E. "Grumble" Jones was relieved of command and sent to the Shenandoah Valley of Virginia, Rosser assumed command of Jones's brigade, which he later dubbed the "Laurel Brigade." Rosser was promoted to brigadier general and led the Laurel Brigade through the campaigns of 1864. He suffered a severe leg wound while leading his Virginia cavalrymen in battle at Trevilian Station on June 11, 1864. After recuperating, he returned to duty with a promotion to major general and the command of a division. Rosser's division was sent to the Shenandoah Valley to face the army of Maj. Gen. Philip H. Sheridan, and Rosser was saddled with the unfortunate moniker—and burden—"Savior of the Valley." Unable to halt Sheridan's men from destroying much of the valley, and after being badly beaten at Tom's Brook, Rosser failed miserably in his efforts to impede Sheridan's progress.

Thomas Rosser was personally brave, and he was popular with the rank and file he commanded. He was a fine battery commander, a good regimental commander, a reliable brigade commander, but a much less effective division commander. He was an overly ambitious ingrate who often quarreled with his subordinates. Rosser and Col. Thomas T. Munford had a severe personality conflict that prevented them from working together effectively, and probably caused Rosser's crushing defeat at Tom's Brook. Ultimately, much of the responsibility for the Army of Northern Virginia's April 1, 1865, defeat at the battle of Five Forks must lie with Rosser, who chose that day to host a shad bake. That meant that the highest-ranking Confederate officers were not with their units when Sheridan's cavalry unleashed a devastating assault. His career was a mixed bag, but Rosser left his mark on the landscape of the Civil War.

Thus, Thomas Rosser became one the highest-ranking officers of the Army of Northern Virginia's Cavalry Corps, but was not competent to command such a large force. Rosser seemed to lack the ability to see the big picture that division commanders needed. His ego led to inadequate preparation. At the same time, he was fearless and popular with the men who followed him into battle. Rosser left a mixed legacy, but it is a legacy that requires further examination.

Rosser's life has been the subject of only one full-length biography that is dated. His story has long needed a modern treatment. Sheridan "Butch" Barringer has finally filled that gap with this book. Barringer explores Rosser's life with an unblinking eye, examining his strengths and weaknesses, placing the big Texan in his proper historical context and within the bigger picture of the American Civil War. Ride along with Rosser and his horse soldiers as they campaign.

Eric J. Wittenberg
Columbus, Ohio

1942 photograph of Catalpa Hill property, originally belonging to the Rosser Family in the 1840s. Photo taken from the hill to the west of the house Buildings: left to right: corn crib, barn (where the Rosser barn once stood), garage, main house, home addition (which included a kitchen or "cook room") added in 1936 (destroyed by fire), well house, woodshed, chicken house, privy, unknown structure. Slave quarters were once near the area of the home addition.

Only the home, remodeled, still stands today. The farm is located near the intersection of Browns Mill Road and Stone's Road, five miles southwest of Rustburg, in Campbell County, Virginia.

Photo by Walter R. Beam, reproduced by permission.

CHAPTER 1

Early Years and West Point

"My training at home had not prepared me for the rigid discipline and arbitrary military dictum of snobs whose only claim to respectability were their shoulderstraps and brass buttons."

Cadet Thomas Rosser at West Point

Thomas Lafayette Rosser was born on October 15, 1836, likely at the ancestral home of his grandparents, Thomas Oglesby Rosser and Nancy (Tweedy) Rosser, at Button Creek, three and a half miles east of Rustburg, Virginia. Out of seven children, he was the second child and first son of plantation owner, farmer, and slave holder, John "Jack" Rosser, who was an intelligent and strong man, standing at six feet two inches and weighing 225 pounds, and Martha Melvina (Johnson) Rosser. His parents married on May 28, 1834. When Thomas was three years old, his family moved to a 789-acre farm called Catalpa Hill. The property stood about a half mile north of Brown's Mill Road, along the waters of Rough Creek, five miles southwest of Rustburg and about 12 miles south of Lynchburg, in Campbell County, Virginia.[1]

Jack Rosser married four times. Tom's mother, Martha, was Jack's third spouse. A woman of English and Scandinavian descent, Martha possessed inner strength, piety, and firmness, traits that had a wholesome influence on her son. Purportedly of French Huguenot descent, Jack may have been from Welsh and English heritage, like most people in the area. During early childhood, Tom Rosser spent little time with his father. Jack was busy building and tending the farm and also engaging in the business of dealing slaves. Tom's mother essentially raised him with minimal help from his father.[2]

---

1. Lyon G. Tyler, ed., *Men of Mark in Virginia: A Collection of Biographies of the Leading Men of the State*, (Washington, D.C., 1906), 1:387; *Campbell County Deed Books, 67 vols.*, 27:343–44, Library of Virginia, Richmond (LVA). The 1830 Federal Census for Campbell County indicates Jack Rosser owned 10 slaves. The 1840 census lists 18 slaves.
2. Thomas L. Rosser, "Reminiscences," 4, Thomas L. Rosser Papers, University of Virginia (UVA), Charlottesville.

Jack Rosser had a checkered marital history. He wed his first cousin Levica Tweedy in 1812, and after her death in 1822, he married Levica's sister, Thirza Tweedy, the following year. It was unlawful in Virginia to marry someone related to you by marriage, so Jack's second marriage was illegal. In April 1824, a grand jury returned "a presentment against John Rosser" for the crime, but the matter eventually died. In 1828, the commonwealth's attorney recommended dropping the prosecution, and Rosser petitioned for and obtained a legislative act legalizing his marriage to Thirza. However, she died in 1834, and he married Martha Johnson. Widowed for a third time in 1859, Jack married Mary Hartley that same year. The couple soon relocated to Arkansas, where Jack Rosser died at 83 years old in 1876.[3]

During the 1830s and 1840s, as a deputy sheriff of the county, Jack Rosser was heavily involved in a practice known as "farming the sheriffalty." For a fee, the county "high sheriff" delegated management of the office (including a cut of the fees and commissions for tax-collecting, licenses, etc.) to a deputy or deputies. It was a lucrative enterprise. Jack served as a deputy sheriff for 12 years. Jack's uncle, Capt. John Rosser, another deputy sheriff, seemed to be a central figure of this practice, enlisting many of the surety bonds required for the numerous deputies. In February 1839, uncle John Rosser petitioned the General Assembly of Virginia, arguing against an earlier petition to transfer the collection of taxes on merchant's licenses in Lynchburg from the county sheriff to the town sergeant. Obviously, this would take a significant bite out of the existing arrangement's profits. In 1847, a large sum of county money, about $22,000, that Sheriff John Rosser (Jack's cousin) controlled, suddenly disappeared. Local lore says that the person Sheriff John Rosser had entrusted to deposit the money in a Richmond bank lost it gambling.[4]

The individuals who had entered into bonds to secure the sheriff's arrangement were forced to indemnify the county, which bankrupted

---

3. Common Law Order Book 4 and 5, 143 and 69, respectively; Petition, John Rosser to General Assembly of Virginia, December 6, 1823, LVA; Ruth Hairston Early, *Campbell Chronicles and Family Sketches: Embracing the History of Campbell County, Virginia, 1782–1926* (Baltimore, 1978), 180; Thomas O. Beane, "Thomas Lafayette Rosser: Soldier, Railroad Builder, Politician, Businessman (1836–1910)," MA Thesis, 1957, UVA, 8; Thomas L. Rosser, "Autobiographical Sketch," 5, Thomas L. Rosser Papers, University of Virginia (UVA).
4. Rosser, "Autobiographical Sketch," 5, UVA; Petition, John Rosser to General Assembly of Virginia, February 23, 1839, LVA; Deed of Trust, John Rosser, Richard Morgan, and Josiah Shepperson, February 10, 1849, "Executors Richard Morgan vs. Bennet Tweedy Etc.," Case 1880-028; John Rosser's Trustees vs. John Rosser, Case 1877-016, Chancery Records of Campbell County, VA, both in LVA; Rob Maurer to author, June 28, 2009, in author's possession.

many of them. Naturally, this process generated a number of lawsuits against uncle John Rosser and litigation that took years to resolve. Apparently, Jack had provided one of the surety bonds in the amount of $8,000, financially wiping him out. Jack embarked on slave selling trips to generate much-needed money. He traveled to Memphis and New Orleans in 1847, trying to sell some slaves that belonged to him, his neighbors, and his relatives. His efforts continued as the financial crisis escalated. In February 1849, as his economic misfortunes mounted, Jack sold half of his farm, 394 acres, along with the house and all the outbuildings, to Joseph H. Stone for $1,600. He later sold the other half to Albert G. Stone for $1,600. The sales helped to settle debts and judgments against him, part of which accrued from the dealing of local slaves and the monies involved.[5]

In the meantime, the United States boundaries had expanded exponentially when Texas entered the Union as a slave state at the end of 1845. A vast new frontier beckoned with cheap, prosperous land for any enterprising families willing to move west. The Rosser family had lived on their Virginia Piedmont farm until its financial problems began squeezing too tightly. Therefore, in 1849, Jack Rosser took his family, which included five of Thomas Rosser's siblings, a half-brother, and three half-sisters, along with eight slaves, to Shreveport, Louisiana—a jumping-off point for Texas.[6]

Jack Rosser had planned to move his family far from Virginia before the full impact of his financial and legal difficulties beset him in early 1849, and then return to Virginia to settle up with his neighbors, sell the family farm, and deal with his legal troubles. However, word of his plans leaked out, and spurred by a petition, the court required Jack to post a $1,500 bond guaranteeing his appearance. Unable to post it, Jack was jailed for several months. Finally, in June 1849, he settled the litigations by selling his land, and left for Texas.

"We marched overland from Campbell County, Virginia to Memphis, Tennessee," Tom Rosser later recalled, "where we took the Steamer *Bulletin* to the Mouth of the Red-River. Thence by a small stern-wheeler *The Creole* to Shreveport, Louisiana. Thence via Prairie

5. Campbell County Deed Book 27:343–44; Campbell County Order Book 25:247, 285; John Rosser vs. John Rosser Etc., Case 1877-016; Morgan vs. Tweedy, Case 1880-028, Chancery Records for Campbell County, all in LVA.
6. Thomas L. Rosser, "Reminiscences," 12, Thomas L. Rosser Papers, UVA. According to a family story, while his father remained behind to close up the family farming business, sell the farm, and sell most of the slaves, 13-year-old Tom Rosser, on horseback, led the wagon train of his mother, five siblings, and eight slaves to Texas. My research indicates that Jack Rosser took his family to Texas in the fall of 1849, arriving in October.

schooners to our new home in the wilderness, three miles southeast of the county seat of Carthage, Panola County, Texas," 40 miles west of Shreveport.[7]

Tom Rosser's extended immediate family included surviving siblings Janet Florence, Milicent Fyke, James Harris, John Carper, and William Edward. Thomas also had 11 half-brothers and half-sisters; three of the latter lived with the family in Carthage. The Rossers owned 11 slaves on their Texas farm, ranging in ages from 11 months to 56 years old.

A section—640 acres, equivalent to a square mile—was a standard land grant on the American frontier in the 1800s. In Texas, Rosser's family settled on a section farm tract in pine-timber country along "Six Mile Bayou," a tributary of the Sabine River in Panola County. Young Rosser soon discovered that life in Texas radically differed from the more urbane, genteel farm life in Virginia. Frontier life was challenging; no roads existed, just trails through a vast, sparsely populated territory teeming with both wild animals and hostile Indians. Accompanied by several of the dozen family hounds that had trekked west, Tom and his father shot deer, bear, and other wild game, often within 100 yards of the house. A family story recounts an alligator coming out of the Sabine River and killing one of their young slave boys.[8]

Rosser, with jet-black hair, dark brown eyes, and a leathery, swarthy complexion, inherited great physical and mental strength from his parents. Muscular, broad-shouldered, with an athletic frame, he was tall like his father, eventually reaching an identical six-foot-two-inch stature. Rosser's greatest loves were his family, horses, and the great outdoors. But he also learned the value of hard work as a farm lad, taking an active interest in agricultural operations, including the tending of livestock, particularly the horses. He became an excellent horseman, which would serve him well in the future. In the new environment of Texas, he adapted to the current imperatives, including

7. Rosser, "Autobiographical Sketch," 5, UVA; Tom Rosser's older half-brother, Robert, probably helped the family move to Texas. He returned to Campbell County, Virginia, and married there in 1852. He then moved south to Arkansas and served as a captain in the 1st Arkansas Cavalry during the Civil War.

8. 1850 United States Federal Census for Panola, Texas, Roll M432, & 1850 Slave Census for Panola County, Texas, both in National Archives (NA), Washington, D.C.; Rosser, "Autobiographical Sketch," 5–6. The "Autobiographical Sketch" lists 13 slaves. Rosser also had a younger brother named Lysander, who died at the age of three while their family still lived in Virginia, supposedly from a fall from a hayloft. In the toddler's memory, a small headstone and a footstone, neither of which survive today, were situated under an apple tree between the barn and the house.

clearing the land and building living quarters. He, along with his father, brothers, and slaves, cleared the land and built a spacious two-story mansion—including a one-story addition, the kitchen, connected by a covered walkway—as well as a cotton gin, gristmill, slave quarters, and other buildings. All the structures were substantial. Several of the slaves were good carpenters.[9]

The frontier family earned income on small crops of cotton and corn, along with sales of pine timber. Usually, Rosser, accompanied by a slave or two, took crops to market in Shreveport where the goods were shipped down the Red and Mississippi rivers to New Orleans.[10]

His father realized the importance of education, insisting that his son receive the best available schooling he could afford. When Rosser was 16 years old he was sent to a boarding school at Mount Enterprise, in nearby Rusk County, Texas. However, he didn't stay long. During a debating society event, Rosser got into a brawl with his opponent. Rosser claimed he badly whipped the fellow, which brought on attempted retaliation from the boy's two brothers and their friends. Rosser remembered, "I soon had so many fights on my hands and was kept in such hot water that my father was requested by Mr. Campbell to take me from his school, which was well, for had I remained, pistols would have taken the place of fists, and serious trouble would have grown out of it. I was, however, exonerated... I really left the school in Triumph." These impetuous, impulsive, and combative personality traits remained with him throughout his life.[11]

Despite his hot-headed nature, the young man grew to love books, particularly biographies of great men such as Napoleon Bonaparte and George Washington. The lives of these famous men helped motivate young Tom Rosser to achieve recognition of his own. Fortunately for Rosser, an excellent opportunity to get started on such a goal soon came along. He received an appointment to the United States Military Academy at West Point. The agents of his good fortune were Samuel McClory Fite, a relative and future Tennessee congressman, and a neighbor, E. Henderson. Fite secured the nomination through Texas Congressman Lemuel Dale Evans, while Henderson sent a letter of

9. Millard K. & Dean M. Bushong, *Fightin' Tom Rosser* (Shippensburg, PA, 1983), 2; Rosser, "Reminiscences," 13–14, UVA.; Deed Book A, Grantor: S. Holland - Grantee: Martha M. Rosser, July 24, 1851, & Grantor: John Rosser-Grantee: E. Bolling, February 6, 1849, Panola County Courthouse, Carthage, TX; Rob Maurer to author, June 28, 2009, in author's possession.
10. Thomas O. Beane, "Thomas Lafayette Rosser: Soldier, Railway Builder, Politician, Businessman," 3, MA Thesis, 1957, University of Virginia (UVA); Rosser, "Reminiscences," 17, UVA.
11. William Griffith Thomas III, "Under Indictment: Tom Rosser and the New South," MA Thesis, 1991, UVA, 4; Rosser, "Autobiographical Sketch," 7, UVA.

recommendation to Secretary of War Jefferson Davis, who forwarded it to President Franklin Pierce, approving the nomination. Rosser received Evans's appointment letter on March 26, 1856, and he left for the academy in April.[12]

Rosser's class of 1861 graduated only 34 cadets out of the 93 who reported to the academy. Twenty-two entering candidates did not pass the physical examination and washed out. John Pelham of Alabama, Rosser's roommate, became the most popular man in the 1861 class. George Armstrong Custer, who was a year behind Rosser, became the most popular cadet in his class. Unlike Pelham, Custer became the class "goat," academically finishing dead last.[13]

To his dismay, Rosser, through a misunderstanding, arrived at West Point several months before he was expected, much too early to enter. Returning to Texas was not a good option, so he settled in nearby Buttermilk Falls, New York (now Highland Falls), and spent his time studying. According to Rosser, Pelham also arrived early, joining him at Buttermilk Falls. Lieutenant William H. Terrell, a future Union artillery officer who was killed in the war, tutored the young men during this critical period. The extra study time helped Rosser pass the entrance examinations, which he might have otherwise failed. "Had it not been for Lt. Terrell's careful instructions," Rosser recalled, "I should have not been able to pass the preliminary exam." Rosser entered West Point on June 2, 1856.[14]

West Point, a small and isolated village 50 miles north of New York City, was essentially cut off from the outside world during the winter months. The academy sat on 40 acres atop a high plain overlooking the Hudson River. Established with congressional approval by President Thomas Jefferson in 1802, it had by the mid-1850s already become encrusted with a raft of hallowed traditions.

Plebes, or first-year cadets, were required to sign an oath of allegiance and pass prescribed physical and mental examinations. In 1856, there were only four companies of cadets, each having fewer than 70 members. The incoming plebes, along with upperclassmen serving as instructors, went into camp in mid-June for two months where the cadets were taught the rudiments of army life. This encampment, alongside the Revolutionary War's Fort Clinton, was meant to separate the men from the boys. The typical day began with reveille at 5 a.m., followed by drill from 5:30 to 6:30 a.m., then roll call, and a 30-minute

12. Lyon G. Tyler, *Men of Mark in Virginia* (Washington. D.C., 1908), 387–88.
13. Mary Elizabeth Sergent, "The West Point John Pelham Knew," *The Cannoneer Newsletter,* John Pelham Historical Association (Nov. 1985), 4:8, Jacksonville Public Library, Jacksonville, AL.
14. Rosser, "Autobiographical Sketch," 8, UVA.

Cadet Thomas Rosser at West Point – Circa 1858

Fun loving cadet who, like George Custer, "marched to his own drum beat."

Albert and Shirley Small Special Collections Library, University of Virginia.

march to the mess hall for a scant breakfast. More drill ensued with sparse breaks until another march to the mess hall for a 1 p.m. dinner. After a short lull, drilling resumed until a 7 p.m. dress parade, followed by a meager supper. Then the plebes cleaned up before another roll call and preparation for bed. Tattoo sounded at 9:30 p.m. Those who could not adapt to the endless roll calls, prompt obedience to orders, and frequent changes of clothes were deemed unfit and dismissed from the academy.[15]

Hazing, of course, was already an established practice, which Rosser encountered during the encampment. Rosser experienced something called "pulling out." Alanson Randol, a yearling, or second-year cadet, threatened to pull a sleeping Rosser out of his tent at night and drag him around on the parade ground. Rosser, who did not get along with this particular yearling, retorted, "You are not man enough to pull me out and I dare you to try it." Sure enough, one unusually chilly, rainy evening in August, Randol and five other yearlings slipped a rope over one of Rosser's legs while he slept in his tent, and then dragged him all around the parade ground. The red-headed Randol, a cadet officer, kicked him severely. Finally, after the rough treatment ceased, Rosser got up and attacked the instigator. As the yearling's buddies pulled Rosser off Randol, a corporal of the guard appeared and arrested Rosser for being out of quarters after lights out.[16]

Released almost immediately, Rosser returned to his tent, and after reveille the next morning he challenged his attacker to a gentleman's duel. Randol declined on grounds that Rosser, not officially a cadet yet, had no right to issue a challenge. Rosser insisted on satisfaction, so a boxing match was arranged. Against a man even larger and stronger than himself, things went badly at first for Rosser, but at last, he wore him down with sheer endurance. Rosser gloated, "I turned on him with all the fury of a wounded wild beast and before he was much hurt, he bled like the cowardly calf that he was and called out, 'Take him off, take him off.'" The fight was stopped, and both men were taken to the hospital. For his misconducts, the plebe was charged with striking a superior officer, and for the next six months he spent weekends in the guardhouse.[17]

15. Bushong, *Fightin' Tom Rosser*, 5; Rosser, "Reminiscences," 19; Jerry H. Maxwell, *The Perfect Lion: The Life and Death of Confederate Artillerist John Pelham* (Tuscaloosa, AL, 2011), 12–13.
16. Rosser, "Reminiscences," 21, UVA; "Autobiographical Sketch," 11, UVA. Randol became a captain in the 1st U.S. Artillery, and then took a commission as colonel of the 2nd New York Volunteer Cavalry. He faced Rosser in battle at Aldie, Middleburg, and Gettysburg.
17. Rosser, "Reminiscences," 21, & "Autobiographical Sketch," 11, 24, UVA; William J. Miller, *Decision at Tom's Brook: George Custer, Thomas Rosser and the Joy of the Fight* (El Dorado Hills, CA, 2016), 37–38. Rosser's

After the two-month encampment, the survivors moved into barracks on the academy grounds. Rosser and Pelham roomed together in the south end of the west barracks in their austere and gloomy quarters. Each cadet had an iron bedstead with a mattress and two blankets, a small table, a lamp, mirror, washstand with pitcher and bowl, and an uncomfortable straight-backed chair.[18]

One contemporary described Rosser as a "great, swarthy-looking cadet, who seemed altogether too big for his bobtailed coat and turned-over white collar." Nevertheless, Rosser seemed to adapt easily to cadet life. "My health is very good and has been all this time. But I study so hard that I am very thin, but that is nothing," he told his mom. "I am getting on very well with my studies. We have completed Grammar and will now commence Geography. We are doing our best in Algebra, have finished the most difficult portion. . . . I have but ten or twelve demerits out of my one hundred and fifty which are allowed me by January."[19]

Rosser had embarked on a five-year course of studies. The five-year curriculum at West Point was first established in 1854 during Jefferson Davis's tenure as secretary of war, as well as Robert E. Lee's tenure as the academy superintendent. It returned to the four-year scheme in October 1858, but six months later switched back again. In June 1860, a congressional commission recommended retaining the five-year course. Thereafter, the course of study at West Point was five years, instead of four, for the classes of 1859 through 1861. The men who had become cadets in 1856 were due to graduate in May 1861, just ahead of the 1857 class's graduation in June. After the war began, the four-year course was re-instituted.[20]

Cadet life was austere, to say the least. During the five-year curriculum, the cadets were granted but one furlough, from the mid-June after their second year to August 28. There were no weekend passes or downtime at the academy. Cadets did not leave their post

---

roommate John Pelham got into a remarkably similar fight with similar results. Pelham's antagonist, embarrassed by losing the fight, resigned from the academy, see Maxwell, *The Perfect Lion*, 20. Rosser was admitted to the hospital on July 2, 1856, for contusion and released two days later. There is no record of Randol being admitted; see RG 94, Records of the Adjutant General's Office, 1762–1984, Field Records of Hospitals, 1821–1912, U.S. Military Academy (USMA), West Point, NY, 109.

18. Maxwell, *The Perfect Lion*, 14.

19. Mary Elizabeth Sergent, *They Lie Forgotten: The United States Military Academy, 1856–1861* (Middletown, NY, 1986), 177; Rosser to his mother, October 23. 1856, Thomas Rosser Papers, UVA.

20. Sergent, "Classmates Divided," *American Heritage Magazine*, February, 1958, 9:2; Paul Kensey, "West Point Classmates—-Civil War Enemies," American Civil War Roundtable of Australia Symposium, Melbourne, October, 2002, Symposium Slide #5.

unless granted leave by the secretary of war, and then only due to death or serious illness at home. Rosser's furlough began on June 14 and ended on August 28, 1858. Loathing saying goodbye to his family at the end of his furlough, he crawled out of his bedroom window and left during the night. The next year his mother died of typhoid fever.[21]

The only organized cadet recreations were dancing, riding, and fencing. On Christmas night, the fencing academy was crowded until lights out, and the cadets, mostly dancing with each other, performed waltz, polka, and quadrille to the academy band's music. Only during the brief summer break did ladies enter the post, enlivening the place with dancing, picnicking, and strolling along the river paths. Cadets wrote home and hugely enjoyed receiving mail. Many read to pass the time.

What little time there was, that is. In the summer they used it to swim, and in winter they skated. They also hiked and rode horseback. Some painted, while others just dawdled around the old ruins of the Revolutionary War's Fort Putnam. The cadets worked hard, played hard, and occasionally settled their differences with their fists in the cold morning dew beneath the ramparts of Fort Clinton.[22]

And, of course, Benny Havens, a tavern and favorite watering hole only a mile from West Point, always beckoned the cadets. Officially, it was strictly off limits for them. Havens, a former West Point employee, had been forever banned from academy grounds for selling cadets hot rum flips (a drink that combined egg, sugar, and rum) instead of coffee and ginger cakes. However, the contract-catered West Point food was terrible, and Mrs. Havens's buckwheat cakes and roast turkey were worth the risk. And Benny Havens still made the best hot rum flip in the Hudson Valley.[23]

---

21. Beane, "Thomas L. Rosser: Soldier," 8, UVA.
22. Sergent, "Classmates Divided," 4.
23. Ibid.; Kensey, "West Point Classmates–Civil War Enemies," Symposium Slides #4–5; Jay Monaghan, *Custer: The Life of George Armstrong Custer* (Lincoln, NE, 1971), 24. In fact, visits to Benny Havens were considered to be the favorite pastime of the future president of the Confederacy. On one occasion a drunken Davis, dodging a raid on the tavern, nearly killed himself when he fell into a deep gulley while fleeing hurriedly from the pub. On another occasion, Davis had been found drinking at Benny Havens, and he faced a court-martial for being absent from duty. Four other cadets caught there that night were dismissed from the academy, but Davis's "silver tongue," or more properly his "touching eloquence," saved him. Davis accumulated so many demerits during his four years at the academy that he almost failed to graduate. Only his academic accomplishments saved him. The authorities often raided the place, of course, trying to catch cadets breaking the rules. But Rosser and his good friend Custer had many a drink there. And like Ulysses S. Grant and Jefferson Davis before him, Custer received multiple demerits for visiting the Benny Havens tavern.

Rosser spent his happiest hours as a cadet with his roommate John Pelham of Alabama, James Dearing of Virginia, Pierce Young of Georgia, and George Custer of Michigan. Pelham, who did not apply himself to his studies, ranked just below the middle academically but was one of the best-liked men in his class. He became the most celebrated artilleryman of the war, immortalized by General Robert E. Lee as "the gallant Pelham." Custer and his roommate, James P. Parker of Missouri, lived next door to Rosser and Pelham. Pelham and Custer were purportedly the most handsome men in the cadet corps. Custer, with his free-flowing blonde hair, was called by the nickname Curly or Fanny, names that stuck with him long after he became famous. His family and friends called him Armstrong or by his baby name, Autie. West Pointers called Rosser by the nickname Tex or Tam, a play on his real name.[24]

Cadets were assigned to companies according to their height. Rosser, along with Pelham, stood in the ranks of the first squad, D Company of the 8th Division. But Pelham was shorter, and hence the real possibility of the roommates becoming separated at formations. Rosser devised a scheme to keep that from occurring; he gave Pelham foot padding to put between his socks and shoes to increase his height just enough to keep them in the same company.[25]

West Point had done little to temper Rosser's combative nature or his frequent disdain for authority. "My training at home had not prepared me for the rigid discipline and arbitrary military dictum of snobs," he said, "whose only claim to respectability were their shoulderstraps and brass buttons. I was frequently punished for disrespectful conduct towards superior officers and once court-martialed for striking the senior Cadet Captain of the Corp of Cadets... my reputation was established."[26]

But the academy also generated enduring friendships, and one of the most long-lasting was that between George Custer and Tom Rosser, kindred spirits and natural leaders. Three years older and a member of the May graduating class—as opposed to Custer's June class—Rosser was imposing in stature and strong in everything but studies. Along with Pelham, the two men were probably the best

24. Joseph Mills Hanson, "Thomas Lafayette Rosser," *Journal of the Unites Stated Cavalry Association*, (1934), 43:22. Pelham was mortally wounded March 17, 1863, at the battle of Kelly's Ford, in Virginia.
25. Ibid.
26. William Griffith Thomas, "Under Indictment: Tom Rosser and the New South," MA Thesis, UVA, 1991, 5; Rosser, "Autobiographical Sketch," 11, UVA; Miller, *Decision at Tom's Brook*, 38. The senior cadet captain that Rosser struck was William C. Paine. Rosser was officially reprimanded and sentenced to four months in solitary confinement when not on duty.

horsemen in the corps. Rosser's other close friendships were with Pelham, Pierce Young, and James Dearing. Dearing, also from Campbell County, Virginia, stood in the top half of his class academically, well ahead of Rosser and Pelham. He was mortally wounded at the battle of High Bridge during the Appomattox campaign.[27]

The cavalry was especially a young man's branch of service, as Custer noted in his memoirs. Custer wrote, "Among those joining the Confederate force who rose to distinction were Joseph Wheeler, Rosser, Pierce M. B. Young, Beverly Robertson, and John Herbert Kelley [sic] . . . . It is somewhat remarkable that these five general officers held commands in the cavalry...I might add my own name—thus showing that the cavalry offered the most promising field for early promotion."[28]

Rosser was hardly a scholar. In 1860, out of 50 cadets, Rosser ranked fortieth in ethics, forty-third in infantry tactics, thirty-sixth in artillery tactics, forty-first in cavalry tactics, forty-seventh in chemistry, and eighteenth in drawing. One year he earned 136 of the 200 maximum demerits. Like Custer, too fun-loving and mischievous to be a serious academic, Rosser earned his share of demerits for: "talking in a loud and boisterous manner to a new cadet;" because the "walls of his room were grossly defaced by spots and marks;" for "entering the guard room before release from quarters, A.M.;" and for "laughing in ranks at parade." Rosser was also frequently late for the 5:10 a.m. formations. He racked up a total of 547 demerits as a cadet and was on the sick list 48 times in his five years at West Point. Records indicate that he suffered a serious bout of gonorrhea during October 1858.[29]

The academy considered character-building a prime directive in its mission, and enforced its efforts by a strict code of honesty and obedience. Breaches of discipline earned demerits, of course. Custer

27. Sergent, "Classmates Divided," 8–9.
28. Ralph Kirshner, *Class of 1861*, (Carbondale, IL, 1999), 4.
29. Official Register, Officers and Cadets, & Records of Hospitals, Ledger, 212; Weekly Class Reports, October 1858, both USMA; Miller, *Decision at Tom's Brook*, 39. Rosser was on sick list with symptoms of gonorrhea that entire month. This helps explain why he had so many days of sickness recorded. Cadets sometimes contracted this disease after their summer furloughs. Rosser's friend, George Custer, suffered the same malady in August 1859, shortly after his summer furlough. Custer later said that future cadets might study his own days at West Point as an example to be avoided. Just before graduation, while duty officer, Custer failed to break up a fight between two cadets. He was subsequently court-martialed and placed under detention at the time of his graduation, unable to attend the ceremonies. See Louise Barnett, *Touched by Fire: The Life, Death, and Mythic Afterlife of George Armstrong Custer* (Lincoln, NE, 1996), 18.

lost count of the number of demerits he received. Ulysses S. Grant once received eight demerits for not attending church. J. E. B. Stuart, Jefferson Davis, and George Pickett were all constantly in trouble. George McClellan, on the other hand, was a relative angel, receiving few demerits, and Robert E. Lee received none at all—other cadets dubbed him the "Marble Model."[30]

One hot August morning, an exciting event occurred during the cadets' second summer as they marched back from breakfast. William C. Paine, labeled as "our dog of a first captain," was assailed by three cadets armed with swords that they had taken from cadet officers. Charles Jesup, a first classman, started the brawl and was soon joined by Edwin Stoughton of Vermont. When Stoughton called to "turn out more swords," the impetuous Tom Rosser was among the first to heed. While Paine fenced with all three of them, the astonished sentries just watched. Finally, one of the sentries declared, "Turn out the guard." Jesup, Stoughton, and Rosser were placed under arrest, charged with "violating the 7th Article of War—inciting to mutiny—the penalty, death, or such lesser penalty as a court martial shall decide." Jesup was at first expelled from the academy, but on September 16 the war department overturned the general court's decision and reinstated him. Rosser, Stoughton, and Jesup were "restricted to ordinary cadet limits for four months," including serving alternate weekends in solitary confinement in the guardhouse, when they were not in class or on duty.[31]

An officer's academic rank in his class upon graduation bore greatly his future career prospects. The highly ranked cadets in the graduating class could choose their career path. The academy ranking also had a significant influence on career advancement opportunities throughout their service.[32]

Pre-War Tensions at the Academy

When Robert E. Lee was superintendent of West Point in 1852, the issue of slavery was steadily rending the United States apart. Lee frequently reminded the cadets they were like a band of brothers, and

30. Kensey, "West Point Classmates–Civil War Enemies," Symposium Slide #4; Douglas Savage, *The Last Years of Robert E. Lee: From Gettysburg to Lexington* (New York, 2016), 156.
31. Bushong, *Fightin' Tom Rosser*, 8; Sergent, *They Lie Forgotten*, 68–70.
32. Despite these motivating factors, there were those who gained notoriety as class goats, with the poorest academic performance at graduation. George Pickett (1846), Henry Heth (1847), Laurence S. Baker (1851), and George Custer (1861) each finished last in their respective graduating class.

admonished them to remember first and foremost that they were all Americans. But the decade of the 1850s placed severe strains on that brotherly notion and Lee's advice.

Throughout the 1850s, conflicting opinions amongst Americans deepened to a point that the political differences between the North and South could no longer be contained or mitigated. The Compromise of 1850, followed by a steady escalation of con- troversies—the Kansas-Nebraska Act, Bleeding Kansas, abolitionist John Brown's attack on Harpers Ferry—ultimately led to Lincoln's election in 1860, the secession of seven Southern states, and a complete breakdown of the country's national bonds. Harsh words turned into harsh actions. The most notorious West Point altercation was a fistfight between New Yorker Emory Upton and South Carolinian Wade Hampton Gibbes, with the whole corps of cadets looking on, cheering for their respective man.[33]

As the political situation deteriorated, Rosser, along with many others, pondered what course of action to take if war broke out. On November 5, 1860, he wrote to Texas Governor Sam Houston offering his services should Texas secede from the Union. Houston, an avowed Unionist, deplored the possibility of a civil war, and in a strongly worded response urged Rosser to "give your whole time and attention to your studies in order that you may be prepared to assume the position to which your graduation would entitle you."[34]

Still contemplating what to do in December, Rosser wrote to Senator Jefferson Davis declaring he would never accept a commission from President-elect Abraham Lincoln. Nonetheless, Rosser believed he could enhance his future military career if he were to remain at the academy a few more months, in order to graduate. Rosser still felt obligated to resign and fight for the Confederacy if Texas left the Union or if several other states seceded. But in the interim, he would guard both his flanks.

With the secession of Texas and Alabama, followed by the formation of the Southern Confederacy in February 1861, Rosser, Pelham, and other cadets struggled to decide their strategy. On February 27, Rosser again wrote Davis, now president of the newly- formed Confederate States of America, offering his service. He was prepared after 49 months of stringent study at West Point "to assume any position in your army" for which Davis might think him worthy. Indeed, he wanted to devote his entire life to the military service of the

---

33. Thomas Fleming, "Band of Brothers: The West Point Corps" in Robert Crowley, ed., *With My Face to the Enemy: Perspectives on the Civil War* (New York: 2001), 30–31, 33.
34. Sam Houston to Rosser, November 17, 1860, Thomas Rosser Papers, UVA.

Confederacy. Although he felt he would be better qualified for such service if he remained at West Point until receiving his diploma in June, he would promptly obey any orders "to return to my country" if his services were "more needed at home than here."[35]

In January 1861, Louisianan Col. P. G. T. Beauregard was appointed West Point's superintendent, and Southern cadets sought his counsel about secession and resignation from the academy. "Don't jump too soon," Beauregard advised. "When you see me go, you go." Once the secretary of war heard about the instructions, he immediately relieved the colonel of his position, automatically bestowing upon Beauregard the dubious distinction as the officer having the shortest tenure as superintendent.[36]

The wavering Southern cadets had to confront their problems directly on February 22, 1861, when President James Buchanan tried to prevent a mass resignation of West Point cadets before Lincoln's inauguration, directing that the young men listen to a reading of "The Friendly Counsel and Prophetic Warnings Contained in Washington's Farewell Address to His Troops." Marched into the chapel, as was the tradition on George Washington's birthday, the cadets listened as one of the staff members delivered the first president's message about the need for unification. Southern cadets were not inspired. All classes had been canceled for the holiday, and after the chapel service, cadets spent the rest of the day discussing politics and the impending war. At the end of the day the band marched across the parade ground playing "Washington's March," and then swung into "The Star-Spangled Banner." Suddenly, all hell broke loose. Cadets rushed to every window. Rosser, a Virginia native and son of Texas, called out: "Secession, Secession—Dixie, Play Dixie!" As the Southerners broke into singing "Dixie," on the other side of the quadrangle, Custer led the singing of "The Star-Spangled Banner."[37]

---

35. Thomas Rosser to Jefferson Davis, Dec. 17, 1860 & February 27, 1861, in Thomas L. Rosser Service Record, General and Staff Officers, Roll M331, NA. It was Rosser's typical behavior to protect his own interests by trying to get Davis to tell him which way would garner him the best position in the Confederate service—to leave immediately or to graduate.

36. Thomas J. Fleming, *West Point: The Men and Times of the United States Military Academy* (New York, 1969), 151–52; Morris Schaff, The Spirit of Old West Point, 1858–1862 (Boston, 1907), 207–209; Mark Van Rhyn, MA Thesis, "An American Warrior: Thomas Rosser, 1836–1910," (Lincoln, NE, 1998), 6.

37. Kensey, "West Point Classmates–Civil War Enemies," Symposium Slide #7.

In March 1861, Pelham wrote a disheartened letter to a cousin:

> I have worked almost five years for my diploma, and it pains me to give up the undertaking now—besides all this, it chagrins me to be forced to leave an undertaking unfinished. I believe there is only two Cadets here at present from the Seceded States—Myself and a classmate from Texas. We will leave together—in June—or before, as the fates will it. We have been living together for three or four years, and I feel like we are inseparable—like his presence is necessary to my happiness.[38]

The day after the firing on Fort Sumter, South Carolina, on April 12, 1861, Secretary of War Simon Cameron directed that all West Point cadets take a new oath of allegiance. Previously, each had taken an oath as a citizen of an individual state. Now, they were required to swear fidelity to the United States as paramount to any state, county, or other political entity. With the academy staff all present in full uniform, the new oath was administered in the chapel. Ten cadets from the South refused to take it.[39]

John Pelham of Alabama was the first to refuse swearing the oath. Some applauded, while others hissed at his action—never before had a cadet refused to take an oath! Of the 278 cadets at the academy at the beginning of 1861, 86 were Southerners, and of these men, 65 resigned. Following South Carolina's secession in December 1860, 313 officers left the army, reducing its active officer corps on the eve of the Civil War to 767. The vast majority of the remaining officers, totaling 637, were West Point graduates—475 were Northerners and 162 were Southerners. Of the 297 Southerners who left the Federal army to join the Confederacy, 168 were West Pointers. Sixteen West Point Northern graduates, all married to Southern women, also went south.[40]

Once Virginia seceded on April 17, Rosser and other Southern cadets decided to forego graduation and leave the academy at once. On April 22, 1861, Southerners Rosser, Pelham, Dearing, and George Thornton, along with several border-states cadets, resigned and left West Point to offer their service to the Confederacy. Departing with a flock of Virginians and North Carolinians, they took the ferry to Garrison's Landing and then New York Central railcars to the city. Their classmates carried Rosser and Pelham down to the South Dock on their shoulders.

38. John Pelham to Mariann Pelham Mott, March 26, 1861, Garrison Family Papers, Sophia Smith Collection, Smith College, Northampton, MA.
39. Brian R. McEnany, *For Brotherhood and Duty: The Civil War History of the West Point Class of 1862* (Lexington, 2015), 82–83.
40. Kensey, "West Point Classmates–Civil War Enemies," Symposium Slide #7.

Perhaps no other group reflected the nation's discord more starkly than West Point's classes of May and June 1861. The outbreak of war forced the June class's graduation to occur six weeks sooner than scheduled; the following June class of 1862 graduated a whole year earlier. Secession, which demanded loyalty to one's state, had complicated the lives of many of the cadets. The academy had drilled in the notions of duty and loyalty to the United States. Once one's home state seceded, the young cadet faced the stark, difficult decision: country or state?

Robert E. Lee, who after much agonizing joined the Confederate cause, rejected the offer to command the Federal army because he could not draw his sword against his beloved state of Virginia. Clashes of loyalty even split West Point families. Virginian Philip St. George Cooke, class of 1827, for example, remained loyal to the Union while his son, John Rogers Cooke, and son-in-law, James Ewell Brown (J. E. B.) Stuart, class of 1854, both fought for the Confederacy. By the time President Abraham Lincoln's second secretary of war, Edwin M. Stanton, took office, loss of West Point officers to the Confederacy had become a blotch on the academy itself. Radical Republicans described it as a "bastion of Southernism."

While an officer had the luxury of resigning from the army, a soldier would be shot dead for desertion. In the Confederacy, where the president himself was a West Pointer, academy graduates were appointed to command as fast as they volunteered. The situation differed in the Union; in the initial days of the war, West Pointers tended to be overlooked for senior appointments in favor of political appointees. However, academy officers did form the nucleus of the depleted Federal army expansion, which was at least recognized as an established organization. The Confederacy, with no existing army, had to raise one from scratch, on the basis of state militia systems. The South had to train an army of more than a million, many of them only farm boys... and quickly.[41]

---

41. Previous paragraphs based on Sergent, *They Lie Forgotten: The United States Military Academy, 1856–1861,* 7–8, 95, 177. The first recorded academy resignation came from South Carolinian Henry Farley, followed four days later by James Hamilton, also from South Carolina, 95. Farley submitted his resignation on November 10, 1860, but it was not approved until November 17, 1860. Farley, a lieutenant in the Provisional Army of South Carolina, fired the first shell as the signal to begin bombardment of Fort Sumter, South Carolina, on April 12, 1861.

CHAPTER 2

Tom Rosser, Artilleryman

"Come see me at daylight in the morning and I will give
you the particulars [of your promotion]...
Come a-runnin'."

J.E.B. Stuart to Thomas L. Rosser

When Tom Rosser, who would have graduated on May 6, 1861,
resigned from West Point in April, he and classmate John
Pelham headed south to the Confederacy's capital in Montgomery,
Alabama, to offer their services. Generally, Federal authorities did not
interfere with departing cadets and their trips home. Some young
soldiers, however, found the journey a difficult one. Police and
marshals were searching southbound trains for secessionists carrying
weapons. Rosser and Pelham's train from New York City to
Philadelphia was stopped and searched twice. They were wearing their
West Point uniforms, and when authorities questioned the men,
Pelham claimed they were on their way to Washington, D.C., to report
for duty. To prevent the unpleasant experience from occurring again,
they decided to make a long, circuitous journey in order to avoid areas
where anti-secession feelings ran high.

After visiting Pelham's cousin, Marianna Mott, in Philadelphia,
the pair detoured via Harrisburg, Pennsylvania, to lessen the likelihood
of local authorities detaining them or violent unionists setting upon
them. Passing through Pittsburgh, Pennsylvania, and Cincinnati, Ohio,
they crossed the Ohio River at Louisville, Kentucky, before heading
south to Jacksonville, Alabama, arriving there on May 1. At Pelham's
home in Alexandria, they received a warm welcome. The *Jacksonville
Republican* reported the arrival of the new lieutenants "last night on
their way from West Point to Montgomery. They both received
appointments in the Confederate Army... Pelham and Rosser are a
couple of handsome, well educated and promising young officers, and
will be quite an acquisition to our army at this time. We predict for
them a brilliant future."[1]

1. *Jacksonville Republican*, May 2, 1861; Maxwell, *The Perfect Lion*, 46–47;
   Robert J. Trout, *Galloping Thunder: The Story of the Stuart Horse Artillery
   Battalion* (Mechanicsville, PA, 2002), 13–14. The Philadelphia Press

At the Pelham home, the young men enjoyed several days of hunting, parties, drilling with the local militia, and the hospitality of Alabamians. They left Pelham's home for Montgomery on May 10, setting out to volunteer their services to the new Southern nation.[2]

Once in the capital, it took Rosser and Pelham almost a week to get an appointment with any high-ranking Confederate official. On May 16, Rosser, now 25 years old, commissioned as a lieutenant to serve under Brig. Gen. Theophilus H. Holmes, who commanded the coastal defenses of North Carolina. However, as part of his responsibilities he first had to serve on recruiting duty in Wilmington, North Carolina. Anxious for active service, Rosser requested a transfer and was elated when he received orders to report to Maj. James B. Walton's battalion of the Washington Artillery of New Orleans on June 7, 1861. Promoted to first lieutenant on June 7, he was placed in command of the 2nd Company on June 27.[3]

Composed of prominent men of the "Crescent City," the South's largest at the time, the Washington Artillery organized in 1840 and served in the Mexican–American War. It was the oldest and best-known military organization in Louisiana. The unit drilled in both artillery and infantry tactics. Of the five companies raised, the first four would serve in the Army of Northern Virginia, while the fifth would be assigned to the Western Theater, initially under Maj. Gen. P. G. T. Beauregard's command.[4]

On April 11, even before the first shots of the war, Walton led his Washington Artillery in seizing much-needed rifles and cannons from the Federal arsenal at Baton Rouge, Louisiana. Some weeks later, the unit was mustered into Confederate service at Lafayette Square in New Orleans. Arriving in Lynchburg, Virginia, on June 2, the men boarded a train the next day for Richmond. On June 4, the battalion's four

reported on May 9, 1861, that a train from New York City to Philadelphia had been stopped, and 45 cadets were taken into custody for suspicious activity. The report stated that the apprehended cadets were headed to join the Confederacy and had purchased arms in New York. Briefly detained and disarmed, the cadets were allowed to proceed on their journey. The cadets were actually headed for Washington, D.C., to join the Union army. Incidents like that, however, caused great anxiety for southern cadets trying to return to their homes.

2. Rosser, "Reminiscences," 59, UVA; Sergent, *They Lie Forgotten*, 97.
3. Rosser, Reminiscences," 67, UVA; Special Orders No. 6, AIG's Office, June 7, 1861, Rosser Papers, UVA; AGO to Annette Tanquary, June 30, 1934, Rosser Compiled Service Record, Roll M331, NA. Pelham, commissioned a first lieutenant, was assigned as an artillery ordnance officer and headed for Lynchburg.
4. William Miller Owen, *In Camp and Battle with the Washington Artillery of New Orleans* (Baton Rouge, LA, 1999), 1–3, 8; Albert A. Nofi, *The Civil War Treasury* (Boston, 1992), 92.

companies, with a 12-piece brass band and their cooks and servants, arrived in Richmond. On July 3, the *Richmond Dispatch* duly reported:

> **The Washington Artillery of New Orleans, are now encamped in a very picturesque spot, called Mitchell's Ford, 3 miles from Manassas Junction. The locale is open, elevated and salubrious, bordered by dense woods, so that you can see the tops of the stately trees in the distance, forming, as it were, a magic circle around the camp...This battalion numbers 500 men, rank and file, 325 of whom are now in Viginia, the remainder being in New Orleans. Its... ordnance consists of fourteen field-pieces... [:] rifled cannon, howitzers and six-pounders, the last of which are from the original Ringgold battery.**[5]

Major Walton placed Rosser in charge of the one fully-equipped and manned battery (two companies) left behind at "Camp Louisiana"—about 100 men and eight guns, plus 120 horses and four mules. Rosser drilled the men twice in the morning and listened to "sweet music" in the afternoon. "Oh, how I love music—don't know what I would do without this fine Band away off here in this lonely place," he told a friend. A young lady he met also charmed him. He complained that he saw few people who were not soldiers. But "[w]ithin sight is a beautiful young lady. See her but seldom, her curls remind me of Ellen, now far away." It had been three years, during his sole furlough from West Point, since Rosser had last seen his beautiful friend Ellen R. Lape, step-granddaughter of Thomas Hinds, a famed War of 1812 general. He had met her aboard the Mississippi steamer *E. H. Fairchild*.[6]

Finally arriving in Richmond on June 25 with the two companies, Rosser was happy to rejoin his West Point classmates James Dearing and John J. Garnett, who were members of the battalion. All three served as instructors, training the gunners in artillery tactics. In fact, Rosser had secured the positions for his West Point friends, much to the dismay of other battalion officers. Rosser simply dismissed complaints about his favoritism as "worthless." As he rose through the ranks, Rosser often used his influence to promote friends. Intense loyalty to his friends was, in fact, one of his primary characteristics. In turn, he expected reciprocal loyalty. Much of his later animosity toward others, especially his superiors, originated from the reciprocity Rosser expected or perceived did not meet his expectations.[7]

5. *Richmond Dispatch*, July 3, 1861; William Miller Owen, *In Camp and Battle with the Washington Artillery of New Orleans* (Baton Rouge, 1999), 16.
6. Rosser to unidentified friend, July 4, 1861, & Rosser, "Reminiscences," 86, both UVA.
7. Owen, *Washington Artillery*, 16.

On July 17, the Washington Artillery marched to McLean's Ford, near Bull Run at Manassas, Virginia. Comprising 284 officers and men, the battalion was armed with 13 guns: six smoothbore, three rifled brass 6-pounders, and four 12-pounder howitzers. The following day, Rosser, commanding the 2nd Company with the four howitzers, marched toward Union Mills Ford, south on Bull Run by a crossing railroad bridge. This was the extreme right of the Confederate line, which ran eight miles upstream to the stone bridge on the Warrenton Turnpike. Rosser wanted to shell a group of Union Zouaves that had come into view, but Brig. Gen. Richard Ewell, commanding that section of the Confederate line, forbade it.[8]

Rosser's battery, busy accompanying Ewell's brigade at 2 p.m. toward Fairfax Court House, missed the first major battle of the war on June 21. They arrived back at Bull Run too late to take part in the battle. The other batteries of Walton's battalion had been heavily engaged during the clash, which ended in a chaotic Federal retreat.[9]

While rushing his battery to the front after the battle ended, Tom Rosser was handed a letter from Ellen, of all people. He read it after the battery had bivouacked for the night. She had received all the letters from him after he returned to West Point, but she was not allowed to write back, and after a while her romantic interest dimmed. She had, however, reread Rosser's letters many times, and the flame still flickered. Ellen had hoped "he might call to see me on your way home after graduation," but with the advent of war, she could no "longer suffer my desire to hear again from you to tell you of the deep interest I feel now... I pray for your safety, and should you survive [the war], may I hope that you will come to me?" Why did Ellen have a sudden interest in reestablishing ties with Tom Rosser?[10]

Whatever the reason, Rosser was astounded and quickly wrote a reply he wanted telegraphed immediately. But the corporal he sent to post the wire got lost and then did not have enough money to send it.

8. Owen, *Washington Artillery*, 24–25; Bushong, *Fightin' Tom Rosser*, 16.
9. Owen, *Washington Artillery*, 43.
10. Rosser, "Reminiscences," 86, UVA. Determining the identity of Rosser's girlfriend was challenging. He identified her only as "Ellen" who lived on the plantation of "General H." near Fayette, Mississippi. Census data revealed the only "General H." living in that area of Jefferson County was Gen. Thomas Hinds, who served in the War of 1812. In 1840, Howell Hinds inherited the plantation named Home Hill from his famous father. Locals still knew it as "the General Thomas Hinds estate." Ellen R. Lape was the stepdaughter of Howell and the daughter of Mary Ann (Coleman) Lape Hinds. I feel confident that Ellen R. Lape was indeed the "Ellen" whom Rosser courted. Howell Hinds was a major and assistant adjutant general of Albert Sidney Johnston's 1st Division. In 1866, Ellen married widower Dr. Charles Manuel Currell.
11. Ibid., 87–88.

Rosser had to send him back, this time with sufficient money to send the telegraph. Though he could not personally go to her yet, he certainly wanted to at the first opportunity.[11]

The next day, Rosser and Walton's adjutant, William Owen, rode out along the Warrenton Turnpike, the route the Federals had taken while fleeing the Manassas battlefield toward Washington. The two gathered as much abandoned Federal property—blankets, overcoats, and other supplies—as they could carry on their horses. Rosser even salvaged what he thought was New Hampshire Congressman John P. Hale's abandoned carriage. Hale was one of many who had come down to "see the fun" of the anticipated Federal victory.[12]

Rosser had his eyes on other ladies besides Ellen. A charming woman from Fairfax County, Virginia, named Antonia Ford, the flirtatious 24-year-old daughter of Edward R. Ford, a well-to-do Fairfax Court House merchant and secessionist, purportedly had been involved in intelligence-gathering activities before the Manassas battle. According to Rosser, Maj. Gen. Irvin McDowell had for a short time made his headquarters at the Ford family's home. Allegedly, Antonia had overheard a council of war and was anxious to get the critical information to Major General Beauregard. She was the object of many a suitor, but preferred to "play the field." Her brother Charles served in Col. J. E. B. Stuart's horse artillery. A civilian named Peter Wilson Hairston wrote about Antonia's exploits, and he was one of the first members of Stuart's inner circle; Hairston was also Stuart's cousin and brother-in-law.[13]

On September 4, 1861, Hairston told his wife Fanny about the encounter between Rosser and Antonia:

> **I heard yesterday one of the most romantic incidents of the war. Miss Ford of Fairfax Court House having received information thro' the Federal officers who took up quarters in her mother's house, that the enemy intended to make an attack on the 18th of July on Manassas and their plan of attack, procured permission the night before to visit her grandmother who lived six miles off. She then procured an old and rough-going horse and made her way to Manassas where she was**

12. Owen, *Washington Artillery*, 42–43.
13. Rosser, "Autobiographical Sketch," 13–14, UVA; Lisa Tendrich Frank, ed., *An Encyclopedia of American Women at War: From the Home Front to the Battlefields* (Santa Barbara, CA, 2013), 2 vols., 1:227–28; Larissa Phillips, *Women Civil War Spies of the Confederacy* (New York, 2004), 53–60; Peter W. Hairston to "Fanny," September 4, 1861, Peter W. Hairston Papers, Southern Historical Collection, Chapel Hill, NC; hereinafter SHC/UNC.

Antonia Ford Willard

In October 1861, Miss Ford was made an honorary aide-de-camp by J.E.B. Stuart in appreciation for her spying. Miss Ford was arrested for spying in March 1873, but released that same year once she signed the Oath of Allegiance. She married Major Joseph Willard, in 1864. Willard was co-owner of the Willard Hotel in Washington. The couple had three children, but only one survived. Antonia died in 1871, at age 33, from the lingering effects of imprisonment and child bearing.

taken prisoner by Capt. Rosser of the Washington Artillery from New Orleans. He carried her to Genl. Beauregard and she revealed to him their plan of attack which enabled him to place his men in ambush and commit such havoc on the enemy on the 18th [21st] . . . Yesterday I saw a beautiful bouquet which she had sent Capt. Rosser and I would not be surprised if the matter ended by her leading him captive. She is said to be beautiful and accomplished and I know him to be a brave and gallant man. It was said that while Confederates still held the area near Alexandria, Rosser invited Miss Ford to Munson's Hill, close enough to peer through a spyglass at the skeleton of the Capitol dome in Washington.[14]

The Reconnaissance Balloon

The Confederate army remained in the vicinity of Centreville, Virginia, for eight weeks after the first battle of Manassas. After the battle, Maj. Gen. George B. McClellan replaced Maj. Gen. Irvin McDowell as commander of the Federal army, and throughout the next several months, he proceeded to reorganize and train the army into a well-prepared fighting force. One of his initiatives was to have Professor Thaddeus Lowe construct an aerial reconnaissance balloon to observe the movements and disposition of the Confederate forces. Although a source of considerable irritation to the Confederate commanders, they could not do much about it. The balloons and their aerial observers were out of small arms range.[15]

Writing many years later, Tom Rosser claims that he himself came up with an ingenious solution for the pesky balloons. He realized that no cannon could be elevated more than a few degrees on its carriage, and it would require a firing angle of at least 45 degrees to reach an elevated target such as an observation balloon. So, on September 2, he had a pit dug in order to elevate the gun's muzzle and provide room for some of its recoil. No range tables existed to establish the proper firing angle, so he estimated the angle to hit the balloon. His first round missed the target, but the second shot reportedly either hit the balloon's rigging or just nearly missed it, forcing the Federals to haul their craft down quickly. Thereafter, when the Confederates employed balloons, they ascended well behind the front lines, out of artillery range.[16]

Rosser further distinguished himself during a small skirmish on September 11 in Fairfax County. Brigadier General William F. Smith sent a 2,000-man Federal reconnaissance force, which occupied Lewinsville, Virginia, across the Potomac River. Colonel Stuart's Confederate force opposed him with 305 men of the 13th Virginia, two companies of the 1st Virginia, under Capt. William Patrick's command, and Rosser's two guns. Major James B. Terrill led the Union infantry, accompanied by Capt. Charles Griffin's battery of eight guns and a small detachment of cavalry. Stuart moved his force from his headquarters at Munson's Hill toward Lewinsville, approach-

14. Peter W. Hairston to Fanny, September 4, 1861, Peter W. Hairston Papers, SHC/UNC; Ernest B. Furgurson, *Freedom Rising: Washington in the Civil War* (New York, 2005), 230.
15. Bushong, *Fightin' Tom Rosser*, 16.
16. Rosser, "Reminiscences," 89, & "Autobiographical Sketch," 25–26, both UVA.

ing the Federals from their left and rear. His cavalry pickets had reported the Federals there in large numbers. Securing a safe retreat route by using the woods surrounding the town as a screen, Stuart sent out about 100 skirmishers. Meanwhile, Rosser's artillery surprised "a cluster of the enemy a quarter of a mile away, sending the enemy in full retreat." His shells, Stuart recounted, were "bursting directly over their heads, and creating the greatest havoc and confusion on their ranks."[17]

Rallying after retreating about a mile and a half, the Union artillery unlimbered and poured round after round up the road where they anticipated the Confederate pursuit. Stuart's small force, however, had not revealed its location for most of the conflict and safely avoided the exploding shells. The Confederates fired from many positions, trying to convince the Federals that they were a much larger force. Finally, they charged part of the Union line. Some of the Yankees scattered, but some attempted to flank the Confederate left. Sent to support the infantry in that sector, a howitzer of the Washington Artillery dispersed the Federals after several shots. Although facing a numerically superior force, Stuart's Confederates had driven the enemy from the field.

Pleased with his soldiers' performance, Stuart also took notice of Rosser's diligence, writing on September 11 that "having no enemy left to contend with" Rosser had requested "to view the ground of the enemy's flight, and found the road plowed up by his solid shot and strewn with fragments of shells; 2 men left dead in the road, 1 mortally wounded, and 1 not hurt being taken prisoner. The prisoners said the havoc in their ranks was fearful, justifying what I saw myself of the confusion."[18]

Stuart complimented Rosser's contribution to the Confederate success by his skillful handling of his two guns. Rosser reported his guns had fired 66 rifle and 41 spherical cases. Reportedly, his success in forcing down McClellan's observation balloon combined with his actions at Lewinsville won him promotion to captain on September 27, 1861.[19]

---

17. *The War of the Rebellion: A Compilation of the Official Records of the Union and Confederate Armies,* 128 vols. (Washington, D.C.: Government Printing Office, 1880–1901), vol. 51, part 1, 43. All references are to Series I unless otherwise noted. Hereafter cited as follows *OR* 51/1:43.
18. *OR* 5:184.
19. Ibid.; Charles Preston Poland, Jr., *The Glories of War: Small Battles and Early Heroes of 1861* (Bloomington, IN, 2006), 99; *OR* 5:183 & 51/1:42–43; Owen, *Washington Artillery,* 54.

Nonetheless, poorly manufactured ordnance severely limited the Confederate artillery units' firing accuracy. Early in the war, after the Lewinsville fight, Rosser's 2nd Company complained of the:

> **inefficiency of the case and shell projectiles [for] the rifled guns... not one of them exploding. The 'Boarman' fuze, with which the spherical case and shell for the howitzer were served, showed, in their manufacture, great deficiency. There was no uniformity whatever in their burning. Some cut for five seconds did not burn, in many cases. Two others cut at two, burnt as long as four or five seconds.**[20]

Artillery commanders found that drill was continually needed. Untrained substituting soldiers were required to fill various positions on the crew as cannoneers were disabled or killed during battle or fell out of ranks from illness. All men in a gun crew needed to know how to perform the duties of each cannon position. Artillery work was exhausting, requiring endurance.

In the fall of 1861, a picture of Rosser was emerging as a young artillery officer studiously and carefully learning his craft, as well as experimenting and honing his skills as an artillerist. Cool under fire and seemingly fearless, no one questioned his bravery.

Upon Rosser's promotion to captain, he was assigned outpost duty in command of the 2nd Company. Still attached to Stuart's command, Rosser's company was stationed at the most advanced position in the Confederate states, within sight of the Federal capital at Washington, D.C. The battalion received three 24-pounder howitzers, thereby increasing its armament to 16 guns, four batteries of four guns each. Normally only 350 yards apart, some of the opposing pickets advanced to within 100 yards of each other to get off a good shot. Rosser had not forgotten how to shoot. While out on reconnaissance on September 23, he took a rifle shot at an enemy picket leaning on a tree and brought him down "like a black bird before a fowling piece."[21]

After the battle of Manassas, Lieutenant George Custer participated in the fights defending Washington. In October he became ill and was absent from his unit until February 1862. Custer recuperated in Monroe, Michigan, where his brother-in-law and half-sister lived and where he met his future bride, Elizabeth Bacon. Custer began his lifelong avoidance of alcohol after meeting Elizabeth.

20. *OR* 51/1:43; Owen, *Washington Artillery*, 55–56.
21. *The Charleston Mercury*, September 24, 1861.

Stuart's brigade, pulled from outpost duty as Union pressure increased, returned to Fairfax Court House. There, on October 14, 1861, a reporter from the Richmond Dispatch penned a nice description of Captain Rosser:

> **a strong, well-made, athletic man, something over six feet in height; a naturally dark complexion, browned by exposure; dark hair, eyes and whiskers; a full, expressive face; broad, massive shoulders, and limbs that show... the military training that has shaped them. The head is covered with a black felt hat... a navy blue sash belted around the waist, the light blue pants of the corps, with red cord, and heavy top boots... The tout [ensemble] of the man is decidedly picturesque. Imagine the blending of a Texas hunter with an Italian bandit—one of those glorious, noble-looking fellows [Spanish painter Bartolomé Esteban] Murillo has made famous—and you cannot form a very bad mental picture of him who is stalking with manly stride before me. As I have stated previously, his characteristics are very similar to those of General Stuart, his present friend and commander. Sagacious, vigilant, attentive to duty, well skilled in his profession, he is said to be the best artillery officer in the service, of his age.**[22]**

When the Federals made a strong demonstration at Fairfax Court House on October 19, 1861, the Rebel forces withdrew to Centreville to consolidate their lines and construct fortifications. Then, as the weather turned bad and the roads became mired in mud, virtually all campaigning ended. The ensuing inactivity opened opportunities for social activities. Rosser, like his commander, enjoyed relaxing. While the enlisted men, as was their lot, endured the cold, rain, and snow as best they could in their tents or rough cabins, the officers made themselves comfortable living quarters, transporting a framed house from the outposts to Centreville. Around a roaring fire, they enjoyed hot punch and various goodies, and entertained each other with their favorite music. Rosser added his favorite tune, "Dragoon Bold," to the song list.[23]

In November, Stuart inquired of the Adjutant and Inspector General (AIG) Office if his requested appointment of Lt. John Esten Cooke to captain of an artillery battery had been made.

---

22. *Richmond Dispatch*, October 18, 1861.
23. Owen, *Washington Artillery*, 59–60, 64–65; Bushong, *Fightin' Tom Rosser*, 17.

"If they would not make him Captain," Stuart wrote, "I wanted him senior 1st Lieutenant. John Pelham wants it and he may get it, and next to Rosser probably no graduate would do better."[24]

In mid-December, with winter settling in, the troops had to prepare sturdier quarters. The officers selected a site at Blackburn's Ford on the same grounds the Federals had occupied before the battle of Manassas. With plentiful wood available, the men built log huts to replace their tents. The soldiers named their quarters Camp Waltonville, in honor of the Washington Artillery's commander.[25]

Solid winter quarters allowed more time for social events. J.E.B. Stuart, as well as Rosser, flirted with many beautiful ladies from the area. The colonel was especially taken with Laura Ratcliffe—Antonia Ford's neighbor in Fairfax County—who reportedly also spied for the Confederacy. Stuart met Ratcliffe when she ministered to wounded soldiers at Frying Pan Church, in eastern Fairfax County. "A Happy New Year," he greeted her in January 1862. "I send you a nice beau Capt. Rosser (Miss Ford's friend)—he will escort you here to dinner, and hence to [Fairfax Court House] to spend a night with Mrs. Ford. Be assured I sacrifice a great personal pleasure in foregoing this visit for your sake and Capt. R's."[26]

The Washington Artillery had suffered heavily in recent fighting, needing replacements by December. As the new year began, Rosser was ordered to proceed to New Orleans to gather recruits and bring them back to Virginia. This offered him an opportunity to see Ellen R. Lape, who resided near Fayette, Mississippi. Because Federal gunboats had closed the Mississippi River to passenger steamer travel, Rosser had to ride the trains. Leaving the rails at Brookhaven, Mississippi, the closest rail point to Fayette, he hired a team and driver and set out directly for Ellen's residence, a 40-mile trip. Rosser recalled that on the first night traveling from Brookhaven to Fayette, he spent the night with a planter who happened to know Ellen and the Hinds family. Rosser, excited and in love, "kept his host up most of the night talking about her." The next morning he started for the Hinds's plantation. Rosser remembered going out of his way to be friendly with the locals; he intended to marry Ellen and wanted good relations with her neighbors. Knocking at the door of Ellen's home, he felt "sure that all heard the thumping of my heart." A servant announced his presence, and soon Ellen, "a tall, handsome woman," appeared.[27]

24. J. E. B. Stuart to Flora, November 24, 1861, J. E. B. Stuart Letters, Emory University (EU), Atlanta, GA; Adele H. Mitchell, ed., *The Letters of Major General James E. B. Stuart* (Stuart-Mosby Historical Society, 1990), 225, Alexandria, VA.
25. Owen, *Washington Artillery*, 68–69.
26. J. E. B. Stuart to Laura Ratcliffe, January 6, 1862, Library of Congress (LC).
27. Rosser, "Reminiscences," 104–105, UVA.

She led Tom to a sofa in one corner of the room, and he sat next to her. He presented her with a solitaire engagement ring he had purchased in Richmond. But to his consternation, it would not slip over her knuckle when he tried to put it on her left ring finger. Ellen reminded him of the promise she had made in her letter: that if he should survive the war, "I might then claim her." He tried to convince her that the war was nearly over already, but she refused his marriage proposal. After staying a few days, trying to change her mind, Tom Rosser had to proceed to duty in New Orleans without having won her hand. He must have been hurt deeply and was probably angry too. He did not handle rejection well. After completing his recruiting duties, a dejected Rosser returned to Virginia.[28]

By the beginning of March 1862, all signs pointed to the Union army making a massive movement southward along the coast toward Richmond. With improving roads, the men of the Washington Artillery likewise prepared to break camp and head southward. Confederate commander Gen. Joseph E. Johnston assigned the Washington Artillery to Brig. Gen. James Longstreet's infantry division. On March 6, the Confederate army left the Centreville area and headed 100 miles south for Orange Court House, where, upon arrival, they found an abundance of food and a bevy of pretty girls. With the bands of the Washington Artillery and the 1st Virginia providing music, the officers enjoyed dancing at the local tavern. Celebrating a promotion, Brig. Gen. Ambrose P. Hill, along with Rosser and several others, was there.[29]

Rosser's performance, up to this point, had so impressed J.E.B. Stuart that he felt the young captain deserved a field promotion. Accordingly, on April 4, 1862, he recommended the promotion to Confederate president Jefferson Davis; Rosser, he averred, had "extraordinary merit, unsurpassed ability, and conspicuous gallantry displayed in action." He was not alone in his observations. Colonel Beverly H. Robertson, commander of the 4th Virginia Cavalry, reported at a later engagement that "Rosser displayed much judgment in placing his pieces, which, under his personal supervision, were served in the most handsome style."[30]

Rosser's battery was, in fact, establishing quite a reputation. Brigadier General William N. Pendleton, Johnston's chief of artillery, took notice, requesting the battery be detached from the Washington Artillery to serve temporarily with Brig. Gen. Robert Toombs's

---

28. Ibid.,105–06. Rosser claimed the ring was too small for Ellen because she had gained weight.
29. Owen, *Washington Artillery*, 75–76.
30. Ibid.; *OR* 11/1:663–64.

infantry brigade; the request was approved. After two months of service with Toombs, the battalion commander, Major Walton, sharply protested to headquarters about the disruption in his command. "[I]f this policy of detachment, except for temporary duty, was continued," Walton complained, "his battalion would be dissolved, and he would be without a command."[31]

The Peninsula Campaign

As the Confederate artillery officers attended church in Richmond one beautiful Sunday morning on April 6, they received orders to move out at once. On the march the next day, they encountered sleet and snow. Miserable already with no provisions, shelter, wood, or rations, their morale suffered another blow when they received orders to retrace their steps back to Richmond. Major General McClellan's seaborne movement of his army to the Virginia Peninsula, between the York and James rivers, and his plan to march up the peninsula to capture Richmond had necessitated adjustments. With the movement of horses and artillery almost impossible over the drenched, wretched roads, the persistent Confederates finally reached Richmond on April 13. About a week later, the men, horses, and artillery pieces were ferried down the James River to near its junction with the Warwick River. From there they marched to Yorktown. When the battalion reported to Longstreet at Yorktown, Walton left Rosser and the 2nd Company there and took the rest of the battalion to Williamsburg.[32]

On the lower Virginia Peninsula, Confederate Maj. Gen. John B. Magruder, commanding 13,600 soldiers, devised an ingenious ruse to fool McClellan and the Army of the Potomac's 55,000-man vanguard. In charge of delaying the Federal march up the peninsula until Confederate army commander Johnston could assemble reinforcements, Magruder marched his soldiers back and forth across the peninsula, demonstrating noisily. McClellan became convinced that a force superior to his own would dispute his advance. The subterfuge worked for a while, holding the line at Yorktown, but it finally became necessary to withdraw farther up the peninsula. Even with reconnaissance from the hot air balloons, McClellan was not getting accurate intelligence. Plus, the Federal commander typically overestimated his enemies' numbers and strength, and therefore advanced slowly and cautiously in pursuit. Finally, he shelled Yorktown and took possession of it on May 4—after the Southerners had already left. The Confederate artillerists continued their retreat

31. *OR* 51/2:546–47, 572–73.
32. Owen, *Washington Artillery*, 76, 78.

until they reached a position called Blakey's Mill Pond, only two miles south of the Southern capital, Richmond.[33]

Rosser was seriously wounded during a small skirmish at Mechanicsville, Virginia, on May 24. The Richmond Dispatch reported:

> After fighting for some time, and while engaged in posting a piece to protect it from the enemy's fire, he was struck by a fragment of a shell, which tore the flesh from the right arm [above the elbow], causing a severe lacerated wound. His horse was also shot under him. About this time, the order came [for] our force to fall back, and the artillery withdrew from the field in beautiful style, in the face of enemy fire... Capt. Rosser is now at the house of Dr. Gibson, on Franklin Street [Richmond]."[34]

Incapacitated for more than two weeks, Rosser was not fit for the field until June 15. Upon his return he discovered he had been appointed lieutenant colonel of the Washington Artillery five days earlier. Two days later, now assigned as Brig. Gen. Henry Wise's chief of ordnance, Rosser wrote, "I was fond of Artillery... I soon began to see visions of glory on the battlefield with sixteen instead of four guns." On June 18, 1862, Rosser was officially promoted to lieutenant colonel.[35]

Rosser took command of four batteries stationed at Chaffin's Bluff, on the north side of the James River, south of Richmond. Expecting Federal cavalry to attack, and lacking cavalry of his own, Brigadier General Wise sent orders through a subordinate that if enemy cavalry appeared, Rosser's artillery batteries were to charge them. Rosser was flabbergasted but promised to follow orders. The incident prompted Rosser to request to be relieved of further service under the 55-year-old general, whom he did not respect. The request was granted, and he transferred to the reserve artillery.[36]

While Rosser's military fortunes waxed and waned, McClellan's forces steadily advanced up the peninsula toward the Confederate capital, with Johnston's army giving way before them. McClellan already had a numerical advantage of nearly two to one, and he anticipated receiving McDowell's 40,000 troops, stationed at Fredericksburg, which according to plan, would soon be sent to him. Instead, Gen. Robert E. Lee, Davis's military advisor, conceived a plan whereby Maj. Gen. Thomas J. Jackson—nicknamed "Stonewall" since

---

33. Ibid., 78.
34. *Richmond Dispatch*, May 26, 1862.
35. SO 34 & 65(7), both in Rosser Service Record, NA.
36. Rosser, "Autobiographical Sketch," 26–29, UVA.

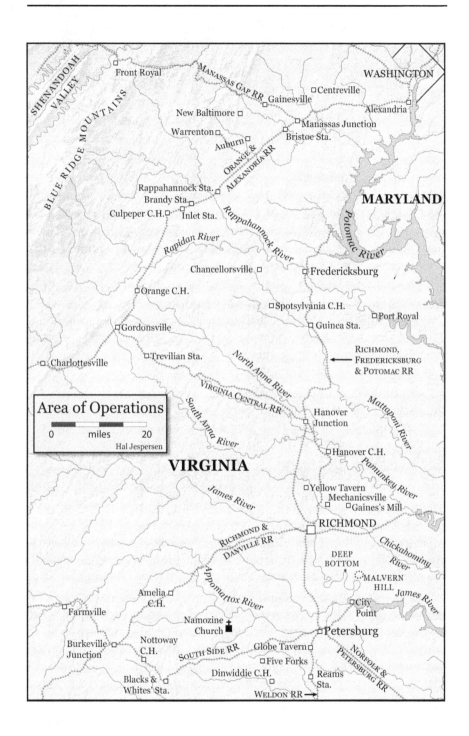

Area of Operations

0   miles   20

Hal Jespersen

the battle of Manassas—would create a major diversion in the Shenandoah Valley. Jackson's battles and maneuvers, including a stunning victory at Winchester, Virginia, were so successful that the Federals, perceiving a threat to Washington, halted releasing McDowell's forces to McClellan.

With his five corps within striking distance of Richmond, McClellan then made a strategic blunder by isolating two of his corps south of the Chickahominy River. Seeing an opening, Johnston endeavored to attack McClellan's left wing with the bulk of his army. The battle began on May 31 at Seven Pines, but the Confederate attacks started late and were executed in piecemeal fashion. A bloody draw resulted with severe losses on both sides, and Johnston himself was seriously wounded. On June 1, Lee was appointed commander of the Confederate forces, and immediately withdrew his army to the defenses of Richmond to reorganize and regroup.[37]

For the next several weeks, the Washington Artillery saw little action during the Peninsula campaign. Longstreet visited the unit's camp and informed Colonel Walton that Rosser had been appointed chief of artillery on the right wing of Longstreet's forces. Walton retained command of the Washington Artillery itself, but then detailed it as reserve artillery for Longstreet.[38]

On June 22, Rosser received a letter from Stuart thanking him for the battery's gift of a "beautiful kepi." Stuart wrote, "I know that the most appropriate response from one is the assurance that when the red tempest of battle lowers, that cap shall be seen, where the Washington Artillery would have it, at the foremost in the charge and last in the retreat." But to Rosser's astonishment, the following day he got another letter from Stuart, informing him that he had been promoted to colonel and transferred to Stuart's cavalry brigade as commander of the 5th Virginia Cavalry Regiment. "Come see me at daylight in the morning & I will give you the particulars," Stuart instructed. "Come a-runnin'." The next day Secretary of War John Randolph officially notified Rosser of his promotion.[39]

Rosser wrote in his unpublished memoir, "Reminiscences," that he declined Stuart's offer. The general never imagined Rosser would resist a transfer to the cavalry, decline a personal invitation from its commanding general, and forfeit promotion to colonel and regimental command. Rosser had also spurned the highly respected Fitzhugh Lee,

37. *OR* 11/1:992.
38. Owen, *Washington Artillery*, 85.
39. J. E. B. Stuart to Rosser, June 22–23, 1862, UVA; Mitchell, *The Letters of James E. B. Stuart*, 251, 257; Rosser's Service Record, NA; Rosser, "Autobiographical Sketch," 29, UVA.

who had lobbied Stuart for him. "This note [offer] greatly displeased me," Rosser recalled years later, "for I had a very poor opinion of the Cavalry, as I had seen it in the Confederate service and I was too well pleased [with the artillery] to desire a change." Rosser probably adjudged the cavalry as having a little too much fun and not being attentive enough to business. He may have also been displeased about the idea of leaving his friends Pelham and Garnett. Although his ambitions would increase dramatically in the near future, at that point, Rosser may not have envisioned anymore for himself than commanding an artillery battalion at the rank of colonel.[40]

General James Ewell Brown Stuart

Stuart took notice of Rosser and had him transferred to his cavalry to take command of the 5th Virginia Cavalry.

Courtesy: Library of Congress

Rosser's uncorroborated rejection of Stuart's invitation did not end the matter. On June 24, Secretary of War Randolph summoned Rosser to Richmond. The officer arrived in Randolph's office and greeted him with deference, thanking him for the promotional opportunity and expressing "assurances of due appreciation of the honor, as well as the joy he had conferred so undeservedly." Randolph, however, was in no mood to accept any rejection of his orders. "I have promoted you again and understanding that you are too well satisfied with your present command to accept another," Randolph said, "notwithstanding that it carries promotion with it, and I wish to say that you have already been transferred, your successor to command of your battalion of Artillery has already been appointed."[41]

---

40. Rosser, "Reminiscences," 167, UVA.
41. There is no other documented evidence of Rosser's account of this event. It is entirely from Rosser's memory, recorded many years afterward in his unpublished "Reminiscences." The entire episode appears self-serving in creating a certain image of Rosser, and should be assessed with caution. It is

Randolph's words caught Rosser off guard, but as the surprise weakened, he became angry. Randolph's actions violated Rosser's "code of honor," by which he believed officers were not to be treated in this manner, that they had the right to refuse capricious transfers made without their knowledge. Rosser would not accept his commission document from the secretary. "You refuse to accept," Randolph challenged angrily. "Yes," came the response, "I prefer to remain where I am. I don't like the cavalry, and while I thank you, I must decline the honor."

Randolph then launched into a demeaning harangue. "I don't ask you to accept it, but as I have seen fit to transfer you from the artillery to another branch of the service, your consent is not necessary and you have got to accept it, or you have got to leave the service as there is no other place for you." Rosser started to reply, but Randolph cut him off, saying, "Which will you do, accept promotion or resign?" Rosser, stunned at such disparaging treatment, let his temper get the best of him: "Then, sir, I'll leave the service," he replied, and walked abruptly from Randolph's office, leaving his commission behind.

Fortunately for Rosser's military future, J. E. B. Stuart intervened. The general listened intently and sympathetically to Rosser's recounting of the disastrous meeting. The general told him he had taken the only honorable course under the circumstances and urged him to wait while he tried to mediate the dispute with Randolph. Rosser recalled, "Stuart soon returned and stating 'that it would never do to leave the Secretary in such a frame of mind' toward you (me) as he was in, and begged me to go back with him and have a further talk with the Secretary of War. Of course, that meant surrender, and I was not in condition to yield."

Realizing Rosser needed time to get his temper under control, Stuart took him for a leisurely walk. Stuart made a number of "fair promises" to the young officer if he would change his mind and return with him to talk with Randolph, surrendering to the promotion. Stuart's promises are unknown, but they probably hinted at a future promotion to command a brigade. Rosser relented and returned to Randolph's office where Stuart initiated and led the conversation. Randolph, for his part, remained silent until he recognized a moment for reconciliation, which came when Rosser asked how well the 5th Virginia was armed. "Poorly," Randolph replied.

---

difficult to believe that young Rosser, a lowly captain who could be colonel, would transgress his station and ignore his West Point training to adhere to the hierarchical command structure. This is Rosser's version of the events, which may be exaggerated.

I'll give you the first arms that come through the blockade—and I'm expecting a cargo at Wilmington every day."[42]

Randolph's gesture allowed Rosser to ameliorate his previous actions in an honorable, face-saving way. The upshot of the entire affair was prosaic: Rosser joined Stuart's cavalry command as a colonel commanding the 5th Virginia Cavalry.

The entire Rosser-Stuart-Randolph episode, recorded years after the event, is cut whole-cloth out of Tom Rosser's memory. No other evidence exists. Hence, one might observe, Rosser appears favorably as an officer of rather crusty, but determined, values. The bare facts of the case suggest a more cautious approach to the story: a brand new 26-year-old lieutenant colonel, now promoted to full colonel and given his own command, defies his penultimate superior and spurns his designated commander in militant disregard of his rigorous West Point training and the basic hierarchical principle foundational to all military organizations.

Rosser's promotion to command of the 5th Virginia came with controversy. In spring 1862, Capt. Henry Clay Pate first conceived the idea of a new cavalry unit, the 5th Virginia, when returning with his Petersburg Rangers (Letcher Mounted Guards) to Richmond from service in the western part of the state. Pate's idea was to build one independent command of enlistees from every Virginia county, which would serve anywhere in the state that it was needed. Familiar with all areas of the state, they could act as scouts, harass enemy supply lines, and gather intelligence on enemy dispositions and movements. Secretary of War Randolph was so pleased with the idea, he immediately ordered Pate to implement it. Recruiters for his regiment blanketed the state, and in short order, seven companies, about 900 men, volunteered. Pate established a camp at Allen's Grove, near Richmond, and began drilling the men. The 2nd Battalion Virginia Cavalry was officially organized on May 25, 1862.[43]

Brigadier General Stuart visited Pate's command several times, always expressing pleasure at the soldierly appearance and progress of the battalion. On June 23, Pate received a request to immediately report to Stuart's headquarters where he received one of the shocks of his life: the general informed him that his battalion no longer existed. Pate's battalion, plus another few companies, had been formed into the 5th Virginia Cavalry Regiment under a new commander, Col. Thomas L. Rosser. Pate, a hard-fighting, eccentric, and sometimes erratic,

---

42. Previous paragraphs based upon ibid., 167–69; Rosser, "Autobiographical Sketch," 29–30, UVA.
43. Robert J. Driver, *5th Virginia Cavalry. Virginia Regimental Series.* (Lynchburg, VA, 1997), 22.

officer, was named the regiment's lieutenant colonel. An inconsolable Pate remained at Stuart's headquarters all night. On the return trip to inform his men of the changes, Pate questioned a companion, adjutant Robert S. Morgan, asking, "What shall I do? How can I meet my men and tell them a stranger has been ordered to command them?" Pate continued to struggle with the new arrangement until just before he reached camp when he said, "I think I see my way clear, now: the Confederate Government has treated me badly; but I belong to Virginia, and to her I devote my life." He proceeded to inform his men that very day at dress parade. Pate's men were troubled and protested vigorously to headquarters. One word from Pate likely could have ignited a revolt, but Pate succeeded in quelling the potentially dangerous situation.[44]

The following table shows the organization of the new regiment.

5th Virginia Cavalry Regiment - June 1862[45]

Company	Name	Commander	Origin
A	Gloucester Light Dragoons	Capt. John W. Puller	Gloucester Point
B	[Independent]	Capt Frederick R. Windsor	[SC, GA, LA]
C	Danville Cavalry	Capt. William K. Mebane	Danville
D	Petersburg Rangers (Letcher Mounted Guards)	Capt. John W. Bullock	Petersburg
E	King & Queen County Cavalry	Capt. Marius P. Todd	King & Queen County
F	Shields Lancers or Dragoons	Capt. John Eells	--
G	Randolph Cavalry	Capt. McNairy Hobson	Randolph, VA
H	The James City Cavalry	Capt. James H. Allen	James City County
I	--	Capt. Rueben B. Boston	Companies B/F 3rd VA Artillery
K	--	Capt. Charles Pannill	Petersburg

Rosser "was well received" when he officially took command on June 27, 1862. Morgan recalled, "Pate invited him to his table, and lent him horses. Colonel Rosser at once commenced the organization of the regiment into squadrons. In this matter, he held no consultation with his Lieutenant Colonel."[46]

---

44. Ibid., 582; John Lipscomb Johnson, ed., *The University Memorial; Biographical Sketches of Alumni Who Fell in the Confederate War*, Pate biography by Robert S. Morgan. (Baltimore, 1871), 581. Hereinafter cited as "Johnson, ed., Biographical Sketches of Alumni Who Fell in the Confederate War."
45. Driver, *5th Virginia Cavalry*, 23, 27.
46. Johnson, ed., *Biographical Sketches of Alumni Who Fell in the Confederate War*, 582.

Meanwhile, upon receiving reinforcements, General Lee seized the offensive in what collectively became known as the Seven Days Battles, occurring from June 25 to July 1, 1862. McClellan quickly lost the initiative as Lee began a series of successive attacks at Beaver Dam Creek (Mechanicsville) on June 26, at Gaines's Mill the following day, and at Savage Station on June 29. McClellan's Army of the Potomac fell back toward the safety of Harrison's Landing on the James River. Poorly executed orders at the battle of Glendale on June 30 blunted Lee's final opportunity to intercept the Union Army, which escaped and established a strong defensive position on Malvern Hill. During the battle of Malvern Hill on July 1, which brought the campaign to a close, Lee launched futile frontal assaults, suffering heavy casualties in the face of strong infantry and artillery defenses.[47]

Rosser's regiment played only a minor role in the campaign. The 5th Virginia, along with a squadron of the Hampton Legion, and the 1st North Carolina, commanded by Col. Laurence S. Baker, were ordered on June 26 to "watch the enemy's movements toward James River." They were instructed to notify the nearest at-hand commander of any enemy attempt to move from White Oak Swamp to the James River and "to harass and delay him en-route 'till our forces could fall upon him." Two days later, Rosser reported to Maj. Gen. Benjamin Huger a considerable force of the enemy near Willis's Church and also small elements of Yankees moving toward the James River.

On a scout the next morning, Rosser encountered the 1st North Carolina and 3rd Virginia, both under Baker's command, returning to camp after an earlier fight that morning at Willis's Methodist church, on the Quaker Road, 10 miles southeast of Richmond. The 3rd Pennsylvania, 2nd Rhode Island, 7th Massachusetts, as well as Battery C of the 1st Pennsylvania Light Artillery, had ambushed Baker's troopers. The Rebels lost 15 men, killed or wounded, and had 48 captured. Rosser recalled that his scouts had recaptured 15 of the 1st North Carolina's horses from the enemy before he marched his troopers and the Hampton Legion to the junction of the River and Long Bridge roads.[48]

The following morning, June 30, Rosser's entire command got involved in a brisk skirmish when the Federals drove in his pickets on the Long Bridge Road, near Willis's Church. After reestablishing the picket line, Rosser reported:

47. David G. Martin, *The Peninsula Campaign* (Conshohocken, PA, 1992), 131–33, 143–45; Stephen W. Sears, *To the Gates of Richmond* (New York, 1992), 189, 209–10, 242, 249, 269–74, 308–12, 336.
48. *OR* 11/2:13.

[I] then dismounted one company and deployed them as skirmishers, giving them a squadron for support, and sent them forward, and after driving in the enemy's picket still pressed upon him, and strange to say, this gallant little band, commanded by Capt. John W. Bullock, of my regiment, drove them back within a few hundred yards of their main force, and was still pressing upon them when General Longstreet's advance came up, and with his infantry and artillery attacked them. [49]

At the same time, Rosser's pickets reported Union infantry advancing toward River Road, and Longstreet ordered Rosser to take his command in that direction. Rosser's subsequent reconnaissance found the head of the retiring Federal column moving hurriedly toward the James River. About 1 p.m., Rosser duly passed on his observations to Longstreet and Brig. Gen. Theophilus H. Holmes (commanding the Department of Fredericksburg and attached to Lee), but Rosser stated that "for some reason, no one paid attention to this report." Rosser then recounted what he saw to General Lee, who came himself to observe and who quickly ordered Holmes to attack the enemy. Holmes, however, arrived late in the day, about 5:00 p.m., and the dust he stirred up revealed his presence to the enemy. With support of the gunboats on the James River, the Federals launched an attack on Holmes's troops and drove them back. Rosser then withdrew his command, sending scouts toward the river to observe the movements of the gunboats.

Early the next morning, July 1, Rosser encountered the Union line of battle at Malvern Hill. "I was near enough to hear loud and prolonged cheering," he remembered, "as if reinforcements or a general had arrived." He reported this to Huger, but Baker assumed command upon his arrival "and soon moved with my command over to the left to support the attack...Magruder was about to make." Rosser and his command were held on the left. Rosser did not particularly like what he saw. Whenever Southern troops "were thrown in contact with the enemy I could but observe the great want of proper discipline necessary to insure implicit confidence. They had not been drilled and most of them had never been under fire before." Despite a certain ineptitude, Rosser's troopers captured several prisoners and collected many arms. The 5th Virginia lost only four men, one by desertion. The regiment continued on picket duty and followed McClellan's retreat to White House Landing. [50]

---

49. Previous paragraphs based on *OR* 11/2:513, 532.
50. Ibid. After the Seven Days Battles, McClellan's army sought relative safety next to the James River, having suffered almost 16,000 casualties during the retreat. Lee's army, which had been on the offensive during the Seven Days, lost more than 20,000 men.

McClellan's Peninsula campaign had failed with the end of the Seven Days Battles, and the Confederate capital had been saved. And in light of his campaign in the Shenandoah Valley that had stymied three Federal armies, Stonewall Jackson's star ascended, despite his subpar performance on the Virginia Peninsula.

On June 26, 1862, President Abraham Lincoln, exasperated at his generals' failures, reorganized the armies into a unified command called the Army of Virginia, and, passing over several senior Eastern Theater generals, named Maj. Gen. John Pope from the western army to head it. The physically imposing but boastful and obnoxious Pope meant to proceed aggressively and announced his intention to make short work of the Confederates. On July 11, Lincoln completed the top-level shakeup by ordering Maj. Gen. Henry W. Halleck, also from the west, to come to Washington, D.C., to serve as general-in-chief of the United States armies.[51]

Barely two weeks into his command, Pope issued a series of general orders that, although generally acceptable to the Union rank and file, provoked bitter resentment in the South and sparked shock among his more conservative fellow officers. The directives encouraged his troops to seize food and supplies from Virginia farmers, raze to the ground any house from which shots were fired at his army, and threatened to shoot, without trial, anyone suspected of aiding the Confederates. Lee would later call the blusterous Pope "a miscreant who needed to be suppressed." Stonewall Jackson even proposed a "black flag" war policy—which would "give no quarter" to the enemy—to strike back at Pope, but it was never approved or implemented.[52]

Convinced that McClellan would not resume his threat against Richmond, General Lee decided to move north.

51. John William Thomason, *Jeb Stuart* (New York, 1929), 211–12. Walter E. Clark, ed., *North Carolina Regiments and Battalions from North Carolina: in The Great War, 1861–1865*, 5 vols. (Goldsboro, NC, 1901), 1:420; *OR* 11/2:532; John J. Hennessy, *Return to Bull Run: The Campaign and Battle of Second Manassas* (Norman, OK, 1993), 3–6.
52. Peter Cozzens, *General John Pope: A Life for the Nation* (Chicago, 2000), 86–87, 89.

CHAPTER 3

Colonel Thomas L. Rosser:
Commander of the 5th Virginia Cavalry Regiment

"Just then Colonel Rosser, with his sword drawn and dripping with blood, rode up to General Stuart, who was close by, and said in his own emphatic language: 'General, I have been giving them hell, cutting and slashing right and left.'"

4th Virginia Cavalry trooper recounting Rosser's words at the battle of Catlett's Station

Tom Rosser overcame the pushback he received from taking command of the newly created 5th Virginia Cavalry. In the following year, he drilled his troopers, increased his regiment's efficiency, and took part in daring fights under the command of his mentor, Maj. Gen. J. E. B. Stuart. The friendship between the two men underwent some trying moments, but Stuart liked his mentee, looking after him and pushing for his advancement in rank.

A natural cavalryman and one of the best horsemen in his West Point class, Rosser, nonetheless, had been dragged" into the cavalry service. Again in favor with the general after a rocky start, he was now considered Stuart's protégé and friend. Rosser experienced rapid promotion thanks to Stuart's favoritism toward him. His developing love of the cavalry was owed partly to his farming background when he worked with horses; his love of horses never lessened. He was also thrilled that Stuart's brigade included his friend and former academy classmate Capt. John Pelham, commander of Stuart's Horse Artillery.

Foot soldiers envied the cavalrymen's evidently easy way of life—free of harsh discipline, riding wherever they went, and seemingly doing little by comparison to the infantry's way of tough fighting. "Whoever saw a dead cavalryman or a dead mule?" was the standard refrain among the infantry. And the fact that prima-donna cavalrymen tended to brag about their exploits did not endear them to the hard-slogging infantrymen either.[1]

Following Gen. Joseph E. Johnston's serious wounding on May 31 at the battle of Seven Pines, during the Peninsula campaign, the Confederate president, Jefferson Davis, appointed Gen. Robert E. Lee as the commander of the newly designated Army of Northern Virginia. Lee pulled his forces back to Richmond before setting out to counterattack during the battles of the Seven Days, which occurred from June 25 to July 1, fought against Federal commander Maj. Gen. George B. McClellan's Army of the Potomac. The battles of the Seven Days effectively ended the Peninsula campaign, as McClellan failed to capture the Confederate capital, Richmond. Although the campaign saved Richmond, Lee's army suffered substantially more casualties than McClellan's. After the battles, McClellan retreated, and on July 2, he reached his new base at Harrison's Landing on the James River. Lee called off the pursuit, recognizing his inability to exact additional damage to the Union army.

During this period, before McClellan received an August 3 order to abandon the Virginia Peninsula, the Union army looked for ways to renew its attack on Lee. During ensuing Union and Confederate cavalry probes and reconnaissance missions, skirmishes broke out. Stuart's cavalry screened army movements, reported enemy positions, and looked for opportunities to inflict damage on McClellan's army.

Stuart reported that from July 6 to 8 the Federals had persistently annoyed his pickets on the River Road, south of Westover, trying to dislodge his cavalry from its position. Rosser and his well-positioned regiment resisted so "that the enemy failed in the effort within three-quarters of a mile of his men and in his rear." At sundown on July 8, the Confederates withdrew from the Federal's position, with the cavalry screening the withdrawal. At daybreak the next day, Stuart's horsemen proceeded north of Turkey Creek, where they established a line of cavalry outposts for reconnaissance and to allow the men early response to enemy movements from the vicinity of Shirley, 17 miles southeast of Richmond, to the Chickahominy River.[2]

On July 10, Rosser's troops, along with other regiments, received a well-deserved respite. On that day, some officers of the regiment petitioned Lt. Col. Henry Clay Pate to bring charges against Colonel Rosser for allegedly being drunk on duty. This was the first formal complaint

---

1. John Lamb, "The Confederate Cavalry: It's Wants, Trials, and Heroism," Southern Historical Society Papers (SHSP), 38 vols, 26:363; Millard Kessler Bushong, *General Turner Ashby and Stonewall's Valley Campaign* (Verona, VA, 1980), 49.
2. *OR* 11/2:521.

about Rosser's drinking, but it would become increasingly obvious that Rosser had a problem with alcohol. Captain Reuben Boston was one of the leaders of the movement to formally charge Rosser. Pate hesitated sending the charges forward, but pressed by his officers as second in command, he did. Violating military discipline, Pate sent the charges directly to Stuart, not through the chain of command to Rosser first. Stuart had one of his staff officers look into the matter and, upon receiving the officer's report, dismissed the affair.[3]

Rosser's regiment proceeded to Hanover Court House to link up with Stuart. Rosser recalled that just before arriving they passed "a very pretty plantation home, 'Courtland,' and from the pretty lawn we were greeted by the waving of handkerchiefs by several bright rosey-cheeked young ladies." After conferring with Stuart, Rosser positioned his regiment in camp on the large grass field in front of Sarah Gregory Winston's mansion, located a mile and a half from Hanover Court House. William O. Winston, who had died the previous year, and his wife, Sarah, had long been prominent citizens of

Courtland

The mansion of William O. and Sarah G. Winston in Hanover County, Virginia. In July, 1862, Rosser's 5th Virginia Cavalry camped in the front yard, and Colonel Rosser met the Winstons' attractive daughter, Elizabeth.

By permission of Eleanor Cochran and Douglass Cochran, Jr.

---

3. Johnson, ed., *Biographical Sketches of Alumni Who Fell in the Confederate War*, 582. There is no indication that Rosser's problem with alcohol affected his leadership in battle.

eastern Hanover County, Virginia. Their 600-acre estate had been in the family for generations.[4]

Captain James Allen reported:

> **The 5th Virginia camped in Mrs. Winston's field, which was dotted over with wheat stalks, affording shelter and food for an innumerable host of harvest bugs. These bugs put themselves upon terms of great familiarity with the men, crawling over them and seeming to have a fancy for exploring the depths of the ears of the sleepers. The shrieks and groans of the sufferers oft-times made nights hideous and aroused the whole camp. The aid of the surgeon was invoked, and his skill was tested in extracting the bores.[5]**

Rosser undoubtedly sympathized, but he had other problems. "Having no facilities for writing a requisition to the Quartermaster for forage, I walked over to the mansion, struck the old brass knocker on the front door and was admitted by the servant, who said that 'Ole Misses' ain't home, but Miss Bettie's here. Take a seat 'till I call her.'" Soon a "stately and very pretty young lady of about 18 summers entered." Rosser rose, introduced himself, and apologetically explained that he needed paper and ink. "[S]he returned a sweet smile, showing the prettiest dimpled cheek I had ever seen." He further noticed that she was "tall, willowy, pale, dignified and pretty—and, from the first sight of her for the first time...I have been her slave and idolater." Rosser's regiment camped in front of the Winston home for two weeks, and before leaving, Rosser said, "I had two uncles and a brother of the beautiful young lady on my staff. I had become reconciled to the pain of losing fair Ellen down on the Mississippi and begun to cherish new hopes." Although he was saying nothing to "Miss Betsy" yet, when the regiment left on August 16, he had "begun a plan and scheme for her capture."[6]

Meanwhile, at the 5th Virginia's camp, Rosser issued orders enforcing strict military law, demanding all officers to report to him at reveille and tattoo, for example. Another order forbade any member of

---

4. Rosser, "Reminiscences," 173, & "Autobiographical Sketch," 40, UVA; Driver, *5th Virginia Cavalry*, 31.
5. Driver, *5th Virginia Cavalry*, 31; James H. Allen, "The James City Cavalry: Its Organization and First Service," SHSP, 38 vols, 24:354; *Richmond Dispatch*, June 16, 1896.
6. Rosser, "Reminiscences," 173–74, & "Autobiographical Sketch," 41, UVA. Elizabeth "Betty" Winston's brother, Philip B. Winston, enlisted as a private in Company E of the 5th Virginia, and he would later serve as an aide-de-camp to Brigadier General Rosser. Philip went on to become a wealthy man and a mayor of Minneapolis, Minnesota, after the war.

the regiment from sleeping away from camp without his permission. While Lieutenant Colonel Pate's wife was staying with a family about a quarter mile from the regiment, Rosser granted Pate permission to visit her and return in the morning for dress parade. Pate thought that Rosser's permission was valid for every night his wife remained in the area; Rosser remembered otherwise—granting permission for one night only. When Pate returned on the morning of August 1 after staying with his wife, Rosser had him arrested and confined to camp, charged with "disobedience of orders" and conduct unbecoming an officer. Pate claimed, probably correctly, that Rosser was exacting revenge on him for attempting to bring the colonel up on charges of drunkenness on duty.[7]

From the day he took command, Rosser claimed that Pate had been "non-cooperative and... an obstruction to harmony and discipline," necessitating the arrest for the sake of order and discipline in the unit. With open war now between the two, Stuart and most of the regiment's officers backed Rosser, while Pate had the bulk of the rank and file's support. Obtaining the legal services of J. Randolph Tucker, Virginia's attorney general, Pate mistakenly counted on Stuart's support. He was tried by a general court-martial at the Hanover Court House, but before the proceedings were completed, the army was ordered to move out on August 16. Pate applied for release from arrest, either to go with the army or to some point where he could settle with his family and regain his health. Stuart, however, refused to grant Pate's petition. The court adjourned indefinitely with Pate still under arrest.[8]

Some officers, such as Lt. William R. Staehlin of Company I, sympathized with Pate, or, more precisely, did not like Rosser. The colonel, Staehlin thought, was "jealous of his [Pate's] popularity" and a man of "petty spite [and] mean disposition." The lieutenant was not surprised about the arrest:

> **for I believe he would resort to any mean [and] low act to gain his insatiate ambition [and] greed for office and promotion, that was all he fought for but he gained at the**

7. Proceedings of the General Court Martial in the case of Lieut. Col. H. Clay Pate, 5th Va. Cavalry, "Confederate Imprints, 1861–1865," No. 2535, Reel 82, Film 3556, LVA, 5, 7, 56, 67, 73. Hereinafter cited as "Pate, Court Martial Proceedings." Pate was an avid states' rights and pro-slavery ideologue who had led a pro-slavery faction in a skirmish with abolitionist John Brown in Kansas before the war. Brown captured Pate, and Stuart, serving in the army, secured his release. Stuart did not like Pate, and he tried to get rid of him when the regiment formed, but Secretary of War John Randolph overruled him.
8. Johnson, ed., *Biographical Sketches of Alumni Who Fell in the Confederate War*, 583; Rosser, "Autobiographical Sketch," 31, UVA.

risk of his life which was all right but not at the sacrifice of the lives of his men. He was a man without regard for the feelings of others. I believe he would put aces up his sleeve [and] would stand in his way of promotion and I don't believe he thought the good Lord put him here either for that purpose. He said he was a native of Va but went to Louisiana [Texas], in infancy but I can't think he had one instinct of a well-bred Virginian.

As the war dragged on, others started discerning unbecoming facets of Rosser's personality too.[9] President Abraham Lincoln, dissatisfied with McClellan's leadership, wanted a new commander for the Army of the Potomac, but he left the recommendation and final decision to newly appointed chief of the Union army Maj. Gen. Henry W. Halleck. Lincoln wanted to unite the Army of the Potomac with the recently formed Army of Virginia, under Maj. Gen. John Pope's command, with the Army of the Potomac in a subservient role. When General Robert E. Lee found out that the two Federal armies were combining, he realized he would be vastly outnumbered in any offensive operations.

The failure of the Peninsula campaign left Washington, D.C., vulnerable. Once it was obvious that McClellan was retreating, Lee was free to move his army north toward Pope's Army of Virginia. If McClellan moved slowly, then Pope's unreinforced army would be in great danger. In early August, Halleck visited McClellan. He offered McClellan limited reinforcements, but after listening to McClellan's lack of plans and reinforcement demands, he lost confidence in McClellan. On August 3, Halleck ordered McClellan to withdraw from the peninsula and move to northern Virginia to support Pope.[10]

Pope's mission was to protect the capital and the Shenandoah Valley, as well as draw Confederate forces away from McClellan by moving toward Gordonsville, Virginia. Based on his experience from fighting McClellan in the Seven Days Battles, Lee perceived that McClellan was no longer a threat to him on the Virginia Peninsula, so he felt uncompelled to keep all of his forces defending Richmond. This allowed him to relocate Stonewall Jackson to Gordonsville to block Pope and protect the Virginia Central Railroad. Lee had larger plans in mind. Because the Union army was split between McClellan and Pope, and they were greatly separated by distance, Lee saw an opportunity to destroy Pope before returning his attention to McClellan. Pope was strung out along the Rapidan and Rappahannock rivers. Lee ordered

9. Driver, *5th Virginia Cavalry*, 34.
10. David G. Martin, *The Peninsula Campaign, March–July 1862* (Conshohocken, PA, 1992), 236–37.

Maj. Gen. Ambrose P. Hill's 12,000-man division to join Jackson. Along with Brig. Gen. James Longstreet's corps, Lee marched to bolster Jackson. On the Rapidan River, Pope successfully blocked Lee's attempts to gain the tactical advantage, and then on August 18, Lee withdrew his men north of the Rappahannock River, establishing a base at Warrenton. Lee knew to defeat Pope he would have to strike before McClellan's army arrived in northern Virginia.[11]

Lee left two weaker brigades to defend Richmond, and on August 7, he dispatched 24,000 of Longstreet's troops to join Jackson at Culpeper, Virginia. J. E. B. Stuart's cavalry kept Pope's right flank busy, while Jackson, who left Maj. Gen. Richard S. Ewell's division and the 5th Virginia at Bristoe Station, proceeded through Thoroughfare Gap with the rest of his command to Manassas Junction.[12]

The 5th Virginia was generally poorly armed. Some had Jenks breech-loading carbines, while others carried a few privately owned shotguns and pistols. Secretary of War Randolph had promised Rosser new arms from the next shipment to land in Wilmington, North Carolina, but those arms had never arrived. Instead, the regiment was issued green lances with a 24-inch farmer's scythe attached to one end. Many of these, scornfully called "butterfly poles" because of the bright pennon attached to the end, were unwieldy and out of balance. Nevertheless, the regiment's luck would soon change.[13]

On July 24, the 5th Virginia was assigned to Brig. Gen. Fitzhugh Lee's brigade, along with the 1st, 3rd, 4th, and 9th Virginia and Capt. John Pelham's battery of horse artillery. Moving northward, the brigade camped for the night near Davenport's Bridge on the North Anna River, near Beaver Dam Station. Fitz Lee had orders from Stuart to join him at Raccoon Ford on the evening of August 17. But he arrived late, apparently not comprehending the urgency of the directive. Fitz Lee's tardiness permitted Federal horsemen to approach Verdiersville, Virginia, via the Orange Plank Road undetected in the predawn light—the very road Fitz Lee was expected to arrive on. Spotting horsemen in the distance, Stuart and his staff thought the tardy general and his troopers had come, but the Union troopers soon disabused them with shots fired.

Stuart barely escaped capture by abandoning his cloak and newly gifted hat, speedily mounting his horse and bolting across a yard and over a rear fence. Meanwhile, Fitzhugh Lee had followed his wagon train via Louisa Court House to resupply, and by not taking a more

11. Joseph W. A. Whitehorne, "The Second Battle of Manassas," Center of Military History, United States Army, Washington, D.C., 1990, 1–5.
12. Ibid.
13. Rosser, "Reminiscences," 172, UVA.

direct route he arrived one full day late. Because of the ambush, Stuart had to delay his march northward across the Rapidan River, losing critical momentum as McClellan moved closer to reinforce Pope.[14]

Robert E. Lee detailed in Special Order 185, dated August 19, his plan to position Longstreet's command as the right wing of Fitz Lee's northern marching army, ordering them to cross the Rapidan River at Raccoon Ford and move in the direction of Culpeper Court House. Jackson's command, constituting the left wing, would cross at Somerville Ford and move in the same direction, keeping to the left of Longstreet. Major General Richard Anderson's division was ordered to follow Jackson and act in reserve. Colonel S. D. Lee's battalion of light artillery would also follow Jackson's and Anderson's route. Stuart's cavalry was ordered to cross at Morton's Ford, pursue the route by Stevensburg to Rappahannock Station, destroy the railroad bridge, cut the enemy's communications and telegraph, and then move toward Culpeper Court House, taking a position on Longstreet's right.[15]

On August 20, Stuart ordered Rosser to take his command at daylight the next day to Beverly Ford on the Rappahannock River, as the advance guard of the army. Stuart commanded him to seize the opposite bank and hold as much of the country as possible. Rosser's troopers crossed Beverly Ford and took the north bank, opposite the Union center at Warrenton. The Confederate horsemen launched a surprise attack, capturing prisoners and 50 still-stacked muskets, abandoned in the Federals' hurried departure. Stuart hoped he had seized enough ground to permit an unmolested crossing for Jackson's infantry. Stuart's cavalry led the way forward, but quickly found itself in a fight with superior infantry, artillery, and cavalry enemy forces when Longstreet's army followed too slowly. Stuart's cavalry and two artillery pieces fought the Federals most of the day, during which "a brilliant charge as foragers [loose column of riders] [was] made by Colonel Rosser's cavalry, dispersing, capturing, and killing a number of the enemy, losing but one captured."[16] The Federals forced Stuart, although reinforced by Brig. Gen. Beverly Robertson's brigade, to withdraw back across Beverly Ford in the evening. Jackson's infantry could not cross; attacking Pope would have to wait for another day. Robert E. Lee reported that Rosser "gallantly accomplished the object of the operation." Stuart's and Rosser's relationship had really warmed over the past couple of months. They were becoming fast friends, but things were about to change.[17]

---

14. *OR* 12/2:725.
15. Ibid., 729.
16. *OR* 12/2:730.
17. Ibid., 552, 730; Clifford Dowdey and Louis H. Manarin, eds., *The Wartime Papers of Robert E. Lee* (New York, 1991), 275–85, 286; Henry Brainerd

Catlett's Station

Lee wanted Stuart to strike the rearguard of Maj. Gen. John Pope's Federal army and cut its supply line coming down the Orange and Alexandria (O&A) Railroad (which extended from Alexandria to Gordonville, with another section from Charlottesville to Lynchburg), forcing them to retreat. On August 22, Stuart led his two brigades, about 1,500 troopers, across the Rappahannock River at Waterloo Bridge and Hart's Mill in Faquier County, Virginia. They marched through Auburn Mills, 15 miles southwest of Manassas Junction on the O&A Railroad, toward Union-held Warrenton Junction. Stuart planned to attack Catlett's Station, north of Warrenton Junction on the O&A Railroad. After a brief respite in the pouring rain, Stuart's command proceeded to cross rain-swollen Cedar Creek. Stuart wanted to destroy the bridge across Cedar Creek, located just southeast of Catlett's Station, thereby severing Pope's supply line. The torrential rains continued as the troopers reached Auburn. Fitz Lee's brigade led the column toward Catlett's Station, with the 5th Virginia in the advance. Stuart rode up alongside Rosser and became alarmed when he saw that the 5th Virginia was so poorly armed to be in the advance position. According to Rosser, Stuart pulled him aside, saying, "We are near the enemy and shall have hard fighting. You are not well armed and you must give place to a regiment which is better armed."[18]

According to Rosser, writing many years later in "Reminiscences," he stubbornly refused to yield, stating that a withdrawal so close to the enemy would be dishonorable and a disgrace to his regiment and to himself. Stuart, dealing with Rosser's inflexible code of honor again, had to think of what was best for the command. He then ordered Rosser to halt the regiment and "form it on the side of the road and allow the column to pass." Rosser became extremely angry. "My whole nature revolted! I could not submit," Rosser declared. "I rose in my stirrups and in the most defiant manner, thus addressed the commander of the Cavalry Corps of the Army of Northern Virginia—'You well know, sir, that I am not under your command from choice—I left the Artillery only to gratify you. That my regiment is not armed is more your fault than mine, to yield the post of honor, which I now rightfully hold would be cowardly. It is best for us, for you, and for the service that I and my regiment should be utterly

McClellan, *I Rode with Jeb Stuart: The Life and Campaigns of Major General J.E.B. Stuart* (Bloomington, Indiana, 1981), 92.
18. Rosser, "Reminiscences." 175–176, & "Autobiographical Sketch," 42, UVA.

wiped out in battle, than to admit inferiority by declining the responsibilities which duty now imposes.'"[19]

An exasperated Stuart replied, "Then you refuse to obey me." "Yes, Sir. You may arrest me for disobedience of orders, but you shant disgrace me or my regiment," Rosser quipped. Stuart barked back, "Rosser, you had better yield and let the next regiment take your place—that would not disgrace you." Rosser still refused to yield, and Stuart, after contemplating the situation, let his cooler head prevail, allowing Rosser's regiment to remain in the front of the advance. (Rosser penned the only version of this event, so it cannot be substantiated.)[20]

Fitz Lee ordered Col. W. H. F. "Rooney" Lee and the 9th Virginia to rush Pope's supply depot, while Rosser's 5th Virginia, along with the 1st Virginia, made a diversion at the camp next to Pope's headquarters near Catlett's Station. Rooney Lee's troopers rode into the Federal camp, catching them by surprise, slashing and firing at them with borrowed shotguns. The encampment guards fled, and Pope's quartermaster and other staff officers were captured. Rosser's men raided other nearby camps, guided only by lightning flashes during the dark, stormy night. They caused enormous destruction and captured bluecoats, horses, and booty. One Confederate trooper recalled, "I never saw it rain so hard before or since... [After the storm] it was laughable to see the men standing on their heads or getting their feet up in the air to let the water run out of their boots."[21]

Unable to destroy the bridge across Cedar Creek because of the torrential rain, high water, and its sturdy construction, Stuart decided they had accomplished enough and left by way of the Auburn Road to the vicinity of Catlett's Station. Stuart, holding no enmity toward Rosser for his insubordination, reported, "Rosser being again in front, by his good address and consummate skill, captured the picket, and we found ourselves in the midst of the enemy's encampments, but the darkest night I ever knew." Rosser recalled, "To my delight, I found it to be an Ordnance Train, and soon my men were all armed with carbines, pistols, saddles, bridles—halters and everything we needed and the 'butterflies' were thrown away." The incident at Catlett's

19. Rosser, "Reminiscences." 175–176, & "Autobiographical Sketch," 42–43, UVA. It is hard to imagine Stuart letting Rosser get away with this blatant insubordination. Rosser's account is uncorroborated and should be assessed with caution.
20. Rosser, "Reminiscences," 177, & "Autobiographical Sketch," 42–43, UVA.
21. William W. Blackford, *War Years with Jeb Stuart* (New York, 1946) 107; Richard L. T. Beale, *History of the Ninth Virginia Cavalry, in the War Between the States* (Cornell University Library, 2009), 32–33; *Lexington Gazette*, April 26, 1899.

Station damaged the men's friendship, but Stuart was the type of man to rise above the conflict for the good of the service. He continued to extol Rosser's valor in battle, recommend him for promotion, and keep the best interests of his subordinate at heart.[22]

A private of Company G of the 4th Virginia, who participated in the fight at Catlett's Station, described an encounter between Major General Stuart and Colonel Rosser. "Just then [when Rosser joined Stuart at Pope's headquarters] Colonel Rosser, with his sword drawn and dripping with blood, rode up to General Stuart, who was close by, and said in his own emphatic language: 'General, I have been giving them hell, cutting and slashing right and left.'" (Rosser had taken possession of Pope's horse, and would ride him until a bullet wound to the head disabled the magnificent animal during the battle of Kelly's Ford in March 1863).[23]

During the Catlett's Station raid, Rosser's casualties numbered four killed, one wounded, and one missing. A careless remark, however, made by the naiveté cavalry commander had almost cost him his life. During the ferocious fight, sometimes hand-to-hand, Rosser's troopers captured Federal infantrymen, and someone asked Rosser, "What shall we do with the prisoners?" Either preoccupied with the fighting and not thinking clearly or speaking sarcastically, Rosser retorted, "Kill them." One prisoner heard the comment and told his fellow prisoners. The prisoners, fearing for their lives, revolted and attacked the gray-clad troopers with fence posts, rocks, and anything else they could get their hands on. One prisoner, who had not been completely disarmed, viciously attacked Rosser himself with a bayonet. A surprised Rosser recalled:

> **[The Yankee] made at me with the wildest savagery. I had my pistol in my hand...[I] used it as best I could in parrying his thrust. He was a German and his mutterings ring in my ears to this day. In parrying his thrust I was badly cut above the wrist and hand and face, and my horse was very badly wounded. He doubtless would have killed me, but Lieut. [Private Edward] Hall of Maryland...rushed upon the poor fellow, shot him and saved me.**[24]

Finally, after many prisoners had been killed because of Rosser's reckless remark, the Confederates assured the Federals' protection, and the revolt ended.[25]

22. *OR* 12/2, 731–732; Rosser, "Reminiscences," 181, UVA.
23. *Richmond Dispatch*, April 16, 1899, in SHSP, 27:304; Rhyn, "An American Warrior: Thomas Lafayette Rosser," MA Thesis, 1998, UVA, 23.
24. Rosser, "Reminiscences," 184, UVA.
25. Ibid; William N. McDonald, *A History of the Laurel Brigade* (Baltimore and

After the raid at Catlett's Station, Stuart withdrew his command to a wooded area and bivouacked for the night. He sent about 300 prisoners and Pope's baggage to Robert E. Lee's army. On August 24, he led his command back across the Rappahannock River. The Federals intended to destroy Waterloo Bridge, but Stuart had assigned about 100 of Rosser's men, including sharpshooters, to protect the structure. They succeeded in preventing the bridge's destruction. Infantry relieved them the next day.[26]

Battle of Second Manassas

At 2 a.m. the next morning, August 25, Stuart led his cavalry in following Stonewall Jackson's wagon train, joining Jackson near Gainesville. When Stuart deployed his cavalry on August 26, he left the 5th Virginia with Maj. Gen. Richard S. Ewell's infantry division near Bristoe Station, about five miles southwest of Manassas Junction. Following Ewell's fight the next day, the 5th Virginia served as rearguard for Ewell's infantry march to Manassas. On August 28, Rosser's command acted as rearguard for Maj. Gen. A. P. Hill's division near Centreville and picketed Blackford's Ford. When Hill's division moved the next morning, he ordered Rosser to report to Jackson. While marching parallel to Hill's infantry, Rosser discovered a Federal wagon train moving on a nearby road. Rosser borrowed a section of artillery from Col. Bradley T. Johnson, commanding the 1st Maryland Regiment (Line) of infantry and artillery of Ewell's 3rd Division, and drove the Federals back. Jackson joined him, ordering the 5th Virginia to picket in front on the Warrenton Turnpike.[27]

Meanwhile, Stonewall Jackson brought up his infantry and attacked Pope's troops marching on the turnpike toward Alexandria. Rosser positioned the 5th Virginia to the right, taking prisoners and guarding the flank before bivouacking for the night. The next morning, Rosser marched to Gainesville. His regiment had been reduced by detachments and details, so it was placed on picket duty. Rosser left Maj. Beverley B. Douglas in charge and took command of artillery pieces in support of Maj. Gen. John B. Hood's division. Rosser, applying his West Point artillery training and his prior

London, 2002), 198. Rosser remembered it differently, as he apparently told the men, "Don't encumber yourselves with prisoners; whip the enemy!" Addresses of Gen'l T. L. Rosser at the Seventh Annual Reunion, Association of the Maryland Line, Baltimore, February 22, 1889 & Staunton, Virginia, June 3, 1889 (New York, 1889), 30; Rosser, "Autobiographical Sketch," 47–48, UVA.
26. *OR* 12/2:733.
27. Ibid., 734.

experience with the Washington Artillery, drove back the Federal assaults and supported Hood's advance.[28]

On August 29, Stuart decided to bluff Union Brig. Gen. Fitz-John Porter to delay his advance while awaiting Longstreet's arrival. He ordered Rosser to have some of his horsemen drag bushes and limbs fastened to their horses' tails to simulate great clouds of dust that large columns of marching soldiers would make. Rosser employed several companies for the task. Porter fell for the ruse, thinking Longstreet's corps was reinforcing the Confederates. Rosser continued the subterfuge for four hours until Longstreet arrived. Porter was court-martialed for disobeying orders to move in the direction of Gainesville in order to be in a position to attack. Instead, Pope charged Porter with avoiding the fight all day. At that time Maj. Gen. Irvin McDowell received intelligence from his cavalry commander, Brig. Gen. John Buford, who reported that 17 regiments of infantry, one battery of artillery, and 500 cavalry were moving through Gainesville at 8:15 a.m. Buford's report had described Longstreet's wing arriving from Thoroughfare Gap, and it warned the two Union generals that trouble lay to their front.[29]

Early on August 31, Rosser returned to his regiment, withdrew his pickets, and went in pursuit of the Federals. Stuart joined Rosser in the chase. In the afternoon Rosser was ordered to Manassas, and he reported, "I proceeded with my command . . . and one piece of the Washington Artillery to Manassas, which I found abandoned, save by over 400 stragglers, which I captured, with a large lot of small-arms, five elegant ambulances, with horses and harness complete, and a quantity of medical stores." The 5th Virginia rejoined the brigade the next day near Germantown (Midland), southwest of Manassas.[30]

At the battle of Second Manassas, August 28 to 30, Maj. Gen. John Pope mistakenly thought he had Stonewall Jackson trapped and assumed he would shortly destroy the Confederate commander's army. Jackson was anything but trapped. He was right where he wanted to be, and on August 28, Jackson launched a head-on attack against Pope. The fighting occurred at close quarters, lasting for more than two hours. More than 1,000 Federals fell—a third of all those engaged. Pope skirmished with Jackson on August 29 in a series of uncoordinated attacks. Unbeknownst to Pope, Robert E. Lee and Longstreet, along with 30,000 reinforcements, marched through Thoroughfare Gap and

28. Ibid., 12/2:750.
29. Ibid., 69, 736; Hennessy, *Return to Bull Run*, 233–34; Rosser, "Autobiographical Sketch," 49–50, UVA. Porter's conviction was reversed in 1886.
30. *OR* 12/2:738, 743, 751.

joined Jackson on August 30. That same day Pope launched a massive attack against Jackson's soldiers, who were protected by a railroad cut, allowing the Confederates to slaughter the Federals. As the Union soldiers fell back, Lee unleashed Longstreet's forces against Pope's left. The retreating Yankees pieced together two brief defensive stands, giving Pope enough time to escape across Bull Run. Federal losses were estimated at nearly 16,000, while Confederate casualties numbered almost 8,600.[31]

The soon-to-be famous partisan ranger Capt. John S. Mosby complained to his wife about the press coverage of the fight at Manassas from August 28 to 30. Mosby wrote, "My dearest Pauline: Enclosed I send a copy of my report to General Stuart of my scout down to Manassas when, with nine men, I stampeded two or three thousand Yankees. I see the Richmond papers give Col. Rosser the credit of it. He had nothing to do with it, and was not [with]in twenty-five miles of there."[32]

After Second Manassas, Pope retreated across Bull Run, establishing a defensive position at Centreville. On August 31, Robert E. Lee sent Jackson's 20,000-man force on a wide-flanking march to intercept the Federal retreat headed toward Washington. Meanwhile, Longstreet's corps kept Pope in place. Rain slowed Jackson's progress, and Pope anticipated his turning movement. He fell back to Germantown to cover the intersection of Warrenton Turnpike and Little River Turnpike. A fight on September 1 at Chantilly, Virginia, west of Washington, D.C., was tactically inconclusive, but the Federals had foiled Jackson's turning movement, and he was unable to block the Union retreat or destroy Pope's army. The Union army resumed its retreat toward Washington. Robert E. Lee no longer viewed Pope's army as a threat, so he turned his sights northward to Maryland.[33]

Lincoln's extreme dissatisfaction with the general resulted in the president sending Pope to fight the Indians as commander of the newly minted Military Department of the Northwest. Lincoln turned to McClellan again in an effort to raise the sagging morale of the army after Pope's debacle. The president appointed McClellan commander of the forces around Washington, D.C., creating a larger Army of the Potomac.[34]

---

31. Frances H. Kennedy, ed., *The Civil War Battlefield Guide* (New York, 1998), 111.
32. Charles Wells, ed., *The Memoirs of Colonel John S. Mosby* (Boston, 1917), 147.
33. Kennedy, *Civil War Battlefield Guide*, 112.
34. Ibid.

The Maryland Campaign:
September 4–20, 1862

The compelling success against Pope at Manassas encouraged Robert E. Lee to strike a blow at the enemy on their foe's own turf. He devised a plan, approved by Confederate President Jefferson Davis, to cross the Potomac River near Leesburg, Virginia, and march into Maryland. Lee's objectives were to resupply his 55,000-man army outside of the war-torn Virginia theater, damage Northern morale in anticipation of the November elections, and increase the chances of European recognition of the Confederacy. Lee undertook the risky maneuver of splitting his army so he could continue north into Maryland while simultaneously attempting to capture the Federal garrison and arsenal at Harpers Ferry. For his plan to succeed, the Confederates would have to dislodge the Federal troops at Harpers Ferry in order to secure his rear and the lines of supply and communication needed to support the invasion.

Meanwhile, Rosser still enjoyed relatively widespread popularity among his troopers and reveled in it. Expressing his elation to Betty Winston on September 5 in a letter, he wrote, "Yesterday I went within 3 miles of Alexandria. I am happy to say that I am now universally popular in my Regiment. The service I have rendered has set all things right [and] I assure you this is a happy change." Rosser evidently felt that the hard feelings the Lt. Col. Henry Clay Pate situation provoked had healed.

Colonel Rosser also recalled in his letter to Betty that he had seen his friend Antonia Ford, who purportedly had spied briefly for J. E. B. Stuart and whom Rosser was quite fond of himself. He wrote, "I met my old friends [at] Fairfax Court House. Miss Antonia you have doubtless heard me speak. She is as lovely as ever—Oh! How glad they were to see us!"[35]

Stuart's cavalry would play a critical role in Robert E. Lee's invasion plan. They were absolutely essential to guarding Lee's rear, protecting communication lines, and maintaining a safe route of retreat, if that should prove necessary. On September 5, Stuart's horsemen crossed the Potomac River into Maryland with Fitz Lee's brigade leading the advance. They moved eight miles to Poolesville, Maryland, and camped for the night. The next morning the Southern horsemen, with the 1st North Carolina leading, marched to Urbana, 37 miles northwest of Washington, and occupied the town until

35. T. L. Rosser to Betty Winston, September 5, 1862, UVA.

September 10. Some sympathized with the invaders and openly socialized with them. It was there, on September 8, that Stuart and his officers held a ball for the eligible ladies of the town. However, a skirmish at an outpost manned by some troopers of the 1st North Carolina interrupted the dance. Officers at the ball left to aid in the fight but soon returned, and the dance resumed. It became known as the "Sabers and Roses Ball." For the several days following the ball, Stuart's horsemen skirmished with Federal cavalry at nearby Hyattstown, Maryland.[36]

During the march to Antietam, Rosser's men screened Robert E. Lee's left flank. During the subsequent fighting against Union cavalry commander Maj. Gen. Alfred Pleasonton, Rosser temporarily assumed command of Fitzhugh Lee's cavalry brigade, because he was ill. On September 11, Rosser and his 5th Virginia made a raid around the Union army, taking possession of the post office and train depot. They spent the night in Westminster at the home of Judge John Brooke Boyle, who had two sons serving in the Confederate Army. According to a Union army surgeon, Rosser and his troopers "treated the inhabitants with respect and consideration. They made large purchases and paid promptly, even for the food for their horses." Another resident stated that the "rebels proceeded to lay hands on all the boots, shoes, and clothing that they could find in the stores, for which they tendered in payment Confederate money." Rosser remained overnight and succeeded in arresting Dr. J. L. Billingslea, the Union provost marshal, but paroled him immediately upon his promise not to function in that office thereafter. Rosser destroyed enrollment books for the Union army draft, much to the pleasure of a number of young county residents. Riding a splendid horse that had belonged to Pope, Rosser established his main encampment one mile from Westminster, Maryland.[37]

Confederate leaders had overestimated the Southern sympathies of Marylanders in the western part of the state. The Rebels were greeted with reactions varying from a cold reception to open hostility, rather than with liberators' cheers. Robert E. Lee was disappointed at the state's resistance, a condition he had not foreseen. Although Maryland was a slaveholding state, Confederate sympathies among the civilian

36. Heros Von Borcke, *Memoirs of the Confederate War for Independence* (London, 1866), 2 volumes, 1:193–97; W. W. Blackford, *War Years*, 140–41; J. H. Person to his mother, September 27, 1862, Presley Carter Person Papers, DU.
37. Thomas T. Ellis, *Leaves from the Diary of an Army Surgeon* (New York, 1863), 244; *Baltimore Clipper*, September 13, 1862; *The New York Herald*, September 13, 1862. The John Brook Boyle house is still known as "Rosser's Choice."

population were considerably less than anticipated. These people generally supported the Union cause, differing from the pro-secession Maryland legislature. Furthermore, many of the fiercely pro-Southern Marylanders had already traveled south at the beginning of the war to join the Confederate army in Virginia. Few Marylanders joined Lee's columns in Maryland.[38]

Fate was on McClellan's side September 13 when he gained possession of the infamous "Lost Order" that Robert E. Lee issued on September 9. Special Order 191 laid out Lee's entire plan for the Maryland offensive. Even though McClellan was convinced that the order was genuine, he moved too slowly to keep Lee's divided forces from concentrating along the banks of Antietam Creek near Sharpsburg, Maryland. McClellan finally pushed forward, and on the afternoon of the 13th, he approached the pass in South Mountain, on the Boonsboro and Fredericktown Turnpike. The cavalry Stuart commanded fell back before him, using its gallant resistance to materially impede his progress and gain time for preparations to oppose his advance. During the fighting at Crampton's Gap, the battle of South Mountain, Stuart's cavalry and 1,200 infantrymen delayed the advance of Union Maj. Gen. William B. Franklin's VI Corps for two hours, with help from Capt. John Pelham's artillery. Eventually, the Federals' greatly superior numbers prevailed, and the Confederates fled.[39]

Knowing the disposition of the Confederate forces by virtue of the "Lost Order," McClellan decided that by penetrating the mountains at Crampton's Gap, he would reach the rear of Maj. Gen. Lafayette McLaws's column and be able to relieve the garrison at Harpers Ferry. To prevent this, Maj. Gen. D. H. Hill, with five brigades, guarded the Boonsboro Gap to impede the Federals from debouching. Lee ordered Longstreet to march from Hagerstown, Maryland, to support Hill. On September 13, Hill sent back the brigades of Brig. Gen. Samuel Garland and Col. Alfred H. Colquitt to hold Turner's Pass, but subsequently ascertaining the enemy was near in heavy force, he ordered his division to rest. Early the next morning, Colonel Rosser, with the 5th Virginia and Pelham's battery, occupied Fox's Gap (Braddock's Gap), one mile south of Turner's Gap on the Sharpsburg Road. On the rugged terrain, Rosser dismounted his men, and Pelham positioned his artillery just north of the end of Rosser's line.[40]

38. George Edward Moon, *Wagon Tracks* (Bloomington, IN, 2014), 58–59.
39. Jeffrey D. Wert, *The Sword of Lincoln: The Army of the Potomac* (New York, 2005), 153. After the war ended, Rosser claimed to know the identity of the soldier who lost Lee's order, but he never actually revealed the name, only hints.
40. Bushong, **Fightin' Tom Rosser**, 28; Trout, *Galloping Thunder*, 98.

Upon observing the approaching Union advance on the Sharpsburg Road, Garland moved south along the crest of the mountain, joining Rosser. A large body of the enemy attempted to force its way to the rear of Hill's position by way of a road south of the Boonsboro and Fredericktown Turnpike. Garland's brigade repulsed the attack after a severe conflict in which the brave and accomplished young Garland was killed. The remainder of the division arrived shortly afterward; Colquitt's brigade positioned itself across the turnpike road. Brigadier General G. B. Anderson's forces, supported by Brig. Gen. Roswell S. Ripley, were placed on the right, and Maj. Gen. Robert E. Rodes's infantry division occupied an important position on the left. Garland's brigade, suffering heavily in the first attack, withdrew, and the 5th Virginia and Rosser, who reported to D. H. Hill with his regiment and some artillery, were entrusted to defend the road.[41]

Robert E. Lee expected Col. Dixon S. Miles's 14,000-manned Federal army at Harpers Ferry to withdraw in the face of a superior force of 24,000 men, which included 14,000 seasoned veterans under Stonewall Jackson's command. Miles, ordered to stay put, made a fight of it before designating Brig. Gen. Julius White to arrange surrender terms with Jackson on September 15. Jackson captured 11,000 prisoners, 73 pieces of artillery, 11,000 small arms, and 200 wagons.[42]

Upon securing Harpers Ferry, Jackson rejoined Robert E. Lee at Antietam on September 16. The following day, September 17, the bloodiest battle of the war occurred. In the fierce daylong fight, the Confederates managed to fend off McClellan's much larger army's poorly coordinated frontal attacks. The casualties were horrific: about 10,000 Confederates and 13,000 Federals were killed, wounded, or missing.[43]

Artillerist Frank Labrano of the 1st Company of the Washington Artillery recalled, "Fighting commenced at daylight. We went in at 7 a.m. and continued fighting until dark. Our Company repulsed 3 charges of the enemy besides fighting 40 pieces of artillery. On the 4th charge we gave out of ammunition. We went after more, and came back. We held our ground. The loss of the 1st, 2nd, [and] 3rd Cos. amounted to 39 killed [and] wounded. I [had] rammed 253 shots in succession."[44] Robert E. Lee expected McClellan to launch an attack

41. Dowdey and Manarin, eds., *The Wartime Papers of Robert E. Lee*, 307, 312–324; Bushong, Fightin' Tom Rosser, 28; OR 19/1:146, 1020; Trout, Galloping Thunder, 98–99.
42. *OR* 19/1:951.
43. Stephen W. Sears, *Landscape Turned Red: The Battle of Antietam* (New York, 1983), 294–98, 306–07.
44. Frank Labrano Diary, Sept. 17, 1862, Special Collections, Howard Tilton Library, Tulane University, New Orleans.

the next day, but it never came. During the evening of September 18, Lee's battered army retreated across the Potomac River at Blackford's Ford. Fitz Lee's troopers successfully covered the withdrawal to the safety of Virginia.

Back in Virginia

Once again in Virginia, Robert E. Lee's Army of Northern Virginia took a much-needed rest between Winchester and Bunker Hill. The infantry stayed in the vicinity of Martinsburg and Winchester, a section of Virginia still rich in food supplies. The cavalry kept a watchful eye on the Potomac River by establishing its headquarters along the banks of Opequon Creek, a small tributary of the Potomac River. The rundown horses of the artillery recuperated, feeding on the rich grasses of the rolling meadows of the Shenandoah Valley. Lee had fought at Antietam with 40,000 troops, but by October 10 he had built up his command to about 70,000 men through recruiting, gathering stragglers, and by adding soldiers who had either been worn out from the incessant campaigning or who had been without shoes to accompany their commands north.[45]

J. E. B. Stuart next posted his cavalry for a month-long rest at his friend Adam Stephen Dandridge's estate, "The Bower," in Jefferson County. Stuart's stay was interrupted several times for missions lasting one to three days, but he and his men always received an enthusiastic welcome upon returning. The Bower was an old-fashioned Virginia mansion that Dandnridge's father built in 1806. Sited on a hill, around which flowed the waters of the Opequon Creek, it was eight miles from Martinsburg and about 10 miles from Charlestown. Dandridge's son, Adam Stephen Dandridge II, served in the 1st Rockbridge Artillery. Ample time allowed for socializing, and Rosser and Pelham often visited Stuart's headquarters, spending time with Adam and Serena Catherine (Pendleton) Dandridge's five attractive daughters and seeing cousins. Formal teas in the afternoon were followed by music and dancing at night. Rosser became romantically involved with Lilly Dandridge, and the family hoped that they would marry.[46]

Major Heros von Borcke, a fun-loving Prussian staff officer and favorite of Stuart's, recalled that near the end of their stay at The

45. Emory M. Thomas, *Robert E. Lee: A Biography* (London, 1995), 265; Jennings Cropper Wise, *The Long Arm of Lee: Bull Run to Fredericksburg* (Lynchburg, 1915), 2 vols, 1:327–29, 345.

46. Blackford, *War Years*, 154, 296, 304; Lt. Robert T. Hubart, Jr., Thomas P. Nanzig, ed., *The Civil War Memoirs of A Virginia Cavalryman* (Tuscaloosa, 2007), 63. Rosser stayed at The Bower from September 28 to October 10, 1862.

Bower their supplies began to run low in the country around the plantation. It became necessary to make long excursions into the woods and fields to keep the mess table furnished. Major von Borcke remembered, "I was therefore very much gratified when my friend Rosser appeared early one morning at my tent, with the news that there was to be a large auction sale of native wines and other supplies that very day, at a plantation only eight miles off in the direction of Charlestown." All was quiet along the lines at that time, so Rosser and von Borcke decided to attend the sale. The horses were hitched to a yellow wagon, and they soon proceeded at a rapid trot over the rocky road amid the loud outcries and bitter complaints of Rosser who was riding in the wagon, declaring that "he had never in his life experienced such joltings."[47]

Rosser and von Borcke arrived at their destination and bought a large quantity of wine. After sampling the Corinth and blackberry varieties, they returned to camp with the wagon well filled with stores of various kinds. The major recalled:

> **Among our purchases was an immense pot of lard, which we placed in the back part of the wagon, regarding it as an acquisition of great value for our camp biscuit-bakery. We had not, however, counted on the melting influence of the sun upon the lard, and the consequence was that with every jolt of the wagon over the frequent stones in the road, the fluid mass sent its jets of grease in a fountain over the hams, potatoes, and apples that covered the bottom of the vehicle.[48]**

Rosser and von Borcke, however, mellowed by their frequent samplings of the country wine, continued their rapid pace while having a "good ole time." Suddenly, not heeding the roadway before them, von Borcke ran the wagon over a large stone with "so severe a shock that Rosser was thrown out far to the left, while I settled down, after a tremendous leap, far to the right." Fortunately, they were not injured nor did the horses run off, so the men continued their drive back to headquarters, albeit at a much slower pace.[49]

Music was an important means of keeping up morale during the war, and J. E. B. Stuart loved music. He actually put together a kind of early jazz band. On October 9, at 1:00 a.m., Stuart put on an impromptu concert for a group of ladies at The Bower. Stuart and his

47. Heros von Borcke, *Memoirs of the Confederate War for Independence* (Philadelphia, 1867), 219–220.
48. Ibid.
49. Ibid.

band performed 14 different pieces during the performance, ending with Sam Sweeney's rendition of "Old Grey Mare."[50]

On October 9, Stuart again left The Bower, this time on a daring expedition to Chambersburg, Pennsylvania, a mission in which Rosser did not participate. Returning to Virginia with 1,200 horses for the Confederate army, Stuart arrived at The Bower on October 14. The following night, he held a grand ball to celebrate the successful expedition. Finally, on October 29, Stuart's troopers left The Bower amidst tears from their hosts and started for the Blue Ridge Mountains. The next night they camped near Bloomfield. The following day, October 31, the 9th and 3rd Virginia captured three companies of the 1st Rhode Island at the hamlet of Mountville. In the fight, Pelham's guns fired from Hibb's Bridge over Beaverdam Creek. The Confederate horsemen pursued to Aldie before withdrawing.[51]

Meanwhile, after the indecisive battle of Antietam, McClellan, content to "declare victory," sent a few cavalry patrols across the Potomac River, but he did not seriously threaten the Confederates. This was terribly frustrating to President Lincoln, who on October 6 instructed Halleck to order McClellan to cross the Potomac and either engage the Confederates or drive them from the Shenandoah Valley. McClellan took his time, though, finally getting his entire army across the Potomac at Brunswick by November 2. His objective was Warrenton, Virginia.[52]

Robert E. Lee matched McClellan's movements by ordering Longstreet's corps, covered by cavalry, to march from Winchester to Culpeper Court House. He left Jackson's troops in the valley to threaten the Federal flank. Separated by 40 miles, Lee counted on his cavalry to keep communications between Longstreet and Jackson open.[53]

Meanwhile, on November 3, a strong Federal force of infantry, cavalry, and artillery advanced on Stuart's position in the Blue Ridge Mountains near Ashby's Gap. Stuart's horsemen, backed by horse artillery, delayed the attack long enough for Longstreet's corps to escape. The attack started about 9 a.m., and Stuart's horsemen were able to resist for almost the entire day before yielding the field. During the battle, Col. Williams C. Wickham, commanding the brigade in

50. Burke Davis, *The Civil War: Strange & Fascinating Facts* (Fairfax, VA, 1982), 48.
51. Blackford, *War Years with Jeb Stuart*, 181, 183.
52. Ezra Ayers Carman and Joseph Pierro, *The Maryland Campaign of September 1862: Ezra A. Carman's Definitive Study of the Union and Confederate Armies at Antietam* (New York, 2008), 387, 392–93; *OR* 19/1:10–11, 2: 395.
53. *OR* 19/2:392, 545.

Fitzhugh Lee's absence, was struck in the neck by a shell fragment, and Rosser took over command.[54] In a letter to his wife, Stuart stated, "Rosser is in command of [Fitz] Lee's brigade and is my right-hand man now."[55]

Facing an attempted turning of his left flank, Stuart withdrew through Upperville, dispatching the 1st and 5th Virginia to Piedmont to act as rearguard for the wagon trains. Through a misunderstanding of Stuart's orders, the 5th Virginia, with Maj. Beverley B. Douglas commanding, and the 1st Virginia left Piedmont that evening. When Rosser approached Piedmont from Paris after dark, he found it in the Federal's possession. Rosser was able to circumvent the village and move on. He must have been thrilled at his first taste of high command.[56]

With Jackson remaining in the valley on McClellan's flank, Stuart moved toward Markham to link up with Maj. Gen. Wade Hampton's brigade, but found it also in the Federals' occupation. Stuart reported, "I learned that Colonel Rosser had moved from his position at Markham that evening, the enemy having advanced upon him with such a force as to compel him to withdraw, without however, any serious loss."[57]

When Stuart reached Barbee's Cross Roads, he was greatly annoyed that Rosser had retreated to Orlean. Von Borcke went to Orlean to rouse a sleepy Rosser with orders to return to Barbee's Cross Roads. On the morning of November 5, Stuart's cavalry fought Maj. Gen. Alfred Pleasonton's cavalry at Barbee's Cross Roads, 12 miles northwest of Warrenton. Fitz Lee's brigade, with Rosser commanding, held the right, and Hampton's brigade was on the left. Pelham's guns were on a hill north of town. A fierce engagement of artillery and sharpshooters ensued for several hours. Stuart received incorrect information that Federals were in Warrenton, and he thought—considering the lack of a vigorous overall attack—that the fight at Barbee's Cross Roads was only a demonstration to divert his attention from the Federals' move on Warrenton. Accordingly, he ordered Hampton to withdraw via Flint Hill Road and Rosser to retire along Orlean Road, where he bivouacked for the night.[58]

The next morning, Stuart sent a portion of his command, under Colonel Rosser, to occupy Warrenton. Stuart reported, "Rosser, having reached Warrenton, found that the enemy was advancing on his rear as

---

54. *OR* 19/2:143.
55. J. E. B. Stuart to Flora Stuart, November 6, 1862, VHS; Mitchell, Ed., *The Letters of James E. B. Stuart, Stuart-Mosby Historical Society*, 259.
56. *OR* 19/2:143.
57. Ibid., 144.
58. Ibid.

well as front, and was therefore compelled to leave the place. Meeting the enemy in his path, he skillfully eluded him, bringing off his little band without loss to the south side of the Rappahannock." Stuart noted "what a fine officer Tom Rosser has become and how much help he was in battle."[59]

On November 7, Lincoln removed McClellan from command position again and replaced him with Maj. Gen. Ambrose E. Burnside. On November 10, 1862, Stuart's cavalry reorganized under Special Order 238, and Rosser's 5th Virginia, along with the 9th, 10th, and 15th Virginia, as well as the 2nd North Carolina, were assigned to Brig. Gen. W. H. F. "Rooney" Lee's brigade. It appears Rosser's 5th Virginia stayed with Fitz Lee, at least temporarily, even though it was officially assigned to Fitz's cousin.[60]

On November 12, Rosser skirmished with Federal cavalry near Waterloo Bridge and Amissville, where he found a strong Union force. He captured about 30 prisoners, with no loss of his own men, before being pushed back. One of Rosser's officers, however, complained that the colonel "did not handle the brigade very well, because he lacked the directing hand of Stuart."[61]

The 5th Virginia remained on duty in the area for several weeks until moving eastward, while Burnside's Federal army approached the Rappahannock River north of Fredericksburg. The regiment marched to Fredericksburg during the battle, which occurred from December 12 to 14, but it was not actively engaged. They moved to Spotsylvania Court House on December 19.[62]

While the 5th Virginia was not actively engaged at the great battle of Fredericksburg, Colonel Rosser was certainly busy during the fight. Early on the morning of December 13, Major General Stuart secured 10 batteries from the reserve field artillery and moved them onto the Massaponax flats. He had the horse artillery, now under Maj. John Pelham's command, join them, and placed Rosser in command of them all. As soon as Union Maj. Gen. William B. Franklin began to move his column out on the Richmond Road, Rosser positioned the artillery so he could enfilade the advancing Federals. Franklin's column had become so strung out in its advance that he signaled across the Rappahannock River to Brig. Gen. Henry J. Hunt, who was in command of the Federal heavy artillery on the heights below Fredericksburg, asking him to concentrate his fire upon Rosser's

59. Ibid.; J. E. B. Stuart to Flora Stuart, November 6, 1862, VHS.
60. *OR* 19/2:712–13.
61. *OR* 19/2:147; McClellan, *Life and Campaigns of Stuart*, 140; Blackford, *War Years*, 165–168.
62. Driver, *5th Virginia Cavalry*, 42.

batteries in order to get them out of the way. Major Pelham had succeeded in getting a 12-pounder Napoleon gun in a strong position at the intersection of the Richmond and River roads. A ditch had been cut on each side of these roads for the purpose of draining the farms and making a dirt bank of about four feet high on which a row of willow saplings had been planted to act as an enclosure. Soon after, the Union heavy guns across the river opened on the Confederate artillery. One after another of Rosser's batteries became so disabled that he had to withdraw them, including all but one of Pelham's guns, which was the gun positioned at the Richmond and River roads intersection. With this single gun, the "Gallant Pelham," as Gen. Robert E. Lee forever called him afterward, remained all day doing splendid work.[63]

After all of Rosser's other guns had been withdrawn, he visited Pelham and his single gun to ascertain his condition and to render him any assistance needed. Rosser recounted, "I found him coolly directing the operations of his gun. All his horses had been killed and also many of his men, but all that he asked for was some assistance in supplying the details of squads of two men each which he said he should keep running to the rear for ammunition." Rosser fulfilled the need after leaving Pelham.[64]

After leaving Pelham, Rosser remembered an encounter with Stonewall Jackson, which he would never forget:

> **That I might see the effect of the shots from Pelham's gun, I galloped up on the hill above Hamilton's Crossing, and as I rose [up] the hill a man who was lying down behind the low breast works with the men in front of me seeing me come galloping my horse up the hill half rose and raising his hand called out: "Get off that horse—get off that horse."**[65]

Not accustomed to being spoken to in such a preemptory manner, Rosser paid no attention to the impertinent fellow and rode on. He recalled, "The bullets were hissing about my head and it was evident that I was riding into the zone of danger, and as this fellow seemed excited and more persistent, rising on his elbow, called out: 'I said get off that horse sir!' I then recognized the man in the ditch. It was Stonewall Jackson and I sprang off my horse, threw the bridle reins on the ground and started towards him in a brisk trot—when he again commanded: 'Get down, get down sir!'" Rosser dropped down and crawled up to him, and Jackson remarked, "Your horse would have been killed had you ridden him much higher up the hill, and you see

63. Rosser, "Reminiscences," 243–44, UVA.
64. Ibid., 244.
65. Ibid., 245.

from the fire that a man can't stand erect here." Rosser continued, "Then as I lay by his side upon the line of battle, he pointed out the enemy, praised the gunmanship of the cannoneers at the lone gun at the forks of the road, and pointing to the large reserves of the enemy who were not participating in the attack, exclaimed: 'Thank God, they have 3 lines idle and I shall soon dispose of the feeble effort they are making on me.'"[66]

Rosser then crawled back to his horse, but was much too interested in the fighting going on around him to leave the scene. He put his horse far enough down the hill for safety, then went back to the nearest point of fighting and watched the advance of Maj. Gen. George Meade's divisions. The ensuing battle was a disaster for the Federal army. Their frontal assaults against the entrenched Confederates resulted in one of the most one-sided victories of the war.[67]

After Fredericksburg, Stuart successfully led several cavalry raids across the Rappahannock River during December. He planned and executed a raid, which became known as the "Apple Jack Raid," well into the Union rear, striking them at Dumfries, Virginia. Stuart organized his raiding force of 1,800 troopers, including 100 men of the 5th Virginia and four guns from the Stuart Horse Artillery. On December 25, Rosser directed the force to Ely's Ford on the Rapidan River. The next morning, Stuart led his horsemen across the Rappahannock at Kelly's Ford and bivouacked near Morrisville that evening. Stuart split his command in order to inflict almost simultaneous attacks on Federal supply trains along the Telegraph Road, minimizing the possibility of the Federals learning of the raid and risking them retreating to Dumfries. In the meantime, Rosser proceeded toward Dumfries, capturing six 4-horse and three 2-horse supply wagons, along with 22 Yankees who were guarding them. Upon reaching Dumfries, Rosser's sharpshooters engaged the Federal infantry before withdrawing across the river in the face of a superior force. Stuart realized it would be too costly to capture Dumfries against an entrenched infantry and called off the assault.[68]

On December 28, Fitz Lee's brigade led Stuart's cavalry toward Occoquan. Lee's troopers drove two regiments of Federal cavalry from Greenwood Church back across the Occoquan River at Selectman's Ford. Lee discovered Federal dismounted sharpshooters along the northern bank of the river. Stuart reported, "Without waiting to exchange shots, they were gallantly charged by file, the Fifth Virginia, under Colonel Rosser, leading across a narrow, rocky, and very

---

66. Ibid., 246.
67. Ibid.
68. *OR* 21/2:732–733.

difficult ford; but in spite of heavy volleys directed at our men, they pressed on, crossed the stream, suffered no loss, and captured or dispersed the whole party." Fitz Lee then took possession of the Federal's abandoned camps, capturing many spoils, including horses, mules, and loaded supply wagons. Fitz Lee called Rosser's attack across the Occoquan River "one of the most admirable performances of cavalry I have ever witnessed."[69]

Stuart next pushed his command to Burke's Station on the Orange and Alexandria Railroad. After burning the bridge over the Accotink River and menacing Fairfax Court House, he turned westward to Middleburg, passing by Fairfax Station, Vienna, and Frying Pan. On December 30, Stuart detached Rosser with 15 men to make a reconnaissance into the Shenandoah Valley. Rosser discovered the disposition of Federal forces, and captured the Federal picket at Leetown. Stuart led the rest of the raiding party back through Warrenton to Culpeper Court House on December 31. By January 1, 1863, Stuart's whole command was back in Fredericksburg.[70]

69. Ibid., 733, 739.
70. *OR* 12/2:736.

CHAPTER 4

1863: Wounded at Kelly's Ford; Marriage; Gettysburg Campaign; Rosser turns on Stuart; Rosser's promotion to brigadier general

> "I ask this appointment because no officer I have met within the Confederacy combines in a more eminent degree the characteristics of the Cavalry Commander than Rosser. He is an officer of superior ability, possesses in an extraordinary degree the talent to command and the skill to lead with coolness and decision of character."
>
> **J. E. B. Stuart, recommending Colonel Thomas Rosser for promotion to brigadier general**

Tom Rosser had performed well during the Peninsula, Second Manassas, and Maryland campaigns. Major General J. E. B. Stuart's protégé continued to impress him, and the cavalry commander proceeded to mentor him and urge for his promotion. But as 1863 progressed, Rosser found more and more fault with his commander, condemning Stuart's performances at the battles of Brandy Station and Gettysburg. He also blamed Stuart for failing to secure his promotion to brigadier general, even though Stuart put pressure on his superiors in Richmond for Rosser's career advancement.

Stuart believed his friend and commander of the 5th Virginia had performed extraordinarily in 1862, and on January 13, 1863, he recommended Rosser for promotion to brigadier general in command of a new cavalry brigade. Stuart wrote to Samuel Cooper, adjutant and inspector general of the Confederate army, saying:

I ask that this appointment be made because no other officer that I have met with in the Confederacy combines in a more degree the characteristics of the cavalry than Col. Rosser. He is an officer of superior ability, possesses in an extraordinary degree the talent to command and the skill to lead with coolness and decision of character... I urged his appointment as Col. of 5th Virginia Cavalry... This command was raw and undrilled and Rosser took command just at the beginning of the Battles before Richmond. Yet raw and undisciplined as was his material, he has made of it a splendid regiment and has commanded it with brilliant success through the campaigns of Virginia and Maryland.[1]   Stuart also communicated with Army of Northern Virginia Chief of Staff R. H. Chilton, penning:

> **I consider Colonel Thomas L. Rosser the most suitable for such a command [over Munford and Wickham]... I give to Rosser the preference, which I consider due to the generalship I have seen him display on several very critical occasions, to which he unites a noble self-reliance and a tenacity of purpose, and I would feel safer with him in command of a Cavalry Brigade than any other Colonel I know of.[2]**

General Robert E. Lee did not support Stuart's recommendation, dismissing it with: "Return to War Department." He did not think there were enough cavalry regiments to warrant a new brigade and a new brigadier to lead it.[3]

Rosser welcomed Stuart's recommendation, and he was entirely confident in his abilities to lead such a command. He was very ambitious and anxious to be promoted to general officer rank. As the months dragged on, he became increasingly impatient and paranoid, thinking there were those who were blocking his promotion. Frustration and a bit of political posturing led him to try other means to accelerate the process. On March 15, Rosser wrote to a friend, Alexander R. Boteler of the Confederate Congress, asking him if he could determine what was holding up his promotion and whether or not there was any possibility of a successful outcome. If the promotion in Stuart's command was not forthcoming, Rosser let it be known to his close colleagues that Brig. Gen. Beverly H. Robertson had offered him command of six regiments in North Carolina, which would make a fine brigade. If neither of these promotions occurred, Rosser was interested in commanding an infantry brigade, namely that of Brig. Gen. Robert A. Toombs's. Toombs had just resigned his brigade

1. J. E. B. Stuart to Samuel Cooper, January 13, 1863, Thomas L. Rosser Papers, UVA; Rosser's Service Record, General and Staff Officers, Roll M331, NA; Mitchell, ed., *The Letters of James E. B. Stuart*, 275.
2. J. E. B. Stuart to Gen. R. H. Chilton, February 4, 1863, VHS; Mitchell, *The Letters of Major General James E. B. Stuart*, 291–292.
3. Lynda Lasswell Crist, Mary Seaton Dix, and Kenneth H. Williams, editors, *The Papers of Jefferson Davis: January–September 1863* (Baton Rouge, 1997), 10 vols., 9:53.

command to enter politics. Because Rosser's promotion in Stuart's command would not occur until October, he became increasingly disgruntled. Promotion in hand or not, Rosser would stay in Stuart's cavalry and in Brig. Gen. Rooney Lee's brigade as a cavalryman.[4]

Following the 1862 fall campaigns, the weather had turned bitterly cold, resulting in harsh conditions for the soldiers and their horses. Lieutenant Thaddeus Fitzhugh, Company F of the 5th Virginia, wrote:

> **The winter was unusually severe and as we had not tents, we prepared a shed to sleep under by putting two forked posts, and a cross pole with fence rails placed obliquely, with blankets and oil cloths spread to shed off the rain and snow, but for beds we procured straw and spread our blankets overlapping each other under which six of us slept. A big log fire was in our front and when one wanted to turn the order was given 'all turn.'[5]**

After the Union's disastrous battle at Fredericksburg, Maj. Gen. Ambrose E. Burnside, pressured to advance on Richmond, attempted an envelopment of Robert E. Lee's army by way of Banks's Ford, on the Rappahannock River, on January 20. Unfortunately for Burnside, the elements sided against him; rain began on January 20 and continued for two days, making roads and streams impassible. The operation became known as the "Mud March," and the weather forced Burnside to abandon the effort. On January 26, President Abraham Lincoln replaced Burnside as army commander with Maj. Gen. Joseph Hooker, who had been critical of the Federal attack at Fredericksburg.[6]

On March 9, Col. Edwin H. Stoughton, commander of the 2nd Vermont Infantry Brigade, found himself a prisoner of Col. John Singleton Mosby, who hustled him to the Confederate cavalry headquarters where Tom Rosser warmly greeted him. Stoughton, along with Charles Jesup, and Rosser, had been involved in a fight with an upperclassman officer during their time at West Point. They all had been arrested and sentenced to four months in the guardhouse. Rosser treated his captured friend fondly, and Mosby began to feel as though his prisoner was getting more attention than he. The exasperated Mosby took the train to Culpeper, catching Stuart and Maj. John Pelham in the railroad station where he proceeded to pour his woes

4. Thomas L. Rosser to Col. Alexander R. Boteler, March 15, 1863, Rosser Service Record, General and Staff Officers, Roll M331, NA; Brig. Gen. Beverly H. Robertson to Secretary of War James A. Seddon, March 24, 1863, Rosser's Service Record, General and Staff Officers, NA.
5. Driver, *5th Virginia Cavalry*, 45.
6. Spencer C. Tucker, ed., *American Civil War: The Definitive Encyclopedia and Document Collection* (Santa Barbara, CA, 2013), 1345-46.

into Stuart's ear. Pelham likely found Mosby's anguish humorous, for he must have recalled the incident at the academy.[7]

On March 10, a private returning from leave wrote, "We arrived in camp last Saturday evening, [and] found things in a bad state. Men very little to eat [and] horses starving. Col. Rosser has acted by reporting the whole reg. unfit for duty... It is snowing now."[8]

Conditions remained rough during the weeks preceding spring. Private Louis C. Haney of the 5th Virginia penned, "The horses are starving, they only get a little hay every other day and we don't get much ourselves—we get a quarter pound of bacon a day. There are a great many of the horses a dieing [sic] here, and they say all who don't furnish horses has to go to the infantry."[9]

On March 12 the delayed court-martial of Lt. Col. Henry Clay Pate resumed at Culpeper Court House. Instead of the original two charges, there were now five charges and twelve specifications. The trial continued from March 12 until April 22 and, of course, was often interrupted by the war. Pate responded that "Colonel Rosser came to the command prejudiced against me—that by repeated acts he attempted to degrade me as an officer, and, as I verily believe, has sanctioned, aided, and abetted a conspiracy to rob me of my command." Pate stated, "Colonel Rosser, I fear, has so prejudiced the mind of General Stuart against me, unfairly and ungenerously, that he [General Stuart] has his sympathies enlisted against me." Stuart denied any prejudice against Pate. Pate also recalled that before charges were brought against him, he had filed a report against Colonel Rosser for intemperance, but nothing had come of it because of the bias against him. He accused Stuart of suppressing the report, which Stuart denied. Stuart recalled that he gave Rosser the option of being tried on the charge or enter "a written obligation to abstain from intoxicating drink whilst in the army of the Confederacy," and Rosser chose the latter option. The court adjourned on March 16, because Federal forces were nearby.[10]

Battle of Kelly's Ford

During March, the 5th Virginia moved to Culpeper County and camped near Brandy Station. The Federal cavalry, improving with

---

7. Mary Elizabeth Sergent, "The West Point John Pelham Knew," speech to the John Pelham Historical Association, in Newburgh, New York, September 6, 1985; *The Cannoneer Newsletter,* John Pelham Historical Association, 1985, vol. 4, No. 3:8.
8. Ibid., 45–46.
9. Louis C. Haney to his sister, March 14, 1863, Jacob B. Click Papers, Perkins Library, DU.
10. Pate, "Court Martial Proceedings," 5, 7, 11.

Brig. Gen. Alfred Pleasonton's command, attacked across Kelly's Ford on the morning of March 17. Union cavalry Brig. Gen. William W. Averell led 2,100 troopers across the Rappahannock River, scattering the Confederate pickets guarding the ford. Brigadier General Fitzhugh Lee gathered all able-bodied men and horses in camp, numbering about 800, and rode toward the scene of the crossing. Beforehand, Fitz Lee had sent half of his command home to obtain replacement horses. Fitz Lee's brigade encountered Averell's command as it approached Carter's Run, so he formed his troopers with the 5th Virginia on his left flank. Rosser's 5th Virginia charged across Carter's Run, but the Federals drove them back by concentrated fire. Fighting continued throughout the day with each of Fitzhugh Lee's regiments mounting a charge, only to be repulsed. Fitz Lee sent Lt. Harry W. Gilmor, of the 12th Virginia, with orders for Rosser to make a charge around the Federals' extreme left flank and capture the ford. Rosser led the charge, only to run into concentrated fire from Federal horsemen. Troopers and horses went down in a hail of fire. Gilmor recalled, "Rosser strove hard to keep the regiment in order, but owing to the nature of the ground and the severe fire from the fence, they went back in some confusion."[11]

Gilmor recounted, "As I was going out, trying to get the men together, I heard Rosser call out, 'Major Puller, why, in the name of God, don't you assist me in rallying the men?'" John W. Puller had recently been promoted when Maj. Beverley B. Douglas had resigned to take his seat in the Virginia legislature. Gilmor continued, "I turned in my saddle and saw Puller, bent forward on his horse's neck, coming along just behind me. As he turned his head and spoke, I saw death plainly stamped on his features. He said, as if to rebuke Rosser, 'Colonel, I'm killed.' Rosser seemed petrified, and said, 'My God, old fellow, I hope not; bear up, bear up!' . . . he made an effort to straighten himself in the saddle; but as soon as he let go of his horse's mane and tried to rise, he pitched off head foremost, and his horse ran away." Several men succeeded in carrying him to an ambulance, but he soon expired.[12]

Soon after Puller fell, Maj. John Pelham, the "Gallant Pelham" of Stuart's Horse Artillery, was killed when charging with the 3rd Virginia Cavalry. Stuart, who had just returned from Colonel Pate's resumed court-martial, had called Pelham back from his planned three-day trip to Orange Court House. Pelham had not even had the

---

11. *OR* 25/1:48, 58–61.
12. Driver, *5th Virginia Cavalry*, 48–49; Harry Gilmor, *Four Years in the Saddle* (New York, 1866), 69. John W. Puller was the grandfather of Lt. Gen. Lewis Burwell "Chesty" Puller of World War II fame.

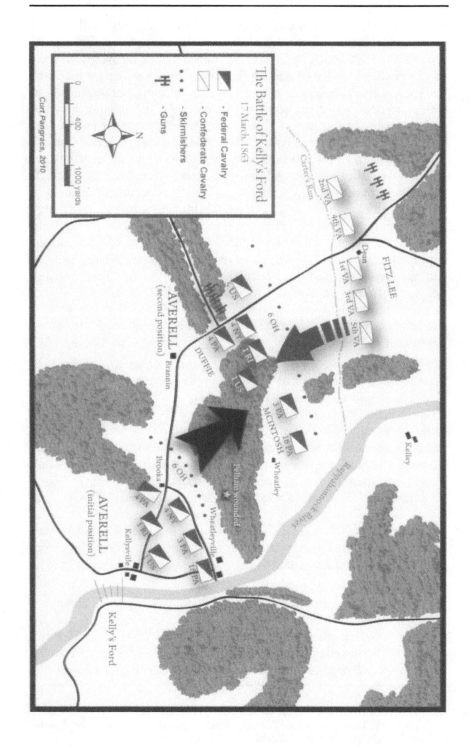

The Battle of Kelly's Ford
17 March, 1863

- Federal Cavalry
- Confederate Cavalry
- Skirmishers
- Guns

Curt Pangracs, 2010

opportunity to join his artillery force yet. He had been hit in the head either by a piece of shrapnel or by a musket ball. The last message in the tragedy came from an enemy—a former classmate and a current Union cavalry commander. After Pelham was dead, a note came forth from the Union lines. "After a long silence, I write," the message began. "God bless you, dear Pelham; I am proud of your success." It was signed "George A. Custer." Rosser later described Pelham as "young, and handsome and as modest as a girl, he was withal as brave and as bright as the trusty saber which his manly arm wielded. The army loved him, and his fall left a blank in our midst, like that which is occasioned in the deep blue sky above us, by the setting of a bright and beautiful star."[13]

In the fight at Kelly's Ford, Rosser, "who, though severely wounded [in the foot] at 2 p.m., remained in command at the head of his regiment until the day was won, and nightfall put an end to further operations." Rosser had been shot in the foot, and the ball lodged between the small bones and was not immediately extracted. He was in extreme pain. Surgeon John Fontaine requested a 60-day leave of absence for Rosser.[14]

As darkness fell the Federals retreated back across the Rappahannock. The Union horsemen had acquitted themselves well—from now on, they would be a force to be dealt with. Rosser's command lost two men killed and 11 wounded. Sixteen horses had been killed and 11 had been wounded. Fitz Lee praised Rosser's conduct on the battlefield for "his habitual coolness and daring, charging at the head of his regiment." No one ever doubted Rosser's bravery, but questions later arose as to whether he unnecessarily risked too many of his troopers' lives to achieve glory for himself. Pelham's death affected Rosser deeply, and he later named one of his sons John Pelham Rosser. Stuart wept when hearing the news of Pelham's passing. Before his final journey home to Alabama for burial, Pelham's body lay in state in the capitol at Richmond where many paid their final respects to perhaps, up until that time, the best artilleryman of the war.[15]

Pate's court-martial resumed on March 20, 1863, but Rosser was excused after his wounding at Kelly's Ford. The court continued to examine other witnesses in Rosser's absence. Colonel Rosser's delayed

13. *Richmond Times-Dispatch*, March 28, 1937; "The Cavalry, A.N.V., Address of General T. L. Rosser, at the Seventh Annual Reunion of the Association of the Maryland Line, Academy of Music," Baltimore, Maryland," February 22, 1889 (Baltimore, 1889), 25.
14. Ibid., Robert J. Trout, *With Pen and Saber: The Letters and Diaries of J.E.B. Stuart's Staff Officers* (Mechanicsburg, PA, 1995), 182–83.
15. *OR* 25/1:59, 62; *Richmond Sentinel*, March 23, 1863.

The "Gallant" Major John Pelham (1838 – 1863)

Killed at Battle of Kelly's Ford, March 17, 1863. Pelham and Rosser were roommates at West Point. Pelham was considered one of the best artillerymen of the Civil War from either side.

Photo Courtesy Library of Congress

cross-examination occurred on April 2, and the court moved to Hanover Court House to be near Richmond, where Rosser was convalescing. Rosser was on the stand through April 3, and the defense then presented its case. From their testimonies, both Stuart and Rosser appeared to suffer from selective memory loss. They denied ever discussing the case amongst themselves. Pate and his attorney put on an excellent defense. When the case was finally submitted for a verdict, "Lieutenant Colonel Pate was honorably acquitted, and by order of General Robert E. Lee, 'resumed his sword.'"[16]

Battle of Chancellorsville

After the battle at Kelly's Ford, the new commander of the Army of the Potomac, Maj. Gen. Joseph Hooker, reorganized his army. He

16. Pate, "Court Martial Proceedings," 21, 48–54.

eliminated the cumbersome Grand Divisions structure that Burnside had created and replaced them with army corps. He established a cavalry corps under the command of Maj. Gen. George Stoneman. The cavalry corps consisted of three divisions led by brigadier generals Alfred Pleasonton, William Averell, and David Gregg, along with a reserve brigade under John Buford.[17]

On April 28, the Federal army crossed the Rappahannock River at Kelly's Ford. Stuart notified Robert E. Lee who then amassed his cavalry near Brandy Station. Rosser was still recuperating from his foot wound. On April 30, the 5th Virginia was routed in a fight with the 6th New York Cavalry near Spotsylvania Court House, a small village 20 miles north of Richmond. Stuart believed that the 5th Virginia's poor performance in the battle stemmed from Rosser not leading them.[18]

Rosser did not rejoin the command until May 12, and thus missed Gen. Robert E. Lee's greatest victory at the battle of Chancellorsville on May 2 and 3. Lee had gambled by splitting his command and sending Stonewall Jackson on a successful, long flanking maneuver. Jackson rolled up the unanchored Union right flank, defeating Hooker, who had twice Lee's number of troops at his command. With Rosser still on the mend, the 5th Virginia accompanied Jackson on his flanking march. Lee's splendid victory was a very costly one indeed, as Jackson was mortally wounded by friendly fire, dying of pneumonia eight days later. When Rosser told Stuart that the dying Jackson had expressed the desire that Stuart succeed him in the command of his corps, the cavalry commander proclaimed, "I would rather know that Jackson said that, than have his appointment." Stuart ably led Jackson's corps on May 3, the second day of the battle.[19]

After the great victory at Chancellorsville, Colonel Rosser wrote to his now fiancée, Elizabeth Winston:

> **The army is quiet, and unless Gen. R. E. Lee advances, I think there will be no fighting for some time. Stuart commanded Gen. Jackson's corps after Jackson was wounded and seemed to have shown great skill in the management of it. He read me a portion of a letter from**

17. Walter H. Hebert, *Fighting Joe Hooker* (Lincoln, NE, 1999), 175–77.
18. Thomas L. Rosser to Elizabeth Winston, May 12, 1863, Rosser Papers, UVA; Bushong, *Fightin' Tom Rosser*, 40.
19. Jay B. Hubbell, ed., "The War Diary of John Esten Cooke," *The Journal of Southern History*, Southern Historical Association, Baton Rouge, LA, 77 vols., 1941, vol. 7, No. 4:537; Henry Brainerd McClellan, *I Rode with Jeb Stuart: The Life and Campaigns of Major General J.E.B. Stuart* (Bloomington, Indiana, 1981), 438, hereafter cited as H. B. McClellan, *I Rode with JEB Stuart*.

Gen. R. E. Lee last night in which he was very highly complimented indeed—I think Stuart will be made Lt. Gen. of Cav'y [Cavalry] very soon and in such an event I will expect to get the much talked of Brig... It is only on your account that I desire to be promoted as a general.[20]

After the battle of Chancellorsville, both armies reorganized. The Army of Northern Virginia, with additional men obtained by conscription, was divided into three corps and commanded by lieutenant generals James Longstreet, Richard S. Ewell, and Ambrose P. Hill. By the end of May, Robert E. Lee had 76,000 men and 270 artillery pieces. Each corps had three divisions, and each division (except the third) had four brigades. The corps of the Army of the Potomac were about half the size of Lee's corps. On May 22, Maj. Gen. Joseph Hooker replaced his cavalry chief, Maj. Gen. George Stoneman, with Brig. Gen. Alfred Pleasonton, after Stoneman had been discredited at Chancellorsville. Pleasonton enhanced the effectiveness of the Union cavalry by virtue of his skills as a gifted administrator and organizer.[21]

During this post-Chancellorsville period of sinking morale following the deaths of Jackson and Pelham, Tom Rosser was engaged to Elizabeth Barbara Winston. Earlier in the war, upon meeting "Betty" Winston, a beautiful 19 year old with an attractive personality, Rosser at once became smitten. He had been courting her since the previous summer, and on February 19 he wrote her to say that he did not believe in long engagements. He explained that his friends believed his promotion was forthcoming. He also told her that if he were to transfer from Virginia, he wanted her to accompany him.[22]

On May 20 Rosser told J. E. B. Stuart about the impending wedding, but the cavalry chief had already heard about the engagement. Stuart wanted to grant Rosser's request for a furlough and wished to attend the wedding himself, but he was afraid military events would interfere with the nuptials. Rosser invited Col. Pierce Young to be a groomsman, reporting to Betty, "He seemed delighted and promised certainly to do so." Rosser told Betty that Antonia Ford was nearby and was "quite melancholy in consequence of my engagement." Rosser, popular with the ladies, exhibited his vanity with statements like this to his soon-to-be bride.[23]

20. Kirshner, *Class of 1861*, 49; Thomas L. Rosser to Elizabeth Winston, May 12, 1863, UVA.
21. Ibid., 44.
22. Thomas L. Rosser to Elizabeth Winston, February 19, 1863, UVA.
23. Thomas L. Rosser to Elizabeth Winston, May 20, 1863, UVA.

Rare photos of Thomas and Barbara Winston Rosser, probably taken at their wedding.

Holsinger Collection, Albert and Shirley Small Special Collections Library, University of Virginia

Soon a lull in the fighting occurred, so Thomas Rosser and Betty Winston planned their wedding for May 28 at Courtland, the Winston estate. The wedding was a gala occasion and the social event of the season. A guest recalled that there was "music, laughter, soft Southern speech; and in the velvet dusk the summer stars looking down upon gray frock coats and white gowns side by side beneath the trees where the air was heavy with the scent of old-fashioned garden flowers." The Winstons were a prominent family in Hanover County. The guests at the wedding included many leading Confederate officers and their wives, including Maj. Gen. and Mrs. J. E. B. Stuart, Brig. Gen. Fitzhugh Lee, Maj. James Dearing, Maj. Heros von Borcke, Col. Pierce Young, and Capt. Roger P. Chew, as well as Senator and Mrs. Louis T. Wigfall and many others. The wedding party included 12 bridesmaids and 12 groomsmen. Sally Madison was the maid of honor, and Maj. James Dearing was the best man. Also mingling amongst the guests was an officer that everyone assumed to be a friend of either the bride or the groom, but was in fact a Union spy trying to overhear conversations.[24]

24. Biographical Material, Thomas L. Rosser Papers, 1171a.b., UVA; Thomas L. Rosser to Betty Winston, February 19, 1863, UVA. Mrs. Rosser met the Union spy years after the war in Minneapolis, Minnesota.

The day after the wedding, Fitzhugh Lee, who considered Colonel Rosser one of his favorite officers, threw a picnic for many of the wedding guests at his headquarters at Culpeper Court House. According to one guest, "all the young ladies from the neighborhood" attended, and "music and refreshments were on hand and all went off very merrily."[25]

Rosser's marriage occurred at a period when he was personally disgruntled about not receiving the promotion he so coveted. The Confederate authorities in Richmond felt there were not enough troopers in Stuart's command to form a new cavalry brigade. The foot wound he received only served to make Rosser's mood worse. His intemperance may have been a factor, too. Pelham's death was especially hard on Rosser. His West Point roommate would almost certainly have served as best man at his wedding.[26]

Gettysburg Campaign

Following Chancellorsville, Robert E. Lee, with Confederate President Jefferson Davis's approval, decided again to carry the war into the Northerner's territory. The first northern invasion had resulted in the terrible battle at Antietam and subsequent retreat back into Virginia. It was assumed that an invasion northward would relieve Virginia of the enemy's presence by drawing the Federals north of the Potomac River. Also, Union troops might move away from the coasts of Virginia and North Carolina, and potentially alter their Mississippi and Tennessee campaigns (Vicksburg, Mississippi, was then under Gen. Ulysses S. Grant's seige) to meet the new Confederate offensive. Equally important, Virginia, ravaged by war for two years, was unable to feed Lee's troops much longer. Finally, the South needed a major victory on Union soil to obstruct Lincoln's reelection and boost chances for European recognition.[27]

On May 11 Robert E. Lee had ordered Stuart to move his cavalry from Orange County north to Culpeper County in preparation for his planned invasion of the Keystone State. After his success at Chancellorsville, Lee planned to lead his army through the Shenandoah Valley for his second invasion of the North. Lee was

25. Edward G. Longacre, *Fitz Lee: A Military Biography of Major General Fitzhugh Lee, C.S.A* (Cambridge, MA, 2005), 113; Halsey Wigfall to his brother Louis Wigfall, June 4, 1863, Louis T. Wigfall Family Papers, Library of Congress, (LC). Louis T. Wigfall was a Confederate senator from Texas.
26. Bushong, *Fightin' Tom Rosser*, 43; Crist, Dix, and Williams, eds., The Papers of Jefferson Davis: January–September 1863, 14 vols., 9:53, Rice University, Houston, TX.
27. Edward G. Longacre, *The Cavalry at Gettysburg* (Lincoln, Nebraska, 1993), 35–36.

determined to strike north to capture horses, equipment, and food for his men. He was also hoping to threaten as far north as Harrisburg, Pennsylvania, or even Philadelphia, and to influence Union politicians to give up their prosecution of the war. By May 22, Stuart had moved nearly 7,000 troopers of Wade Hampton's, Rooney Lee's, and Fitzhugh Lee's brigades to Culpeper, and by June 5, another 3,000 troopers from brigadier generals Beverly Robertson's and William "Grumble" Jones's brigades joined them. Robertson's brigade was camped southwest of Brandy Station near John Minor Botts's farm, called Auburn, while Jones's brigade had shifted from the Shenandoah Valley. Robert E. Lee's invasion plan called for Stuart to position his Confederate cavalry on the right flank of his army to screen the infantry and protect its rear.[28]

Robert E. Lee's army was at Fredericksburg, across the Rappahannock from Falmouth. Lee was intent on marching north to Pennsylvania. Hooker was unable to resolve what Lee's plans were and needed to know his objectives. Was he heading north, or would he suddenly turn east and move toward Washington, D.C.? Hooker assigned his cavalry corps and two brigades of infantry to conduct a raid and determine Lee's intentions.[29]

On June 5, General Stuart held a review of his corps on an open field near the little hamlet of Inlet Station, four miles northeast of Culpeper. The review was not only a military parade but also one of those splendid social events the flashy Stuart loved to stage. The entire corps passed in review with three bands playing and a flag waving at the head of each regiment. Then the column divided into brigades and regiments that performed drill. In a climactic finale, the troopers, with yells and sabers drawn, charged at the artillery, which was posted at intervals around the perimeter of the field. The artillery fired blank cartridges at the charging horsemen in a noisy conclusion. The day ended with a ball "on a piece of turf near headquarters, and by the light of enormous wood fires, the ruddy glare of which upon the animated groups... gave the whole scene a wild and romantic effect."[30]

Not all were happy with these reviews. Some, such as Wade Hampton and the irritable Grumble Jones, considered them to be a waste of resources. Jones was in no mood for revelry, as his brigade had just arrived on June 3 and 4; the men and horses were tired and needed rest, which the review on June 5 did not permit.[31]

28. Heros von Borcke, *Memoirs of the Confederate War for Independence*, 2 vols., 2:264–65; *OR* 25/2:792.
29. Longacre, *The Cavalry at Gettysburg*, 103.
30. Von Borcke, *Memoirs of the Confederate War for Independence*, 2:264–65.
31. Eric J. Wittenberg, *The Battle of Brandy Station: North America's Largest Cavalry Battle* (Charleston, SC, 2010), 67.

Robert E. Lee had been invited to review the troops, but he was unable to attend. General Lee ordered another review for June 8, where he surveyed all of his cavalry, some 9,500 troopers, at Inlet Station. Rosser, who had also missed the June 5 review, participated this time.[32]

The next day, just 12 days after Rosser's wedding, the great battle at Brandy Station occurred. Some 20,000 cavalry and 3,000 infantry soldiers participated in the daylong battle. Rosser missed the epic battle because the 5th Virginia stood picket duty at Freeman's Ford on the Rappahannock, upriver from the battle.[33]

Lee ordered Stuart to cross the Rappahannock on June 9 and screen the Confederate army from observation or interference as it moved north. Unknown to the Confederates, 11,000 of Pleasonton's men were amassed on the other side of the Rappahannock River. Hooker interpreted the Confederate cavalry presence around Culpeper to be in preparation for a raid of his army's supply lines. Responding, he ordered Pleasonton's force on a preemptive raid. Pleasonton's attack plan called for a two-pronged thrust at the enemy. Pleasonton anticipated that the Southern cavalry would be caught in a double envelopment—surprised, outnumbered, and beaten. However, he was unaware of the precise disposition of the enemy, and he incorrectly assumed that his force was substantially larger than the Confederates he faced. Lieutenant Colonel George Custer was Pleasonton's officer of the day, dutifully awaking his commander at 2 a.m. to prepare for a 4 a.m. crossing of the Rappahannock. The Federal predawn attack surprised Stuart at Brandy Station, but after an all-day fight the Confederates held the field upon suffering substantial losses. Stuart's reputation was tarnished in the eyes of the press; his aura of invincibility was destroyed. The Union cavalry fought on even terms that day, and it would be a force to be reckoned with for the rest of the war.[34]

Union cavalry chief Pleasonton reported that Robert E. Lee was headed north. Lee always maintained that the Confederacy could not win the war by remaining on the defensive, but must achieve a decisive victory on Northern soil. The morale of Lee's soldiers was high after the victories at Fredericksburg and Chancellorsville. The Southern soldiers and their commanders thought they were more or less invincible.[35]

---

32. Bushong, *Fightin' Tom Rosser*, 44; *Confederate Veteran Magazine*, 40 vols., 4:74.
33. Bushong, *Fightin' Tom Rosser*, 45.
34. Longacre, *The Cavalry at Gettysburg*, 62–63, 87; Monaghan, *Custer*, 123.
35. Longacre, *The Cavalry at Gettysburg*, 62.

At the onset of the invasion, Maj. Gen. Richard S. Ewell's II Corps led the Confederate advance to Pennsylvania, while Lt. Gen. James Longstreet's I Corps marched to Culpeper. Lieutenant General A. P. Hill's III Corps remained at Fredericksburg until the Confederates could ascertain Hooker's intentions. Hooker, ordered to protect Washington, soon left the Fredericksburg area. J. E. B. Stuart would operate on Lee's right flank, screening the Army of Northern Virginia's movements from the Union army. Pleasonton would fight through Stuart's screen to determine Lee's movements.[36]

Wade Hampton's and Grumble Jones's cavalry brigades remained at the Rappahannock River in order to maintain contact with A. P. Hill. Meanwhile, Stuart took Robertson's, Fitz Lee's, and Rooney Lee's troopers to guard Longstreet's right and front. Colonel John R. Chambliss had replaced Rooney Lee after he had suffered a severe wound at Brandy Station and was recuperating at Hanover County. A Federal raiding party discovered Rooney Lee's location and captured him. However, he was later exchanged. Fitz Lee was also absent, suffering from a bout of rheumatism, and Col. Thomas T. Munford, a reliable, experienced cavalry officer, took over command of his brigade.[37]

Rosser had not shared J. E. B. Stuart's optimism at the outcome of the battle of Brandy Station on June 9. Even though the fight was a draw, Rosser complained in a letter to his sister-in-law, written two days after the fight, that Federal troopers had won the engagement even though they withdrew after accomplishing their mission. On June 14, he wrote his wife, Betty, that he felt remiss in living up to her expectations of a husband. He promised to become a better man and join her church. He believed it imperative to become a confirmed Christian. He informed Betty that he had recently dined with the wife of a mutual friend, Lt. Col. John Shack Green. Mrs. Green told Rosser she thought he had acted foolishly in getting married during the war. Rosser told Betty that he convinced her otherwise, saying it was better to have a husband in the army than an affianced one. He felt marriage removed any doubt of gaining a woman's hand and heart, allowing a soldier to concentrate better on fighting the war. In the letter, he also expressed his lack of confidence in Richard S. Ewell, successor of Stonewall Jackson's II Corps.[38]

36. Stephen W. Sears, *Gettysburg* (New York, 2003), 98–99.
37. Edward G. Longacre, *Gentleman and Soldier: A Biography of Wade Hampton III* (Lincoln, NE, 2003), 132. 138; Tom Hatch, *Clashes of Cavalry* (Mechanicsburg, PA, 2001), 146.
38. Thomas L. Rosser to his sister-in-law Sally Winston, June 11, 1863, UVA; Thomas L. Rosser to Betty W. Rosser, June 14, 1863, UVA.

Several cavalry actions preceded the July 1 to 3 battle of Gettysburg. The first involved Pleasonton's Federal troopers who were trying to penetrate Stuart's screening of Lee's northbound army. This cavalry fight occurred on June 17, 1863, at Aldie, Virginia, when Brig. Gen. Judson Kilpatrick's 2nd New York drove in Col. Thomas T. Munford's pickets in Loudoun County. Munford, in command of Fitz Lee's brigade, was ordered to defend Aldie Gap. Stuart defended Ashby's and Snickers Gaps in the Blue Ridge Mountains, preventing the Federals from observing Confederate troop movements in the Shenandoah Valley. Munford spent the night of June 16 between Upperville and Piedmont Station. The next morning, Stuart directed him to Aldie. Aldie was a strategically located 10 miles southwest of Leesburg where two macadamized turnpikes diverged, one leading almost due west to Ashby's Gap and the second leading northwest to Snickers Gap—both were principal crossings of the Blue Ridge Mountains. In need of forage for his horses, Munford sent most of the 2nd and 3rd Virginia to procure feed from the B. Franklin Carter farm, about 5 miles away. Colonel Williams C. Wickham continued with the rest of the brigade along the Ashby's Gap road to Dover, where he dismounted the 1st and 4th Virginia to water the horses. A detached company of the 2nd Virginia continued scouting to Aldie Gap, with Rosser's 5th Virginia following in column. At Middleburg, Munford divided his command. He sent elements of the 1st, 2nd, 4th, and 5th Virginia to Dover, three miles east of Middleburg, to hold off Kilpatrick, while he brought up the rest of his brigade. Munford's troopers held out for four hours under heavy Federal attack before Stuart ordered him to retreat westward to defend Middleburg.[39]

Rosser, coming from Middleburg and then Dover, moved east to defend an intersection and the gap. As the 2nd Virginia's pickets fell back from Kilpatrick's 2nd New York near Aldie, the Union horsemen met Rosser's troopers. Rosser reported:

> **I caused sabers to be drawn and charged immediately, at the same time sending the information to the rear... I drove the enemy upon his main body, which was in the town of Aldie. His sharpshooters got possession of the heights on my left, in the wood and behind fences, and it was impossible for me to engage him further with saber; consequently, I deployed my sharpshooters to the front [on a low ridge east of the Adam house and orchard, under Captain Reuben Boston], and withdrew the regiment beyond the range of the enemy's rifles. Boston's sharpshooters took cover in drainage ditches**

---

39. Driver, *5th Virginia Cavalry*, 52–54.

that traversed the field and amid scattered haystacks on the hillside and began to harass the Federal skirmishers. As soon as this was done, he [the 6th Ohio and the 2nd New York] charged my skirmishers, who were doing terrible execution in his ranks, endeavoring to dislodge them, but, by a counter-charge, I gave them immediate relief.[40]

Captain Reuben Boston's squadron of about 50 men faced two regiments of Federal cavalry. The squadron repulsed two charges before requesting Rosser's help. Rosser's replied, "Stand your ground. If they charge you, charge them again." The Federals charged Boston's troopers in three lines, and the dismounted Yankee skirmishers pressed Rosser's own skirmishers until the "fighting became desperate and close." Rosser reported: "most of the horses of the dismounted men had been killed, and the enemy, seeing that my force was small (the brigade not yet gotten up), made a desperate effort to capture them, charging them in flank, right and left... I charged the regiment which was threatening the right, drove it back, and the gallant Boston drove his assailants back in confusion and dismay, after emptying many of their saddles."[41]

The Federals brought up artillery and the remainder of their large force, which kept Rosser from supporting his sharpshooters. Rosser ordered Boston to hold his position "at all hazards." Lieutenant Colonel William Stedman's 6th Ohio finally subdued the Confederates. Boston was wounded and lost one-third of his 58 men, either killed or wounded. Overwhelmed, Boston surrendered.[42]

Rosser reported to Colonel Wickham, who was supporting the horse artillery in his rear, that Union cavalry had advanced on the left flank of the brigade. Rosser moved the 5th Virginia to the Snickers Gap Pike "just as [the] enemy had charged and was pursuing one of our regiments. I charged with my entire regiment [along with the 2nd, 3rd, and 4th regiments], with a view of cutting the enemy off and capturing him, but as soon as I was discovered, he escaped through the field, with the exception of a squadron, all of which were killed, wounded, or captured—with their horses and arms." Rosser declared, "The gallant and heroic manner in which Captain Boston and his men acted in this, one of the most vigorous cavalry fights I ever engaged in, makes them take the pride of their regiment." However proud Rosser was of Boston, Stuart was furious that one of his cavalry units had

40. Ibid., 54; *OR* 27/2:747.
41. Driver, *5th Virginia Cavalry*, 54; *OR* 27/2:747.
42. *OR* 27/2:748.

surrendered. Some blamed Rosser for leaving Boston and his men in such an exposed position, but after Boston's exchange later on, Stuart had him face a court-martial.[43]

During the close-quarter fighting with pistols and sabers at Aldie, Colonel Rosser "shot [Cpl. Howard O.] Fisk dead with his self-cocking pistol." Rosser and Union Maj. Henry Lee Higginson, 1st Massachusetts of Kilpatrick's command, fought each other hand-to-hand. Rosser's sword struck Higginson in the face, and someone else shot the major in the back. He was severely wounded and left on the roadside, but managed to crawl into the woods where Union troopers eventually rescued him. Years after the war, at the dedication of the Joseph Hooker statue in Boston, Massachusetts, Rosser went over to Higginson and cordially remarked, "I want to see how good a job I did on your face, that day at Aldie." With that said, the two gentlemen reminisced like old friends for a long while.[44]

The day after the fight at Aldie, Rosser wrote boastfully to his wife:

> **I thank God that I have safely passed through another battle. We met the enemy at Aldie yesterday and after a warm conflict of about four hours, we were compelled to fall back. I had my black horse shot under me. I lost about 100 men killed, wounded or taken prisoner. My loss was heavier than anyone else. I was first to begin and last to retire from the field. Had it not been for me, there would have been another surprise... it was soon discovered that five regts. [regiments] could not hold the position which I had been holding for all hours.[45]**

Rosser was referring to Stuart's being surprised at Brandy Station. Tom Rosser, certainly not a humble man, continued:

> **I am almost completely exhausted. At one time yesterday, I could scarcely lift my hand and now find it difficult to write... Oh Betty, how earnestly do I pray for your happiness and that we may soon again be joined... I feel that I am growing a better man and I know it is the influence which you exercise over me that induces me to change my moral condition.[46]**

43. *OR* 27/2:748; Driver, *5th Virginia Cavalry*, 55.
44. Ibid.; Henry Lee Higginson and Bliss Perry, *Life and Letters of Henry Lee Higginson* (Freeport, New York, 1972), 196.
45. Thomas L. Rosser to Betty W. Rosser, June 18, 1863, UVA.
46. Ibid.

Rosser was much happier when near his wife, and when separated from her, he often took to drinking in an attempt to bolster his sinking morale.[47]

Another cavalry fight of the Gettysburg campaign occurred on June 19 near Middleburg, when Union Cavalry Gen. David M. Gregg advanced from the west against Stuart, forcing him back about a half mile. It was there that a Federal sharpshooter wounded Stuart's 250-pound Prussian aide, Heros von Borcke, in the neck. He recovered and returned to the army, but he never resumed the aggressive lifestyle he had lived up until the wounding.[48]

In the meantime, Pleasonton dispatched Col. William Gamble, who had replaced Col. Grimes Davis after Davis's death at Brandy Station, to outflank the Confederate position west of Middleburg. Stuart's scouts detected Gamble's flanking movement, and Munford, commanding in place of the ailing Fitz Lee, ordered Rosser's 5th Virginia to meet Gamble's threat. Arriving at a crossroads called Pot House at New Lisbon, Rosser found Gamble's men deployed in line of battle with skirmishers thrown forward. Rosser dismounted some of the 5th Virginia and assumed a defensive stance behind stone walls. Gamble, employing the superior Union horse artillery of Lt. John H. Calef's battery, dispersed the Confederates with a few well-placed shells. Rosser's troopers retreated into the woods, and Gamble's command pursued them for several miles toward Upperville before withdrawing as a result of outdistancing their available support. Skirmishing continued on June 20 when Rosser's 5th Virginia attacked the rear of the Federal cavalry and "drove the enemy's force across the stream [Goose Creek] in handsome style."[49]

When the morning mist cleared on June 22, it became evident to Stuart that the Federals were retiring from Upperville, and Stuart ordered the cavalry to pursue the Northerners. The Confederate horsemen pursued the Union cavalry to within a short distance of Aldie. The 5th Virginia, reconnoitering across from Snickers Gap, charged the Federals beyond Goose Creek to reestablish the 1st Virginia's broken picket lines at White Pump.

Stuart asked for guidance regarding the raid into Pennsylvania, receiving vague suggestions from Longstreet and orders from Robert E. Lee, stating:

47. Ibid. Rosser's letters to Betty reveal his desire for her support, so he could change his ways.
48. *OR* 27/2: 690.
49. *OR* 27/1:908–09, 27/2:690. Rosser claimed that a mule kick had disabled Fitzhugh Lee; Rosser, "Autobiographical Sketch," 56, UVA.

> **If you find that he [Hooker] is moving northward, and
> that two brigades can guard the Blue Ridge and take care
> of your rear, you can move with the other three into
> Maryland, and take position on General [Richard]
> Ewell's right, place yourself in communication with him,
> guard his flank, keep him informed of the enemy's
> movements, and collect all the supplies you can for the
> use of the army.**[50]

Three cavalry brigades would march with Stuart: Fitz Lee's,
Rooney Lee's, and Wade Hampton's. They rendezvoused near Salem
Depot on June 24. Fitz Lee, recovered from his aliment, took
command of his brigade. Stuart ordered the brigades of Beverly H.
Robertson and Grumble Jones to guard the passes in the Blue Ridge
Mountains, certain that he would join Robert E. Lee before any battle
ensued. Robertson's brigade was small, consisting of two under-
strength North Carolina regiments. Stuart despised Jones, and
Robertson outranked Jones by date of promotion; thus, Robertson led
the two brigades in their mission. These brigades would not be able to
do the necessary scouting and screening Lee needed. General Lee had
given Stuart a wide latitude and had not planned on a general
engagement for Gettysburg. Now in Pennsylvania, Lee's army became
blind to the disposition and movement of the Northern army. Stuart,
ordered to report to Ewell, took a circuitous raid around the Union
army, planning to meet with Ewell later. The Federals' movements
forced Stuart so far east, however, that he had to cross the Potomac
River at a point only 20 miles from Washington, D.C. Stuart captured
a Union supply train and 400 prisoners at Rockville, Maryland, which
greatly slowed his pace moving north. He reached Hanover,
Pennsylvania, on June 30.[51]

On June 30, 1863, Stuart, still trying to locate Ewell, encountered
Brig. Gen. Judson Kilpatrick's Third Division near Hanover. The
cavalries of both sides, including Rosser and his 5th Virginia, entered
into fighting as they arrived on the scene. Part of the Michigan Cavalry
Brigade, under Bvt. Brig. Gen. George Armstrong Custer, broke
through Stuart's line twice on the Union right, but countercharges
drove them off. Pressured to join Lee, Stuart held on until dark, and
then quietly slipped away.[52]

Stuart pushed on to York, Pennsylvania, where Maj. Gen. Jubal
Early's division had been the day before. Arriving at Carlisle, he fired

50. *OR* 27/2:691.
51. Robert E. Lee to J. E. B. Stuart, June 22, 1863, *OR* 27/3:913; Sears,
    Gettysburg, 106, 139, 153.
52. Longacre, *The Cavalry at Gettysburg*, 174–178.

artillery shells into the Union-held town and burned the barracks. His troopers also destroyed a Federal supply depot. On the evening of July 1, Stuart, learning Lee's army was concentrated at Gettysburg, immediately set out with his command for the scene of the main battle. When he arrived on July 2, he and his men and horses were exhausted from hard riding and frequent fighting—no condition in which to effectively battle the Federal army. Rosser recalled:

> **Stuart had been marching constantly, almost day and night, on scant forage and little rest for man or horse, for eight days, within the enemy's lines, and while his conduct displayed a daring almost to recklessness, he accomplished little, save the wear and fatigue of long marches. He had undoubtedly impaired the strength and vigor of his command.**[53]

Major General George Gordon Meade now led the Army of the Potomac; Meade had replaced Hooker almost two months after the fiasco at Chancellorsville. Hooker had resigned after a dispute with general-in-chief Henry Halleck. Stuart's assignment for July 3 was to guard the Confederate left flank and to be prepared to exploit any success the infantry might achieve on Cemetery Hill by flanking the Federal right and hitting their trains and lines of communication. At noon, Stuart's troopers rode along the York Pike north of the main battle, but Gen. David Gregg's stubborn cavalry, with generals John Buford and Judson Kilpatrick as reinforcement, confronted them. Custer served as brigade commander under Kilpatrick. After a hard-fought battle lasting for several hours, both sides withdrew, leaving the East Cavalry Field in Federal hands. General Wade Hampton was seriously wounded in the fight. Rosser's 5th Virginia missed the main fight as they were on picket duty.[54]

The Confederates were defeated at the three-day battle of Gettysburg. Many blamed Lt. Gen. James Longstreet for General Lee's failure there. Longstreet, Lee's "Old War Horse," had disagreed with Lee's battle plan, recommending Lee move around the Union's right between Meade's defensively well-positioned army and Washington, D.C. Such a maneuver might have drawn out the Army of the Potomac, possibly providing Lee with more favorable fighting terms. Lee rejected Longstreet's advice, however, and ordered the July 2 attack, which Longstreet did not get underway, some say half-

---

53. Thomas L. Rosser, *Addresses of Gen'l T. L. Rosser, at the Seventh Annual Reunion of the Association of the Maryland Line, Academy of Music, Baltimore, Md., February 22, 1889, and on Memorial Day, Staunton, Va., June 8, 1889* (New York, 1889), 41.
54. Driver, *5th Virginia Cavalry*, 58; Jeffrey D. Wert, *Gettysburg, Day Three* (New York, 2001), 25.

heartedly, until 4:00 p.m. On July 3, Lee ordered Longstreet to renew the attack using Maj. Gen. George Pickett's division, which he did so begrudgingly and then was repulsed with heavy casualties.[55]

Long after the war, Kirkwood Otey of the 11th Virginia, among others, questioned Pickett's courage, casting doubts about Pickett's whereabouts during the soon-to-be-famous charge; Otey even suggested that Pickett might have been drinking. Rosser, a nonparticipant in the charge, added to the controversy in a letter he wrote to Republican politician Aurestus S. Perham, claiming Pickett's division was supposed to attack the Federal center, but for some unaccounted reason "obliqued to the left, leaving a dangerous gap between it and [Cadmus] Wilcox's brigade, and thus exposing [James L.] Kemper's right flank." After talking with others who participated, Rosser apparently learned that as Kemper advanced with his right exposed, Union Gen. George J. Stannard sent two of his Vermont regiments on Kemper's flank while enfilading his whole line with "murderous fire." Rosser questioned whether Pickett was on the field close enough to his troops to correct the gaping hole and support his right flank. He concluded, "Gen'l. Pickett was not on the field when the critical conditions were presented." Rosser further stated:

> I have never heard an officer or private soldier (and I have seen many who were in the attack) who was in that attacking column, who says he saw Gen'l. Pickett after his command emerged from the clouds of smoke, from bursting shells, which had enveloped it as it crossed the field to the foot of Cemetery Heights, and I feel sure that he had been detained in the rear, for some unknown cause, and was not on the field, near enough to command the attacking column, when the enemy was reached.[56]

Others participating in the attack on July 3 witnessed Pickett, at the rear and flanks of his advancing troops, directing their movements through couriers. From his rear position he had a virtually unobstructed view until his soldiers reached the Emmitsburg Road. At

55. Wilmer L. Jones, *Generals in Blue and Gray: Davis's Generals* (Westport, CT, 2004), 2 vols., 2:193.
56. Thomas L. Rosser to A. S. Perham, February 2, 1903, A. S. Webb File, Box 4, of the Brake Collection, Copy on file at the United States Army Heritage and Education Center, Carlisle, Pennsylvania, Original at Yale University; *Richmond Times*, November 7, 1894. Rosser, lacking solid evidence, was probably looking for scapegoats to protect Lee's and Longstreet's reputations, so he blamed Pickett. Kirkwood Otey, who had been court-martialed for drunkenness on duty, held a 30-year-long grudge against Pickett. Aurestus S. Perham served in the 7th Maine Light Artillery and after the war served in the House of Representatives and as Special Examiner for the United States Pension Office.

that point, according to his orderly and courier, Pvt. Thomas R. Friend, Pickett must have passed to the far right of the column to the edge of the peach orchard. From the orchard, Pickett "rode off from his staff in a left [oblique] direction," heading toward Gen. James L. Kemper's rear. He then dismounted, walked a distance, remounted, and rode toward his division. After getting a good view of his troops as they reached Cemetery Ridge under "murderous fire," Pickett wheeled and rode back to the flank and out of the line of fire. Accounts from that point on are more vague. It appears that as his men closed with the Federals, Pickett and his aides gathered on the Wentz farm, near the intersection of Emmitsburg Road and the road from the wheat field. From this position, Pickett could view the entire length of his command. Arguments later emerged as to whether he should have been with his advancing troops, or was it appropriate for him to be where he was, essentially out of the line of fire?[57]

After Pickett's repulse, Lee withdrew to Seminary Ridge to await an expected counterattack from General Meade; it never came. Meade's army was physically exhausted and nearly out of ammunition, requiring resupply from Westminster, Maryland. Many of Meade's soldiers had not been fed since July 1. Meade did not know Robert E. Lee's plans, and thus proceeded cautiously. Pleasonton's cavalry took up the chase, fighting with retreating Confederate cavalry all the way to Williamsport at the Potomac River, while Lee's army escaped to Virginia.[58]

Rosser was not among those blaming Longstreet for Lee's defeat at Gettysburg. He defended Longstreet, blaming Pickett and Stuart and, long after the war, Lee himself. After Longstreet's death, Rosser stated, "Longstreet came out of the war with a record for courage and loyalty second to none." Continuing to a reporter of the *Washington, D. C. Star*, he said:

> **When Lee's army was beaten from the fatal attack which he ordered on the 3d of July, he [Lee] rode among the fleeing soldiers, begging them to rally and reform on Seminary Ridge, telling them that it was his fault that they had failed and not their own. No criticism was made**

57. Thomas R. Friend to Charles Pickett, December 10, 1894, Charles Pickett Papers, VHS; Edward G. Longacre, *Pickett: Leader of the Charge* (Shippensburg, Pennsylvania, 1995), 122–125.

58. For a detailed description of the Army of Northern Virginia's retreat and the Army of the Potomac's pursuit, see Eric J. Wittenberg, J. David Petruzzi and Michael F. Nugent, *One Continuous Fight: The Retreat from Gettysburg and the Pursuit of Lee's Army of Northern Virginia, July 4–14, 1863* (El Dorado Hills, CA: Savas Beatie, 2008).

of Longstreet at that time. Longstreet was retained in the most important corps of Lee's army and served honorably and faithfully under Lee to the end.[59]

Years after the war, Rosser blamed Robert E. Lee, stating, "Lee will be held responsible at the bar of history for his fatal blunder by neglecting in the first day's fight to immediately occupy the heights around Gettysburg, after driving the advance of the northern army from the field." Rosser also recalled:

> After the war I went to Lexington to study [law] and saw [Robert E.] Lee practically every day and night. We often discussed comrades and enemies, but I never heard him speak of Longstreet but in the most affectionate manner... no man ever heard him say one word against Longstreet.[60]

Rosser wrote his wife after Gettysburg saying that he had escaped being wounded, but his regiment had suffered greatly in the hand-to-hand combat at Aldie and Hanover. He assured her that he was a changed man and that he constantly prayed to a just God for protection and deliverance. He told Betty he longed for the war to end so he could enjoy her companionship, stating:

> This trip to Penn. Has done us no good—indeed I feel that it is quite a disaster. . . . Sometimes I think that if this war does not end soon, that I will leave this country in order that I may enjoy undisturbed your society—as soon as our army returns to VA—and that will be soon I will send for you.[61]

Back in Virginia, during early August, an interesting incident occurred, bringing Rosser and George Custer together. At the Lacy House in Falmouth, Virginia, Lt. Samuel Harris, along with his Company A of Custer's 5th Michigan, had experienced Confederate sharpshooters constantly firing at them. General Custer visited Lieutenant Harris at the Lacy House to see how things were going on Harris's picket line along the Rappahannock River. Upon hearing Harris's report, Custer ordered Harris to send one of his troopers down to the river under a flag of truce to find out if Colonel Rosser was on the other side. If Rosser was there, Custer wanted arrangements made so that he could visit his West Point friend. Fearing

59. Helen D. Longstreet, *Lee and Longstreet At High Tide: Gettysburg in the Light of the Official Records* (Gainesville, Georgia, 1904), 254; *Kansas City Semi-Weekly*, March 22, 1901; Herman Leonard Papers, Emory University; Glenn Tucker, *Lee and Longstreet at Gettysburg* (Indianapolis, 1968), 253.
60. Ibid.
61. Thomas L. Rosser to Betty W. Rosser, July 7, 1863, UVA.

complications, Harris went himself, asking for Rosser to come down to the riverbank and guarantee Custer's safe visit and return. Rosser met Harris, and agreed to the arrangement, saying, "Send him over," and he ordered his troopers, "no firing." Rosser sent a boat to fetch Custer, and the two friends had a good visit for several hours. About 4:00 p.m., Custer returned, reporting, "Had a fine time over there."[62]

By August 14 Rosser's command had moved to Spotsylvania County, Virginia. On August 20, Rosser received secret orders to march to Saluda, in Middlesex County, 82 miles from their current position. Two days later, he met Lt. John Taylor Wood of the Confederate navy, whom he was to support. The evening of August 22, Lieutenant Wood captured two Federal gunboats—the Satellite and the Reliance—with about 85 prisoners. Rosser sent the prisoners to Richmond under guard. With about 30 of Rosser's sharpshooters aboard one of Wood's ships, Wood captured three transports out in the bay of the Rappahannock, along with their crews and cargo. Wood determined he could accomplish little more in the presence of a large Federal fleet. He then landed at Urbana, unloading Rosser's sharpshooters. Rosser returned to Fredericksburg, reporting, "Many of my men who were from the lower counties deserted and went home while I was near Urbana and it became necessary to leave a lieutenant and 6 men behind to collect them and bring them up."[63]

In late August Rosser checked with the War Department about potential promotions. He discovered there were no recommendations for promotion of either colonels Munford or Wickham on file, but two recommendations were on file for him. Paranoid, he convinced himself that Stuart would somehow prevent his promotion. He wrote to Betty:

> **Somehow or other I can't help [but] suspect Stuart of some trick to get Wickham promoted, not on his account but [by] Gen. R. E. Lee. I have always liked General Stuart and have supported him in every instance and it is very hard for me to believe he would ever desert me—I am now one of his oldest Colonels and I feel that I... deserve promotion.[64]**

---

62. Samuel Harris, *Personal Reminiscences of Samuel Harris* (Chicago, 2008), 46.
63. *OR* 29/1:76. Lieutenant John Taylor Wood had served as an officer in the newly converted ironclad USS Virginia, serving under commander Franklin Buchanan. During the battle of Hampton Roads, Wood had commanded the stern pivot gun, firing the shot that seriously wounded Captain John Worden, commander of the Monitor.
64. Thomas L. Rosser to Betty W. Rosser, August 31, 1863, UVA.

At home Betty was also dealing with difficult circumstances. Responding to a letter from Betty complaining about the loss of her slaves to a group of Union soldiers operating near Courtland, Tom Rosser offered little comfort, replying, "The loss of servants it is true is a great inconvenience, but pshaw before the war is over all [of] you will have to go and it makes no difference how soon they start." After the Emancipation Proclamation, slaves began fleeing their Southern masters in increasing numbers. Wealthier families, in order to save their slaves, often abandoned their homes and moved to a more secure inland location or across the Mississippi River.[65]

Betty, in one of her rare extant letters, wrote to her husband, pleading, "Please do not urge Gen. Stuart any further to have your promotion, for I think it shows impatience as well. . . . I strongly suspect that if he is irritated [and] provoked that he will withhold his recommendation simply to have his revenge. I hope my dear husband that you will not say in this case—'Betsy, don't interfere with my affairs,' for you must know that whatever concerns you must intimately concern me."[66]

On September 3, Rosser told Betty that his relations with Stuart were "still as they have always been, entirely friendly, even familiar." He scolded Betty for suggesting in her August 31 letter that he had asked Stuart for a promotion: "You mistake your husband very much when you suppose he would ask every power on Earth for a promotion. I have never asked or even intimated such a thing as my promotion to Gen. Stuart. The matter has always been discussed by him alone and with him it rests."[67]

The Confederate cavalry reorganized again on September 9, resulting in two division commanders, major generals Fitzhugh Lee and Wade Hampton. The list of new brigadier generals conspicuously did not mention Rosser's name. The 5th Virginia was assigned to Brig. Gen. Lunsford L. Lomax's brigade, along with the 1st Maryland Battalion and the 11th and 15th Virginia regiments. The brigade was at Verdiersville on September 15 and at Orange Court House from September 19 to October 5. On September 23, the brigade again camped at Verdiersville. Drilling and dress parades resumed, and the supplies improved for both men and horses. On October 1, the brigade moved to the vicinity of Orange Court House.[68]

65. Thomas L. Rosser to Betty W. Rosser, August 31, 1863, UVA; Joseph T. Glatthaar, *General Lee's Army: From Victory to Collapse* (New York, 2008), 306.
66. Betty W. Rosser to Thomas L. Rosser, August 31, 1863, UVA.
67. Thomas L. Rosser to Betty W. Rosser, September 3, 1963, UVA.
68. Driver, *5th Virginia Cavalry*, 61.

Camp rumors circulated that Rosser was about to be promoted to brigadier general, with Henry Pate being promoted to colonel of the 5th Virginia. It appeared Rosser's promotion would have to wait until Stuart could get rid of Grumble Jones, with whom he had been feuding for some time. Jones was a capable brigade commander who had won the respect of his men. He had increased the efficiency of Brig. Gen.Turner Ashby's former brigade. Yet, in spite of his war record, Stuart wanted Jones transferred out of his command. Way back in October 1862, Stuart had written, "I do not regard Brigadier General Jones as deserving this command or as a fit person to command a brigade of cavalry." Stuart instead had praised Rosser, recommending him for promotion to command a new brigade to be formed:

> I ask this appointment because no officer I have met within the Confederacy combines in a more eminent degree the characteristics of the Cavalry Commander than Rosser. He is an officer of superior ability, possesses in an extraordinary degree the talent to command and the skill to lead with coolness and decision of character.[69]

As far back as February 1863, Stuart had written to Army Headquarters requesting Jones's transfer, stating, "He does not possess the qualities essential to a successful cavalry leader and commander." In the very same letter, Stuart recommended that Rosser should receive promotion to brigadier general. He indicated his preference of Rosser to colonels Munford and Wickham:

> I give to Rosser the preference, which I consider due to the generalship I have seen him display on several critical occasions, to which he unites a noble self-reliance and tenacity of purpose, and I would feel safer with him in command of a Cavalry Brigade than any Col. I know of and have already recommended him for promotion separately, in case a new Brigade recommended be authorized.

Munford had predicted that junior officers, such as Rosser and Wickham, would be promoted rather than him because they were members of the West Point elite Virginia clique, whereas he was considered an outsider as a graduate of the Virginia Military Institute.[70]

69. J. E. B. Stuart to Robert E. Lee, October 24, 1862, VHS.
70. J. E. B. Stuart to Brig. Gen. R. H. Chilton, February 4, 1863, Jeb Stuart, C. S. A. Miscellaneous Confidential Papers, VHS; Longacre, *Lee's Cavalrymen*, 245.

Stuart's displeasure with Jones was in part from Jones's failure to adequately protect the passes of South Mountain during the Gettysburg campaign. As a result, Union General Kilpatrick was able to capture 45 wagons and 1,000 Confederate prisoners from Ewell's corps. Jones offered to resign, but Robert E. Lee still needed him, and the commander was able to defer his departure from the army. Strained relations between the two strong-headed cavalrymen continued until culminating with a verbal clash in September. Stuart had Jones arrested and court-martialed. Jones let it be known that even if he were acquitted, he would never serve under Stuart again. The military court found him guilty of disrespect to a superior officer, stripping him of his command and ordering him to take charge of the cavalry in southwest Virginia.[71]

Rosser wrote Betty in mid-September, still tired of waiting for his promotion to general rank. He took out his hostility on Stuart, declaring that recent campaigning had applied "the finishing stroke to Stuart's declining reputation. I can't sympathize with him now." He blamed Stuart for not securing his promotion by then, and became determined to leave his command, stating, "Nothing will keep me." However, Rosser went nowhere.[72]

Near the end of September, Rosser brought charges against Pate again, asking to establish a board of review to examine the colonel "with a view of having him removed from the field and his commission cancelled." Rosser complained that Pate had not been with the regiment since June 17, but he conveniently failed to mention that Pate had been wounded on that date. Rosser further complained, "He [Pate] has been in action with this regiment, and is totally inefficient, and lacks every qualification of an officer. Present, or absent, he seems to take no interest whatever in the good of the command; and if such an officer be allowed to hold his commission, all discipline is gone, and the efficiency of the command in which he is attached will be destroyed." General Lee appointed a board of officers to decide the case, consisting of generals John R. Chambliss and Lunsford Lomax and Col. Thomas H. Owen of the 3rd Virginia. After questioning witnesses, of which 18 out of 20 supported Pate, and reviewing Pate in the field on tactics and drill, the board concluded, "There is not shown any reason why Lieutenant-Colonel Pate should be removed from office; and the Board do recommend that he be promoted to the

---

71. William N. McDonald, *A History of the Laurel Brigade* (Baltimore and London: 2002), 168.
72. Thomas L. Rosser to Betty W. Rosser, September 15, 16, and 24, 1863, UVA.

Colonelcy of the 5th Virginia Cavalry." Rosser had been rebuffed a second time in trying to get rid of Pate.[73]

Given the vacancy that accompanied Jones's transfer, Stuart recommended to Lee that Rosser be promoted. In a September 30 letter to Rosser from Stuart, the cavalry chief stated:

> **Should another vacancy occur in my command, it is my earnest desire to have you fill it, and I have written to Col. Munford, who felt himself slighted at Wickham's promotion, that I should recommend you in preference to him. There is no difference of opinion with General officers under whom you have served that on the field of battle, in coolness or capacity to 'control happening events', and wield troops, you have no superior... You deserve promotion more than any Col of a Va Regt in my command, and if Brig Gen Jones should be sent elsewhere, you are my choice for the post this made vacant.[74]**

Rosser refused consolation and turned on his friend and commander, viciously and irrationally writing to his wife, "Stuart has been false to me as he has ever been to his country and his wife. I will leave him in his glory." Rosser was determined to transfer from Stuart's command and told Betty that only she knew his true feelings. "I don't speak of it myself. I seem cheerful and speak of General Stuart as usual. I will never give him an opportunity of deceiving me again." When Stuart tried to explain why Rosser had not yet been promoted, Rosser wrote to Betty: "His arguments I thought quite silly. He seems to hate the way that he has treated me, but it is too late now you know." Rosser looked for opportunities to criticize his commander's performance in combat, saying, "Gen. Stuart is badly whipped." Rosser stated that he had options to leave the cavalry. General Ewell offered him a position as his chief of artillery with the rank of colonel. Stuart probably never suspected the depth of Rosser's loathing of him, because Rosser kept his vitriol of Stuart to his wife in confidence. Within a month, Stuart managed to push Rosser's promotion through. On Rosser's birthday, October 15, 1863, he was promoted to brigadier general, to rank from September 28.[75]

73. Driver, *5th Virginia Cavalry*, 61; Johnson, ed., *Biographical Sketches of Alumni Who Fell in the Confederate War*, 586–87.

74. J. E. B. Stuart to Thomas L. Rosser, September 30, 1863, Mitchell, ed., *The Letters of James E. B. Stuart*, 349.

75. Thomas L. Rosser to Betty W. Rosser, September 15, 16, and 24, 1863, UVA. The cavalry chief's enemies spread rumors about his alleged infidelities. Certainly, there were plenty of opportunities, but no credible evidence exists that Stuart strayed from his wife.

Brigadier General Thomas Lafayette Rosser – 1863
Rosser felt that only certain men were endowed to be generals.
Albert and Shirley Small Special Collections Library, University of Virginia

CHAPTER 5

Brigadier General Thomas L. Rosser, commander of the Laurel Brigade: Bristoe campaign cavalry fights at Auburn and Buckland; Fighting along the Rappahannock and Rapidan rivers; Dispatched to Shenandoah Valley to aid General Jubal Early.

Rosser referring to the Partisan Rangers:
"They are a nuisance to the Service."

Tom Rosser, remaining in Maj. Gen. J. E. B. Stuart's favor, fought in the fall of 1863 Bristoe campaign cavalry fights at Auburn and Buckland, skirmishing along the Rappahannock and Rapidan rivers, before he was dispatched to Maj. Gen. Jubal Early in the Shenandoah Valley. In doing so, Rosser gained the confidence of his brigade's troopers, displaying courage and skill in leading them. He continued, however, to sour on Stuart and struggle with alcohol. In the Shenandoah Valley, Rosser, accompanying Early on raids, performed admirably, providing a glimpse of his talent for the upcoming surprise raids against Federal bases. Impressed by his performance, Early pressured Richmond for confirmation of Rosser's promotion to brigadier general.

When Brig. Gen. Tom Rosser took command of Brig. Gen. William E. Jones's brigade in October 1863, he found himself in command of a unit immortalized by the late Brig. Gen. Turner Ashby. Ashby had been killed by friendly fire near Harrisonburg, Virginia, on June 6, 1862. Brigadier General Beverly H. Robertson had taken command of the brigade after Ashby's death. Although Ashby had lacked administrative and disciplinary skills, he had been a brave and daring warrior. When Gen. William E. Jones took over the brigade after Robertson had been transferred to North Carolina at the behest of Stuart, he added necessary complementary skills that Ashby had lacked. The brigade consisted of the 7th Virginia, Col. Richard H. Dulany commanding; 11th Virginia, Col. Oliver R. Funsten commanding; 12th Virginia, Col. Asher W. Harman commanding; 35th Virginia, Lt. Col. Elijah V. White commanding; and Capt. Roger Preston Chew's battery of horse artillery. There were 26 companies in all, most recruited in the Shenandoah Valley, including several companies from Maryland, plus others from Loudoun County and other counties east of the Blue Ridge Mountains.[1]

Rosser believed only certain men were destined to become generals. In a speech after the war, he stated:

> **A man may acquire, by long training, an accurate knowledge of tactics, the rules and usages of war, and all the regulations governing armies in the field—such as methods of attack, and defense, systems of outposts, pickets, vedettes, flankers, spies and scouts—but with all these, he is not a general unless nature has bestowed on him genius and physical endowments of a high order, for no man of mere ordinary talents can by any amount of training become a general.[2]**

Obviously, Rosser was egotistical and filled with ambition to climb to the top of the Confederate hierarchy, eager for greatness and glory. Even in defeat or falling short, he never let obstacles interfere with his drive to prominence.

Originally known as "Ashby's Cavalry of the Army of Northern Virginia and Chew's Battery," General Rosser renamed the brigade the "Laurel Brigade." A yellow patch with a green laurel branch embroidered upon it became a part of their uniforms. The ancient Greeks used laurel foliage to crown victors of the Pythian Games. Mothers, wives, sisters, and sweethearts generally made the green silk patch. The men usually chose to wear the badge of honor on their hats. The brigade's prowess as a fighting unit and as a brigade intensely proud of its previous commanders had influenced Rosser. Rosser also desired to increase his own standing and to improve the "esprit de corps" of his brigade. Typically, brigades in the Confederacy were known by the last names of their commanders. Division commanders occasionally used the "Laurel Brigade" title, but other cavalry brigades did not generally reference the designation. Some viewed it as bit arrogant.[3]

According to Capt. Frank M. Myers, the troopers of Col. "Lige" White's 35th battalion soon found Rosser to be a "handsome, soldierly-looking man, very different in manner, language and appearance from Gen. Jones, though not a whit behind that officer in the maintenance

---

1. McDonald, *Laurel Brigade*, 17-18; H. B. McClellan, *The Campaigns of Stuart's Cavalry*, 91fn1; *Thomas L. Rosser Scrapbook*, Thomas L. Rosser Papers, UVA.
2. "The Cavalry, A.N.V.," *Address by Gen. T. L. Rosser at the Seventh Annual Reunion of the Association of the Maryland Line, Academy of Music, Baltimore, Maryland, February 22, 1889* (Baltimore, 1889), 8.
3. McDonald, *Laurel Brigade*, 18.

of discipline in his brigade; but, it did not take them long to find that he was a genial, warm-hearted gentleman, and they respected and loved him accordingly." Many soldiers, including Myers, would lose respect for Rosser as the war progressed.[4]

In September 1863, rumors circulated in Hanover County, Virginia, that Tom Rosser had been married before wedding Betty Winston. This naturally upset Betty who wrote her husband about it. Rosser became irate, denying the rumors and chastising Betty, writing, "It gives me no little pain to see that you are annoyed by the basely false reports in circulation concerning me and another wife. These reports are should you know basely false but until I can ascertain who it is that is putting them in circulation, I have no means of putting them at an end." Rosser implied that if he determined the culprit then he would challenge him to a duel, saying, "If I can ascertain who it is that is spreading the report, I will punish him, provided he is a gentleman." He suspected Lt. Col. Henry C. Pate behind the gossip, but could not prove it.[5]

Betty suggested to her husband that he publish a public denial of the false allegations, but Rosser disagreed, stating, "I think it likely that it would make it worse." Apparently, the rumors reached the officers in Stuart's command. Stuart, amused, told Rosser that "Miss Bull and some officers had quite a warm discussion on the subject." Miss Bull thought Rosser had two wives. Stuart's amusement at the subject probably added to the list of reasons why Rosser soured on his commander.[6]

Major Cavalry Fights During the Bristoe Campaign: Auburn and Buckland, Virginia

Regardless of the rumors circulating, on September 13, Union cavalry commander Maj. Gen. Alfred Pleasonton attacked and defeated J. E. B. Stuart's cavalry at Culpeper Court House, situated halfway between Richmond and Washington, D.C. The Union victory opened the Culpeper region to Union control, ushering in the Bristoe campaign. During this campaign, several significant cavalry actions

4. Frank M. Myers, *The Comanches: A History of White's Battalion, Virginia Cavalry*, (Marietta, Georgia, 1956), 176.
5. Thomas L. Rosser to Betty W. Rosser, September 18 and October 5, 1863, Thomas L. Rosser Papers, UVA.
6. Thomas L. Rosser to Betty W. Rosser, September 24, 1863, Thomas L. Rosser Papers, UVA. The author has been unable to determine the identity of "Miss Bull."

occurred, including the battle of Auburn on October 14 and the battle of Buckland Mills on October 19, 1863.[7]

On October 11 Stuart attempted to assault the Federal rear at Brandy Station in order to gain the high ground at Fleetwood Hill. Stuart sent the 12th Virginia to attack Union cavalry near Fleetwood Hill, but a Federal cavalry squadron struck the flank of Stuart's 4th and 5th North Carolina, routing them and forcing their retreat. The Federals established a strong position on Fleetwood Hill, and were able to thwart all Confederate attacks with artillery. Regardless of their success, at nightfall the Federal cavalry, under Pleasanton, re-crossed the Rappahannock River to safety.[8]

During the cavalry fight at Brandy Station, Maj. Gen. Fitzhugh Lee's cavalry division and two brigades of infantry forced Union Brig. Gen. John Buford back across the Rapidan River at Morton's Ford. A trooper of the 6th Virginia recalled:

> Presently we saw a magnificent sight. The colonel of the Fourth [Fifth] Virginia Regiment, mounted on a beautiful black horse, moved forward, calling upon his regiment to follow him. It was Colonel, afterward General Rosser. As the regiment moved toward the enemy's lines, at a gallop, the cry went up and down the ranks, "Look at Rosser, look at Rosser." Everybody expected to see him tumble from his horse, shot to death. But he went forward, leading his men, and when the enemy discovered that we were coming in earnest, they turned on their heels and fled.[9]

Lieutenant George W. Beale of the 9th Virginia observed Rosser's actions and recalled:

> I was in a position to see Colonel Rosser with his men in the line of breastworks, from which our infantry had retired, and to do so at the moment he was struck by a spent bullet. He began at once to retire, supposing his wound was serious, but had gone but a few rods towards the rear when, having seen some slight wavering in his line, he turned around quickly and went forward again as if no ball had touched him.[10]

Rosser had been wounded in the forearm during the Brandy Station fight. When Maj. Gen. George Meade learned that evening

7. "Bristoe Campaign," NPS.
8. *OR* 29/1:442–44, 448.
9. Luther W. Hopkins, *From Bull Run to Appomattox: A Boy's View* (Baltimore, 1908), 120–21.
10. G. W. Beale, *A Lieutenant in Lee's Army* (Boston, 1918), 128, 131.

that Confederate infantry was attempting to outflank him, he with-drew northward to protect his rear.

On October 12 Stuart left Rosser's 5th Virginia with only one piece of artillery near Brandy Station, with orders to picket the Rappahannock. He ordered Col. Pierce Young to move Maj. Gen. Matthew C. Butler's brigade from James City to Culpeper Court House. He then proceeded with the remainder of his command toward Warrenton, 15 miles southwest of Manassas in Fauquier County, Virginia. Stuart had succeeded in screening Gen. Robert E. Lee's army from the prying eyes of the Union cavalry. Meade mistakenly thought Lee was at Culpeper Court House, and on the afternoon of the 12th, he dispatched the II, V, and VI Corps with Buford's cavalry for Culpeper, intending to fight Lee there. Meade's advance struck Rosser's regiment midafternoon, forcing Rosser to fall back in the face of a vastly superior force. He fought a stalling action as best he could while retreating, delaying the Federal advance from reaching a wooded ridge called Slaughter's Hill, north of Culpeper Court House, until nearly nightfall.[11]

Meanwhile, Young had arrived from James City, bringing five pieces of artillery along. Young dismounted every available man and positioned his guns in advantageous positions. Rosser's troopers joined his line of battle. Severe cannon fire surprised Buford's approaching cavalry, ceasing their advance. Buford bivouacked for the night, as did Rosser and Young. Rosser's troopers lit many campfires in an attempted ruse to fool Buford into thinking the Confederate force was larger than it appeared. During the night, Meade received information that General Lee was in fact moving on the Orange and Alexandria Railroad, so he moved his army to confront the Confederate commander. Buford also moved back across the Rappahannock River.[12]

On October 13, General Lee ordered Stuart to conduct a reconnaissance toward Catlett's Station, southwest of Manassas on the O&A Railroad. Lee's main army concentrated at Warrenton, and when Stuart reached within eight miles of Catlett's Station and Warrenton Junction, he discovered Meade retreating toward Manassas. Stuart spotted a large number of Federal wagons near the railroad between Warrenton and Manassas. However, two Federal corps along the road protected the wagons. Stuart realized he could not attack with his cavalry command alone. He sent his inspector general, Maj. A. Reid Venable, to Lee with the information, but Lee responded by sending a courier to Rosser telling him that Auburn was in the Federals' hands. Stuart then realized he was cut off from the main

11. H. B. McClellan, *The Campaigns of Stuart's Cavalry*, 383.
12. Ibid, 384.

army, stranded between two Federal corps. He had two choices: fight through or ride around the Union forces. He chose to hide his two brigades of cavalry and seven artillery pieces until Lee could arrive to attack the Federals. Stuart found a small secluded valley for this purpose, just 175 yards from where the Federals bivouacked for the night.[13]

Before dawn on October 14, Stuart heard a volley of musketry on Warrenton Road, assuming it was General Lee advancing to attack. Responding, Rosser assaulted the Federals camped near him with cannon fire, and then attempted to break through the Union lines. Lee was not attacking, however, and Stuart suffered substantial losses while breaking free of the Federals and proceeding toward Warrenton.[14]

A few days later, Stuart's and Fitz Lee's commands withdrew from Bristoe by separate routes, planning to meet in the vicinity of Warrenton. On October 18 Brig. Gen. Judson Kilpatrick attacked Stuart's outposts, forcing the Confederate cavalry commander to withdraw his troopers to the south bank of Broad Run at Buckland on the Warrenton Turnpike. Here Stuart planned to make a stand until Fitz Lee could join him. Rosser's brigade camped in the area of Haymarket for the night. Early on October 19, Gen. Wade Hampton's cavalry division, which included Rosser's brigade, joined in defending Buckland against Kilpatrick's attacking cavalry. Stuart, commanding Hampton's division in his absence, received a suggestion from Fitz Lee for Stuart to withdraw from Kilpatrick, enticing him to follow. At a given signal Stuart would turn and attack Kilpatrick, while Fitz Lee would attack from the south against the Federal left flank.[15]

Stuart sent Hampton's division to Chestnut Hill, only two and a half miles northeast of Warrenton. The unsuspecting Federal cavalry-men fell for the subterfuge, approaching to within 200 yards of the Confederate position, whereupon the Confederates, hearing Fitz Lee's signal, turned and attacked Kilpatrick's leading brigade, which Brig. Gen. Henry E. Davies commanded. The Federal horsemen were completely surprised, fleeing in confusion. Located in the rear, Bvt. Brig. Gen. George Armstrong Custer's brigade did not fall for the trap, but defended the Broad Run position from Fitz Lee. While Custer's troopers were holding off Fitz Lee, Stuart led Hampton's division in pursuit of Davies along the Warrenton Turnpike. Brigadier General James B. Gordon led his North Carolina cavalry in a frontal attack on the Federal column, while brigadier generals Thomas Rosser and Pierce Young attacked Federal cavalry on both sides of the Warrenton

---

13. *OR* 29/1:448.
14. Ibid.
15. *OR* 29/1:451. Hampton was still recovering from his Gettysburg wound.

Turnpike. During Kilpatrick's rapid flight, he abandoned all of his division's transport, including Custer's headquarters wagons and personal effects. The fleeing Federals overran Custer, but he retired in good order. Kilpatrick's division continued its flight until it reached safety behind Meade's I Corps. Ultimately, Stuart captured about 250 prisoners and a few wagons. Custer would not soon forget his humiliating defeat at the hands of Rosser's horsemen. The fighting moved toward Haymarket where an aggressive Stuart, with Rosser's and Gordon's troopers, drove off the Yankees in a night attack.[16]

Fighting Along the Rappahannock and Rapidan Rivers

After the Bristoe campaign and the cavalry fight at Buckland, the Confederate and Union armies reoccupied their previous positions on the Rappahannock and Rapidan rivers. Rosser's brigade fell back to the Hazel River on October 19, and the following day marched to near Rixeyville, remaining there until October 26. They continued marching to Gaines Crossroads, going into camp to enjoy a brief respite. Rosser was then ordered to picket along the fords on the Rappahannock River between Germanna and Fredericksburg. The Federal army crossed the Rappahannock at Kelly's Ford on November 7, reoccupying its former position at Culpeper Court House. Robert E. Lee withdrew to the south bank of the Rapidan, preparing to go into winter quarters. Meanwhile, during a nighttime attack, the Federal III, V, and VI Corps, the latter two under Maj. Gen. John Sedgwick, overran Maj. Gen. Jubal Early's division at Rappahannock Bridge. The Confederates lost 1,630 killed, wounded, or captured; in comparison, Federal casualties totaled only 419.[17]

On November 10, 1863, Rosser's cavalry brigade reorganized to consist of the 6th, 7th, and 12th Virginia Cavalry regiments and the 17th and 35th Virginia battalions. Hampton, sufficiently recovered from his wounds, returned to duty on November 3. Hampton ordered Rosser's command to break camp near Flint Hill on November 17 and march to Chancellorsville. During the night, Hampton, with Rosser's command, crossed the Rapidan River at Germanna Ford, proceeding toward Stevensburg. Here, near daylight, Rosser's troopers attacked the 18th Pennsylvania's encampment, scattering them toward Stevensburg and capturing 60 prisoners, about 100 horses and mules, and some

16. Richard L. Armstrong, *7th Virginia Cavalry* (Lynchburg, Virginia, 1992), 61; OR 29/1:451–52.
17. *OR* 29/1:624; Douglas Southall Freeman, *Lee's Lieutenants*. 3 vols. (New York, 1942), 3:267.

equipment, while losing one killed and two wounded. Rosser's brigade then re-crossed the Rapidan and returned to Hamilton's Crossing, near Fredericksburg, to resume picketing at the various fords on the Rappahannock.[18]

Rosser's troopers had just grown comfortable when they found themselves back in the saddle as word spread that the Army of the Potomac made a general advance. General Meade and his entire army crossed the Rapidan at Germanna Ford on November 26, proceeding up the Plank Road toward Orange Court House. Upon receiving scouting reports, Rosser moved his brigade to near Todd's Tavern at the intersection of Catharpin and Brock roads, four miles southeast of Chancellorsville, to guard the roads leading toward the Central Railroad and the flank of General Lee's army. The scouts reported a large Federal wagon train of the I and V Corps located on the Plank Road. Meade was taking a route that became known as "The Wilderness," 10 miles west of Fredericksburg. Meade had pickets out, but they missed seeing the Confederate cavalry at the Brock and Orange Plank intersection, which crossed Meade's marching line and led to Todd's Tavern. The Wilderness was a 150-square-mile expanse of virtually uninhabited land containing poor soil, allowing only stunted trees and nearly impenetrable underbrush to grow.[19]

On the morning of November 27, Rosser approached the Federal column cautiously. As the rattle of the Federal wagon train became audible, he attacked. Confederates captured more than a dozen of the V Corps's wagons, and took them on the Brock Road toward Todd's Tavern. In the confusion of the minutes-long attack, many wagons were stampeded and abandoned. Federal infantry came from two directions in an attempt to save the wagon train. Exposed to fire coming from two directions, the Confederate raiders made a hasty retreat into the cover of the Wilderness. Between 35 and 40 wagons were broken or destroyed on the Plank Road, but the Confederates secured the mules and equipment. The Southerners brought about 15 to 20 wagons and 130 mules to Todd's Tavern, along with roughly 95 prisoners. Rosser had lost two men killed and three wounded.[20]

Colonel Rufus Dawes of the 6th Wisconsin Infantry of the Iron Brigade, recently returning from a leave of absence and rejoining his regiment near Chancellorsville, recalled the same event. "Soon

18. *OR* 19/2: 712; McDonald, *Laurel Brigade*, 203–4; *Philadelphia Weekly Times*, March 22, 1884; Armstrong, *7th Virginia Cavalry*, 61–62; *Richmond Enquirer*, November 19, 1863.
19. McDonald, *Laurel Brigade*, 204–05; *OR* 29/1:904; *Philadelphia Weekly Times*, March 22, 1884.
20. *OR* 29/1:904, 51/2:789; *Philadelphia Weekly Times*, March 22, 1884; Armstrong, *7th Virginia Cavalry*, 62.

afterward, musketry was heard on his [Dawes's] front and his regiment was ordered forward double quick," Dawes said. "They deployed as skirmishers in the woods. His regiment had been marching on a narrow road through thick woods in advance of the I Corps. Ahead of them was a wagon train of the V Corps."[21] Dawes continued:

> **Most of the wagons were loaded with ammunition. The rebel cavalry under Colonel Rosser came in by a cross road through the woods and attacked this wagon train, driving away the guards. It was a bold dash to come in between two army corps. We hurried forward through the thick woods and opened fire on the rebels as they were trying to hurry off the wagons. They promptly returned our fire and, for a few moments, the shots cracked and whizzed around our heads. We quickly drove them away, killing and wounding several of their men. Before they retreated, they set fire to a number of ammunition wagons which blew up with loud and continued explosions, scattering shot, shell and wagon wheels all over the country. One of our men was shot. A rebel cavalry man took fair aim at me and his bullet cut a hole in my hat.**[22]

Two days later, on November 29, Stuart, with Hampton's division and Rosser's brigade leading, made a reconnaissance around the left of Meade's army. The cavalry column often marched in single file through the dense underbrush of the Wilderness. An abandoned railroad bed, nearly parallel to the Plank Road, ran across the marching path. A Federal camp, consisting of a regiment of Gen. David M. Gregg's cavalry, sat just across the road at Parker's Store. The Federals were also picketing in the railroad bed. Parker's Store was located a couple miles east of New Hope Church on the Orange Plank Road. Captain Harry Hatcher, of Company A of the 7th Virginia, discovered Union pickets while leading the advance guard. The Confederates charged with Rosser's brigade in front and the 7th Virginia leading; they captured or killed every picket, about 10 to 15 total. Shortly thereafter, the Federal camp situated on the right of Plank Road came into view. Rosser led a charge of the camp. Before long, Rosser's troopers were strung out on the narrow road, resulting in the brigade losing its formation. For a brief period, the Federals managed to pour fire into the attacking Confederate horsemen, keeping them at bay. Rosser's brigade, however, soon closed up, successfully attacking the

21. Rufus Dawes to M. B. G. (My Best Girl), December 4, 1863, Rufus Robinson Dawes, *Memoir of Rufus Dawes, in Service with the Sixth Wisconsin Volunteers* (Marietta, OH, 1890), 227–28.
22. Ibid.

camp. The Laurel Brigade's losses amounted to three killed and 15 wounded. In a report, Rosser overemphasized his brigade's contribution to the battle. Refuting Rosser, Gen. Wade Hampton reported, "Without detracting in the smallest degree from the credit due this brigade, I think General Rosser underestimates the services performed by the other two, the arrival of which was most timely, and whose share in this fight I regard as quite equal to that of Rosser's gallant brigade."[23]

The fleeing Federals had abandoned supplies in the woods, including an unfinished breakfast, to which the cold and hungry Confederate troopers helped themselves. In the meantime, the Federal army received heavy reinforcements and sent out skirmish lines on the Confederate flanks, attempting to recover the field. For more than two hours a fierce struggle ensued, with neither side prevailing. The fighting mostly occurred between dismounted men, as the dense undergrowth prevented mounted squadrons from moving advantageously. Rosser fell back until Brig. Gen. James B. Gordon's 2nd and a portion of his 5th North Carolina cavalry regiments showed up as reinforcement, allowing Rosser's troopers to rejoin Col. Pierce Young's horsemen. Finally, Rosser made a charge on the Plank Road with elements from all his regiments, and a fierce pistol and saber fight ensued. The Federals stood their ground for a time before becoming overwhelmed and fleeing with Rosser's horsemen in pursuit. The chase continued for several miles with the Federals losing many killed or wounded and more than 100 captured. Rosser had three killed and 15 wounded.[24]

The Confederate army expected Meade to attack the next day, but Meade had no intention of doing so, re-crossing the Rappahannock River to go into winter quarters. Rosser's brigade returned to camp at Hamilton's Crossing, near Fredericksburg, on December 5. A barren wasteland with little forage surrounded the camp. Troopers were exposed in their tents to the cold and received meager rations. While the citizens of Fredericksburg tried their best to aid the hungry soldiers by hosting "starvation parties," the troopers longed for a more hospitable camp location in the Shenandoah Valley.[25]

23. McDonald, *Laurel Brigade*, 206–7; *OR* 29/1:905–6; Armstrong, *7th Virginia Cavalry*, 62.
24. McDonald, *Laurel Brigade*, 206–7; *OR* 29/1:900; Roger H. Harrell, *The 2nd North Carolina Cavalry* (Jefferson, N. C., 2004), 215–16.
25. McDonald, *Laurel Brigade*, 208.

To the Shenandoah Valley

General Robert E. Lee learned one or two regiments of Federal cavalry were moving into the Shenandoah Valley from Winchester toward Staunton. On December 16, he ordered Rosser to cross the Shenandoah River in the rear of the Federal force to prevent its escape. This Federal contingent acted as a diversion to aid Brig. Gen. William Averell in attacking the Virginia and Tennessee Railroad.[26]

Newly minted as a brigadier general, Rosser had commanded his brigade for only two months. Stuart wrote his cousin before Rosser's arrival in Augusta County, stating, "General Rosser is a cavalier of the right stamp—very different from Jones. I promise you people of Augusta no stampedes or false alarms from him."[27]

Rosser marched his command to Fredericksburg before crossing the Rappahannock during low tide at twilight, but some of the troopers still had to swim their horses. Rosser's horsemen were happy to be moving toward the Shenandoah Valley. They rode through the late campground of Maj. Gen. Ambrose E. Burnside's army. Soon Rosser's troopers spotted the campfires of Meade's army and stopped to rest for the night. Rain started at a drizzle but quickly became a downpour, drenching the men, filling the streams, and making the roads muddy quagmires that were difficult for advancing. The rain continued the next day, creating miserably slow marching conditions. Three days' rations were prepared and all too quickly consumed.[28]

With the 7th Virginia leading, followed by the 12th and 11th Virginia, along with Col. Lige White's battalion, Rosser's brigade approached the Occoquan River at nightfall. The Confederate horsemen found a passable ford at Wolf Run Shoals, an important crossing point for travelers between Richmond and Alexandria. Rosser felt eager to reach the Shenandoah Valley quickly, as they had lost time from the bad weather. Instead of taking routes that avoided Federal outposts, he decided on a more direct course along a road leading to Sangster's Station on the O&A Railroad, even though he knew Federal forces guarded the railroad bridge. He procured a local guide to aid him through the countryside where there were no roads, avoiding the loss of valuable time from fighting Federal guards.[29]

26. Armstrong, *7th Virginia Cavalry*, 63.
27. Theodore Stanford Garnett, *Riding with Stuart: Reminiscences of an Aide-de-Camp.* (Shippensburg, PA, 1994), 13, 19; J. E. B. Stuart to My Dear Cousin, December 18, 1863, Stuart, Alexander Papers, VHS; Mitchell, ed., The Letters of James E. B. Stuart, 357.
28. McDonald, Laurel Brigade, 209–210; *Philadelphia Weekly Times*, March 22, 1884.
29. Ibid.

Nearing Sangster's Station, Rosser found a deep stream to ford. The rainstorms continued; thunder and bright lightning lit up the pitch-black surrounding area revealing features of a stockade fort, and, unfortunately for Rosser, a garrison of Federal forces inside had already discovered his presence. With the element of surprise lost, Rosser ordered the 7th Virginia, led by Col. Richard H. Dulany, to cross the stream and attack. At first only Capt. Daniel C. Hatcher's First Squadron gallantly plunged across and attacked the stockade. The squadron went around the stockade and crossed the railroad, but large forces in the Federal breastworks prevented them from returning. Blinded by darkness, the remainder of the 7th Virginia passed the stream by without crossing. Rosser ordered the 11th Virginia, commanded by Lt. Col. Mottrom Ball, to charge the fort. Forming in close column, while guided by lightning flashes, they crossed the roaring stream. Rosser reported, "Although by this time, the enemy was thoroughly aroused, and was pouring sheet after sheet of fire into the head of Ball's column, the gallant old regiment went cheering through water, and in a moment was up the hill on the other side—and the stockade was ours." Shielded by darkness, most of the Federal garrison had escaped. The Sangster's Station raid left a lasting impression on Rosser's troopers for its fierce fighting, suffering, and horrors.[30]

According to the *Richmond Whig*, Rosser reviewed the Corps of Cadets at the Virginia Military Institute in Lexington after the fight at Sangster's Station. The newspaper reported: "He was accompanied in the review by Governor [William] Smith and Ex-Governor [John] Letcher, and a large number of ladies and citizens. After the review General Rosser inspected the barracks, and the cadets were presented to him." Four days later, a regiment of Rosser's brigade, under Lieutenant Colonel Ball, visited the institute for the purpose of presenting a flag they had captured at Sangster's Station. New York City citizens presented the flag to the 164th New York. After the ceremony finished, the cavalry made two mock charges over the grounds and consumed a meal prepared for them.[31]

Next, Rosser's command marched through rain and darkness toward Upperville, northeast of Manassas in Loudoun County. Rosser's troopers continued marching all night. In the morning the weather turned cold and the rain changed to sleet, increasing everyone's misery. The horses were jaded and hungry, and the troopers were freezing and numbed into semi-slumber, but somehow kept their

---

30. McDonald, *Laurel Brigade*, 210–11; *Philadelphia Weekly Times*, March 22, 1884; Armstrong, *7th Virginia Cavalry*, 63.
31. *Richmond Whig*, April 18, 1864.

place in the column. Arriving at Upperville at sunrise on December 18, the column stopped to breakfast and to feed and rest the horses. Some of the men were literally frozen in their saddles and had to be broken loose. After a mere hour's respite, Rosser resumed the march. Eventually the skies cleared, and the welcome sight of the Blue Ridge Mountains cheered the half-frozen troopers.[32]

A few hours later, Rosser's command crossed Ashby's Gap and approached the banks of the Shenandoah River. Rainwater, however, had swollen the river too much to cross. With the Federal cavalry in hot pursuit, Rosser decided he would have to cross the river or face the Union cavalry at Luray or Front Royal. He opted to cross the river, and started moving up the right bank to find a practical crossing point. Rosser's weary troopers marched between the river and the mountains on a narrow road, one made rougher by the recent weather. The brigade finally reached Front Royal. A halt was called, and the troopers went into camp for the first time in two days, after marching for 72 hours and covering more than 230 miles.[33]

Rosser and his staff spent the night of December 19 at the home of Thomas Almond Ashby in Front Royal. Ashby recalled, "I have never seen men so worn out and dilapidated in appearance. After a hearty supper they went to their rooms and slept like dead men. The next morning when Rosser and his staff appeared at the breakfast table they were much refreshed by sleep."[34]

Rosser's column resumed marching, reaching Luray a few hours before the Federal cavalry passed through Thorton Gap in their rear. The river was still raging, making a difficult crossing for Rosser's command at Conrad's Store. They reached Maj. Gen. Jubal Early's army in the valley on December 20. Rosser then learned the Federal raiding party he had been sent to fight had returned to Winchester. Rosser's brigade went into camp and rested.[35]

It was Christmas time in the valley, and the hungry troopers of Rosser's brigade enjoyed a bounty from the women at the home front, trying to forget the horrors of war for a time. Resting was good for all; the horses were shod, and their strength returned on the abundant forage of the valley. During this downtime, Tom Rosser's problem with alcohol became obvious. He was able to forgo drinking for long periods, only to succumb again to the temptation of liquor. In

---

32. McDonald, *Laurel Brigade*, 212.
33. McDonald, *Laurel Brigade*, 212–13; Rhyn, *Thesis*, 45; *Philadelphia Weekly Times*, March 22, 1984; Armstrong, *7th Virginia Cavalry*, 63.
34. Thomas Almond Ashby, *The Valley Campaigns: Being the Reminiscences of a Non-Combatant While Between the Lines in the Shenandoah Valley During the War of the States* (New York, 1914), 264.
35. McDonald, *Laurel Brigade*, 213.

February of 1863, he had joined other officers in signing a pledge to forever give up alcohol. Subsequent letters to his wife, Betty, reveal the difficulty of abstaining. In a Christmas Eve letter to Betty, Rosser reflected on their relationship and his failings as a husband. He promised to do better, stating:

> **I am just learning my duty to my dear wife, and my darling, you must not entertain any fear concerning my behavior in your absence. As God lives my dear wife I promise most solemnly that I will not drink again. The promise I gave to you last, I did not, while at Fred's, fully fulfill. God forgive me! I have repented and will never repeat... I will never drink again, I most solemnly promise![36]**

Continuing in his reflective state of mind, Rosser wrote Betty from near Mount Jackson:

> **I have sinned grievously of late and there is one thing which you must pardon. Remember my precious wife, you are to know everything I do—well, as I came through Fredericksburg, I accidentally got very drunk, this too at Mr. Alsop's. So very badly did I behave, that all the ladies knew it... I have quit. So help me God—and now when all around me are drinking their Christmas 'Nogs' I feel proud that I am no longer a slave to passion and am free![37]**

The rest time for Rosser's troopers ended too soon. In late December, Early ordered an expedition west of the mountains to secure cattle for General Lee's army, meanwhile capturing any detached Federal troops and damaging communications on the Baltimore and Ohio Railroad. Major General Fitzhugh Lee led the expedition on December 27, and upon arriving at Moorefield, West Virginia, he learned that between 800 and 900 Federals were strongly fortified behind the entrenchments in Petersburg. The rain had ruined much of his small arms ammunition and he lacked artillery, so Fitz Lee decided not to attack the position and instead make a move on the Union-held B&O Railroad. On the morning of January 2, 1864, Fitz Lee marched his command down the south branch of the railroad and began to cross Branch Mountain at Mill's Gap. Rosser's brigade, only about 400 troopers, led the advance with the 11th Virginia in front, followed by 181 troopers of the 7th Virginia. Upon nearing the top of

---

36. Ibid; Thomas L. Rosser to Betty W. Rosser, December 24, 1863, Thomas L. Rosser Papers, UVA.
37. Thomas L. Rosser to Betty W. Rosser, December 27, 1863, Thomas L. Rosser Papers, UVA.

Branch Mountain, they found fallen trees blocking the road, forcing the men to axe open a path. While engaged in chopping down trees, scouts reported a Federal wagon train moving toward New Creek, West Virginia, in the direction Rosser marched, where Branch Mountain Road forked with the Petersburg and New Creek roads.[38]

Rosser hurried his forces to near the front of the column. After rounding a curve in the road, the wagon train came into view. It moved slowly with a small force guarding it. The train consisted of about 40 wagons; a team of six mules pulled each one, which were loaded with ammunition and sutlers' stores. Rosser ordered Maj. E. H. McDonald's 11th Virginia to charge with Colonel Dulany's 7th Virginia following in support. Just as Rosser's troopers cleared the concealing woods the train quickened its pace, which resulted in many collisions as faster wagons tried to pass slower ones, and mules became entangled in the melee. The *Richmond Enquirer* reported, "Every [Union] wagoner could see Rosser, with his brigade, dashing like a thunderbolt down the mountain side after them, with a war-whoop that penetrated to their very souls as it echoed and reechoed along the valley." It appeared Rosser would make an easy capture, considering the guards escaped through the nearby woods. Then, suddenly, the train halted. About 75 infantrymen jumped from the wagons, ran up a hillside, and began firing on the Confederate horsemen. A portion of the 11th Virginia charged after the Federal infantrymen, capturing most.[39]

Meanwhile, Fitz Lee moved down Patterson's Creek, gathering cattle and sheep for the Army of Northern Virginia. At Burlington he captured additional sutlers' stores. The cavalry often served as foragers for the army. After a short stay in Burlington, Fitz Lee marched to Ridgeville, six miles from New Creek, and camped. A severe snowstorm set in that night, and the next morning Lee returned to the valley, traveling by way of Romney and Brock's Gap to Harrisonburg, taking with him 110 prisoners and 400 cattle.[40]

Rosser wrote Betty from New Creek, reporting his brigade had captured 40 wagons, 500 head of cattle, 300 horses, and about 100 prisoners. He explained he was cold and frostbitten. Rosser also complained that Fitz Lee went along on the New Creek raid, and added, "I did as usual all the work." He continued to wrestle with his drinking problem. Seemingly trying to convince himself as much as his wife, he declared, "I am a changed man... I have refused everything to

38. McDonald, Laurel Brigade, 215–16.
39. Frank Moore, ed., *The Rebellion Record: A Diary of American Events* (New York, 1865), 8 vols., 8:326–27; *Correspondent report for the Richmond Enquirer*, dated January 9, 1864; McDonald, *Laurel Brigade*, 215–16.
40. McDonald, *Laurel Brigade*, 215–16

drink. All seemed surprised to see it. Yet I feel proud of my power to resist. I have never felt a desire to break my resolve—nor have I regretted making it—so my darling you must rest assured."[41]

Soon after returning from the New Creek raid, Fitz Lee and his command rejoined the Army of Northern Virginia, while Rosser's brigade remained with General Early who commanded the Valley District. Rosser had left Stuart under difficult circumstances concerning his promotion, and what Rosser saw as Stuart's failings at Brandy Station and Gettysburg. Robert E. Lee agreed to keep Rosser in the Shenandoah Valley. As time went on, Rosser and Early grew to detest each other. Rosser and Brig. Gen. John D. Imboden, commanding another cavalry brigade under Early, often found themselves in disputes with Early. Early developed a strong dislike of the cavalry, and this prejudice hurt the performance of his army in the final year of the war.[42]

In mid-December, when Brig. Gen. William Averell pulled off a successful raid on Confederate stores at a Salem, Virginia, railroad depot, Early's Confederate cavalry pursued the Federals, only to soon be driven off, with Averell's troopers escaping to Beverly, West Virginia. When Early made his report of the unsuccessful attempt to capture Averell, he criticized Rosser's brigade, writing, "Rosser's horses were broken down and his men a good deal scattered, he having accomplished nothing toward interrupting the enemy's communications."[43]

In January 1864, Early expressed his dissatisfaction with Imboden's brigade in a letter to Robert E. Lee. Early stated that Imboden's brigade had a reputation as being "wholly-inefficient, disorganized, undisciplined, and unreliable." The general claimed the cavalry's failure greatly impeded his operations, and Imboden's brigade did not make the necessary reconnaissance to determine Federal troop locations. Early told General Lee he would hate to rely on Imboden's undisciplined command during an emergency. When Imboden, who had been absent during part of the commotion, learned of Early's derogatory remarks about his troopers, he fired off a letter directly to General Lee. He asked Lee to appoint a court of inquiry and to publish the results for all to read. Imboden's protest had to go through various channels, beginning with Jubal Early. Early disputed Imboden, but supported the idea of a board of inquiry, stating that "it may result

41. Thomas L. Rosser to Betty W. Rosser, January 8, 1864, Thomas L. Rosser Papers, UVA.
42. Gary W. Gallagher, ed., *Struggle for the Shenandoah: Essays on the 1864 Valley Campaign* (Kent, OH, 1991), 23–24.
43. *OR* 29/1:970.

in materially improving the condition of the command." Lee thought all the charges and counter-charges would do more harm than good, and refused to convene a court of inquiry.[44]

During the same period, Early complained to General Lee that Rosser had gone to Staunton to see his wife without authorization. Betty had stayed with friends in Staunton during the winter. Early was a crusty old bachelor with no interest in marital matters involving his men. He would never grant a leave of absence for one of his officers to get married. He considered a newlywed too cautious to be of use in battle, and many were killed early on. Of course, Rosser greatly resented Early's complaint to Lee, and wrote Betty: "I intend calling his attention to it tomorrow. A miserable old rascal."[45]

Rosser Describing the Partisan Rangers: *"They are a nuisance and an evil to the service."*

Tom Rosser's experience with the partisan rangers in the Shenandoah Valley led him to form a negative opinion of the numerous bands of irregulars operating throughout the mountains and valleys of Virginia. With his West Point training, he could not accept the partisans' independent operations, lax discipline, and lackadaisical attitude. Early agreed with Rosser, and after the war described Maj. John S. Mosby as a ranger "whose idea was that the highest motive that can influence a soldier is the desire for plunder, and whose post bellum history is in accordance with his war experience—still fighting for plunder." On one occasion, Rosser and partisan ranger Capt. John H. McNeill engaged in a bitter dispute about the role of the rangers. This particular argument involved McNeill's criticism of Rosser's treatment of horses and the humaneness of forcing animals over icy roads. McNeill had refused to cooperate in a January foraging expedition. Unrelenting, Rosser and McNeill each thought their own argument was correct. A low-ranking partisan criticizing a West Point officer incensed Rosser.[46]

Upon his return to the Valley, after the raid at New Creek, West Virginia, Rosser wrote to Gen. Robert E. Lee:

> They [irregulars or partisans] are a nuisance and an evil to the service. Without discipline, order, or organization, they roam broadcast over the country, a band of thieves

44. *OR* 33/1:1066–67, 1167–68.
45. Thomas L. Rosser to Betty W. Rosser, January 25, 1864, Thomas L. Rosser Papers, UVA.
46. Bushong, *Fightin' Tom Rosser,* 72.

stealing, pillaging, plundering, and doing every manner of mischief and crime. They are a terror to the citizens and an injury to the cause. They never fight; can't be made to fight. Their leaders are generally brave, but few of the men are good soldiers, and have engaged in this business for the sake of gain. The effect upon the service is bad, and I think, if possible, it should be corrected.[47]

Then, Rosser wrote specifically of Maj. John S. Mosby, stating:

Major Mosby is of inestimable service to the Yankee army in keeping their men from straggling. He is a gallant officer and is one that I have great respect for; yet the interest I feel in my own and the good of the service coerces me to bring this matter before you, in order that this partisan system, which I think is a bad one, may be corrected.[48]

Rosser's stinging letter found its way into the hands of J. E. B. Stuart who endorsed it and forwarded it to Robert E. Lee. Stuart commented, "Guerilla organizations, as a rule, are detrimental to the best interests of the army at large." Stuart defended Mosby, however, saying Mosby's rangers were "the only efficient band of rangers" he knew. General Lee agreed with Rosser's position, and forwarded the letter to the War Department, urging to abolish the law authorizing the partisan corps. Other influential Southerners agreed, and within a few weeks the Confederate Congress passed the necessary legislation abolishing the partisan ranger organizations. Ideally, the independent partisans would have merged into the regular army commands, but because the waning fate of the Confederates on the battlefield was a more urgent matter, the partisans more or less continued to operate as they had in the past. Mosby, for his part, did not learn of Rosser's letter until after the war, which he then pointedly responded: "There was scarcely a day that our command didn't kill [and] capture more Yankees than Rosser did the whole time he was in the Valley."[49]

Rosser's Raids

On January 28, 1864, Early, with Rosser's brigade, Brig. Gen. Edward L. Thomas's infantry brigade, Maj. Harry W. Gilmor's and Capt. John H. McNeill's partisan rangers, and four guns of Capt. John

47. Thomas L. Rosser to Gen. Robert E. Lee, January 11, 1864.
48. *OR* 33/1:1081–82; Thomas L. Rosser to Gen. Robert E. Lee, January 11, 1864; Douglas Southall Freeman, ed., *Lee's Dispatches: Unpublished Letters of General Robert E. Lee to Jefferson Davis and the War Department of The Confederate States of America, 1862–1865* (New York, 1957), 132–33.
49. *OR* 33/1:1082; James A. Ramage, *Gray Ghost* (Lexington, KY, 1999), 137.

McClanahan's artillery battery, began another cattle raid across Branch Mountain. The raiders first moved from New Market toward Moorefield. The next day, Rosser, along with his cavalry, artillery, and Gen. Early, reached Moorefield in advance of the infantry. Scouts reported a large Union wagon train on its way from New Creek to Petersburg, Early ordered Rosser to cross Branch Mountain and capture the wagon train. On January 30 Rosser's command, with a few pieces of McClanahan's artillery, left Moorefield, proceeding by way of the Moorefield and Allegheny Turnpike. When Rosser reached the top of the mountain, he found fallen trees blocked the road, and Federal infantry held the turnpike gap. Rosser dismounted the 12th Virginia and vigorously attacked. Rosser's troopers forced their way through the gap, and the Federals retreated toward Medley to meet the wagon train, on its way toward Petersburg.[50]

Upon discovering Rosser's approach, the Federals parked their 95 wagons at Medley, preparing to defend them. The train guard consisted of about 800 infantry and a small body of cavalry, which should have been sufficient to deal with the smaller Confederate raiding force. Rosser, despite knowing he was outnumbered with only about 400 troopers, set his mind to attack. He ordered the 12th Virginia to go around and attack the Federal rear, while the other regiments, partially dismounted, advanced on the Union front and flank. Outnumbered and fighting infantry in a defensive position, the Federals at first repulsed the Confederates, but Rosser ordered another attack, this time accompanied by artillery that had just come up. After a couple shells found their mark, Rosser renewed the attack. The dismounted troopers advanced on the Federal left, while Maj. Frank Myers's mounted troopers charged the Union front. The Federals broke and fled in disorder, leaving their wagons behind, while Rosser's command captured 42 prisoners. The retreating Federals managed to save the mule teams because the 12th Virginia was out of position and not in the Federal rear. The captured wagons, however, were loaded with supplies, such as bacon, rice, beans, sugar, and coffee. The raid cost Rosser 25 men, killed and wounded, while the Federals lost 80. After the fight, Rosser told his troopers that "this was the first time he had ever seen cav[alry] whip 3 times their own number of infantry."[51]

After a brief rest, Rosser's command, again with Thomas's infantry brigade as reinforcement, moved against Petersburg on

---

50. *OR* 33/1:43.
51. McDonald, *Laurel Brigade*, 219–20; *OR*/1:33, 45–46, 1133; Diary of James W. Wood, LVA; McDonald, *Laurel Brigade*, 218–19. A correspondent for a Richmond newspaper reported that Rosser's troopers captured 94 wagons and 450 mules (Frank Moore, *Anecdotes, poetry, and incidents of the war: North and South:1860–1865* (New York, 1866), 436.

February 1. Arriving, Rosser found the Federals had left in haste, leaving a substantial quantity of ammunition, including about 13,000 cartridges and commissary stores. Obeying Early's orders, Rosser moved down Patterson's Creek to collect cattle and do whatever damage possible to communications on the B&O Railroad. Rosser also ordered Gilmor's and McNeill's partisans into the Allegheny Mountains to gather any cattle they could find. After sending the 7th Virginia to hold the gap at Mechanicsburg against Averell's 1st New York, Rosser proceeded to Patterson's Creek. At the mouth of the creek, Rosser's troopers engaged a regiment of infantry and cavalry, under Lt. Col. James W. Snyder. After Rosser's troopers charged twice, with 44 men dismounted, the Federals fled for the mountains. Rosser's horsemen captured a company of infantry guarding the railroad, and destroyed a few bridges and a lock on the Chesapeake and Ohio Canal.[52]

With his mission accomplished, Rosser started back by the same route he had come, but found Averell's troopers in his rear after the Federals had forced their way through the gap at Mechanicsburg. Rosser successfully evaded Averell's pursuit, arriving at Moorefield with his prisoners and about 1,200 cattle, including the 300 McNeill procured from citizens on the western side of the mountains. Early led his command across the mountains to the Shenandoah Valley, arriving on February 6. He reported capturing a total of 1,200 cattle, 500 sheep, 78 prisoners, and 50 wagons with their mule teams. Rosser's performance during this raid must have impressed Early. The army badly needed the beef and lamb to feed the hungry soldiers. The Confederate high command did not let General Rosser's performance during the expedition go unnoticed. J. E. B. Stuart endorsed Rosser's report, commenting, "The bold and successful enterprise herein reported furnishes additional proofs of General Rosser's merit as a commander, and adds fresh laurels to that veteran brigade so signalized for valor already." General Robert E. Lee included his own endorsement of Stuart's opinion, adding, "General Rosser acquitted himself with great credit in this expedition."[53]

On February 12 Early wrote Robert E. Lee, pushing for confirmation of Rosser's promotion to brigadier general. Despite spending four months in command of a brigade, the Confederate confirmation process dragged on slowly. Praising Rosser, Early stated, "I should consider it a great loss to the service if he should fail of having his appointment confirmed." General Lee responded to Early's

---

52. McDonald, *Laurel Brigade*, 220–21; *OR* 33/1:33–36, 1166; SHSP, vol. IX, No. 6, 268–71.
53. Ibid., *OR* 33/1:46; Richard H. Dulany to Carlyle Whiting, March 28, 1864, Dulany Papers, VHS.

initiative by expressing his desire to relieve Rosser's brigade of operational duties, "that his whole attention may be devoted to recuperating his command, which will be wanted for hard service in the spring." Lee also wrote Secretary of War James Seddon about Rosser's promotion confirmation. Lee's intercession succeeded, and Rosser's promotion to brigadier general was confirmed on February 17, 1864.[54]

When Rosser's brigade returned to the Valley they went into camp at Weyer's Cave, which Valley native artilleryman George Neese described as "the most beautiful hole in the ground I ever was in, and the environments on the outside are strikingly picturesque." Rosser issued a general order naming his brigade the "Laurel Brigade," and directed each trooper wear a laurel leaf on his hat. Apparently, the troopers did not adopt the name until May, during the battle of the Wilderness.[55]

Learning that a large force of Brig. Gen. George Custer's cavalry and artillery threatened Charlottesville, Rosser ordered his brigade to mount up. His command left camp at Weyer's Cave on February 29. Many troopers left their overcoats behind, as the weather was fine, not knowing a taxing march lie ahead. While marching to pursue Brig. Gen. Judson Kilpatrick near Richmond, drizzle turned into a northeaster, bringing sleet before midnight, engulfing the troopers in sheets of ice. The ghostlike riders marched all night before arriving about sunrise at Charlottesville, where the troopers took a short rest. The cold, wet, and hungry troopers took refuge in woods near the University of Virginia, constructing shelters made from rails and oilcloths and eating as best they could. Rosser and his staff made themselves comfortable in a university hotel.[56]

The Federal force threatening Charlottesville had retreated the evening before Rosser's arrival. Rosser was ordered to march immediately to Hanover County to intercept Kilpatrick on his Richmond raid. Rosser's brigade participated in the pursuit of the fleeing Federal cavalry raiders after the Kilpatrick-Dahlgren Raid, February 28 to March 1, on Richmond. Because of the need to press

54. *OR* 33/1:1167, 1174; Rhyn, *Thesis*, 49.
55. George M. Neese, *Three Years in the Confederate Horse Artillery* (New York, 1911), 52; Frank M. Myers, *The Comanches: A History of White's Battalion, Virginia Cavalry* (Marietta, Georgia, 1956), 340; McDonald, *Laurel Brigade*, 230 note; Andrew C. Gatewood to his mother, April 9, 1864, Andrew C. L. Gatewood Papers, Virginia Military Institute Archives, Lexington, Virginia; Corporal Isaac Ira White to his sister, Ursula J. White, April 9, 1864, Special Collections, University of Notre Dame.
56. Armstrong, *7th Virginia Cavalry*, 66; *OR* 33/1:1159. On February 9, 1864, George Armstrong Custer married Elizabeth Bacon in Monroe, Michigan.

ahead to catch up to the Federals withdrawing from Richmond, Rosser's troopers again went on an all-night forced march before reaching a spot six miles west of Richmond. Union Col. Ulric Dahlgren's raiders had come within two and a half miles of Richmond, but his troopers were driven off, and he was killed. Papers found on his body included a plan to kill President Jefferson Davis and his cabinet. Considerable controversy ensued for several weeks because of the papers.[57]

For the next two weeks Rosser's brigade unsuccessfully scoured the countryside in search of the retreating Federal cavalry. They then rested for two days at Gordonsville. On March 16 the Laurel Brigade began a return trip to the Shenandoah Valley, taking short marches to Lexington, where they arrived on March 31. General Lee felt they needed to rest and recuperate after arduous campaigning. During this period, badly needed conscripts were added to the brigade, along with returning sick and wounded soldiers and fresh horses. The brigade's strength rose from 1,200 to 2,300 men.[58]

Rosser's brigade spent the rest of the winter at Buffalo Forge, near Lexington in Rockbridge County, Virginia, where they enjoyed the hospitality of the local families. Rosser's troopers brought these families stories of camp life, anecdotes of their friends, and news of the war. The troopers were treated to food, tea, good company, and gaiety as the spellbound children listened to their tales. But spring came too soon, and Winchester resident Cornelia McDonald recorded in her diary:

> **Rosser departed, taking with him most of our brightness and pleasure. He could not tarry there though the soldiers and young ladies of the town were happy together, dancing and merrymaking; for the grass in the valley had grown and he must hasten to open the spring campaign, to gallop after the insolent enemy who now ventured further into that valley than they had ever before dared. They could march at any season for they had food for their horses; ours had only the grass, and they had to wait for it to grow.[59]**

---

57. Ibid., 66; Wilmer L. Jones, *Generals in Blue and Gray: Lincoln's Generals*, 2 vols., 1:306.
58. Ibid.
59. Cornelia Peake McDonald, Mimrose C. Gwin, eds., *A Woman's Civil War: A Diary with Reminiscences of the War, from March 1862* (Madison, Wisconsin, 1992), 184.

During 1863 and early 1864, Tom Rosser had gained valuable experience, knowledge and skill that he would need in the remaining campaigns of the war. Recalled to the east, an enemy of superior numbers would severely test him in battle as he faced a foe with fresher mounts, better equipment, and finer arms.

CHAPTER 6

The 1864 Campaigns: Spring through Summer; Wilderness campaign; Stuart killed; Spotsylvania; Rosser wounded at Trevilian Station; Second Reams's Station.

"Give the general [Wade Hampton] my compliments
and tell him we are giving 'em hell."

**Brigadier General Thomas Rosser at Trevilian Station,
June 11, 1864.**

1864 presented new opportunities for Tom Rosser. He and his Laurel Brigade returned east to help Gen. Robert E. Lee's army face new Federal commander Lt. Gen. Ulysses S. Grant's opening campaign. Rosser would continue criticizing Maj. Gen. J. E. B. Stuart, resulting in a strained relationship between the two. Still, Stuart supported Rosser, putting the good of the service ahead of any personal bickering. Rosser, illogical at times, maintained his belief that Stuart was hindering his promotion to major general. The battles of the Wilderness, Trevilian Station, and Second Reams's Station, along with a cavalry reorganization, loomed large in the events during this period. After Gen. Wade Hampton took command of the cavalry corps in August, Rosser remained disappointed concerning his promotion to major general.

With the 1864 spring campaign approaching, President Abraham Lincoln decided to transfer Ulysses S. Grant from the Western Theater to take command of the entire Union Army. Grant was promoted to the rank of lieutenant general, the first United States military man since George Washington to hold that rank. Grant's strategic plan involved attacking the Army of Northern Virginia and Brig. Gen. Joseph E. Johnston's Army of Tennessee, as well as not capturing and occupying cities, a rejection of the prevailing military thinking. Unsatisfied with the Federal cavalry's performance in the East, Grant transferred Maj. Gen. Philip H. Sheridan from Tennessee to take command of the Army of the Potomac's cavalry corps. Grant attached himself to the Army of the Potomac, leaving Maj. Gen. William T.

Sherman with the task of defeating Johnston. Grant reduced the Army of the Potomac from five to three corps—the II, V, and VI—commanded by major generals Winfield S. Hancock, Gouverneur K. Warren, and John Sedgwick, respectively. The IX Corps, with Maj. Gen. Ambrose E. Burnside commanding, was not incorporated into the Army of the Potomac until May 24, 1864, although it served with the unit in the Wilderness and Spotsylvania campaigns. Grant's army in Virginia consisted of about 116,000 men, including the IX Corps.[1]

Meanwhile, General Lee did not reorganize his army in preparation for the spring campaign. The Army of Northern Virginia still consisted of three corps commanded by lieutenant generals James Longstreet, Richard Ewell, and Ambrose P. Hill. The war of attrition took its toll on Confederate manpower, with the number of available recruits declining. Lee's army could only muster about 64,000 soldiers in its ranks.[2]

Stuart's and Rosser's Friendship Ends, as far as Rosser is Concerned.

Stuart's and Rosser's relationship increasingly strained as Rosser became more disillusioned with Stuart. Rosser's disenchantment had begun after the June 1863 battle of Brandy Station when Rosser believed Stuart was unprepared to fight during the surprise Union cavalry attack. His lack of enthusiasm continued after Stuart failed to be where Rosser thought his superior should have been during the Gettysburg campaign. After the war, Rosser blamed Stuart, not Lee or Longstreet, for the Confederate defeat at Gettysburg, stating that Stuart did "on this campaign, undoubtedly, make the fatal blunder which lost us the battle of Gettysburg." Rosser later described Stuart as "a devout Christian, yet an inordinate vanity with all its giddiness and frivolity possessed his very soul and detracted greatly from his otherwise strong character." Obviously paranoid, he unfoundedly thought Stuart had deceived him about his promotion to major general. Just three months before Stuart's mortal wounding in battle, the men's relationship further worsened when Stuart berated Rosser for refusing to accept a new quartermaster. Rosser had his own candidate in mind, but ran afoul of Stuart and Lee regarding the matter. Stuart rebuked Rosser, stating, "Gen Lee says positively he will not consent to an officer from another command receiving this appointment unless it is beyond question that there is no AQM

1. *OR* 36/1:198, 915.
2. Freeman, *Lee's Lieutenants*, 3:345.

[Assistant Quartermaster] in the brigade suitable for promotion." In another incident, Stuart chastised Rosser for failing to obey orders, reminding the brigade commander that "if subordinates undertake to hold all orders in abeyance which make them unpleasantly or do not meet their approval, then good bye to discipline and an effective army." Stuart was fed up with Rosser's constant whining about promotion, among other issues.[3]

Stuart sent Rosser another critical letter reprimanding his subordinate for failing to send a scout he had specifically requested. In the ensuing correspondence, each strong-willed man responded to the other with unrestrained frankness. In part, Stuart wrote:

> **The cases are extremely rare wherein a junior can take the responsibility of disobeying the orders of his superior in command, and it is a practice which will lead endless abuse and difficulty. . . . A very essential portion of the first order was disobeyed without any explanation. In the second order when three persons were specifically called for by name, only two were sent, the third being retained for the reason that he was a valuable non-commissioned officer and could not be spared from his company, which reason is insufficient for he was known to be a non-commissioned officer and was selected with the expressed view of his great value for more important duty. In reply to the inquiry why the order was had not been obeyed, you write that you relied upon the friendly relationship which had existed between you and myself and between you and Maj. [H. B.] McClellan to prevent any animadversion of mine on your failure to comply with the order. I beg leave to inform you that however great my personal regard for you, and however high my estimate of your value as an officer and intimate the relation referred to, neither can be relied upon to the extent of justifying you in disobeying orders of the plainest and most unmistakable import issued from these Hd. Qrs. You will therefore send Sergt. J. W. McCleary without delay to these Hdqrs. I took occasion during the winter to address you in a letter unofficially on the subject, not wishing to make it the subject of an official letter.[4]**

3. Jeffrey D. Wert, *Cavalryman of The Lost Cause: A Biography of J. E. B. Stuart* (New York, 2008), 300; J. E. B. Stuart to Thomas L. Rosser, February 10, 1864, Thomas L. Rosser Papers, UVA; "The Cavalry, A.N.V.," *Address by General T. L. Rosser at the Seventh Annual Reunion of the Association of the Maryland Line, Academy of Music, Baltimore, Maryland, February 22, 1889* (Baltimore, 1889), 38.
4. Ibid.

Continuing Rosser's scolding, Stuart stated:

> **I will not trouble you with enumerating the positive detriments to the public service which have resulted from your failure to comply with the whole of the original letter of March 29, but I trust that your course in regard to such matters in the future will abundantly show a spirit of prompt subordination to authority, and your example will infuse a like spirit throughout your command, and that you will bear in mind that the essential step towards maintaining discipline and subordination in those commanded by you is to exhibit for their example those qualities in your conduct towards those who command you, remembering that every order is to be obeyed in good faith. If there is any objection to be made, let them be made in respectful terms, without delaying the action of the order.[5]**

Rosser, equally headstrong as Stuart, was stubborn and proud to the point of intransigence, and not willing to take such a reprimand without protest. He penned a stinging response to Stuart:

> **I will send Sgt. McCleary to you as ordered, but I do it under protest. I am not reconciled to the justice of such a detail by your letter upon the subject. Whilst I will never again hesitate to obey any order you may give, I will never be convinced that it is right and proper for a Commanding officer to make a detail as you have made choosing the individual yourself mentioning him by name—Thus assuming a prerogative which alone is mine if not by regulation, it certainly is made so by custom and courtesy requires that certain forms be observed. . . . I certainly would treat my Cols. with more respect in a case of this kind than you have extended to me. If I have presumed upon our "friendly relations," I regret it exceedingly and will endeavor not to commit so gross a mistake again.[6]**

Rosser wrote a complaining letter to the Confederate Secretary of War. The letter first had to pass through Stuart who attempted to soothe the wounded feelings of his friend, advising, "I have your complaining letter to Genl. Cooper still on my table hesitating as your friend to forward it knowing that it will do you harm and affect no

---

5. J. E. B. Stuart Miscellaneous Papers, 1833–1864, 55–58, VHS; Mitchell, ed., *The Letters of James E. B. Stuart*, 384–87.
6. Thomas L. Rosser to J. E. B. Stuart, April 27, 1864, Henry B. McClellan Papers, VHS.
7. Rosser Service Record, Generals and Staff Officers, NA.

good. I will keep it 'till I hear from you again." Unlike Rosser, Stuart had the capacity to separate friendship from command. Rosser held grudges, remaining inflexible.[7]

Things seemed to settle down between the two strong-minded generals as no other correspondence followed on the matter. Both men, trained at West Point, resumed the proper code of conduct even though Rosser shared his feelings with his wife, Betty, but apparently to no one else.

In March 1864, William Henry Fitzhugh "Rooney" Lee was exchanged as a prisoner of war. He had recovered sufficiently enough from his June 1863 wounding at Brandy Station to return to active service. Stuart assigned Rooney Lee to lead a new division of cavalry. Brigadier General John R. Chambliss's brigade, from Maj. Gen. Fitzhugh Lee's command, and Brig. Gen. James B. Gordon's North Carolina Cavalry Brigade, from Hampton's division, combined to form the division. Thus, the three cavalry divisions consisted of two brigades each, except for Hampton's division, which included Brig. Gen. Pierce Young's, Thomas Rosser's, and Maj. Gen. Matthew Calbraith Butler's brigades. Rooney Lee was promoted to major general on April 23. Robert E. Lee waited until August 11 to appoint Wade Hampton as cavalry corps commander. Waiting until August to assign an overall cavalry commander was detrimental to army organization.[8]

In April, Stuart denied Rosser's request to visit his wife in Richmond. Rosser complained bitterly to a friend on April 5, stating, "Stuart would not let me go to Richmond, he is now an open enemy of mine." Regardless of Rosser's attitude toward Stuart, the cavalry chief continued to support Rosser for promotion. On May 2 Stuart wrote the secretary of war: "You are aware that troops prefer serving with troops from their own State... General Rosser, being senior to Generals [James B.] Gordon and [John R.] Chambliss, and a highly efficient officer of distinguished service, should be the Senior Brigadier in some Division."[9]

Stuart and Rosser did not reconcile their rift before Stuart's death on May 12, 1864. Writing harshly about Stuart long after the war, Rosser penned, "He [Stuart] did nothing with thoughtful deliberation. He was dashing, daring, enterprising, self-possessed in danger, volatile, and nonchalant in personality, and on the whole a very attractive man, and within limits a good officer, but as a cavalry general, was below the class of N. B. Forrest and Wade Hampton."[10]

8. Bushong, *Fightin' Tom Rosser*, 92.
9. J. E. B. Stuart to James A. Seddon, May 2, 1864, VHS.
10. Thomas L. Rosser to an unidentified friend, Thomas L. Rosser Papers, April 4, 1864, UVA; Rosser, "Reminiscences," 131, UVA.

Wilderness Campaign: Cavalry Fight at Craig's Meeting House

In late March 1864 Grant established his headquarters at Culpeper Court House, while Robert E. Lee set up his at Orange Court House. Lee positioned his army in a defensive arrangement south of the Rapidan River behind well-fortified entrenchments. Grant reasoned he could not make a frontal assault, so he decided to turn one of Lee's flanks. In this way, Grant hoped to force Lee out of his entrenchments to fight or inevitably face a Union attack from his rear. Grant decided to turn Lee's right flank. He hoped to quickly cross the Rapidan to the south side, fleeing the Wilderness undiscovered. If successful, Grant's superior numbers would be more advantageous.[11]

The Wilderness, 50 miles north of Richmond, was a wooded rectangular tract of land, approximately 14 miles long by 10 miles wide, south of the Rapidan River. Most of the original timber had been felled, and the vegetation consisted of second-growth cedar, pine and black oak trees, while the undergrowth made it almost impenetrable. Troop movements and dispositions in the Wilderness were extremely difficult.[12]

Traveling light, the Army of the Potomac left their Culpeper Court House camp at midnight on May 3, crossed the Rapidan River at Ely's and Germanna fords, and approached Chancellorsville. Shortly after noon on May 4, the Federals encountered Lee's army while it moved from Orange Court House toward New Verdiesville on the Plank Road. Lee had anticipated Grant's move, and did not fall for the feints against his left flank. The Confederate commander had set his army in motion to attack Grant's flank before the Federal army managed to escape the Wilderness. By the evening of May 4, Lt. Gen. Richard Ewell's corps had reached Locust Grove on the Orange-Fredericksburg Turnpike, only about five miles from Maj. Gen. G. K. Warren's corps, which had camped at Old Wilderness Tavern. Farther south on the Plank Road, the leading division of Lt. Gen. A. P. Hill's corps stopped only seven miles from Federal cavalry units stationed at Parker's Store.[13]

Rosser's brigade left camp at Wolftown in Madison County on May 4, and joined the Army of Northern Virginia. They passed the Confederate infantry breastworks at Mine Run—a small, winding stream that fed into the Rapidan River five miles south of Raccoon

11. Bushong, *Fightin' Tom Rosser,* 82–83.
12. Ibid., 83.
13. Ibid.

Ford in northern Orange County—and camped on Lee's right. The night had been hot and oppressively humid, and the troopers who mounted their horses the next morning were already tired from a restless night. Rosser's command then moved down Catharpin Road toward Todd's Tavern, where he expected to join Fitz Lee.[14]

Meanwhile, Brig. Gen. James H. Wilson's Union cavalry division, including artillery, reached the Catharpin Road, turned west, and at 7:30 a.m. arrived at a wooden structure called "Craig's Meeting House," five miles west of Shady Grove Church and just north of the Po River. Wilson and Rosser had been West Point classmates, and this was Wilson's first fight in command. Wilson sent a battalion of the 1st Vermont of Maj. Gen. George H. Chapman's brigade to scout ahead.[15]

On May 5 Ewell's corps made first contact with the Federals when it encountered Warren's V Corps in its front while moving along the Germanna Plank Road. Grant ordered Sheridan to march Brig. Gen. David M. Gregg's and Gen. Alfred T. A. Torbert's divisions of cavalry toward Hamilton's Crossing and engage Stuart. Grant sent Wilson's cavalry division to Craig's Meeting House, four miles southwest of Parker's Store, ordering him to reconnoiter the Orange Turnpike and the Plank Road, as well as other roads converging on the Federal army's line of march. Major General George Meade ordered Maj. Gen. Winfield S. Hancock's corps to march via Todd's Tavern to Shady Grove Church, Maj. Gen. Gouverneur K. Warren's corps to march to Parker's Store, and Maj. Gen. John Sedgwick's corps to march to Old Wilderness Tavern. Meade told Sedgwick to leave a division of infantry to protect Germanna Ford until Maj. Gen. Ambrose E. Burnside arrived with the IX Corps. The Federal troops moved out, extending in long columns along the narrow roads. Lee planned to attack Grant's forces while they were strung out on the roads in the Wilderness, but did not want a full engagement until Longstreet's corps arrived on scene.[16]

On the way to Todd's Tavern to meet Fitz Lee, nearly 1,000 of Rosser's horsemen encountered Chapman's 1st Vermont, but quickly forced them back. Chapman dismounted his brigade near Craig's Meeting House, and after a brisk fight and several charges, managed to force Rosser back about two miles west on the Catharpin Road. Chapman's ammunition began to run low, and he was perhaps overextended. Reforming, Chapman dismounted the 3rd Indiana along a ravine that crossed the road, and positioned the rest of his brigade

---

14. *Philadelphia Weekly Times*, April 19, 1884; Armstrong, *11th Virginia Cavalry*, 67.
15. Gary W. Gallagher, ed., *The Wilderness Campaign* (Chapel Hill, 1997), 119.
16. Bushong, *Fightin' Tom Rosser*, 83, 85.

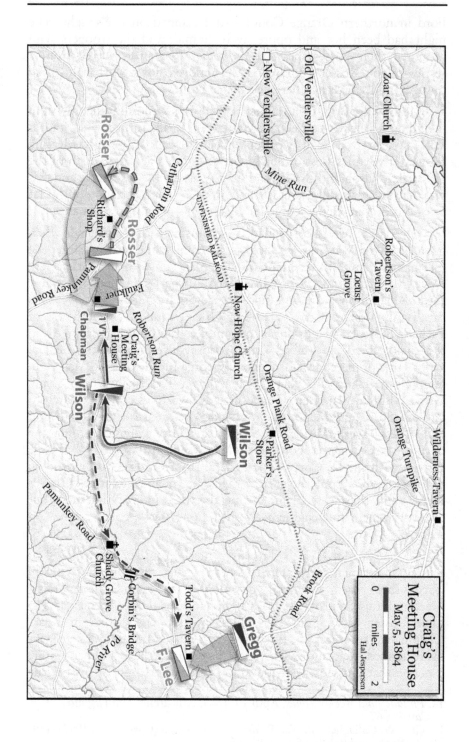

Zoar Church

New Verdiersville

Old Verdiersville

Mine Run

Robertson's Tavern

Locust Grove

Rosser

Catharpin Road

UNFINISHED RAILROAD

Richard's Shop

Rosser

Pamunkey Road

Faulkner

Chapman

Wilson

1 VT

Craig's Meeting House

Robertson Run

New Hope Church

Parker's Store

Orange Plank Road

Orange Turnpike

Wilderness Tavern

Wilson

Pamunkey Road

Shady Grove Church

Corbin's Bridge

Po River

Todd's Tavern

Brock Road

Gregg

F. Lee

Craig's Meeting House
May 5, 1864

0   miles   2

Hal Jespersen

about a half-mile back. Wilson ordered Col. Timothy H. Bryan's brigade to move to Craig's Meeting House, and positioned two artillery batteries nearby.[17]

About 1:00 p.m., however, Wilson discovered Rosser advancing along both flanks of the 3rd Indiana, and ordered them back. Defending the road became untenable as Rosser sent his brigade charging ahead. Chapman beat a hasty retreat with Rosser in pursuit. On both sides of the heavily wooded, narrow road, fighting broke out among dismounted soldiers. A company of the 12th Virginia charged with sabers drawn. The fighting increased in intensity as the Federals added artillery fire with good effect. At an opportune time, Maj. Roger P. Chew's Confederate horse artillery arrived. Chew positioned part of Maj. James W. Thomson's battery, and commenced firing on Wilson's command. Some Federals soon began to yield, but a Union battery on a hill worried Rosser, so he ordered a charge in columns of four. The 12th Virginia, commanded by Col. Thomas Massie, led the advance, followed by the 7th and the 11th Virginia, with Col. "Lige" White's 35th Battalion bringing up the rear.[18]

The 12th Virginia rode over a barricade of abatis, charging the Federals. A vicious hand-to-hand fight with sabers and pistols ensued. The Confederates drove their enemy across the Po River. Union forces resisted from several successive positions, but were unable to check Rosser's horsemen who had been joined by the remainder of Thomson's battery. During the subsequent pursuit of the Union horsemen, Maj. Edward H. McDonald, 11th Virginia, became so enthused he grasped General Rosser around the waist, exclaiming: "General, isn't this glorious!" Rosser and McDonald continued the chase pell-mell to the great amusement of those watching. The Federals retired in good order, thus saving their artillery. They finally checked the charging Confederate troopers when they reached a more open position where they could better use their artillery and have reinforcements. Rosser then realized he was fighting an entire division of cavalry that had artillery support. Undaunted, he ordered the 7th and 11th Virginia to charge in support of the 12th, which had done most of the fighting. Overwhelmed and nearly surrounded, the Federals retreated. Wilson's troopers marched three miles east along a wooded path, and then turned south and entered the Catharpin Road before heading east. Wilson's troopers, barely ahead of Rosser, escaped across Corbin's Bridge, and made for Todd's Tavern, expecting help

17. Gary W. Gallaher, ed., *Wilderness Campaign* (Chapel Hill, 1997), 119–121.
18. McDonald, *Laurel Brigade*, 225–26; *OR* 36/1:903; Gary W. Gallagher, *The Wilderness Campaign* (Chapel Hill, 2006), 119–122.

there from Gregg's cavalry. Rosser pursued them for several miles, losing many prisoners and 146 soldiers, killed or wounded.[19]

Lieutenant Charles H. Vandiver, leading Company F of the 7th Virginia, recalled:

> **I soon observed that the Federal line began to waver and that it was a good opportunity for Company F to win glory. Riding to the front, I said to my men: "Now, Company F, let's make a wedge for them, and drew my saber to lead. Just then a ball struck my horse, a magnificent bay, in the jugular vein of his neck. The blood gushed out in a stream, he fell, and I escaped to terra firma. My noble steed rose to his haunches, lunged, floundered around and straightened out to die. Sergeant Kain quickly brought me his horse and I was quickly remounted."[20]**

In a diary, Pvt. James W. Wood of the 7th Virginia wrote, "Our loss was greater than it had been in any previous engagement this brigade had ever been in and many old members say it was the hardest fight they have ever been in."[21]

Rosser's ordnance train had not been able to keep up with his command's movements, so the men had gone into the fight with little ammunition. Union prisoners had their ammunition seized, but even that amounted to an insufficient supply until the ordnance train could catch up. Some of the men became discouraged by the lack of ammunition. When a Federal cavalry regiment approached, White's battalion positioned on one side of the road, Capt. Franklin M. Myers, commanding Company A, turned to his commander, asking, "Colonel, how can we fight these fellows with no ammunition? We'd as well have rocks as empty pistols." White replied, "What are our sabers for?" Without hesitation, White's men drew their sabers and charged the Federal column, which wheeled about and quickly retreated. Rosser had nicknamed White's battalion "The Comanches," on account of the wild and reckless dash with which they usually charged their opponents.[22]

19. George Baylor, *From Bull Run to Bull Run: or Four Years in the Army of Northern Virginia* (Richmond, 1900), 203; McDonald, *Laurel Brigade*, 226–27; S. Roger Keller, *Riding with Rosser* (Shippensburg, PA, 1997), 20–21; Gallagher, *The Wilderness Campaign*, 119–122.
20. *Confederate Veteran*, February, 1896, 56; *Confederate Veteran*, February 1896, 56.
21. Diary of James W. Wood, Accession 25506, Library of Virginia, Richmond, Virginia.
22. McDonald, *Laurel Brigade*, 228; Myers, *The Comanches*, 197; Keller, *Riding with Rosser*, 20; Wilson, James Harrison, *Under The Old Flag* (New York, 1912), 2 vols., 1:382–83; Dennis E. Frye, *12th Virginia Cavalry*

Rosser pursued the Federals to the vicinity of Todd's Tavern, then began to retrace his steps. Meanwhile, Gregg's division reinforced Wilson and took the offensive in harassing Rosser's rear. Facing two divisions of cavalry, Rosser withdrew and crossed the Po River, where he then headed toward Verdiersville. The Federals inflicted heavy casualties on Rosser's retreating troopers: 114 killed, wounded, or missing. The Federals lost 94 killed, 389 wounded, and 187 missing. Rosser's proud Laurel Brigade had fought two Federal cavalry divisions, including a fight with Brig. Gen. George A. Custer near the Brock Road, and had driven Wilson across the Po River before Gregg came to his aid. It was perhaps Rosser's finest hour as a cavalry commander.[23]

On May 6 J. E. B. Stuart rode into Rosser's camp, ordering him to join Gen. Robert E. Lee's infantry line, already engaged in battle. Rosser's command, with White's battery leading, crossed the Po River, passed the Chancellor plantation, and entered open pine country bordering the Wilderness. Rosser ordered Myers to attack any unit he came in contact with, pushing them back as far as he could. The Comanches soon encountered Custer's pickets, driving them back upon their reserves. White pursued the retreating Federals with Rosser's entire brigade galloping behind the colonel. In the excitement of the pursuit, White's troopers found themselves far in advance of any support—and suddenly in the presence of Federal infantry and dismounted cavalry in a pine forest. White, whose horse was shot out from under him, hastily retreated, whereupon Rosser sent the 12th Virginia to aid the retreating Comanches. The 12th Virginia's commander, Major McDonald, led a charge that turned back the leading Union column through the pines until they came upon Grant's entrenched infantry. Although supported by the 11th and 7th Virginia, Rosser's troopers were unable to withstand the withering fire of Grant's infantry, so they hurriedly retreated. All of Rosser's troopers had "seen the elephant" that day, an expression commonly used to describe the experience of combat.[24]

Rosser, not giving up the offensive, ordered Maj. James W. Thomson to send Lt. John W. Carter's artillery piece forward to fire upon the Federals. The moment Carter opened fire five or six Federal guns deluged him with return fire. The Union artillery fire took its toll among Rosser's cavalry, which had been attempting to reform,

(Lynchburg, VA, 1988), 64; Longacre, *Lee's Cavalrymen*, 279; *Richmond Daily Dispatch*, May 7, 1864; Hubart, Nanzig, ed., *The Civil War Memoirs of a Virginia Cavalryman*, 88.

23. McDonald, *Laurel Brigade*, 234–35; Keller, *Riding with Rosser*, 22; Myers, *The Comanches*, 198.
24. McDonald, *Laurel Brigade*, 235–36; Keller, *Riding with Rosser*, 21.

killing and wounding a great many. Confusion followed, making it impossible to reform his troopers, but Stuart stayed there, calling upon them to be steady. Despite the terrible ordeal for Rosser's cavalry, most of the troopers remained firm. Rosser watched the action from near Carter's gun, expecting at any moment to see a Federal regiment riding over the hill opposite him, but none came. Stuart decided to retreat, allowing the guns of Thomson's artillery to take over the fight. Rosser recalled, "The remainder of the day was spent in wasting ammunition, firing into the woods at an unseen foe."[25]

After the battle with Custer on May 6, Rosser left a note at a nearby farmhouse; it was addressed to "Fannie Custer," one of Custer's nicknames at West Point. It read: "Dear Fannie: Come over to see me and bring your people. Rosser." In a note, Custer replied, "You return my call made this morning. Fannie." Rosser then retired to Shady Grove Church, bivouacking for the night.[26]

When Grant failed to defeat Lee in the battle of the Wilderness, he planned to circumvent Lee's right flank by marching to Spotsylvania Court House. If successful, the maneuver would place Grant between Lee and Richmond. Stuart reported to Lee that the Federals were at Todd's Tavern. Realizing the seriousness of the situation, early on the morning of May 8, Lee ordered Maj. Gen. Richard H. Anderson, who had replaced the wounded Longstreet, to race to Spotsylvania ahead of the Federals. Fitz Lee's division of Confederate cavalry occupied the road between Todd's Tavern and Spotsylvania, while the Federal cavalry, under Maj. Gen. Wesley Merritt, occupied the Brock Road. With an early start, Anderson beat the Federals to Spotsylvania, setting the stage for a major battle. Grant's attempt to flank Lee had failed.[27]

On May 8 Rosser's Laurel Brigade joined with Gen. Wade Hampton at Shady Grove, which would remain so until another cavalry reorganization took place in September. Robert E. Lee would promote Hampton to cavalry corps commander in August, and Maj. Gen. Matthew C. Butler of South Carolina would take over Hampton's division.[28]

Also on May 8, Federal infantry emerged directly in front of Hampton's division, consisting of Young's and Rosser's brigades. Confederate artillery soon checked the Union advance. Robert E. Lee ordered Hampton to vigorously attack the Federals in support of Maj. Gen. Jubal Early, whose division was to attack the Union left at Todd's Tavern. Hampton sent Rosser to strike the Federal right and rear,

25. *Confederate Veteran*, February, 1896, 56; Keller, *Riding with Rosser*, 21.
26. *OR* 36/1:878.
27. McDonald, *Laurel Brigade*, 237–38.
28. Ibid.

while he and Young's brigade pressed their front. Both attacks were well executed and achieved the desired results, driving the Federals into retreat and forcing them to abandon their camp and rations.[29]

During a fierce fight on May 9 Federal infantry drove in Hampton's pickets, gaining possession of the main road leading from Shady Grove Church to Spotsylvania Court House. The Union forces also captured the bridge over the Po River. The next day Early's infantry division dislodged the Federals, with Hampton's division taking part.[30]

Rosser's first engagement in command under Hampton had been of mostly dismounted troops armed with carbines instead of sabers and pistols. Hampton favored this method of fighting, and the cavalry soon adopted his ways. The cavalrymen initially disdained this method of warfare, but began to appreciate its value as they increasingly faced Federal infantry in prolonged fighting.[31]

While the Confederates assimilated new tactics, Maj. Gen. Philip Sheridan had begun a cavalry move that would have far-reaching consequences. Grant ordered Sheridan, with his 10,000 troopers, to threaten Richmond, thus removing the danger Stuart's horsemen posed in moving on Spotsylvania. On May 9 Sheridan started a 16-day raid on Richmond, marching around Fitz Lee's right. On a clear and balmy May 11, Custer's Michigan brigade, many dismounted, charged Stuart at Yellow Tavern, near the intersection of the Brook Turnpike and Telegraph Road, just six miles outside Richmond. Stuart was far outmanned; Sheridan's main force, consisting of Wilson's division and Custer's brigade, pressed Stuart in his front, and another brigade dashed at his left. Before Stuart could reach the embattled flank, Custer had broken through, and most of Stuart's line had collapsed. Stuart desperately tried to rally his men. Along with a few troopers who had stayed put, he fired into the charging Union troopers' flank and rear as they passed. The 1st Virginia valiantly tried to drive Sheridan's horsemen back, but a Federal trooper, remaining dismounted, "turned as he passed the General [Stuart] and discharging his pistol, inflicted the fatal wound." J. E. B. Stuart died the next day. The 5th Virginia's commander, Col. Henry Pate, who had displayed exemplary fighting on the field that day, was killed shortly before Stuart received his mortal wound. The next day another great loss to the Confederate cavalry occurred; one of Stuart's protégés, dependable

29. McDonald, *Laurel Brigade*, 240; McClellan, *The Campaigns of Stuart's Cavalry*, 412–14.
30. Gordon C. Rhea, *To The North Anna River, Grant and Lee, May 13–24, 1864* (Baton Rouge, 2000), 88.
31. McDonald, *Laurel Brigade*, 238–39.

Brig. Gen. James B. Gordon, commander of the North Carolina Cavalry Brigade, was mortally wounded at nearby Brook Church.[32]

With J. E. B. Stuart's death came a reorganization of the Army of Northern Virginia's cavalry. Hampton was the senior ranking division commander; he had proved his value on the battlefield in numerous engagements and was the natural choice to take Stuart's place, but Gen. Robert E. Lee hesitated in naming Hampton as chief of cavalry. Hampton and Fitz Lee were rivals, harboring hard feelings toward one another since Gettysburg. Instead of promoting Hampton to head of the cavalry corps, on May 14 Robert E. Lee announced that "until further orders, the three Divisions of cavalry serving with this Army will constitute separate commands and will report directly to and receive orders from these headquarters."[33]

On May 12 the bloody battle of Spotsylvania Court House began. Hampton's division positioned itself on Robert E. Lee's left, with his sharpshooters in trenches and his artillery posted to impede the Federals' right flank. On the 14th, Robert E. Lee ordered a reconnaissance north of Grant's repositioning lines to determine the Federal commander's intentions. At 5:00 p.m. Rosser's troopers splashed across the Po River, heading for Susan Alsop's farm at the junction of the Brock and Gordon roads. Rosser's horsemen turned east on the Gordon Road toward Archibald Armstrong's farm, Grant's former headquarters. About two miles east of Alsop's farm, Rosser's riders approached "Laurel Hill," the estate and home of 64-year-old Elizabeth Couse, a Union sympathizer from New Jersey.[34]

Major General G. K. Warren had converted Mrs. Couse's yard into a field hospital for the Federal's V Corps, with more than 600 wounded soldiers spread across the grounds. Mrs. Couse and her daughters were carrying meals to the wounded when Rosser's troopers rode up, causing Mrs. Couse's daughter Katherine to later recall, "[It] was a very unwelcome sight to me." Katherine wrote in a letter to a friend that Rosser's men had stolen "everything they could lay hands on." They also took 80 wounded Confederate prisoners who could still walk. When Maj. Gen. Winfield Hancock got word of the raid, he sent the 12th New Jersey to the Couse estate, but Rosser had escaped in the direction of Fredericksburg by the time they arrived.[35]

---

32. *OR* 36/1:780, 791; Perhaps significantly, Rosser's letters to Betty do not mention Stuart's death. Later, Custer cited one of his privates for Stuart's killing.
33. *OR* 36/2:1001.
34. Rhea, *To the North Anna River*, 88; *OR* 36/1:232, 36/2:753; Katherine Couse to a friend, May 4–22, 1864, UVA, Accession #10441.
35. *OR* 36/1:893–94.

After the battle of Spotsylvania, with Grant failing to position himself between Robert E. Lee and Richmond, Rosser's troopers made a reconnaissance as far as the Poor House, northeast of the Mule Shoe, on the road to Fredericksburg, driving off all Federal cavalry they encountered. A short distance south of Chancellorsville, in the pouring rain on May 15, Rosser surprised troopers of the 2nd Ohio, driving them east of the Plank Road, with his troopers then occupying the Plank Road and Catharpin Road intersection at the Alrich's house. Lieutenant Colonel Marshall L. Dempey's 23rd United States Colored Troops formed a line on the Plank Road by the house, forcing Rosser to withdraw. Rosser had captured a few prisoners while discovering the Federal IX Corps in the area. Not wanting to risk a major engagement, he withdrew to behind Confederate lines, reporting what he had learned.[36]

With Grant moving again on Robert E. Lee's right, on May 21 Rosser's troopers skirmished with Custer's cavalry at Wright's Tavern, driving them back on their strong force of infantry and artillery. Rosser learned of Grant's movement to Hanover Junction. His troopers slowly fell back to Hanover Junction, but Rosser maintained his brigade's contact with the Federals until Confederate infantry relieved him. He then positioned his brigade on General Lee's left. An old tale says that before Custer and his Wolverines left the area of Hanover Junction, he visited Betty Rosser, leaving a note with her for his friend. The note expressed the hope that Rosser had recovered from the "thrashing" the Wolverines had administered at Todd's Tavern on May 7. Custer had subsequently beaten Brig. Gen. Lunsford L. Lomax, he added, and he was ready to "serve" Rosser up again.[37]

Custer visited Betty more than once. Custer's wife, Elizabeth, relayed a story that on one occasion when Custer's Third Division had marched by Betty's home, her servant came out to invite Custer inside for a visit. Once inside, Betty told Custer that "she had never supposed that she could bring herself to speak [to], much less invite in a Yankee officer into her home, but that her husband had begged her not to let Custer go if he passed near[by]." Betty apologized to Custer for not having very much to offer him after the Federals had taken almost everything she owned. But the Union general "loved bread and milk as if he were a boy of five and was easily provided for." As Custer was leaving, Betty held baby Sally in her arms. The fun-loving cavalryman held out a gold pencil to the baby, saying, "Give this to your Papa dear, and tell him it is from a friend who whipped him yesterday." Betty

36. McDonald, *Laurel Brigade*, 243.
37. Rhea, *To the North Anna River.* 230 FN45; Elizabeth Bacon Custer, Arlene Reynolds, ed., *The Civil War Diaries of Elizabeth Bacon Custer* (Austin: 1994), 33.

quipped, "She shall not take it." The child grasped it, however, and before Betty could get it from her to return to Custer, he was down the porch steps and in the saddle.[38]

On May 27 Rosser's command made a night march toward Anderson's Ford, passed through Ashland, and camped near Atlee's Station, six miles outside Richmond. The next morning Hampton's division received orders to determine whether all of the Federal infantry had crossed the Pamunkey River. Hampton, accompanied by Maj. Gen. Rooney Lee's division, encountered Federal pickets at Haw's Shop and drove them back on their infantry. Rosser's and Brig. Gen. Williams C. Wickham's brigades led the assault, which turned into a heavy engagement. Private James Wood recorded, "Moved toward Sheridan's raiders. Engage him about 11 o'clock a.m. with sharpshooters. Have a stubborn and determined fight with him until about 3 pm when he was re-enforced with infantry, and we are compelled to fall back, being flanked by them." Rosser lost eight killed and 20 wounded during the fight. Hampton praised the Laurel Brigade's part in the withdrawal: "Rosser's men, being veterans, withdrew without loss and in perfect order under their able commander."[39]

Arriving from South Carolina only a few days earlier, part of Maj. Gen. Matthew C. Butler's brigade, including the 5th South Carolina, joined Wickham's and Rosser's brigades for the fight at Haw's Shop. The untested South Carolinians, fighting with Rosser, performed admirably in the seesaw fight between Fitz Lee's and David Gregg's horsemen, which lasted until mid-afternoon. Fitz Lee ordered a retreat when he encountered dismounted Union cavalry, mistaking them for infantry. Amid the smoke and noise of the Federals using repeating rifles, one bold South Carolina officer, in his first fight, stubbornly refused to pull back as ordered. Rosser argued with him until a shot whizzed between them, nicking the officer's saber knot. Reacting, Rosser told the officer, "If you're fool enough to stay here, you can do so," and departed. The next day the inexperienced officer apologized to Rosser, but the delay in withdrawing had resulted in the capture of one captain and nearly a squadron of the South Carolinians.[40]

Constant fighting since Grant began his May 5 offensive greatly diminished Rosser's brigade. It had lost more than 300 troopers killed, wounded, missing, or captured. The brigade also suffered from a lack of adequate horses, forcing many of the men to join the ranks of the

38. Ibid.
39. McDonald, *Laurel Brigade*, 243–44; Armstrong, *7th Virginia Cavalry*, 68;
    Diary of Pvt. James W. Wood, LVA.
40. McDonald, *Laurel Brigade*, 244–45.

dismounted. The scarcity of food for the troopers and forage for the horses continued to plague the brigade.[41]

Grant, unsuccessful in frontal attacks on Robert E. Lee's army, decided he would launch a series of cavalry attacks on Lee's lines of communication and supply. Accordingly, on May 31 Grant ordered Brig. Gen. James H. Wilson's cavalry division to assault the Virginia Central Railroad and tear up as much of the line as possible. The next day Wilson's troopers attacked Rooney Lee's horsemen near Hanover Court House, forcing them back toward Ashland. Hampton ordered Rosser to attack the rear of Brig. Gen. John B. McIntosh's brigade of Wilson's division. Rosser's vigorous assault was successful. He drove McIntosh into Ashland, and captured about 100

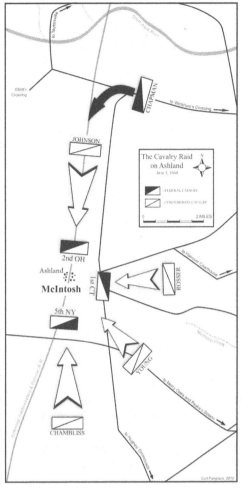

prisoners, including 50 wounded, as well as 200 horses and a cache of arms. The 12th Virginia, commanded by Col. Thomas Massie, led the assault, with Lt. George Baylor's squadrons B and I in the lead. Wilson made a stubborn stand in Ashland, positioning his troopers behind houses and the railroad embankment. Hampton directed Rooney Lee to attack. Rooney Lee sent the North Carolina Cavalry Brigade, which Brig. Gen. Pierce Young temporarily commanded and who dismounted his troopers for the assault. The very first volley Wilson's horsemen fired severely wounded the gallant and capable Young.[42]

Deprived of Young's leadership, the assault failed to dislodge Wilson. Rooney Lee reformed his troopers for another attack, while Hampton took the 10th Virginia, along with part of Rooney Lee's 3rd

---

41. *OR* 36/3:867; *Richmond Daily Dispatch*, June 3, 1864.
42. Ibid.

North Carolina and a squadron of Rosser's 7th Virginia, and attacked Wilson's right flank. At one time during the fight, the Federals poured artillery into the charging 7th and 11th Virginia regiments, causing confusion in the ranks. In the melee mounted Federals charged Rosser's flank with pistols in hand, adding to the chaos. Rosser, unwavering, ordered a counterattack, but his troopers were stunned by the suddenness of the Federal assault. Rosser reported:

> **They failed to obey, but faltered and hesitated until the enemy were well-nigh closed upon me and everything was about to break, when Private Holmes [Conrad], who was at my side, rushed to his old regiment (the 11th Virginia) and seized its colors, and called to his old comrades to save their flag that had waved so triumphantly upon so many glorious fields and rushed with it into the ranks of the enemy. My men roused by this example of daring and chivalry, rushed upon the enemy with the saber, put him to flight, saved the gallant Conrad, their flag, [and] their honor.[43]**

The tide of battle had turned by the action of one trooper, for Pvt. Holmes Conrad of the 11th Virginia, who charged straight at the Federal column. With banner waving, Conrad penetrated the frontal files, turned left, and escaped unharmed. Men had followed Conrad into the breach and soon confronted the astonished Federals who had failed to shoot him. The inspired Confederates drove the Federals back upon their main body. Wilson withdrew his command after leaving many dead, wounded, or taken prisoner. Conrad's brave actions during the fight had earned him promotion to major. Rosser's losses totaled 20 killed or wounded.[44]

In another attempt to outflank General Lee's right, the Confederates butchered Grant at the June 1 to 3, 1864, battle of Cold Harbor. No matter what losses he was willing to endure, Grant realized he could not penetrate Lee's army, so he came up with a new strategy to win the war. He decided to cross the James River and attack Richmond from the south. He began the movement on June 12, with his men facing the Confederate trenches at Petersburg by June 17. Petersburg held the key to Richmond. Grant planned to destroy the railroads supplying Petersburg and Richmond, as well as ravage the countryside where Lee drew supplies and food for his army.[45]

43. McDonald, *Laurel Brigade*, 245–47; *OR* 36/3:867; Thomas L. Rosser to Samuel Cooper, January 2, 1865, Holmes Conrad Papers, VHS.
44. Beane, *Thesis*, 41; McDonald, *Laurel Brigade*, 247–48; *Philadelphia Weekly Times*, April 19, 1884; Keller, *Riding with Rosser*, 28–29.
45. James Marshall-Cornwall, *Grant as Military Commander* (New York, 1995), 181–82.

Trevilian Station

As part of his strategy, on June 7 Grant sent Maj. Gen. Philip Sheridan to the Shenandoah Valley with Brig. Gen. David M. Gregg's and Gen. Alfred T. A. Torbert's cavalry divisions—totaling about 9,300 troopers and 24 artillery pieces—to begin an infamous mission to burn and destroy. The first objective of the operation involved raiding and demolishing the railroads at Gordonsville and Charlottesville. Grant hoped Maj. Gen. David Hunter, who replaced Maj. Gen. Franz Siegel after his defeat at New Market, would advance on Lynchburg and Lexington, and then join Sheridan in Charlottesville. Hampton, with information from scouts and a servant who escaped from Sheridan's camp, correctly concluded the Federals' immediate objectives were the important railroad towns of Gordonsville and Charlottesville. Robert E. Lee ordered Hampton to follow with an additional cavalry division. Hampton ordered Fitz Lee to join him as soon as possible, and on June 8 he proceeded to move between Gordonsville and Sheridan. Hampton, with about 6,400 horsemen and 15 guns in his command, managed to outmarch Sheridan and camped the night of June 10 at Green Spring Valley, three miles from Trevilian Station on the Virginia Central Railroad. Fitz Lee camped that night at Louisa Court House, while Rosser bivouacked two miles west of Trevilian.[46]

Hampton learned during the night that Sheridan had crossed the North Anna River at Carpenter's Ford. He decided to attack at dawn. He ordered Fitz Lee's division to march up the Marquiz Road (present-day Virginia Route 22) from Louisa Court House to Clayton's Store, while Hampton, with his division, planned to assault Sheridan on the road leading from Trevilian Station to Clayton's Store. With this disposition, Hampton hoped to "cover Lee's left flank and my right flank, and drive the enemy back if he attempted to reach Gordonsville, by passing to my left, and to conceal my real design, which was to strike him at Clayton's Store after uniting the two divisions."[47]

---

46. *OR* 36/1:1095–97; *Philadelphia Weekly Times*, April 19, 1884. According to Rosser, the night before Sheridan began to march, a black slave, 19 or 20 years old, who one of Sheridan's officers employed as a servant, left camp, crossed to Confederate lines, and asked to see Rosser. When Rosser was a captain, the slave had been assigned to him as a valet. The slave, whose name is unknown, told Rosser and Hampton the details of Sheridan's plans, as he knew them. Rosser later recalled that when he left the artillery service the slave had gone back to New Orleans with his master. When the Federals captured New Orleans a Union officer employed the slave. Since then the slave had begun to look for an opportunity to escape to Confederate lines; Keller, *Riding with Rosser*, 37. Rosser's account is corroborated by Capt. Thomas Nelson Conrad's story in *The Rebel Scout* (Washington City, 1904), 109–111.

47. *OR* 36/1:1096.

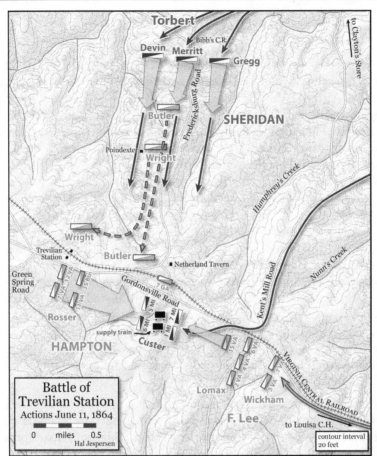

Battle of Trevilian Station
Actions June 11, 1864

0   miles   0.5
Hal Jespersen

contour interval 20 feet

At dawn on June 11 Hampton had his troopers in the saddle. He moved out with Matthew Calbraith Butler's and Pierce Young's brigades, while Rosser's command covered the Gordonsville Road on Hampton's left. Hampton attacked, pressing Union troopers of Torbert's division until 9:00 a.m., pushing them back up the Trevilian Station road toward Clayton's Store. Here they positioned themselves behind breastworks. Meanwhile, Fitzhugh Lee's division, which had bivouacked at Louisa Court House, encountered Custer's brigade on the Louisa Court House road, a few miles east of Trevilian Station. After establishing contact with Custer, Fitz Lee fell back, opening a dangerous gap between himself and Hampton. Thus Fitz Lee failed to fight through Custer and come up to join Hampton as planned. Hampton's staff officers, and perhaps Hampton himself, later regarded Fitz Lee's tardiness as proof of his unwillingness to support any superior other than J.E.B. Stuart.[48]

---

48. Longacre, *Lee's Cavalrymen*, 300; Wade Hampton to Edward L. Wells, January 18, 1900, Wells Manuscript, Charleston Library Society, Charleston,

Meanwhile, at mid-morning, Brig. Gen. George A. Custer's brigade exploited the gap between Hampton and Fitzhugh Lee. Custer interposed his forces between the rail depot and Louisa Court House by way of a diagonal track that ran through the forest, placing them in the rear of Butler's and Col. Gilbert J. Wright's Georgia brigades. Custer had left one of his four regiments to deal with the tardy Fitz Lee, while he proceeded until he was position to strike Hampton from the rear. The remainder of Torbert's troopers pressed Hampton in his front. Custer's 5th Michigan came upon lightly guarded ambulances, caissons, wagons, and 1,500 horses of Hampton's division. Custer spotted Maj. James W. Thomson's battery of Butler's brigade behind him on his right, near Netherland Tavern, and decided to take the unattended battery. Colonel Roger P. Chew, of the Horse Artillery, recalled, "Butler was at this time hotly engaged in front. I went back rapidly and found Custer's men advancing from the rear to capture the guns."[49]

Fortunately for the Confederates, Custer overlooked Thomson's two guns, which Thomson immediately repositioned on the Gordonsville Road. Meanwhile, Butler faced more firepower than he could handle, and retreated toward Trevilian Station, withdrawing Capt. James F. Hart's guns. Chew repositioned the guns on the Gordonsville Road in a spot to damage Custer, provided Chew was to receive cavalry support.[50]

At this stage of affairs, Hampton quickly recalled Rosser, who was on the Gordonsville Road some distance off to the west, to oppose Custer. Hampton ordered his line consolidated around Netherland Tavern. He ordered Butler to send the 6th South Carolina and the Phillips Legion to reinforce the Confederate position near the train station. These troopers charged Custer's horsemen, driving them back from the railroad. Rosser returned rapidly, but Custer was now trying to escape with his captures by traveling off the Gordonsville Road around Butler, Young, and the horse artillery, attempting to get through on their left. Fitz Lee was late in joining Hampton's line, and the Confederate cavalry chief sent a courier after him. Fitz Lee's unexplained tardiness was devastating for the Confederates at Trevilian Station; the delay allowed Custer to drive a wedge between Fitzhugh

SC; Edward L. Wells, *Hampton and His Cavalry in 1864* (Richmond, VA. 1899), 198–99; Keller, *Riding with Rosser*, 38.

49. Longacre, *Lee's Cavalrymen*, 300–302; *OR* 36/1:784–85, 800–801, 806–808, 823–24, 849–51; Eric J. Wittenberg, *Glory Enough For All: Sheridan's Second Raid and The Battle of Trevilian Station* (Washington, D.C., 2002), 101; McDonald, *Laurel Brigade*, 252.
50. Trout, *Galloping Thunder*, 497.

Lee's and Hampton's divisions. In recalling Rosser, Hampton had asked Lt. Wiley C. Howard, Company C of the Cobb Legion, to deliver an oral message to the general. Howard recollected:

> [Hampton] giving me directions as to the location of Rosser's brigade, I put my Yankee steed on his metal and after a time came upon the brigade hotly engaged dismounted. It was powerful uncomfortable where I found Rosser, but I was bound to go to him unless bullets stopped me. When delivered Hampton's message, that gallant commander and superb fighter said, "Give the general my compliments and tell him we are giving 'em hell."[51]

Howard remembered:

> I need not say I rode swiftly away, for it was hot and uncomfortable and I hastened to rejoin our chief who had then been rejoined by staff officers and moved in another direction and nearer a portion of the line. When I saluted and delivered Rosser's message, Hampton snapped his eyes, smiled and said to the staff, "General Rosser is a magnificent fighter and has done much to turn the tide in our favor today."[52]

From his new position Chew opened an effective fire on Custer's troopers, pushing them back toward Trevilian Station and delaying their escape by crippling the horses and stopping the captured wagons. After a considerable delay, Custer tried again to escape, but Rosser heard the firing and brought his brigade at a gallop down the Gordonsville Road. He then wheeled about and attacked the left of Custer's column, doubling it up on Fitz Lee's troopers who were coming up from the other side of the station. Rosser's horsemen attacked vigorously, pressing Custer back and recapturing many wagons and five caissons. Rosser made his well-timed assault in double columns, with the 11th Virginia on the front right of the Gordonsville Road and Col. Lige White's battalion on the front left. Fitz Lee, finally on the scene with Lomax's brigade, captured Custer's headquarters wagon, other wagons, horses, and prisoners. Butler's 6th South Carolina and the Phillips Legion of Wright's brigade attacked Custer from the north. Custer, driven from the field, suffered 11 killed, 51

---

51. *OR* 36/1:1095; McDonald, *Laurel Brigade*, 253; Keller, *Riding With Rosser*, 38; Wiley C. Howard, "Sketch of the Cobb Legion Cavalry and Some Incidents and Scenes Remembered," *Prepared and Read under appointment of Atlanta Camp 159, U. C. V., August 19, 1901*, (Davis Library, UNC-Chapel Hill), 16.
52. Ibid.

wounded, and 299 captured before Maj. Gen. Wesley Merritt and Col. Thomas C. Devin arrived as support. He was fortunate to have escaped at all.[53]

Artilleryman George M. Neese later recalled, "The enemy had already pierced General Hampton's line . . . when General Rosser, who had been hurriedly dispatched for, dashed on the field with gleaming saber at the head of his brigade of gallant trusty veterans, all rushing to the rescue with naked sabers or drawn pistols, with teeth set and knit brow, determined to do or die." After a tough fight, the blue line retreated. Neese concluded, "The timely arrival of General Rosser at the head of his brigade was all that saved our side from sustaining a disastrous defeat." In some soldiers like Rosser and Custer, the frenzy of battle produced an almost mesmerizing state of mind, a rage and audacity, whereby the soldier lost himself, becoming detached from any sense of danger and caught up in what Rosser called "fury's mad delirium." Major General George Meade's aide, Col. Theodore Lyman, observed "most officers would go into any danger when it was their duty, but fighting for fun is rare... [only] such men as... Custer and some others [like Rosser], attacked whenever they got a chance, and of their own accord."[54]

After the war, William H. Payne admiringly wrote Rosser:

> **I always see you, figure you, ready to push into battle. Cheerful, daring full of expedience, knowing no difficulties, arbitrary and despotic too. Loving and admiring brave deeds and brave men so highly as to set all law and precedent aside to show your admiration. Restless, ambitious, but on the battlefield, with more of the "Guadia certaminus" than any man I ever knew.[55]**

Confederate horsemen hotly pursued Custer toward Trevilian Station, 25 miles northeast of Charlottesville. After arriving, Custer

53. *OR* 36/1:1095; *Philadelphia Weekly Times*, April 19, 1884; Trout, *Galloping Thunder*, 495–96; Rod Andrew, *Wade Hampton: Confederate Warrior to Southern Redeemer* (Chapel Hill, 2008), 210; J. H. Kidd, *Personal Recollections of a Cavalryman Riding with Custer's Michigan Cavalry Brigade* (Ionia, Michigan, 1908), 222.
54. George M. Neese, *Three Years in the Confederate Horse Artillery*, 285; Thomas L. Rosser, *Addresses of Gen'l T. L. Rosser at the Seventh Annual Reunion*, Association of the Maryland Line, Baltimore, February 22, 1889 & Staunton, Virginia, June 3, 1889 (New York, 1889), 9; Glenn W. LaFantasie, *Twilight at Little Round Top: July 2, 1863—The Tide Turns at Gettysburg* (New York, 2007), 125; Monaghan, *Custer*, 199; William H. Payne to Thomas Rosser, March 2, 1866, Thomas L. Rosser Papers, UVA; Miller, *Decision at Tom's Brook*, 50. "Guadia certaminus," translated from Latin, means "the joy of the fight."
55. Ibid.

formed his men, controlled the approaches, and positioned artillery. Forming his regiments, Rosser prepared to attack. Colonel Chew informed Rosser he had observed Custer with only about 1,200 troopers. Rosser, who eagerly envisioned capturing Custer, ordered White to charge, but just then Hampton rode up and countermanded the order. Custer remained at Trevilian Station while Sheridan's entire command advanced against Hampton's right flank. If Fitz Lee had been on time and fought aggressively, it is likely that Custer's Wolverines would have been nearly destroyed, along with many captured. Generals Butler and Rosser asked Hampton to seek a court-martial of Fitz Lee, but Hampton would hear nothing of it.[56]

That evening Sheridan unsuccessfully attempted to dislodge Hampton from his new position. After one of the Federals' failed assaults, Rosser, still believing he could drive Custer from his position, ordered a charge, and at once suffered a bad leg wound at the hands of a Federal sharpshooter. Reeling in the saddle, Rosser finally sought safety, ending any thoughts of assaulting Custer.[57]

Sergeant Charles McVicar, of Major Thomson's battery, watched as Rosser swayed in the saddle upon being wounded. Several of Thomson's battery rushed forward to help the wounded general off his horse, and laid him down on the grass. A quick examination revealed Rosser had been hit in the leg, breaking bones below the knee, and his boot was filling with blood. Rosser still tried to direct the fighting even as a tourniquet was quickly applied to his leg. McVicar heard Rosser proclaim "that he could whip Sheridan with his gallant brigade, that God never placed better men on earth."[58]

Rosser's personal surgeon, Dr. Burton, treated the wounded warrior and had him removed to safety. All the while Rosser called for his senior regimental commander, Col. Richard H. Dulany of the 7th Virginia, and issued instructions to him, saying, "Col., fight with the men mounted. Let the other cavalry fight as infantry!" Dulany admired Rosser and knew his commander detested having to fight dismounted, even though the woody terrain sometimes necessitated it.[59]

---

56. McDonald, *Laurel Brigade*, 253–54; Manly Wade Wellman, *Giant in Gray: A Biography of Wade Hampton* (New York, 1949), 151.
57. McDonald, *Laurel Brigade*, 254.
58. Wittenberg, *Glory Enough for All*, 154; McVicar Diary, June 11, 1864, LVA.
59. Wittenberg, *Glory Enough for All*, 154; Keller, *Riding with Rosser*, 38; *Philadelphia Weekly Times*, April 19, 1884.

The Confederate horsemen spent the remainder of June 11 repelling Sheridan's limited assaults. Night closed the action, and both sides entrenched to prepare for the next day's decisive struggle.[60]

At dawn on June 12 both sides faced each other, but nothing happened in the morning. Fitz Lee had attacked Custer on the other side of Trevilian Station the previous day, and rejoined Hampton about noon. About 3:00 p.m. Sheridan began a series of vigorous assaults. His dismounted men, armed with Spencer repeating rifles or carbines, had a tremendous advantage compared to the Confederate troopers who were armed with single-shot carbines or muskets. The fighting on June 12 was chiefly on foot, and the woods provided good cover. Federal fire concentrated on Butler's brigade and on the artillery, which were able to fend off the attacks. Only 250 yards separated the opposing forces. The fighting continued until nightfall. Fitz Lee reinforced Butler's left with Wickham's brigade, taking Lomax's brigade across to the Gordonsville Road to attack the Federals' right flank. Sheridan was unable to force Hampton from his position.[61]

The Confederates heavily pressed on Sheridan's front and attacked on his left. He had had enough. Under the cover of darkness Sheridan slipped away to rejoin Grant's army, abandoning his dead and wounded. Sheridan may have failed to defeat Hampton at Trevilian Station, but he was very successful and brutal in his raids throughout the Shenandoah Valley, where he burned houses and barns, taking anything that might be of use to the Confederate army. Starving Lee's army was part of Grant's plan.[62]

Sheridan claimed victory at Trevilian Station, but some of the Northern newspapers quickly realized he was grossly exaggerating. Rosser was even harsher in his criticism of Sheridan's claims, stating, "Sheridan was fairly and completely beaten, and all of his apologies for his retreat, 'ammunition exhausted and presence of infantry,' are unworthy of a great soldier. Why was he there without ammunition? Didn't he expect to have some fighting? ... These excuses are really too ridiculous to be discussed."[63]

In a speech given after the war, Rosser further ridiculed Sheridan. "Sheridan concentrated his force at Trevilian and exerted his entire strength to the driving of Hampton out of his way, but he could not move him. The fight was conducted more like an infantry battle than a cavalry fight," Rosser spoke. "Sheridan displayed no skill in maneuvering; it was simply a square stand up fight, man to man, and

60. *Philadelphia Weekly Times*, April 19, 1884.
61. McDonald, *Laurel Brigade*, 255–56.
62. Ibid., 256.
63. Keller, *Riding with Rosser*, 39.

Hampton whipped him—defeated his purpose and turned him back." Rosser claimed that on June 12 "Little Phil" had been routed and panicked. Sheridan, despite a numerical superiority of five to one compared to Fitz Lee and three to one compared to Hampton, had failed to exploit his advantage and destroy Butler and Fitz Lee once they were driven apart. Then he failed to follow up when the pressure relaxed.[64]

Rosser convalesced from his Trevilian Station wound in a hospital in Richmond. As a fighting man, he longed to be where the action was, and time seemed to drag by. Restless, he worried about how his Laurel Brigade was doing with Colonel Dulany commanding, but he was fortunate that Richmond was relatively close to Betty's home, "Courtland," in Hanover County. She visited him at the hospital often.[65]

Rosser did not return to his brigade until the end of August. While recuperating he received a letter from Robert E. Lee: "[I] hope that you may soon be restored to your usual vigor and be enabled to return to your command where you have rendered and may still render such valuable assistance to the cause."[66]

On July 5, 1864, a surgeon of the Medical Board examined Rosser in Richmond, granting him leave to go to home, and on July 8 he was granted a 30-day extension. During recovery, Tom's and Betty's first child, a redheaded daughter named Sally Overton Rosser, was born on August 17, 1864. Rosser was a little perplexed as to where the red hair came from, and in subsequent letters requested Betty to "kiss the redheaded rat." He joked it might be necessary to "sit out on the fence and let the woodpeckers feed it." He also expressed his happiness about joining Betty's church before he had returned to camp.[67]

Rosser saw Robert E. Lee before he returned to his command, and "from his manner I am satisfied that he intends promoting me very soon," he told Betty. General Lee also promised "to send my Brigade to the Valley as soon as things became quiet here." Hampton told him General Lee "will give me a division composed of Young's Brigade and my own—that would be very satisfying to me."[68]

64. U. R. Brooks, *Butler and His Cavalry in the War of Secession, 1861–1865* (Columbia, SC, 1909), 256–57; Walbrook D. Swank, ed., *The Battle of Trevilian Station: The Civil War's Greatest and Bloodiest All Cavalry Battle, with Eyewitness Memoirs* (Civil War Heritage, Vol. 4), 28.
65. Bushong, *Fightin' Tom Rosser*, 102.
66. Robert E. Lee to Thomas L. Rosser, July 7, 1864, Thomas L. Rosser Papers, UVA.
67. Clayton Torrence, ed., *Winston of Virginia and Allied Families*, (Richmond, 1927), 52; Special Order No. 12, July 5, 1864 and July 8, 1864; Thomas L. Rosser to Betty W. Rosser, August 23, 1864; August 24, 1864; September 1, 1864; September 6, 1864, Thomas L. Rosser, UVA.
68. Thomas L. Rosser to Betty W. Rosser, August 23, 1864, Thomas L. Rosser Papers, UVA.

Despite the wound not being fully healed, Rosser returned on crutches to Hampton's command on August 22, resuming command of the Laurel Brigade two days later during the battle of Second Reams's Station. The reception Rosser's men gave him upon his return elated the general: "My Brigade is rejoiced to see me and they make the forests wake by their welcoming cheers."[69]

Hampton had been promoted to commander of the Cavalry Corps on August 11, 1864, and his former division needed a new commander. Rosser speculated it might be he who would be promoted to major general to take command. Earlier, Rosser had written Betty that his prospects for the promotion to command Hampton's division upon the anticipated promotion of Hampton to cavalry corps commander were exceedingly good, for "Gen. Lee will be compelled to give Gen. Hampton the Cav'y Corps and I will then be made Division Comdt. Hampton told me today that he had recommended me."[70]

However, Rosser's wound at Trevilian Station and subsequent 10-week convalescence doomed any hope for promotion. Upon Hampton's promotion, the senior brigade commander at the time, Matthew Calbraith Butler, was in line for the command of Hampton's former division. Rosser was again disappointed. After his return to duty, Hampton informed Rosser he would command a division composed of the Laurel Brigade and Young's brigade. When it came time to make the choice officially, however, Hampton recommended his fellow South Carolinian Matthew Butler. Hampton did so "even at the risk of losing the services of the other two brigadier generals of the division, highly as I appreciate their services and anxious as I am to see these services rewarded also by promotion. I hope that in the reorganization of the cavalry both Rosser and Young may be able to obtain larger commands than they now hold."[71]

Butler's promotion wounded Rosser's pride, and he would let his disappointment fester until he turned on his friend—by now a familiar pattern. In an August 27 letter to Betty, from near Reams's Station, he wrote:

> **Gen Hampton has acted very badly I think about my promotion, but there is some difficulty in the way of Butler's promotion and the most of us think that I am that difficulty. Hampton says that Gen Lee will certainly promote me—but I rely upon nothing he says—Gen Lee has been very kind to me and if I can keep the field will**

69. Thomas L. Rosser to Betty W. Rosser, August 24, 1864, Thomas L. Rosser Papers, UVA.
70. Ibid., June 5, 1864, Thomas L. Rosser Papers, UVA.
71. *OR* 42/2:1278–79.

promote me before a great while... My wound is rapidly improving and I think will be well before long. At any rate, it will not lay me up again.[72]

Still simmering, the next day he wrote Betty again, stating his unwillingness to serve under Butler or with any South Carolina troops in the cavalry, feeling Hampton had done him an injustice. In a following letter he wrote that his men all opposed Butler, and were anxious to get away from the division. When Rosser learned the Laurel Brigade might be sent to the Shenandoah Valley to assist a badly outmanned Jubal Early, he said he did not want to go to the valley, rather "I want to get out of this mess. I begin to fear that there is no chance of my immediate promotion."[73]

During this period of disillusionment, in letters to Betty he told her he found great consolation in the almighty God. He relayed to his wife he had heard a good sermon delivered by one of the chaplains, and it did much to revive his sagging spirits. He said he was so glad he had joined the church for this relationship with God made him a happier person and an entirely different man.[74]

Despite his newfound religion, a few days later Rosser expressed doubt about being promoted to major general, still convinced Hampton opposed it. Still suffering from his wound, he wrote Betty that if Butler was instead promoted, then he would ask for a furlough and not return to the army until completely healed. Hampton infuriated Rosser so much that he hoped to be transferred to the West or even to the Trans-Mississippi Department. He knew Betty would be opposed to moving that far from Courtland, but he reminded her that she must not interfere with his interests. Rosser's disaffection with the military seemed to rub off on Betty, as she became gloomy and not her usual self. Not realizing he was the source of her anxiety, he begged Betty to tell him the cause of her unhappiness.[75]

Second Battle of Reams's Station:
August 25, 1864

As soon as Rosser returned to duty on August 25, he was engaged in the battle of Second Reams's Station on the Petersburg and Weldon

72. Thomas L. Rosser to Betty W. Rosser, August 27, 1864, Thomas L. Rosser Papers, UVA.
73. Thomas L. Rosser to Betty W. Rosser, August 28, 1864; September 1, 1864, Thomas L. Rosser Papers, UVA.
74. Ibid.
75. Thomas L. Rosser to Betty W. Rosser, September 6, 1864, Thomas L. Rosser Papers, UVA.

Railroad. Early that morning, Hampton moved out with Butler's division, along with Brig. Gen. Rufus Barringer leading Rooney Lee's division in his absence. Hampton's column crossed Malone's Bridge at 9:00 a.m., driving the Federal pickets back until his troopers encountered a heavy force of Union cavalry. After a sharp exchange, the Federals retreated toward Malone's Crossing, the Confederate horsemen in hot pursuit. Near Reams's Station Federal infantry relieved their cavalry in front, while the latter attempted to turn Hampton's flanks. Hampton checked their attempt at flanking, holding his ground.[76]

At about 5:00 p.m., Lt. Gen. A. P. Hill, commanding about 8,000 soldiers, including cavalry, was ready to attack. Hampton sent his dismounted troopers to attack Hancock's infantry. David Gregg's and Brig. Gen. August V. Kautz's cavalry divisions threatened Hampton's right. The gray troopers steadily advanced against infantry volleys, and the bluecoats fell back behind their earthworks at Reams's Station.[77]

Hampton's line of skirmishers extended across both sides of the railroad. Suddenly, he discovered Hill's infantry attacking on the left and west side. Hampton then moved his line to the right (east side) of the railroad. With his right side far extended, Hampton's troopers swung around to the rear of the Federals to attack. The Confederates attacked and overran the entrenched Union soldiers. The 12th Virginia of Hill's corps and Rosser's 12th Virginia raced in front, with the horsemen reaching the trenches first. The Federal soldiers, under Brig. Gen. Nelson A. Miles, fled the trenches and could not be rallied to stand their ground. During the bruising 12-hour battle the Union forces lost more than 2,700 killed, wounded, or captured.[78]

After dark, Hampton's troopers remained in the abandoned trenches as Hill's infantry withdrew. During the night, the Federals withdrew from the region, with Hampton's cavalry and the 12th Virginia pursuing.[79]

The fight at Reams's Station was a decisive Confederate victory against superior forces. Hill reported the capture of "twelve stands of colors, nine pieces of artillery, ten caissons, 2,150 prisoners, 3,100 small arms, and thirty-two horses. My own loss, cavalry, artillery, and infantry, being 720."[80]

When Rosser took command of Fitz Lee's division on August 30, stemming from Lee's bout with rheumatism, he was ordered to report directly to Maj. Gen. Jubal Early and not to Brig. Gen. Lunsford

76. McDonald, *Laurel Brigade*, 271–72.
77. Ibid., 272, 277.
78. Ibid., 273–74, 280.
79. Ibid., 276.
80. *OR*, vol. 42, part 1, 940–41.

Lomax, the ranking senior officer commanding Early's other cavalry division. Major General Philip H. Sheridan commanded the Federal army in the Shenandoah Valley, while his three cavalry divisions, under William H. Powell, Wesley Merritt, and George A. Custer, were all under the command of Brig. Gen. Alfred T. Torbert. Rosser did not proceed to the Shenandoah Valley to join Early until after Hampton's mid-September "Beefsteak Raid."[81]

After Reams's Station Rosser's troopers rested for a few days, but on September 1 they saddled up for a reconnaissance. The Confederate horsemen rode about four miles beyond Reams's Station where they encountered and drove in Union pickets, pursuing them to their camp. The Federals, though surprised, aptly defended their position in a vigorous fight. After taking prisoners and plunder, Rosser withdrew. The brigade next returned to camp, resting until September 14 when they took part in the Beefsteak Raid.[82]

81. *Philadelphia Weekly Times*, March 22, 1984. Torbert would be promoted to brevet major general on September 9, 1864.
82. McDonald, *Laurel Brigade*, 284.

CHAPTER 7

The 1864 Fall Campaigns:
Wade Hampton's Beefsteak Raid,
Shenandoah Valley Campaign, and Rosser's Raids

> "Tam, do not expose yourself so.
> Yesterday I could have killed you."
>
> -George Armstrong Custer in a letter to
> Thomas Rosser

Following the spring and summer fighting of 1863, Thomas Rosser and the Laurel Brigade participated in Lt. Gen. Wade Hampton's daring cattle raid in mid-September, followed by the 1864 Shenandoah Valley campaign, which included battles at Tom's Brook and Cedar Creek. After the Confederate debacles at Tom's Brook and Cedar Creek, Rosser resumed his hit-and-run strikes, capturing the Federal storage depot at New Creek, and then fought a battle at Lacey Springs. In November Rosser was promoted again, this time to major general.

Hampton's Great Beefsteak Raid: September 14–17, 1864

Rosser, still upset about Matthew Calbraith Butler's promotion to major general, wrote his wife, Betty, penning, "Butler has not yet been promoted, and is now absent and I am in the command of the Division, but he will return tomorrow or the next day." Smarting about Pierce Young's promotion to brigade commander, Rosser also told Betty, "Young has taken command of his Brigade and has a party given him tonight in the neighborhood—none of my staff are invited—but tomorrow night one is given to me and I suppose none of Young's staff are invited."[1]

Rosser complained to his wife, "If Butler is promoted over me whilst my wound is in its present condition, I will procure a furlough." Continuing, he said, "I am not anxious to go to the Valley my darling,

---

1. Thomas L. Rosser to Betty W. Rosser, September 13, 1864, Thomas L. Rosser Papers, UVA.

but I am very desirous to get away [from] these S. Carolinians Troops Butler and Hampton." In the same letter he teased her about their baby Sally having red hair, saying, "The idea of my baby Little Betz having a red head! Betz—where in the world did it get it from? I never had a red head in my life—did you Betz? I wonder if Dorwell ever had had a red head—maybe Betz you looked at him too much." He also recounted that he had "met [Stephen] Dandridge, but he did not speak—none of the Dandridges have been cordial since I failed to marry Lilly." Rosser and Lilly Dandridge once had a romantic relationship when J. E. B. Stuart's cavalry encamped at the Dandridge estate, in late September 1862, following the battle of Antietam.[2]

In a letter to Betty written just one day before the start of Hampton's famous cattle raid, Rosser recounted what he knew about it. Fortunately, the letter did not fall into Federal hands, because the Laurel Brigade commander gave explicit details of the raid to begin the next morning. Rosser complained he was not well, and he would seek a furlough to visit her after returning from the raid behind Federal lines. Again, he talked about his potential promotion to major general:

> **I may not wish to remain in the Army or I may be compelled to do it. I can't tell at this time anything about it. I think that were I get to be a Major Gen. I will be satisfied, or at least until I can make a good reputation as Major Gen. as I now enjoy as Brigadier—But I hope this cruel war will be over before that is the case.[3]**

Petersburg remained under siege in autumn of 1864. The Army of Northern Virginia faced the mounting problem of how to supply food for itself. Based upon intelligence that renowned scout Sgt. George D. Shadburne of the Jeff Davis Legion provided, Hampton developed a plan to steal a herd of 3,000 beef cattle guarded by only 120 soldiers and 30 unarmed citizens near Coggins's Point, Virginia. Coggins's Point was located on the James River, roughly five miles east of City Point, a massive Federal supply storage area and headquarters of the combined Union armies besieging Petersburg. Shadburne added that about 250 men of the 1st District of Columbia Cavalry were at Sycamore Church, less than three miles away from Coggins's Point. Hampton presented his ingenious idea to Gen. Robert E. Lee on September 8, and received approval. Hampton would conduct the raid on September 14 while Lt. Gen. Ulysses S. Grant conferred with Maj. Gen. Philip Sheridan in the Shenandoah Valley.[4]

2. Thomas L. Rosser to Betty W. Rosser, September 6, 1864, Thomas L. Rosser Papers, UVA; Blackford, War Years, 154, 296, 304.

3. Thomas L. Rosser to Betty W. Rosser, September 13, 1864, Thomas L. Rosser Papers, UVA.

4. Horace Mewborn, "Herding the Yankee Cattle: The Beefsteak Raid,

Hampton assembled his cavalry commanders for the expedition, including Rosser, Maj. Gen. Rooney Lee, Brig. Gen. James Dearing, Lt. Col. Elijah White of Rosser's Laurel Brigade, and Maj. Gen. Matthew Butler, and briefed them on his plan. Brigadier General Rufus Barringer's brigade, with the rest of Rooney Lee's division, would guard the rear of Hampton's forces during the raid.[5]

In the early hours of September 14, the majority of 4,000 of the South's finest cavalrymen left for Coggins's Point from their camp, where they had assembled seven miles southwest of Petersburg on Boydton Plank Road, near Gravelly Run. Others, including the 2nd North Carolina and the 9th, 10th, and 13th Virginia, whose camps were farther south, joined the expedition en route later in the day. Hampton's troopers proceeded down the west side of Rowanty Creek. They crossed the Weldon Railroad just north of Stony Creek Station, continuing on to Wilkinson's Bridge on Rowanty Creek, where they bivouacked for the night.[6]

Before dawn on the 15th, the Confederate troopers crossed Rowanty Creek and headed east, turned north on the Jerusalem Plank Road for a short distance, and then veered northeast to Cabin Point. At midday the column reached the site of the previously destroyed Cook's Bridge on the Blackwater River. The Rebels, then only 12 miles due south of Coggins's Point, had not been detected. By dusk Lt. John F. Lanneau's engineers had built a temporary replacement span. All of Hampton's force crossed soon after midnight. The column continued northeast for a few miles, split into three detachments, and approached Sycamore Church from different directions.[7]

Hampton's plan called for Rosser to attack the largest Federal force—more than 250 men—at dawn at Sycamore Church. Rosser needed to quickly suppress the Yankees and proceed north to round up the herd. Meanwhile, Rooney Lee's division would drive away any Federals on the left and hold the roads from City Point. Dearing's brigade would remain to the right of Sycamore Church, and at the

September 14–17, 1864," *Blue and Gray Magazine.* (Summer 2005), 10, hereafter cited as "Mewborn, Herding the Cattle"; *OR* 42/1:26, 42/2: 1234–36; Edward Boykin, *Beefsteak Raid* (New York, 1960), 177–78.

5. Mewborn, "Herding the Yankee Cattle,"12; OR 42/1:26, 43/2:1234–36; Boykin, *Beefsteak Raid*, 177–78.

6. Boykin, *Beefsteak Raid*, 211; Mewborn, "Herding the Yankee Cattle," 12–13; W. A. Curtis Diary, Special Collections, Duke University; OR 42/1:945; Clark, NCR, 3:622.

7. *OR* 42/1:945; Mewborn, "Herding the Yankee Cattle," 12–14; Colonel D. Cardwell, "A Brilliant Coup," *News and Courier* (Charleston, SC), October 10, 1864. Reprinted in the SHSP, vol. 22, 146–157, hereinafter referred to as a "Cardwell, A Brilliant Coup"; W. A. Curtis Diary; Clark, NCR, 3:622.

sound of gunfire it would demolish a nearby Union outpost at Cocke's Mill, as well as hold the roads leading to Fort Powhatan, 25 miles south of Richmond.[8]

Rosser attacked at Sycamore Church before daybreak on September 16, with the 12th Virginia leading the charge. Initially, the 1st District of Columbia Cavalry beat him back. Rosser, however, quickly dismounted the 7th Virginia as skirmishers, clearing the way for the mounted 12th Virginia, followed by the 11th Virginia and White's 35th Battalion. The charging Confederates eventually overcame the stubborn Union cavalry.[9]

Hearing the sounds of gunfire at Sycamore Church at daybreak, Rooney Lee's troopers sprang into action. Colonel Lucius Davis's brigade took the lead, driving enemy guards and picket lines positioned on the Stage Road back toward the small village of Prince George Court House. At the intersection of Lawyer's and Stage roads, Davis's troopers threw up breastworks, thereby controlling both roads.[10]

Barringer's North Carolina Cavalry Brigade, following Davis's troopers, attacked and captured 20 to 25 of the 11th Pennsylvania cavalrymen camped at Prince George Court House. Seeing Davis's horsemen retiring and throwing up breastworks, Barringer's troopers dismounted and constructed defenses of their own to guard the approach of any infantry from the north. Here, the North Carolinians remained until word reached them that Hampton and the cattle were moving.[11]

Meanwhile, after driving off the Yankees at Sycamore Church, Rosser left a strong guard from the 7th Virginia to secure the camp and protect the rear while he went after the cattle. With White's 35th Battalion and the 11th and 12th Virginia, Rosser headed for the cattle, located two miles away. Rosser ordered the 7th Virginia to "run their horses until they got in front of the herd, then to turn upon it and stop it." This was easier said than done as the young steers "ran like buffalo." Rosser's jaded horsemen were forced into a race to stop and turn the herd. After a mile or so, they accomplished their mission by getting in front of the herd to "round them up." After surrounding

8. *OR* 42/1:945; Mewborn, "Herding the Yankee Cattle," 14–15; Wells, *Hampton and His Cavalry in '64*, 289–90; *Raleigh Daily Progress*, September 21, 1864; W. A. Curtis Diary.
9. OR 42/1:28, 836; Boykin, *Beefsteak Raid*, 227–31; W. A. Curtis Diary; Clark, NCR, 3:623; Ben Labree, ed., *Campfires of the Confederacy*, "General Thomas L. Rosser, Capture of Cattle" (Louisville, Kentucky, 1898), 60.
10. Mewborn, "Herding the Yankee Cattle," 16–17.
11. Ibid., 17, 44.

both the herd and the guards, Rosser quickly led them back toward Sycamore Church.[12]

The cattle, numbering 2,468 head, were safely driven back to Hampton's camp at Sycamore Church. Hearing of the successful capture of the cattle, Rooney Lee's division and Dearing's brigade joined Rosser at Sycamore Church. Hampton's reunited command began its return trip with Rosser in the lead, followed by Dearing and Rooney Lee. En route the Confederates destroyed the makeshift replacement span at the site of the late Cook's Bridge, thereby delaying the Federals' pursuit.[13]

During the return trip, White's troopers held off Brig. Gen. Henry E. Davies's horsemens' attack at Ebenezer Church for more than two hours, until Rosser came to their aid. Davies then sent Col. William Stedman's brigade charging into the Confederate line. With the help of Capt. William M. McGregor's and Capt. Edward Graham's guns, the Federals repulsed the Southerners twice. Realizing Brig. Gen. August V. Kautz would not come to his aid in time and knowing that the cattle had already passed Sycamore Church, Davies called off his pursuit. He ordered Col. Charles H. Smith's brigade to pursue by an alternate route, but that also failed.[14]

On September 16 Kautz's column was held up for some time at the Blackwater River. After a skirmish on the Jerusalem Plank Road the following day, Kautz decided it was fruitless to continue. Pursuing the raiders had failed because the Federals had been surprised, slow to gathering their dispersed forces, and late starting the chase. Hampton moved the cattle to a corral at the intersection of the White Oak and Boydton Plank roads. The following day most of the herd moved through Petersburg to a safer location.[15]

Hampton's raiders had covered 100 miles in three days. They captured more than 300 prisoners and 11 wagons, burned three camps, took a large load of supplies, seized three flags, and rustled more than 2,400 fat steers. Hampton had lost 10 killed, 47 wounded, and four missing.[16]

News of the raid shocked Maj. Gen. George Meade's headquarters. Estimates of the raider's strength had run as high as 14,000 men. Panicking, some Federal leaders worried about the safety of City Point

12. Mewborn, "Herding the Yankee Cattle," 44–45; *OR* 42/1:821; Labree, ed., *Campfires of the Confederacy*, "General Thomas L. Rosser: Capture of Cattle," 60.
13. Ibid., 46.
14. Cardwell, "A Brilliant Coup"; Mewborn, "Herding the Yankee Cattle," 46–47; *OR*/1:614.
15. Ibid., 48.
16. *OR* 42/1:946; Boykin, *Beefsteak Raid*, 284.

itself. By 10:00 a.m. the Federals finally figured out what had actually happened, and the alarm subsided.[17] Grant, in a dispatch to Meade, called the captured beef "a rich haul." Indeed, it was; those 2,468 beeves were a blessing for General Lee's starving army. The cattle, deemed "Hampton's steaks," furnished food to the Petersburg defenders for several weeks.[18]

The 1864 Shenandoah Valley Campaign: General Rosser, "Savior of the Valley"

On September 19, 1864, Matthew Calbraith Butler was officially promoted to major general in command of Hampton's former division; Rosser seethed. However, the attitude of most of his troopers at his return to duty encouraged him. In a letter to Betty, he remarked:

> I think Gen [Robert E.] Lee is too just to allow me to be badly treated—but it is difficult to say what will be done in such cases. If I am promoted I will recommend Col. [Oliver] Funsten to command this Brig. The officers of the Brigade would not be willing to serve under anyone else if I should be taken from them.[19]

Virginia's Shenandoah Valley was a key theater in the Civil War. The opposing armies fiercely contested for the Valley throughout the war, as it provided a natural highway between north and south and a richly productive agricultural region, which fed the Confederate troops. More than 300 conflicts took place in the Valley, with Stonewall Jackson's 1862 campaign perhaps known as the most famous series of actions. The Valley lay at the heart of the struggle, and as the war dragged on, the area assumed increasing significance as the "breadbasket" for the Southern cause. Union forces responded by laying waste to this region— burning its fields, farms, and towns in a devastating campaign of total warfare.

17. Wells, *Hampton and His Cavalry in '64*, 294–95; *OR* 42/2:853–54, 876–78; Cardwell, "A Brilliant Coup." Meade's report (*OR* 42/1:86) states that the lowest estimate of Confederate forces was 6,000 men.
18. Wells, *Hampton and His Cavalry in '64*, 294–95; *OR* 42/2:853–54, 876–78; Wells, *Hampton and His Cavalry in '64*, 300; Boykin, *Beefsteak Raid*, 286; Cardwell, "A Brilliant Coup;" *OR* 42/2:853.
19. Thomas L. Rosser to Betty W. Rosser, September 27, 1864, Thomas L. Rosser Papers, UVA.

Custer's Revenge at Tom's Brook: "The Woodstock Races," October 9, 1864

Major General Jubal Early's army, about 8,000 soldiers of all arms, had achieved remarkable successes against Maj. Gen. David Hunter's army of 18,000 at Lynchburg. Early, who had replaced Lt. Gen. Richard Ewell after he had fallen from his horse at the battle of Spotsylvania Court House in May, drove Hunter into West Virginia, and then marched rapidly north to Maryland, where he defeated Maj. Gen. Lew Wallace along the Monocacy River. Early then pushed on toward Washington, D.C., confronting Fort Stevens in the northwest area of the capital on July 11. Grant, in an effort to meet Early's threat on Washington, detached the VI Corps and part of the XIX Corps from the armies besieging Petersburg. Early retreated across the Potomac River into Virginia. Defeating Maj. Gen. George Crook at the battle of Cool Spring and at the Second Battle of Kernstown, Early went into camp along the Opequon Creek.[20]

Early's successes greatly alarmed the Federal high command, and the Union dispatched Sheridan to the Valley to deal with him. The Federal leaders, estimating Early's army to be larger than it actually was, sent about 48,000 men, including 6,100 cavalrymen under Sheridan, to dispose of Early's army. Early could only muster about 12,000 soldiers of all arms, even after receiving reinforcements. Sheridan defeated Early's army at Winchester on September 19, 1864, and three days later at Fisher's Hill.[21]

Major General Fitzhugh Lee, Early's cavalry commander, had just returned to duty after a 10-day bout with rheumatism when he was wounded in the thigh on September 19 at Winchester. Early desperately needed reinforcements in order to fight Sheridan in the Valley and thereby relieve pressure on Richmond. Responding, Robert E. Lee sent Maj. Wilfred E. Cutshaw's artillery battalion, Maj. Gen. Joseph B. Kershaw's infantry division of 2,700 soldiers, and Rosser's undersized 600-man Laurel Brigade as reinforcements.[22]

Rosser's troopers appeared happy at the prospect of returning to the Valley from the Richmond-Petersburg area. Many of the Laurel Brigade's troopers were from the Valley, and reports of Sheridan's burning and plundering unleashed a desire for revenge among the

---

20. Bushong, *Fightin' Tom Rosser*, 111–112; Opequon Creek is a 64-mile-long tributary stream of the Potomac River. It flows into the Potomac northeast of Martinsburg, West Virginia, in Berkley County, and its source lies at the foot of Great North Mountain in Frederick County, Virginia.
21. *OR* 43/1:60–61.
22. Bushong, *Fightin' Tom Rosser*, 112.

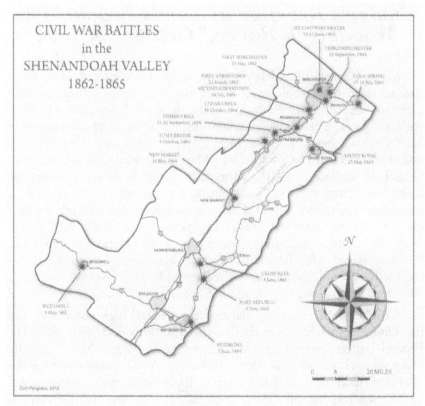

Confederate horsemen. Rosser proceeded by rail to Mount Sidney, and on October 2 arrived at Bridgewater. Rosser relinquished command of the brigade to Col. Richard H. Dulany before taking the train with his staff to Lynchburg and Staunton. The brigade reached the Valley on October 5 and camped at Bridgewater; the arduous journey further depleted their men and horses. The brigade's wagon trains were trailing about 10 miles behind the arriving horsemen. Prideful, Rosser proclaimed: "Order those wagon trains up. I am in the Valley now."[23]

The arrival of Rosser's brigade and Kershaw's infantry brought new optimism to Early and many citizens of the Valley. A trooper from Maryland serving in Brig. Gen. John Imboden's cavalry remarked that Rosser "was one of the bravest and most enterprising of our cavalry commanders, given albeit to perhaps an undue amount of boasting, owing to a superabundance of self-esteem." This same soldier listened as Rosser "very jocularly inquired why we had been permitting the Federal cavalry to misuse us so terribly, stating [that] on the Petersburg lines our people were virtually having their own way,

23. Thomas P. Nanzig, Robert Thruston Hubard, *The Civil War Memoirs of a Virginia Cavalryman*, 201.

and he would now show us how it ought to be done." Rosser's 600-man brigade, however, was merely a shadow of its former stronger contingent. It would be greatly outnumbered in the coming battles with Sheridan's huge cavalry, but Rosser still felt confident his troopers could whip the Federal horsemen.[24]

Upon Fitz Lee's wounding at Winchester, Rosser had taken temporary command of his division, which included the brigades of Brig. Gen. Williams C. Wickham and Col. William H. Payne. Wickham, who had been elected to the Confederate Congress, resigned his commission on October 5, and Col. Thomas T. Munford took temporary command of his brigade. Munford was a capable, efficient, and brave officer who had never been promoted to brigadier general. He had attended the Virginia Military Institute and was not considered a member of the Virginia-elite clique of West Point officers. Munford felt unhappy about serving under the brash and flamboyant Rosser, an officer he had once outranked. Unfortunately for the two officers, they indeed had to cooperate in the months ahead to have a chance of success. Reportedly, neither Rosser nor Munford would even enter the other's tent. The other cavalry division in the Valley, commanded by Maj. Gen. Lunsford L. Lomax, comprised the brigades of brigadier generals John C. Imboden, John McCausland, and Bradley T. Johnson, along with Col. William L. Jackson. All units fell short of their authorized strength from heavy fighting and an inability to add substantial numbers of recruits.[25]

Sheridan's huge cavalry force consisted of Brig. Gen. Alfred Torbert, in overall command, and divisions under brigadier generals Wesley Merritt, William W. Averell, and George A. Custer. While Early prepared to resume the fight at Brown's Gap in the Blue Ridge Mountains, Sheridan had created havoc in the upper Valley. Grant had ordered Sheridan to make the Valley a "barren waste," which he largely accomplished during a 13-day burning spree from late September through early October. Sheridan's troopers concentrated on destroying barns, mills, crops, and farm equipment, as well as driving off livestock— the Federals left nothing behind that could aid the Confederate army. They were also retaliating for Early's burning of Chambersburg on July 30, 1864. Sheridan so efficiently wasted the land that the local farmers could not provide for their own families. When Rosser asked Betty to visit him, he informed his wife that he would have to provide bread and meat for her during the visit, and she

24. George Wilson Booth, *A Maryland Boy in Lee's Army: Personal Reminiscences of a Maryland Soldier in the War Between the States, 1861–1865* (Lincoln, Nebraska, 2000), 152.
25. Bushong, *Fightin' Tom Rosser*, 113.

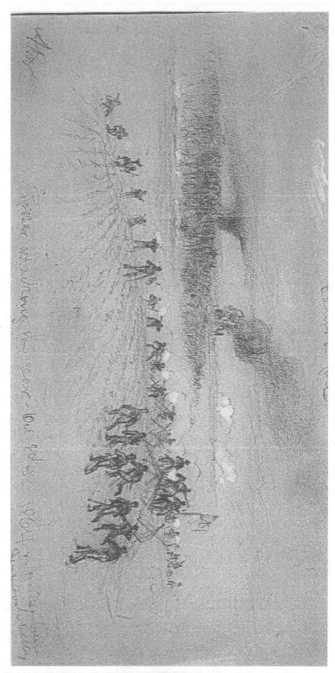

Burning of the Shenandoah Valley.

Rosser Attacking the Rear. October 8, 1864, near Harrisonburg in the Shenandoah Valley.

Drawing by William Waud - Library of Congress

would not be able to stay with neighboring farmers like she had on previous visits to him in the field.[26]

On September 23, a skirmish at Front Royal between troopers of Union Col. Charles R. Lowell's brigade and a contingent of Maj. John S. Mosby's partisan rangers resulted in the execution of six of Mosby's rangers. Sheridan relieved Averell from command of the Second Cavalry Division, replacing him with Col. William Powell. Mosby blamed Custer for the executions. Custer had been present but not in command, and he did not order the executions. Torbert, commanding, probably approved the slayings, supposedly in retaliation for a Union officer's capture and execution. Mosby never believed Custer's innocence, even after the war when an investigation, with Rosser's written testimony as support, appeared to absolve Custer of complicity.[27]

When Sheridan retreated down the Valley, Rosser's horsemen pursued him, vowing vengeance as they eyed the Union general's path of destruction. Three parallel roads ran in this part of the Valley: Valley Pike, Middle Road, and Back Road. The angry troopers of the Laurel Brigade hastened their pace. On October 6 they caught up with Sheridan's rear guard at Brock's Gap, in the geographical area where the North Fork of the Shenandoah River drains before it flows through the gap in North Mountain. A vigorous fight ensued, and Custer's horsemen retreated across Dry River, one of three rivers that drain the eastern slope of the Shenandoah Mountain. Custer posted his artillery on the opposite bank of the river, which kept Rosser's 3,000 mounted troopers at bay until darkness. Custer then joined Sheridan's army.[28]

After the fight at Brock's Gap, Rosser established his headquarters at the home of Joseph Zirkle in Turleytown. Pursing Custer through burnt landscape had taken its toll on Rosser and his troopers, exhausting men and horses. At Zirkle's home Rosser awaited instructions from Early. The next day Early ordered Rosser to continue following Custer, and do "all the damage you can." Early wanted to determine Sheridan's intentions. He ordered that Rosser "must go on as far as Winchester—if you can. If you find a chance to strike a blow do so, without waiting instruction."[29]

---

26. *OR* 43/2:202; Thomas L. Rosser to Betty W. Rosser, October 15, 1864, Thomas L. Rosser Papers, UVA.
27. John S. Mosby to Bob Walker, December 12, 1899, Mitchell, *The Letters of John S. Mosby*, 97–98. One must recall that Rosser and Custer were close friends.
28. Bushong, *Fightin' Tom Rosser*, 114; McDonald, *Laurel Brigade*, 301.
29. Jubal Early to Thomas L. Rosser, October 7, 1864, Thomas Rosser Papers, UVA; Miller, *Decision at Tom's Brook*, 79–80. Early wrote Rosser three messages that day, but only one seems to have reached him.

At dawn on October 7, Rosser's whole command saddled up and began a vigorous pursuit of Sheridan's cavalry. At 3:00 p.m. Rosser's Laurel Brigade horsemen, with Colonel Dulany in the lead, caught up with Custer at Mill Creek. The Federals had posted in force on the opposite bank of the creek. Dulany led about 220 troopers of the 7th Virginia and White's battalion across the stream, but Federal cavalry, consisting primarily of Lt. Col. John Bennett's recently replenished 1st Vermont, soon observed and confronted them. The Union horsemen arrived too late to prevent the crossing, but stood in the way of further advancement. Dulany, however, ordered a frontal charge, with a squadron of the 7th Virginia attacking a Federal flank. The troopers surprised the Federal cavalrymen with their flank attack; the relatively inexperienced Union horsemen fled up the creek until reaching their main body on a hill. Rosser spotted cattle, sheep, and a wagon train belonging to Sheridan just beyond the Federal position. White's battalion charged the Federals on the hill, while Rosser pressed forward with the 11th and 12th Virginia in the front. The Confederate horsemen charged relentlessly, trying to get within sword's distance of their enemy, seeking vengeance as much as victory. The Federals could not withstand the assault and withdrew. Darkness came, and Rosser ceased his pursuit after chasing Custer for almost 25 miles.[30]

Rosser recaptured several hundred head of cattle and sheep in the engagement, as well as several wagons and teams. He also captured several prisoners. On October 8, four Union cavalrymen were caught burning a farmer's barn. Incensed troopers of White's battalion apparently hustled the bluecoats to the road and shot them. Meanwhile, when Rosser tried to return the livestock to the rightful owners, the local populace hailed him with the sobriquet "Savior of the Valley." The press adopted the moniker, and it stuck. Rosser, of course, embraced the nickname and the exaggerated reputation.[31]

After the war, Rosser revealed his feelings about the distinction he noticed between the soldiers who were ordered to burn out farmers and their commander. He stated:

> **The soldiers who were required by Gen. Sheridan to lay waste the beautiful Shenandoah Valley with the torch were brave, good men and were blameless in the part they took, for they only did as they were ordered, and every prisoner seemed heartily ashamed such a cowardly means had been employed in the endeavor to crush a brave people who never declined battle, and who could at**

---

30. *Philadelphia Weekly Times*, March 22, 1884.
31. *Thomas L. Rosser Scrapbook*, Thomas L. Rosser Papers. UVA; *Confederate Veteran*, February, 1909, 53.

all times have been met on the field under the rules and customs of civilized war. Sheridan was retreating before an army, under General Early, much inferior to his own in numbers and equipment, and this wholesale destruction of private property was not a military necessity and Sheridan's boast "that a crow could not fly over the valley without carrying its rations" in the track of his torch was a shameless admission of his cruelty.[32]

Rosser, both brave and blunt, nevertheless became apprehensive about pursuing Custer further; he felt wary about placing increasing distance between his own command and Early's infantry forces. He expressed his concerns by courier to Early, but "Old Jube," presuming Sheridan was leaving the Valley, ordered Rosser to continue the pursuit. Early reported that Lomax was following the Federals on the Valley Pike, and had already past New Market, where the main army encamped. Early figured Sheridan would cross the Blue Ridge Mountains to rejoin Grant's army. He urged Rosser to pursue as far north as Winchester and strike a blow if the opportunity presented itself.[33]

Although apprehensive, Rosser continued following Sheridan and Custer, but he remained mindful that if he went too far north he would be in danger of being cut off from Early's army. Custer withdrew on the Back Road, joining Sheridan on the Valley Pike, while Rosser marched up the Back Road toward Winchester. Scouts then informed Rosser that Sheridan was not leaving the Valley, but instead establishing a strong position at Strasburg. At the same time, scouts reported a large body of Federal cavalry moving from the Valley Pike to the Back Road, intending to cut Rosser off. Rosser quickly backtracked, striking the Federal column at Tom's Brook, six miles south of Strasburg. Making a vigorous saber charge, Rosser's horsemen drove the Federals back across Tom's Brook to Mount Olive, while Rosser established a high position on the Back Road in the vicinity of Coffman's Hill (also known as Spiker's Hill). His 2,500 troopers then bivouacked for the night. Lomax's division of two brigades and a battery of horse artillery, about 1,000 men, bivouacked on both sides of the Valley Pike behind Jordon Run, just south of the hamlet of Tom's Brook.[34]

32. *Thomas L. Rosser Scrapbook*, Thomas L. Rosser Papers. UVA; *Philadelphia Weekly Times*, March 22, 1884.
33. Jubal A. Early to Thomas L. Rosser, October 7, 1864, Thomas L. Rosser Papers, UVA; *Philadelphia Weekly Times*, March 22, 1884.
34. *Thomas L. Rosser Scrapbook*, Thomas L. Rosser Papers. UVA; *Philadelphia Weekly Times*, March 22, 1884. For a discussion of the proper name of the hill, see William J. Miller, *Decision at Tom's Brook: George Custer, Thomas Rosser, and the Joy of the Fight* (El Dorado Hills, CA, 2016), Appendix C.

Sheridan was fed up with Rosser nipping at his heels. Rosser's continuous harassment of Sheridan's rear guard had worn his patience thin. He decided to end Rosser's assaults. Sheridan knew he outnumbered the Confederate horsemen by at least two to one, in addition to having better weapons, equipment, and horses. Starting out at daylight on October 9, Sheridan ordered Torbert: "Finish the 'Savior of the Valley.'" Threateningly, Sheridan told Torbert to "go out there in the morning and whip that Rebel cavalry or get whipped yourself." He also declared to Torbert he would halt his army and personally go to the top of Round Hill to view how his orders were carried out. Torbert got the message—one did not disappoint Sheridan.[35]

Early's army trailed 25 miles in the rear, while Sheridan's army camped on the opposite bank of Rosser at Tom's Brook. The close proximity between the enemies had a sobering effect on Rosser's troopers who had gained some measure of vengeance for Sheridan's burning and plundering. On the evening of October 8, Rosser's horsemen must have wondered what tomorrow would bring, probably unaware they were vastly outnumbered and far from support. Early's orders to Rosser to pursue as far as Winchester, "if you can," certainly left open the possibility of Rosser withdrawing southward in order to close the gap between his command and Early. Rosser, however, convinced himself that if he faced overwhelming Federal forces in the morning, he would be able to safely withdraw—a fatal assumption. Until this point, Rosser had pretty much had his way with the Federal cavalry in the Valley. Rosser's troopers bivouacked overnight on the Back Road south of Tom's Brook, while Lomax's horsemen camped on the Valley Pike near Woodstock, three miles east of Rosser. Unfortunately for Rosser, he had no idea of the Federal cavalry's strength he would soon face on October 9.[36]

The next morning, Merritt's and Custer's divisions, totaling 6,000 horsemen, opposed Rosser's and Lomax's troopers, numbering about 3,500. While many of the Confederate troopers were poorly armed, Federal troopers were well armed with Spencer repeating carbines and rode fresh mounts. Many in Lomax's command had only long rifles, which were exceedingly difficult to handle on horseback, and thus had to fight dismounted.[37]

Merritt's cavalry division, about 3,500 men, had encamped at the base of Round Top Hill at Tom's Brook. Custer's division of two brigades, totaling about 2,500, bivouacked behind Tumbling Run,

35. *OR* 43/1:327, 431; Sheridan, *Personal Memoirs*, 2:56.
36. McDonald, *Laurel Brigade*, 304–5; Longacre, *Lee's Cavalrymen*, 317.
37. Gary W. Gallagher, *The Shenandoah Valley Campaign of 1864* (Chapel Hill, 2006), 146.

northeast of Mount Olive on the Back Road, six miles northwest of Merritt. Torbert planned to bring an overwhelming force against Rosser's division on the Back Road while holding Lomax's troopers at bay with a reinforced brigade on the Valley Pike. Lomax's main battle line, supported by six guns, deployed behind Jordon Run on both sides of the Valley Pike. He dismounted his front line, while maintaining a strong mounted reserve on the Valley Pike.[38]

As Custer, itching for a fight, approached Rosser's position on the Back Road, he recognized his friend from West Point across the way. Private George W. Hunt, 15th New York Volunteer Cavalry, recalled:

> **It was a magnificent place for a cavalry fight. There was room to deploy, smooth ground to ride on; all the rail fences had long ago vanished for soldiers' fires... Out rode Custer from his staff, far in advance of the line, in plain view of both armies. Sweeping off his broad-brimmed hat, he threw it down to his knee in a profound salute to his foe.[39]**

Viewing Custer through field glasses, Rosser returned the gesture, and his men sent up a deafening cheer. Private Hunt described what happened next:

> **Custer replaced his hat, turned to his line of men and the next moment the 3d Division was sweeping on at a trot, the flaming neck tie and bright curls of Custer before all, followed by his staff, all swords out. Now the pace quickens. The rebel guns open at shorter range, bullets and shells whistling over the heads of the men... The trot becomes a gallop, a wild yell from the line and they go racing across the intervening space with waving sabres, the horses wild with excitement as they race for the rebel batteries.[40]**

A few days earlier Rosser had passed a farmer during a brief lull in the fighting. The farmer had handed him a note from Custer who chided his friend for exposing himself to potentially deadly fire on a particular day. The note stated that Custer had observed Rosser and had kept his men from shooting him. Custer had urged Rosser to be more cautious so he would live long enough for Custer to give him a good thrashing. Then the two could get together and laugh about the incident when the war was over. Rosser and Custer seemed to be

---

38. *U.S. Department of the Interior National Park Service, Study of Civil War Sites in the Shenandoah Valley of Virginia*, "Tom's Brook," September 1992.
39. *George W. Hunt Memoir*, George W. Hunt Papers, William L. Clements Library, University of Michigan.
40. Ibid.

Custer Bows to Rosser, on seeing his old friend across Tom's Brook.
October 9, 1864.

Drawing by Alfred Rudolph Waud - Library of Congress

participants in a sort of schoolyard game of one-upping each other. Custer held the poster-boy image of the Union's most dashing and aggressive cavalry officer. Rosser, with the exception of Stuart, appeared to be trying to attain an equivalent status as the South's most flamboyant cavalryman. After Stuart's death in May 1864, the status became more achievable from Rosser's standpoint. It was a contest; neither friend wanted to kill the other, but they wanted fiercely to thrash each other in battle.[41]

At dawn on October 9, Col. Charles Russell Lowell's brigade of Merritt's division advanced to Tom's Brook on the Valley Pike, deployed, and pushed forward a quarter mile to Lomax's main line, and then dismounted behind Jordon Run. Six guns placed on either side of the Valley Pike and a strong mounted reserve supported the Confederate line. While Lowell was engaged, Col. James H. Kidd's brigade of Custer's division rode north along Tom's Brook to connect with Custer. Brigadier General Thomas C. Devin's brigade followed, but veered off on the Harrisville Road, advancing to the vicinity of St. John's Church. Once there, Devin's blue horsemen maintained a connection with the Union force on the Valley Pike. At the same time, they extended a skirmish line to connect with Kidd's brigade on the right.[42]

41. *The Washington Times*, February 8, 1997.
42. *Thomas L. Rosser Scrapbook*, Thomas L. Rosser Papers, UVA;
   Philadelphia Weekly Times, March 22, 1884.

Meanwhile, Rosser dismounted most of his troopers behind Tom's Brook at the base of Coffman's Hill, where they posted amongst stone fences and rudimentary fieldworks. Rosser positioned the brigades from left to right: Munford's on the left, Payne's in the middle, and the Laurel Brigade on the right. Rosser's six guns unlimbered along the crest of Coffman's Hill, slightly behind a second line of barricades. A mounted reserve was maintained on the ridge; mounted skirmishers extended its right toward the Middle Road. Rosser later claimed that White's battalion, which had deployed on Rosser's front and right as skirmishers, charged one of Custer's columns, while the Laurel Brigade drove Custer back across Tom's Brook.[43]

Colonel Munford observed what was happening on the left, and sent for Rosser. When Rosser appeared, demanding to know the problem, Munford informed him Union forces were moving toward them in such numbers that it would be impossible to check them. Arrogantly, Rosser replied, "I'll drive them into Strasburg by ten o'clock." When Munford persisted, warning that the Federals would turn Rosser's left, Rosser angrily retorted, "I'll look out for that." The Federals' approach silenced the conversation.[44]

Custer advanced beyond Mount Olive, pushing forward three regiments of dismounted skirmishers against the main Confederate position. Three other Federal regiments and Col. William Wells's brigade stayed mounted and behind the skirmish line. A Union battery unlimbered on the hill in front of Sand Ridge Church, engaging the Confederate artillery on Coffman's Hill. When Kidd's brigade made contact with Custer's left, Custer extended his right flank along the shoulder of Little North Mountain, supporting the movement with a battery. Kidd positioned his troopers over the hill, driving Rosser's skirmishers before him, and unlimbered another battery to enfilade the Confederate position. The Confederate line gradually fell back into a horseshoe around the front of Coffman's Hill. A regiment of Union cavalry, probably of Devin's brigade, marched on the Middle Road from Harrisville. They topped a hill overlooking Sand Ridge Road, at the intersection of Middle Road and to the right and rear of Rosser's main force. Reacting to this threat, Rosser ordered a withdrawal. The men raced to mount their horses. At this point, Wells's brigade attacked at Coffman's Hill via the Back Road, taking few casualties. Wells encountered Munford's brigade at the crest, and a mounted melee ensued. Rosser's force retreated partly down Back Road to Pugh's Run, and then partially on Sand Ridge and Middle roads toward

---

43. *Philadelphia Weekly Times*, March 22, 1884.
44. SHSP, 13:136.

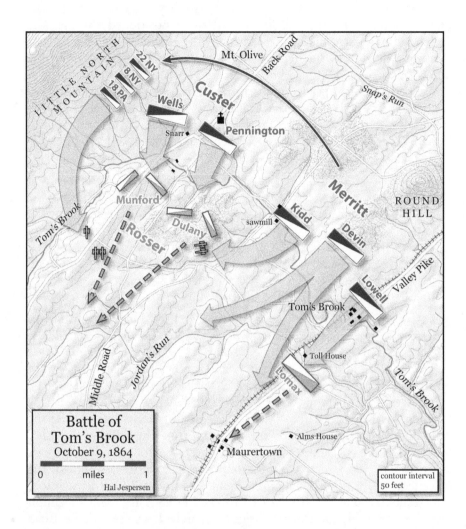

Woodstock. Custer's and Kidd's troopers pursued. Sheridan watched the action from the top of Round Hill.[45]

In the meantime, fighting continued along the Valley Pike. Colonel Charles R. Lowell's 600-man brigade drove Lomax's 800 horsemen back to Jordon Run, deploying on both sides of the pike. Kidd's 1st Michigan Brigade supported Lowell's right flank, while Devin's brigade moved farther to the right along the Middle Road, beyond St. John's Church. As Devin maneuvered, Lomax counter-

45. Jack H. Lepa, *The Shenandoah Valley Campaign of 1864* (Jefferson, NC, 2003), 177.

attacked down the Valley Pike, driving the reserve brigade back to Tom's Brook. Lowell, in turn, attacked until artillery stopped him.[46]

At last, Devin reached a position from which to operate against the flanks of both Lomax and Rosser. He advanced the 9th New York and other elements against Lomax's left and rear, making Lomax's position untenable. The Confederates began to retreat up the pike toward Woodstock. Rosser retreated, losing at least two of his guns at Coffman's Hill. Munford's brigade attempted a stand behind Pugh's Run on the Back Road, but

Colonel Thomas Taylor Munford

Munford and Rosser despised each other and feuded the rest of their lives

Special Collections, University of Virginia

the Federals quickly breached the position. Rosser's cavalry continued a retreat to Columbia Furnace, losing the rest of its artillery and all of its wagons. The Federals captured 150 prisoners during this phase of the retreat. Lomax retreated up the Valley Pike to Woodstock, where a confused portion of Rosser's command joined him. The forces attempted to stand behind Pugh's Run, but soon scattered. Union troopers pressed forward, driving the Confederate cavalry all the way to Mount Jackson, 25 miles away. Lomax lost five pieces of artillery during the rout—two pieces at Woodstock, two at Edinburg, and one beyond Stony Creek. The Union cavalry retired to the vicinity of Woodstock, where it bivouacked for the night.[47]

---

46. Ibid., 148–49; *Philadelphia Weekly Times*, March 22, 1884.
47. Ibid.; Custer estimated he captured 330 prisoners; Lepa, *The Shenandoah Valley Campaign of 1864*, 177.

Rosser hated to lose this fight, claiming it was the first time the Laurel Brigade knew defeat. Merritt and Custer captured more than 300 prisoners and 47 wagons, which included ambulances, caissons, and a battery of artillery, along with the headquarters wagons of Rosser, Lomax, Wickham, and Payne. Rosser claimed, disingenuously, he had lost a battery of artillery, but did not regret it much, for:

I sold it for an excellent prize. It was captured while pouring canister into the ranks of the enemy, and for the sake of performing such service, one can afford to throw away artillery. Many a battle was lost in this war by timid generals who were afraid of losing their artillery and consequently did not expose it to capture. I believe in pushing artillery to the front and using it freely, and if you lose it console yourself with the thought that you could well afford to. And if it was captured fighting you rest assured that its captors paid dearly for it.[48]

Custer also recovered the booty Rosser and Munford had taken from him at Trevilian Station, along with one item Custer particularly prized: Rosser's uniform. He later gave the uniform to his wife, Elizabeth, who apparently presented it to West Point where it is on display at the museum.[49]

Rosser wrote Betty about the defeat at Tom's Brook. "I was completely hemmed in on all sides, and it was with great difficulty that I escaped," he recalled. "I have three regtal [regimental] commanders under arrest for cowardice on this occasion [and] although the troops behaved badly, I think the difficulty was with the officers and they will not do so again."[50]

Brigadier General Bryan Grimes summed up the feelings of disappointment for many infantrymen concerning the cavalry's failure to reverse the trend of defeat for Early's horsemen. Grimes expressed, "There must be something in the atmosphere, or in this valley cavalry for they cause everything to stampede that comes in association with them." In frustration, he remarked, "At least 100 of them ought to have been hanged the next morning."[51]

The disagreement between Rosser and Munford, about Munford's warning to Rosser that he would be flanked, added to the existing acrimony between the two senior officers, which would last until

---

48. *OR* 43/1:521; *Philadelphia Weekly Times*, March 22, 1884; SHSP, 13:139.
49. Ibid.
50. Thomas L. Rosser to Betty W. Rosser, October 10, 1864, Thomas L. Rosser Papers, UVA.
51. Bryan Grimes to his wife, October 10, 1864, Bryan Grimes Papers, SHC; Robert K. Krick, *The Smoothbore Volley That Doomed the Confederacy*, (Baton Rouge, 2002), 211.

Rosser's death in 1910. Munford, resentful of Rosser's promotion to brigadier general while he remained a colonel, criticized Rosser's handling of the division at Tom's Brook. Years later, Munford referred to the fight as "the greatest disaster that ever befell our cavalry during the whole war," and accused Rosser of not reporting its extent to Early. Munford further complained:

> **To make the fight at Tom's Brook was against all the rules of discretion and judgment, and the responsibility belongs to Rosser... It was a trap Sheridan set for him and was successful... We had been incessantly engaged in severe skirmishing; Rosser's head seemed to be completely turned by our success, and in consequence of his rashness, and ignorance of their numbers, we suffered the greatest disaster ever befallen our command, and utterly destroyed the confidence of the officers of my brigade in his judgment—they knew that he could fight and was full of it, but he did not know when to stop, or when to retire.[52]**

Munford claimed, "If Rosser had then retired, as I suggested to him to do, he would have saved his command and his reputation; but pig headed, in he went and ruined his command, losing everything, and then tried to put it off on old Early and two other officers, [Richard W.] Carter and [Henry] Carrington of my Brigade." In another postwar letter, Munford continued his stinging assessment of Rosser: "He is so very unscrupulous and not always truthful, and wants all the glory to himself, and never ought to have any rank than Col. of the 5th Va Cav."[53]

Referring to the battle of Tom's Brook, Lt. Robert T. Hubard of the 3rd Virginia lamented:

> **Under Major General T. L. Rosser, a brave but indifferent officer, our glorious brigade that had never been defeated was subjected to the humiliation and shame of the most disastrous defeat along with the officer's whose command on the 9th of October on upper Cedar Creek. He rushed headlong upon the retreating enemy, some twenty miles ahead of the infantry, leaving his flanks exposed in the most stupid and reckless manner. Our brigade was hemmed in, its entire hospital captured a mile in its rear, while it was fighting in the front and this**

---

52. Driver, *5th Virginia Cavalry*, 90; John T. Phillips to Thomas T. Munford, September 7, 1895, Munford-Ellis Papers, DU.
53. Ibid.

sad news spreading among the men, they broke and fled in confusion... Never was inordinate vanity and conceit more thoroughly punished than in [the] case of this peacock on that occasion.[54]

Sergeant Benjamin J. Haden recalled, "The battle commenced. I said battle, but I will take that back, as there was no battle; for the enemy had nothing to do but drive our skirmish line in and it was all over; as there was nothing in reserve to support anybody or anything. The result was an ignominious rout." Trooper William C. Corson described the fight as "the most complete and disastrous cavalry stampede of the war. We lost our wagons, ambulances and 11 pieces of artillery. The blame rests with Gen. Rosser."[55]

Rosser, looking for scapegoats, blamed Early for the defeat, complaining Early did not have a unified command for the two cavalry divisions. He felt that since Lomax was senior to him, Early should have named Lomax to command the two divisions, allowing him to coordinate the Confederate effort in the same manner as Torbert did on the Federal side. In a letter to Betty, he carped:

Early is the only person that can be censored for the Cav'y disaster. I have all his orders—and they were urging me on all the while—telling me to press on and get in Sheridan's rear and capture his trains, etc. I, at one time, was in his rear and as fortune would have it, an old citizen came to me and informed me that a large Column of Cav'y was coming up in my rear [and] would have been able to destroy me but I rapidly withdrew [and] saved myself—but the next day all the Yankee Cav'y was thrown before me, I was thirty miles from support (Early was at New Market [and] I near Strasburg) and there was no remedy for my loss. I fought my best until whipped! The world may blame me, but Gen Lee cannot.[56]

Embittered at his cavalry's performance, Early reported to Gen. Robert E. Lee, condemning his horsemen as utterly worthless, and added, "It would be better if they could all be put into the infantry;

54. Nanzig, Lt. Robert T. Hubart, Jr., *The Civil War Memoirs of a Virginia Cavalryman*, 201.
55. Sergeant B. J. Haden, *Reminiscences of J. E. B. Stuart's Cavalry* (Palmyra, Virginia, 1993), 35; Robert J. Driver, Jr., *1st Virginia Cavalry* (Lynchburg, VA, 1991), 102; William C. Corson to Jennie, October 13, 1864, William Clark Corson Papers, VHS; Corson, Blake W., Jr., ed., William Clark Corson, *My Dear Jennie: A Collection of Love Letters from a Confederate Soldier to His Fiancee During the Period 1861–1865* (Richmond, 1982), 130.
56. *Thomas L. Rosser Scrapbook*, Thomas L. Rosser Papers, UVA, 1171a.b., Box 2, 26; Thomas L. Rosser to Betty W. Rosser, October 12, 1864, Thomas L. Rosser Papers, UVA.

Major General Jubal Early
Rosser blamed Early for the debacle at Tom's Brook.

Library of Congress

but, if that were tried I am afraid they would all run off." Early also commented, "The Laurel is a running vine."[57]

Rosser published a stunning letter after the war to Early via the press. Concerning the competent but undermanned Early, the letter addressed the issue of whom Rosser thought to blame for the failed Shenandoah Valley campaign:

> I participated in the latter part of your Valley Campaign, and I feel that I not only have the right, but it is my duty, one that I owe to posterity, to explain as far as I am able the cause of the disasters which befell your army in the Valley. Certainly, from the escape of Hunter at Lynchburg to the capture of your little army at Waynesboro, such a series of disasters never occurred in the annals of war. Incompetence is not a crime, and that you failed in the Valley was not due to your neglect or carelessness, for I know you were assiduous, but God did not make you a general, and it was General R. E. Lee's

57. Longacre, *Lee's Cavalrymen*, 317; *OR* 43/1:559; Armstrong, *7th Virginia Cavalry*, 78; McDonald, *Laurel Brigade*, 7.

over-estimate of you, or in other words I may say, it was General R. E. Lee's mistake in trusting so important a command as that you had, to you before you had been fully tried.[58]

Responding to another request for a postwar assessment regarding Early's management of the Valley campaign, Rosser opined: "General J. A. Early is a true patriot; he was energetic, vigilant and brave, but he was unmilitary and lacked enthusiasm, and was utterly unfit to command." Rosser also told a reporter in Minneapolis, Minnesota, that Early should have been hanged for the burning and pillaging of Chambersburg, Pennsylvania. Major General Jubal Early, after a long-running feud with Rosser, called the former cavalryman a "consummate ass" and "falsifier of history," suggesting that Rosser might "emulate Judas Iscariot and consider hanging himself."[59]

Rosser's captured possessions provided Custer with some great amusement. The day after the fiasco at Tom's Brook, Custer, who was considerably smaller in stature than Rosser, donned Rosser's coat and hat, parading in front of his men in the oversized uniform. Displaying his sense of humor, Custer sent Rosser a letter in which he thanked him for providing so many nice gifts, but requested Rosser have his tailor make the coattails of his next uniform somewhat shorter, so it would fit Custer better when he captured it. Rosser and Custer enjoyed bantering back and forth, and Rosser probably saw the humor in Custer's teasing.[60]

In the fight at Tom's Brook Union troopers routed the Confederate cavalry, impairing its morale and efficiency for the remainder of the campaign. Valley residents and victorious Union troopers referred to the Confederates' retreating flight as the "Woodstock Races." Custer boasted, "Never since the opening of this war had there been witnessed such a complete and decisive overthrow of the enemy's cavalry."[61]

Rosser and Custer faced off against each other often. Once, while reconnoitering Union lines in full view of Northern sharpshooters,

58. Thomas L. Rosser to a reporter, March, 1887; Alexander Hunter, *Johnny Reb and Billy Yank* (New York, 1905), 655–59.
59. Thomas L. Rosser to a reporter, March, 1887; Hunter, *Johnny Reb and Billy Yank*, 656; *Springfield Republican*, June 26, 1887; *Wheeling (WV) Register*, June 28; 1887 Newspaper Clippings, no dates or provenance, Jedediah Hotchkiss Papers, LC, Reel 58, Box 70, Frames 436–39; Krick, *The Smoothbore Volley That Doomed the Confederacy*, 203–4; *Springfield Republican*, June 26, 1887; *Wheeling (WV) Register*, June 28, 1887.
60. Gregory J. W. Urwin, *Custer Victorious: the Civil War Battles of General George Armstrong Custer* (Lincoln, Nebraska, 1990), 202.
61. *OR* 43/1:521.

possibly during Custer's attack on Charlottesville, Rosser threw a gray, red-lined cape over his shoulder. Custer, in the Yankee lines, noticed the glow of the bright red in the sunlight, and recognized his friend. He ordered his troops not to fire on the conspicuous Confederate cavalry leader wearing a scarlet-lined cape. The next day Rosser received a note from Custer, which had come through the Yankee lines under a flag of truce. It addressed him as "Tam," a nickname by which his West Point classmates had known him; it read as follows: "Tam, do not expose yourself so. Yesterday I could have killed you."[62]

Rosser sought to rehabilitate his battered reputation. In addition to blaming Early, Rosser heaped his scorn upon Col. Richard Welby Carter of the 1st Virginia and Maj. Henry Carrington of the 3rd Virginia. Carrington was cashiered from the service. Carter had been unable to hold against the initial Federal assault. Rosser pressed charges against Carter for disobedience of orders, leaving his command during the battle, and remaining absent for 24 hours. Court-martialed for cowardice, Carter was convicted and dismissed from the service. Rosser and Early wanted the death sentence, but the court did not oblige. Carter was captured at home and taken to Fort Delaware at Pea Patch Island, on the Delaware River. Carter came from a prominent Virginia family who continued trying, albeit unsuccessfully, to clear his name. Carter's father attacked Rosser as an "unprincipled villain." The court-martial of Carter, one of Munford's regimental commanders, added to Munford's hatred for Rosser. The bitter feelings between the cavalry commanders lasted for the remainder of their lives.[63]

The Battle of Cedar Creek: A Devastating Confederate Defeat, Snatched from the Jaws of Victory

The battle of Cedar Creek was the last major battle of Maj. Gen. Philip Sheridan's 1864 Valley campaign. Cedar Creek is a small stream that rises in the Blue Ridge Mountains; it runs across the Valley, at one point about four miles wide, and pours into the Shenandoah River near Strasburg. It is very crooked and fordable, but its steep banks

62. Story told by Rosser's daughter Mrs. Elliot of Charlottesville. Told in a letter to Rosser's cousin, Mrs. Lucy Rosser Herberick, of Darien, CT; Benjamin Albert Botkin, ed., *A Civil War Treasury of Tales, Legends, and Folklore* (Lincoln, Nebraska, 1960), 580; Brain M. Thomsen, ed., *The Civil War Memoirs of Ulysses S. Grant*, (New York, 2002), 521; Fleming, *West Point*, 187.
63. Krick, *The Smoothbore Volley That Doomed the Confederacy*, 183; Margaret Ann Vogtsberger, *The Dulanys of Welbourne* (Berryville, VA, 1195), 260.

made artillery or wagon crossings difficult, except where a way has been carved out at the fords. Cedar Creek ranks as one of the two largest battles fought in the confines of the Shenandoah Valley. Early's forces consisted of five infantry divisions under command of generals John B. Gordon, Gabriel C. Wharton, Stephen Dodson Ramseur, John Pegram, and Joseph Kershaw, along with Rosser's and Lomax's cavalry divisions, all totaling about 15,265 men. The Federal forces included three infantry corps under major generals Horatio Wright, William Emory, and George Crook, as well as cavalry divisions under Wesley Merritt and George Custer, numbering about 32,000 men.[64]

In an October 12 letter, Robert E. Lee recommended to Early that he move quickly against Sheridan and crush him. General Lee believed Sheridan's infantry and cavalry were not as numerically large as Early thought. Early could either attack or retire to replenish dwindling supplies. Choosing to be aggressive, he planned an assault on forces that were superior to his own, taking advantage of the element of surprise. Examining the Union dispositions behind Cedar Creek, he found an opening. The Union commanders expected an attack across the open Valley floor to the west. Early planned to get his men rapidly across the creek at dawn on the 19th and attack the Union left, rolling up the line and defeating each part in detail.[65]

Shortly before sunrise, Maj. Gen. John B. Gordon, under the cover of a dense fog, struck and surprised Maj. Gen. George Crook's VIII Corps, sending it into retreat. Gordon and Maj. Gen. Joseph B. Kershaw, joining the attack from the west, next routed Maj. Gen. William Emory's XIX Corps. The Confederate assault moved so rapidly that the Federals had little time to prepare, forcing their retreat. Confederate artillery across Cedar Creek bombarded the Union flank. Wright's VI Corps, last in the Union line and forced to fight a defensive battle, withdrew slowly under substantial Confederate pressure.[66]

Meanwhile, Confederate artillery massed on the Valley Pike south of Strasburg to await developments of the attack. Early's orders specified that Rosser, with two brigades and horse artillery, would "occupy the enemy's cavalry," while Early's infantry would charge the enemy's opposite flank. Rosser was not involved in the main assault, which was three and half miles east, near the Valley Pike. Rosser's cavalry, greatly outnumbered, advanced cautiously on the Back Road

---

64. Wert, *From Winchester to Cedar Creek*, 214–16.

65. Robert E. Lee to Jubal Early, October 12, 1864, *OR* 43/2:892.

66. Colonel Benjamin W. Crowninshield, "The Battle of Cedar Creek, October 19, 1864, A Paper Read Before the Massachusetts Historical Society," (Cambridge, MA, 1879), 14–25.

to Cupp's Ford on the west side of the Valley, seeking a diversionary attack on any Federal cavalry in the area. Early sent orders for Lomax's cavalry to move up the Front Royal-Winchester Road and then to cross over to the Valley Pike in the vicinity of New Town. Lomax would interdict any Federal trains and any withdrawals. However, Lomax never received Early's order, and he failed to advance. Brigadier General William H. Payne's small cavalry brigade accompanied Gordon on a planned attack of Sheridan's headquarters at Belle Grove.[67]

Rosser's command, with his and Wickham's brigades, crossed Cedar Creek before daylight, assaulting pickets of the 7th Michigan. Colonel Oliver Funsten commanded the Laurel Brigade. Colonel Thomas H. Owen of the 3rd Virginia led Wickham's dismounted brigade. Rosser advanced after some hard fighting, which Owen's dismounted troopers primarily accomplished. The Confederate horsemen drove the Federals from their camp on the left bank of the creek, forcing them to abandon their killed and wounded. Soon the remainder of Col. James Kidd's Michigan brigade came to the support of the 7th Michigan. Custer's and Lowell's cavalries arrived as additional support for Kidd. Rosser halted, and then retired in the face of the greatly superior force of Union cavalry.[68]

Early routed Sheridan's VIII and XIX Corps infantry in the early phase of the main fight, pressing forward on their exposed left and driving the foot soldiers in confusion down the Valley Turnpike toward New Town. The Federal VI Corps tried to slow Early's onslaught, finally checking the Confederate advance. Uncharacteristically, Early failed to press the attack. For the next several hours a prolonged lull in the fighting happened. Starving Confederates stopped to eat in the camps from which they had just driven the Union soldiers, thus losing their momentum. This pause to fill drawn and empty stomachs gave the Northerners time to regroup. Some Confederate troopers, tired from the morning's work, dismounted and slept. Others gathered shoes from dead soldiers. After the Federal infantry suffered a rout on their left flank, Torbert sent the majority of his cavalry to reinforce the position, leaving only a few cavalry regiments in Rosser's front. Neither Early nor Rosser

67. Donald Silvius, "The Battle of Cedar Creek: The Beginning of the End," *An Appalachian Country Rag*, December 19, 1997; Jeffrey D. Wert, *From Winchester to Cedar Creek: The Shenandoah Campaign of 1864*, (New York, 1987), 213.
68. McDonald, *Laurel Brigade*, 310–11; *Philadelphia Weekly Times*, March 22, 1884; Armstrong, *7th Virginia Cavalry*, 78; Jonathan A. Noyalas, *The Battle of Cedar Creek: Victory from the Jaws of Defeat* (Charleston, SC, 2009), 34.

discerned Torbert's shift of troopers; both men remained convinced that a large Union cavalry force loomed in Rosser's front.[69]

At 3:00 p.m. Union artillery in Rosser's front interrupted the peaceful interlude. The Federal horsemen marched forward menacingly. Confusion among the Confederates ensued. Rosser, assuming he would soon face Custer's entire cavalry, ordered his two brigades to fall back. Colonel Funsten attempted to withdraw in good order, but in the confusion resulting from artillery fire, some of his troopers broke ranks and ran. Seeing the disorder, a column of Federal cavalry launched a spirited charge. One 3rd Virginia trooper wrote:

> **Our men scattered through the deserted camps to plunder... and before we knew it the enemy had rallied and got in our rear. One regiment gave way and then a general stampede commenced, our men running in squads of from 2 to 10, leaving artillery, wagons, ambulances, and everything behind.[70]**

Major E. H. McDonald, commanding the 11th Virginia, fearing a panic might ensue, formed a battle line of about 50 troopers, and attacked obliquely to flank the approaching Federal column. Realistically, McDonald's little band should have been captured; they were alone, their division was falling back, and the large Federal column was attacking in front of them. The small battle line surprised the Federal column, and the front came to a stop, forcing the rest of the column to stop in haste, as well as causing some confusion in the order. The small detachment of the 11th Virginia pressed the startled Federals, forcing them to retreat over a hill where Union artillery had been placed.[71]

Rosser then moved his division across Cedar Creek. Sheridan, about 12 miles away at Winchester, after returning the previous evening from a conference in Washington, D.C., hurried to the battlefield to rally his broken troops. Later in the evening his infantry routed Early, while Rosser held the Back Road against Custer's cavalry. After dark, Early ordered Funsten to hold the infantry trenches at Fisher's Hill, where the Laurel Brigade spent the night. In the morning the Laurel Brigade formed the rear guard of Early's retreating army. The Federals, content with victory, made a feeble pursuit.[72]

---

69. McDonald, *Laurel Brigade*, 311; Armstrong, *7th Virginia Cavalry*, 78.
70. McDonald, *Laurel Brigade*, 311; Armstrong, *7th Virginia Cavalry*, 78–79; William C. Corson to Jennie, October 23, 1864, William C, Corson Letters, VHS; Corson, *Dear Jennie*, 132.
71. McDonald, *Laurel Brigade*, 312.
72. McDonald, *Laurel Brigade*, 312; Armstrong, *7th Virginia Cavalry*, 79.

In terms of casualties during the 1864 Shenandoah Valley campaign, the battle of Cedar Creek ranks only second to the Third Battle of Winchester of September 19, 1864. Casualties numbered 2,910 (320 killed, 1,540 wounded, and 1,050 missing) for the Confederates and 5,665 (644 killed, 3,430 wounded, and 1,591 missing) for the Federals. The Union cavalry captured 43 cannons, more than 200 wagons, and many prisoners. The Confederates lost at least 10 battle flags, suggesting the progressive disintegration of the army.[73]

Cedar Creek dealt a crushing blow to the Confederacy in the Shenandoah Valley. Rarely have the scales of victory and defeat swung to such extremes during a battle. The overwhelming Federal forces and good generalship transformed the Confederate's brilliant morning success into a Union victory by day's end. But even without that fatal respite in the morning, the Confederates probably would have had little chance to carry the day. Early's hungry, ill-supplied troops lacked staying power, and by the end of the day, the Federals drove them from the field.[74]

Rosser described the battle at Cedar Creek: "The sun never rose on a more glorious victory or set on a more inglorious defeat. Had ... the fight continued ... as it was gloriously begun, Sheridan's ride (reference to the poem) of twenty miles away would never have been sung."[75]

About three miles south of Edinburg, the Laurel Brigade's 1,400 troopers went into camp. For the next three weeks they formed part of Early's line on Stony Creek. In spite of the defeat at Cedar Creek, Early reorganized his beaten army, preparing for the next fight. The command instituted more rigorous discipline, especially for the cavalry, which underwent numerous reviews and inspections.[76]

Rosser Resumes Raids

Rosser, dejected by the recent defeat at Cedar Creek, worried people would no longer see him as the "Savior of the Valley," the moniker he had enthusiastically adopted. He hoped recent setbacks would not cost him that distinction. The leg wound he had received at the battle of Trevilian Station still bothered him, and on October 15 he

73. *OR* 43/1:137; Jeffrey D. Wert, *From Winchester to Cedar Creek: The Shenandoah Campaign of 1864* (New York, 1987), 246.
74. John Brown Gordon, *Reminiscences of the Civil War* (New York, 1904), 361. Thomas Buchanan Read wrote a famous poem entitled "Sheridan's Ride," describing Sheridan's ride from Winchester to rally his troopers retreating from Cedar Creek.
75. Ibid.
76. McDonald, *Laurel Brigade*, 313.

Brig. Gen. Thomas Lafayette Rosser

Promoted to Major General on Nov. 1, 1864. Photo by E. and H. T. Anthony, New York

Albert and Shirley Small Special Collections Library, University of Virginia

wrote Betty that he suffered greatly from it. The wound had closed, but it had formed an abscess, necessitating it cut opened and drained. He wanted to take a few days leave, but he worried no one had sufficient experience to take his place commanding the division.[77]

Rosser also became concerned about the arrests he had demanded of three regimental commanders for cowardice after Tom's Brook. He now realized these commanders had their own supporters, and his popularity would inevitably suffer. Furthermore, he worried about the condition of his men and horses. He wrote there was no food for the men and no forage for the horses, and the people of the Valley were starving. Despondent, he wrote Betty of his dissatisfaction. In reply, she encouraged him to resign from the army. He quickly rejected the suggestion, informing Betty that if he quit he would be conscripted as an enlisted man and in a far worse situation. It appears he sought her sympathy, but not her advice.[78]

During this period of reflection, Rosser promised Betty, yet another time, never again to drink, and claimed he was happy about his decision to become a Christian. He even expressed his belief that no man who drinks can be a Christian. He said that since he quit he felt satisfied and happier than he had ever been. Rosser, a fun-loving

---

77. Bushong, *Fightin' Tom Rosser*, 142; Thomas L. Rosser to Betty W. Rosser, October 15, 1864, Thomas L. Rosser Papers, UVA.
78. Thomas L. Rosser to Betty W. Rosser, October 15, 1864, Thomas L. Rosser Papers, UVA.

man, socialized with the top echelon of officers. Giving up drinking must have been a difficult challenge.[79]

One reason Rosser's mood had lightened probably had to do with the fact that Jubal Early, Wade Hampton, and Robert E. Lee had recommended him for promotion. His long-awaited promotion to major general came through on November 4, 1864, to rank November 1. The Confederate Senate, however, did not confirm the promotion until February 20, 1865. Regardless, Early put Rosser in charge of all of the cavalry in the Valley.[80]

Rosser, after his recent promotion, relinquished command of the Laurel Brigade, urging his friend Brig. Gen. James Dearing to apply for the post, inheriting the prestige that went with it. Extremely interested, Dearing planned to discuss it immediately with Hampton. A few days later, Hampton conferred with Robert E. Lee about the appointment. Dearing wrote Rosser that Lee would have difficulty "getting around promoting old [Dennis] Ferebee and [Joel] Griffin. Ferebee's congressman are trying to have him promoted." Frustrated, the aggressive Dearing asked Rosser to write Hampton and Lee again, urging his promotion. Dearing did not attain command of the Laurel Brigade until the Appomattox campaign. In the meantime, he continued to lead another cavalry brigade, consisting of the 8th Georgia Cavalry, 4th and 65th North Carolina cavalry regiments, 7th Confederate Cavalry, and 16th North Carolina Battalion. For the time being, Col. Richard H. Dulany commanded the Laurel Brigade.[81]

After observing what he believed to be a breakdown in discipline, on October 22, 1864, Rosser issued General Orders, stating: "The want of discipline has been the cause of additional disaster to this army. Organizations have been broken up on the Battle Field for the purpose of plundering, and the fruits of victory lost by inefficiency and neglect on the part of Company Officers." He instituted stern measures, including three rollcalls a day. No officer or enlisted man could sleep out of camp without a surgeon's certificate requiring it for health. Anyone found outside of camp limits would be arrested and court-martialed. The company commander, with the approval of the

79. Ibid.
80. Freeman, *Lee's Lieutenants*, 3:668; Robert E. Lee to Secretary of War James A. Seddon, October 31, 1864, Rosser's Service Record for Generals and Staff Officers, NA; *Journal of the Congress of the Confederate States of America, 1861–1865* (Washington, D.C., 1904), IV:350.
81. James Dearing to Thomas L. Rosser, November 24 and 26, 1864, Dearing Family Papers, Albert and Shirley Small Special Collections Library, UVA; William L. Parker, *General James Dearing, CSA* (Lynchburg, VA, 1990), 84.

regimental commander, would make all applications for "horse details." Anyone who brought back an unfit horse would not be allowed to return for another.[82]

Rosser had failed to improve the cavalry's performance in the Valley. With sinking morale and his crackdown on discipline, the troopers commenced to complain. Captain Franklin M. Myers, of the 35th Cavalry Battalion, noted:

> We have fought hard and faithfully and lost heavily, but I can't see why we should have done so. My bright dream that Rosser was one of the finest cavalry Generals in our service is gone. He is no General at all. As brave a man who ever drew a breath, but knows no more about putting a command into a fight than a school boy. We have lost confidence in him so fast that he can't get a good fight out of us anymore.[83]

Another complaining trooper, Mark T. Alexander, wrote from Rosser's camp on November 15:

> There has been quite a commotion at headquarters since the orders for sending back all able-bodied men. Rosser has sent back companies all of Fitz Lee's HdQts thereby treating him very discourteously to say the least of it. He has around him a set of men who would black his boots if necessary. He is extremely unpopular with the Division, they having been whipped in every fight since he has been with us, they say by his bad management. There will be a universal shout of delight when Gen [Fitz] Lee gets back.[84]

One soldier recalled that Rosser was "a dashing and adventurous officer, but in my humble opinion, lacking sometimes in that poise and judgment so essential to the best results in a campaign." And yet another wrote, "Rosser is a very good officer, I expect, but he cannot hold a candle to Genl. [Fitz] Lee."[85]

Quartermaster Daniel C. Snyder, 11th Virginia, exemplified the sinking morale of the Confederate soldiers and citizens in the Valley.

82. Thomas L. Rosser Papers, Broadside, General Orders, UVA.
83. Franklin M. Myers to "Home Folks," May 16, 1864, Frank M. Myers Papers, *Civil War Times Illustrated Collection*, USMHI, Carlisle, PA.
84. Mark T. Alexander to his mother, Sally Park (Turner) Alexander, November 15, 1864, Mark Alexander Papers, Special Collections, Earl Gregg Swem Library, College of William and Mary, Williamsburg, VA;
85. Randolph Harrison McKim, *A Soldier's Recollections*, (Norwood, MA, 1921), 243. McKim served as chaplain to Thomas T. Munford's Brigade; Letter dated November 17, 1864, Charles Minnigerode Papers, 1861-1886, Pearce Civil War Collection, Navarro College, Corsicana, Texas.

Snyder appealed to a "just God," and could not believe "that He will permit such a race of men to subjugate and destroy a people fighting for all that is dear to enlightened freemen." Snyder described the Valley region as a world apart from the year before when its supplies were plentiful. "You can form no idea of how scarce everything is," he warned, "and how much suffering must result the coming winter from the scarcity." Snyder disdained conditions in the army, saying, "Qualification for office [in the army] now seems to be that of whiskey drinking, swearing, deceitfulness and anything else calculated to deceive and take advantage."[86]

Responding to Early's urgent call for reinforcements in the Valley, Gen. George Cosby's brigade of Kentucky cavalry was reassigned to the Shenandoah Valley. Early ordered Cosby's Kentuckians to join Lomax's command in the Luray Valley. Cosby's troopers crossed a mountain and marched through Kershaw's infantry. Generals John B. Gordon and John Pegram were camped near New Market. The Federals were then near Strasburg, some 20 miles distant. At the top of the mountain, on October 29, Cosby's horsemen met troopers of Rosser's Laurel Brigade, "most of them drunk." Brandy was plentiful and cheap in the Valley and practically the only thing that could be purchased. Captain Edward O. Guerrant, of Cosby's brigade, wished "every still house in Va. and the Confederacy was burnt to the ground. The Yankees won't burn them."[87]

Capture of New Creek (Keyser, West Virginia)

The ever-present shortage of food and forage demanded some sort of action. On November 20 Rosser's quartermaster informed him that it would be impossible to feed the horses longer than another week. Rosser knew he needed to act immediately, and asked Early if he could proceed west where his scouts had informed him there was food aplenty. Early approved the request, and Rosser instructed his quartermaster to assemble and ready for travel everything that could

86. D. C. Snyder to wife, October 26 and 31, November 12, December 14,1864, D. C. Snyder Letters, VHS; William G. Thomas, *Nothing Ought to Astonish Us: Confederate Civilians in the 1864 Shenandoah Valley Campaign* (Lincoln, Nebraska, 2006). This paper is posted at Digital Commons @ University of Nebraska - Lincoln. http://digitalcommons@unl.edu/historyfacpub/48. Published in Gary W. Gallagher, ed., *The Shenandoah Valley Campaign of 1864* (Chapel Hill, 2006), 249.
87. William C. David and Meredith L. Swentor, eds., *Bluegrass Confederate: The Headquarters Diary of Edward O. Guerrant* (Baton Rouge, 1999), 565.

carry rations. He took the Laurel Brigade and Brig. Gen. William H. Payne's brigade on the expedition, along with his chief of artillery, Maj. James Breathed.[88]

The poor condition of the horses allowed the two brigades to muster only about 600 effectives, plus some artillerists. They left camp at Timberlake, eight miles south of New Market, on November 26. They passed through Brock's Gap in the Great North Mountains before reaching Matthias on the Lost River, where they camped. The next day they proceeded to near Moorefield, West Virginia, where they halted to rest and feed about 1:00 p.m. Rosser, with Company F of the 7th Virginia, continued on to Moorefield. Arriving, he learned from scout leader Capt. Jesse McNeill that a small Federal force encamped at nearby Old Fields. General Rosser decided to capture them, and moved off with about 75 troopers from McNeill's Rangers and Company F of the 7th Virginia. He sent word for the rest of his command to join him.[89]

Rosser's ultimate objective was the New Creek Depot on the Baltimore and Ohio Railroad. New Creek was located on the south side of the Potomac River at the foot of the Allegheny Mountains, about 20 miles west of Cumberland, Maryland. It had a railroad station, two forts, roughly 20 houses, and a population of about 200. The Union used New Creek for storage of food, forage, and ammunition for its soldiers in Hardy and Hampshire counties. Confederate cavalry had made two previous attempts to raid the post, but both had failed.[90]

Fort Kelley was the main fort defending New Creek. Surrounded by a trench about 12 feet high and 12 feet wide, the work provided a two-mile view up New Creek Valley. Brevet. Major General Benjamin F. Kelley commanded the fort of his namesake. Colonel George R. Latham of the 6th West Virginia led the Federal cavalry. Latham had about 987 soldiers, including 215 artillerists and about 52 infantrymen.[91]

Hoping to conceal his approach to New Creek, Rosser ordered McNeill's squadron and Company F of the 7th Virginia to picket the roads north of Moorefield. He also sent out two scouts to spy on the camp and draw a map of the fortifications. Rosser knew his only hope of capturing New Creek lay in the element of surprise. The people

88. McDonald, *Laurel Brigade*, 321.
89. *Philadelphia Weekly Times*, April 5, 1884; Frances Haselberger, "General Rosser's Raid on the New Creek Depot," *West Virginia History: Quarterly Magazine*, XXVI, No. 2, Jan., 1956, 88–89.
90. Frances Haselberger, "General Rosser's Raid on the New Creek Depot," 88.
91. Ibid., 89–90.

living in the area were Unionists who would inform Latham of Rosser's presence, if discovered. One of the picket squadrons was assigned to Parson's Ford, three miles north of Moorefield, where the main road between Moorefield and New Creek crossed the south branch of the Potomac River. A squadron of Federal cavalry, the advance of the 5th and 6th West Virginia, and a section of Capt. J. O'Rourke's battery, all under Lt. Col. R. E. Fleming, were intent on capturing or destroying McNeill's command. Fleming, hoping to "bag" McNeill, had sent another force through Romney, West Virginia, to enter Moorefield from the east on the Winchester Road.[92]

Unaware of Fleming's trap, McNeill proceeded cautiously along a hidden ridge toward the ford. When McNeill's troopers finally appeared, Federal cavalry fired upon them from a bluff on the opposite bank. Unable to withstand the withering fire, McNeill led his troopers down the river, thus outflanking the dismounted Union horsemen. He led his men across the ford, and started to engage the Federals, who fled in order to avoid being cut off. McNeill's gray-clad men pursued the fleeing Federal cavalry, and even though some of them escaped to warn Latham, the Confederates captured 20 prisoners, some horses, a wagon, an ambulance, and an artillery piece.[93]

When Rosser learned of the fight near Moorefield on November 27, he knew the Federals would be alerted to his presence and the threat on New Creek. It was essential he strike quickly, as Latham was preparing for the defense of the fort. Rosser ordered a night march from Moorefield to New Creek. He proceeded via the Allegheny and Moorefield Turnpike to the head of Patterson Creek, before continuing to the Northwestern Turnpike. He then advanced to Harrison's Gap at Knobly Mountain, approximately six miles from New Creek. It was daylight, and he knew he had been detected. Some of his officers advised abandoning the expedition, but Rosser did not want to return to the Shenandoah Valley without capturing New Creek. Although the Federals knew his whereabouts, he refused to avoid this fight.[94]

Payne requested to lead the assault on the fort, and Rosser agreed. Payne learned from an area resident that a Union scouting party would return back to the fort soon. Using this knowledge to his advantage, Payne hoped that when he advanced to attack the Federals would think it was Maj. Peter J. Potts's returning scouts. Payne ordered 5th Virginia Capt. F. Fitzhugh to put captured Federal overcoats on 20 troopers of

---

92. *Confederate Veteran*, vol. 26, No. 8:350; *Philadelphia Weekly Times*, April 5, 1884.
93. *Confederate Veteran*, vol. 26, No. 8:350; *OR* 46/1:660.
94. Frances Haselberger, "General Rosser's Raid on the New Creek Depot," 95–96.

Capt. R. G. Bourne's Company C of the 8th Virginia, and then approach the fort. The disguised Confederate troopers approached the Federal pickets by walking in a friendly manner. The ruse worked perfectly. Incognito, the men passed nearby residents and even a scouting party, all of whom the Confederate horsemen captured when they followed the disguised men on foot. The pickets were captured in the same manner, without firing a shot.[95]

Payne continued toward Fort Kelley with the 5th, 6th, and 8th Virginia regiments. He sent Maj. William H. McDonald and the 11th Virginia half of a mile to the east side of the fort to sever the telegraph line to Cumberland, West Virginia, and then rejoin his command. With the 6th Virginia in the lead, Payne's troopers approached and entered the fort without difficulty. Courier Clinton Gallaher recalled, "It was raining, and it was a dark and misty morning and when too late they discovered their fatal mistake and every man of them was captured and very quietly too." Many of the garrison's soldiers, resting or eating lunch, were taken completely by surprise. After putting up token resistance, they surrendered. Gallaher remembered he obtained a new wardrobe from the captured stores, recalling, "I got a sutler's trunk and found it full of nice clothing, notably fine woolen outside shirts, a fine pair of trousers, which after the war I wore and called my 'New Creek Pants.'"[96]

While Payne was assaulting the fort, Rosser led his 5th Virginia down the road to take Church Hill, where Col. James A. Mulligan's battery of artillery had posted. A short bluff concealed their approach, and before the horsemen knew it, they were upon the Federal artillerists. Only one piece was readied for fire, and Major Breathed cut the lone artillerist down with his saber. The garrison, numbering about 1,000 men, was so surprised and panic stricken that they fled en masse toward New Creek. Most of the roughly 800 fleeing soldiers, along with 400 horses, were captured, but some, including Colonel Latham, escaped across the river. Rosser destroyed the guns at the fort, and took four of Mulligan's artillery pieces in tow.[97]

The Confederates now took time to enjoy the spoils of victory. Since Payne had led the attack on the fort, his troopers fed first and loaded up with goods from the stores. Rosser's horsemen then took their turn. There was plenty for all: tons of flour, meat, molasses, sugar

95. Ibid., 98.
96. Diary of DeWitt Clinton Gallaher: 1864–1865, Valley Personal Papers, AD1000, UVA; Frances Haselberger, "General Rosser's Raid on the New Creek Depot," 96–98; OR 43/1:656–57.
97. *OR* 43/1:669; Haselberger, "General Rosser's Raid on the New Creek Depot," 99.

coffee, liquor, and munitions. The troopers also took large amounts of clothing, garrison equipment, 167 horses, 40 mules, 700 prisoners (almost half of whom escaped because there were not enough Confederates to adequately guard them), eight artillery pieces, and forage. The Confederate troopers enjoyed their first good meal in a long time. Rosser's Confederates had accomplished a stunning victory, having lost only two killed and one or two wounded. Kelley estimated Federal material losses at about $150,000. When Sheridan learned of the loss at New Creek, he seethed and instituted angry recriminations, including the court-martial of Latham.[98]

Rosser, not content with his rich bounty and success, sent McDonald and 300 men of the 11th Virginia to destroy the machine shops of the B&O Railroad. McDonald accomplished his mission despite resistance from Federal forces, and then his troopers withdrew through the mountains.[99]

Rosser sent his prisoners and captured wagons ahead, and then started back with the rest of his command. He returned by way of Petersburg, though not by the way he had initially come through Moorefield. His foraging parties took advantage of the march up New Creek to gather cattle and sheep. The rich bounty would be a welcome sight to Early's hungry army. Upon returning to the Valley on December 2, the Confederate horsemen went into camp at Timberville.[100]

Back in the Valley, Dr. Harvey Black, visiting Dr. Hunter McGuire (who had been chief surgeon of Stonewall Jackson's corps, and then served with Early in the Shenandoah Valley), relayed a story he had heard about the New Creek raid:

> **As they were coming back, one fellow had bundles all around him. He was trotting along when a bolt of calico came loose and spun out along the road nearly its full length before he saw it. Genl. Rosser came along about this time and ordered the command to "Close up." The poor fellow said most imploringly, "Oh General, do let me wind up my calico. I have but one shirt in the world and that on my back, and I want to take just this little piece along to have me a couple made." The Genl. said, "Why bless my soul. You have nearly enough for your whole regt." They had a lively time of it.**[101]

98. *OR* 43/1:656–57, 43/2:692; 46/1:82, 667–70; Haselberger, "General Rosser's Raid on the New Creek Depot," 101–103.
99. *OR* 43/1:667–68; Haselberger, "General Rosser's Raid on the New Creek Depot," 103.
100. Ibid.
101. Glenn L. McMullen, ed., Dr. Harvey Black to his wife, December 4, 1864, *The Civil War Letters of Dr. Harvey Black* (Baltimore, 1995), 102.

The expedition to capture New Creek pleased Gen. Robert E. Lee, who wrote, "So well were General Rosser's measures taken, and so skillfully executed, that the enemy's pickets were captured and the fort charged before the presence of our troops was known... This expedition was conducted with great skill and boldness, and reflects great credit upon General Rosser and the officers and men of his command." Jubal Early also felt well pleased with the results of Rosser's raid on New Creek. A surgeon visiting with Early remarked in a letter to his wife, "General Early is now in a delightful humor—made so by Rosser's capture of New Creek. I was in his company for a couple of hours while at [Hunter] McGuire's, [and] he was almost amiable."[102]

Early's mood toward Rosser would change when their animus shortly resumed. Rosser assailed anyone who got in his way; they became another on his list of foes. On December 14 he wrote Betty complaining.Early would not allow him to visit her in Staunton. "I fear that I will have great difficulty with General Early this winter about indulgences and the like—he is so perverse and mean. He ... remarked that he had always had great difficulty with Army women—and is very much opposed to my coming to see you," Rosser penned.[103]

Battle at Lacey Springs

On December 16, Early broke camp at New Market, and moved his army to the vicinity of Staunton in order to be near the Virginia Central Railroad. Rosser marched his command to the area of Swope's Depot, seven miles west of Staunton. It was getting too cold for the infantry to make major movements, and Early hoped to settle into winter quarters. The winter would be a bitterly cold one, and the Confederates direly needed food, forage, and warm clothes. Beset by misery, the numbers of troops dwindled. With permission, many troopers went home to seek fresh horses, while others took "French leave." Those who remained looked forward to some rest after the exhausting campaigns. Sheridan, however, was not quite through with his work.[104]

---

102. *OR* 43/1:668; Dr. Harvey Black to his wife, December 3, 1864, McMullen, *The Civil War Letters of Dr. Harvey Black*, 102.
103. Thomas L. Rosser to Betty W. Rosser, December 14, 1864, Thomas L. Rosser Papers, UVA.
104. McDonald, *Laurel Brigade*, 331. Soldiers took "French leave" when absenting themselves for a few days or longer in order to visit friends and family. The term comes from an eighteenth-century French custom of leaving a reception without saying a formal goodbye to the host or hostess.

On December 19 Custer's division, 3,000 strong, marched from Winchester toward Staunton. At Grant's urging, Sheridan planned to raid the Virginia Central Railroad. His main body of Brigadier General Merritt's and Colonel Powell's divisions crossed the Blue Ridge Mountains at Chester's Gap, heading for Charlottesville. Custer would proceed to Staunton and keep Early occupied.[105]

Early learned of the Federal advance from his signal corps on December 20. The Confederate commander moved Gen. Gabriel C. Wharton's division in a hailstorm toward Harrisonburg. He ordered Rosser to summon all the cavalry he could gather and hasten to the front. Rosser gathered everyone on hand, including Payne's brigade, and pushed them through mud and rain toward Harrisonburg, where he found no forage after arriving about 10:00 p.m. After resting only three hours, the weary troopers mounted their jaded and half-starved horses, and Rosser's command moved out to oppose the Federals.[106]

Custer had camped the evening of December 20 at Lacey Springs, just north of Harrisonburg. His 3,000 troopers, well-mounted and fed, confidently expected a restful night before having to fight and defeat the Confederate horsemen. With fewer than 600 horsemen Rosser knew he would have to surprise Custer, whom he was anxious to face, in order to defeat him. On approach, a rain shower worsened the muddy roads, and a stiff wind froze them solid, making travel miserable. The troopers soon became coated with ice, and the frost-covered horses assumed a ghostly appearance. The column followed the Middle Road; at Krotzer's Spring it turned east toward Lacey Springs.[107]

Approaching Custer's camp, Payne and Rosser rode forward to reconnoiter. The site of the numerous Union campfires told Rosser it would be impossible with his small force to surprise the entire camp. However, Rosser had no alternative; he had to try to surprise Custer. Returning to their nearly frozen men, Rosser and Payne silently led the column "down on the half-sleeping foe like an avalanche."[108]

Surprised, the closest Federals scattered, but more distant ones, hearing gunfire, mounted up for a fight. A short skirmish ensued in which the Confederates bested Custer's horsemen, sending them in retreat down the Valley. After pursuing a short distance, Rosser thought the better of it and turned toward Staunton. He had chased Custer off, although outnumbered about four to one. Custer reported

105. Ibid., 331–32.
106. Armstrong, *7th Virginia Cavalry*, 82.
107. *Philadelphia Weekly Times*, April 5, 1884.
108. Ibid.

the fight occurred before daylight and 230 of his troopers suffered from frostbite.[109]

Before heading back to Harrisonburg, Rosser and staff officers Charles Minnigerode, Robert M. Mason, Archie Randolph, and Francis Dawson were alone following the rapid withdrawal of Rosser's troopers. Rosser suggested that the five of them proceed down the turnpike to find out what Custer was doing. They followed Custer's rear guard at a respectable distance. Suddenly, they spotted 30 to 40 men approaching from several hundred yards away. Rosser thought they were Confederate cavalry, but as they drew nearer, all realized they were Union troopers. Dawson recalled:

> **The imperturbable Rosser remarked very serenely: "Well, Dawson, you are right; those fellows are Yankees, but there are not many of them. Let's charge them." And we four [five] did charge them; and, to our amazement and relief, the Yankees put spurs to their horses and galloped off down the Valley. As often happens in war, audacity had saved us. Nothing would have been easier for those Yankees than to have gathered us in, for we were half frozen, and our horses were worn out with hard riding.[110]**

Custer failed to get within 40 miles of Staunton, so Early had Wharton's division return there. On December 23 he sent a portion of Wharton's division by rail to Charlottesville. That same day, Early ordered Rosser to the same destination. Rosser marched through Rock Fish Gap, and the next morning arrived in the vicinity of Charlottesville where he learned the Federals had returned to Staunton. After a day's rest, Rosser marched his command back to Swope's Depot, arriving on December 26.[111]

On December 27 Rosser went to Hanover and returned with Betty and their baby to the Gallaher home as guests. They remained for some time with the Gallahers, the Rossers' family friends. Rosser took Betty and their daughter to Swope's Depot for a visit on December 31. The year ended on a happy note for the general and his family.[112]

109. Trout, Galloping Thunder, 317; OR 43/1:38–39, 825; Philadelphia Weekly Times, April 5, 1884.
110. Francis Warrington Dawson, *Reminiscences of Confederate Service, 1861–1865* (Baton Rouge, 1980), 138.
111. McDonald, *Laurel Brigade*, 333–34; Armstrong, *7th Virginia Cavalry*, 83.
112. Diary of DeWitt Clinton Gallaher: 1864–1865, Valley Personal Papers, AD1000, UVA.

CHAPTER 8

1865: Rosser's Raid on Beverly, West Virginia, the Appomattox Campaign, and the War Ends

"I want these to be put on his [Elijah V. White's] coat."
-General James Dearing,
before dying after the battle of High Bridge, requested Rosser present his brigadier's stars to Elijah White.

1865 would bring the close of the horrific Civil War. After the Confederate fiasco at the battle of Five Forks on April 1, 1865, the Confederacy lost Petersburg and Richmond. The war shifted westward as Lt. Gen. Ulysses S. Grant pursued Gen. Robert E. Lee's army to Appomattox Court House, where Lee surrendered to Grant on April 9, 1865. Tom Rosser, held in reserve at Five Forks, was a prominent figure in the final fight at High Bridge during the closing Appomattox campaign.

After New Year's Day 1865, many members of Rosser's command went on leave. On January 1, the men of Lt. Col. Lige White's battalion headed to their native counties east of the Blue Ridge Mountains. The 1st Squadron of the 11th Virginia went on leave on January 3 to McDowell, 30 miles northwest of Staunton. Rosser granted similar leaves to many in the 7th and 12th Virginia. By mid-January only part of the Laurel Brigade remained in camp west of Staunton at Swope's Depot, where they suffered greatly from lack of food. Private Beverly K. Whittle of the 2nd Virginia recalled, "Feed is very scarce, [and] we have to move about to get it. The horses are in wretched condition, nearly starved to death all the time; if Rosser stays in Command much longer, our division will be utterly ruined by spring."[1]

Raid on Beverly, West Virginia

Rosser, still in command of Maj. Gen. Fitzhugh Lee's division, sought answers to the mounting problems he faced. No help came from others; the famine-stricken countryside could offer nothing. The

---

1. Notebook, September 12, 1864 to February 18, 1865, Beverly Kennon Whittle Papers, UVA.

Confederate government could not do much either. Gloom hung heavy. However, Rosser heard from his scouts that at Beverly, West Virginia, west of the Allegheny Mountains, the Federals had stored a large quantity of army supplies. Particularly compelling, the garrison numbered only about 1,000 soldiers of all arms. With Rosser's interest piqued, he decided to make a raid on the post. Beverly was about 75 miles from Staunton, as the crow flies, but Rosser's troopers would have to travel winding roads through the war-ravaged Alleghenies, offering almost nothing in the way of sustenance. Most roads were nearly impassible, with the route strewn with raging streams. Snow blocked many gorges, some to a depth of 25 feet. Citizens living along this route were fiercely anti-Confederate.[2]

With Fitz Lee approving his raid in Maj. Gen. Jubal Early's absence, Rosser summoned Col. Thomas T. Munford to his headquarters. Once there, Rosser ordered him to select a number of "volunteers" for the expedition, which would begin the next morning. Munford, a capable officer, told Rosser he expected his quartermaster to arrive from Richmond with supplies and shoes for the horses. Considering the fatigued horses and dispirited men, who had been on continuous duty for an extended period, Munford suggested postponing the raid until the fresh supplies arrived and the weather moderated. Rosser adamantly denied the request, repeating his intention to leave the next morning. Munford returned to his command, informing his officers of the orders. Captain John Lamb and Maj. Charles Old asked Munford for permission to travel to Rosser's headquarters to intercede on behalf of the dejected men. Permission granted, Lamb and Old journeyed to Rosser's command, but Rosser remained unyielding and refused their request. Lamb and Old reported they were "very indignant at his [Rosser's] reception of them, and it was evident that they had no confidence in him or his care for his men."[3] Munford reluctantly instructed his detail to report in the morning to Col. William A. Morgan, commander of the 1st Virginia.[4]

Since Munford had reported his brigade unfit for duty, Rosser sought volunteers from the Laurel Brigade and Brig. Gen. William H. Payne's brigade. He received responses from all brigades in the division, but could find only 300 horses suitable for the trip. Some men volunteered to march on foot, but Rosser refused the offer. He

2. McDonald, *Laurel Brigade*, 334–36.
3. Thomas P. Nanzig, *3rd Virginia Cavalry* (Lynchburg, VA, 1989), 69; Handwritten article by Thomas T. Munford published in the *Philadelphia Weekly Times*, May 17, 1884, Munford Papers, Munford-Ellis Collection, Box 17, DU.
4. Ibid; SHSP, vol. 13:143–44.

divided his 300-man force about equally between Colonel Morgan and Col. Albert W. Cook, who led the 8th Virginia. The expedition started as scheduled on January 7, 1865.[5]

On the morning of the raid's start, Munford received a visit from Capt. R. B. Kennon, Rosser's Inspector General. Kennon asked where Munford's detail had gone, and Munford referred him to Morgan's headquarters. Shortly, Kennon returned to Munford with a paper Rosser had signed informing Munford that he should consider himself under arrest; he would be tried by court-martial on charges of sedition, conspiracy, and efforts to thwart Rosser's plans. Upon Rosser's return from Beverly, a military court was convened and a trial was held, but Munford was acquitted. Rosser received admonishment from the court, which recommended charges not be made against officers without sufficient foundation.[6]

Rosser and his troopers marched through Buffalo Gap, proceeding along the Staunton and Petersburg Turnpike. The men ascended the mountains, passed through Monterey, and about dusk reached the peak of the Allegheny Mountains, where they camped for the night. They rode down the western slope of the mountain, encountering no inhabitants for 20 miles. Deep, drifted snow obstructed the gorges, and a torrential rain fell during the night, making the streams difficult to ford. The rains stopped about dawn, and the troopers continued on to Jackson River, which they had great difficulty crossing. Meanwhile, Early, who had returned to the Valley after meeting with the Confederate high command, sent a courier to call off Rosser's dangerous mission. The courier made it to Jackson River, but could not cross and returned to camp without reaching Rosser.[7]

Rosser's raiders had to ford more streams, and a thunderstorm drenched them as they crossed Cheat Mountain. A cold front brought strong winds, dropping the temperature to nearly zero degrees Fahrenheit. Captain Cornelius B. Hite of the 6th Virginia recalled:

> **Our direction was north, right in the face of the wind. I thought I would perish from the cold, but my cousin and I, by taking turns in dismounting and running along to keep up with our command, each in his turn leading the others horse, managed to keep from being frost-bitten... The weather was below zero and the Confederates had been in a rain the preceding day. Their overcoats being wet, were frozen stiff, the capes rattling like boards.**[8]

5. *Philadelphia Weekly Times*, April 5, 1884.
6. SHSP, vol. 13:143–44.
7. *Philadelphia Weekly Times*, April 5, 1884.
8. Daniel Amon Grimsley, *Battles in Culpeper County, Virginia, 1861–1865: And other Articles* (Culpeper, Virginia, 1900), vol. 21:42; *OR* 46/1:448;

Another trooper remembered the miserable night in camp: "We were not allowed to build fires ... all night long we stood there in the pelting rain, driven by the gusts of wind until it seemed to penetrate the very marrow of our bones; the soldiers fretting, fuming, quarreling, cursing, and damning everything in general upon the face of the earth, and the man who suggested the expedition in particular." The next morning the troopers headed north, and on January 10 reached the swollen Tygart River in Randolph County. They bivouacked for the night on a mountainside in Devil's Hollow. Choosing not to challenge the Tygart River, Rosser's raiders took a longer route by following a rough mountain road to Beverly. They marched all the next day and night, finally reaching the outskirts of Beverly at 4:00 a.m. on January 11. A short distance from Beverly, they halted and fed for a few hours. Early that morning, Rosser's horsemen approached the Federal camp at Beverly. Rosser dismounted all of his troopers except one squadron. The sounds of crunching snow beneath the dismounting men's feet alerted a Federal picket. One picket challenged the troopers, but Rosser's raiders quickly overpowered the man before he could sound an alarm. Rosser attacked quickly; the Federals were completely surprised, getting off few shots. Rosser lost one trooper killed and several wounded. Colonel Nathan Wilkinson, commanding the 6th West Virginia Infantry, reported an inflated number of 700 troopers wearing United States army greatcoats.[9]

The Federal force protecting the fort consisted of the 8th Ohio Cavalry and the 34th Ohio Infantry, totaling about 1,000 men. Surprisingly, the officers of the 34th Ohio were at a ball in a nearby village, away from the garrison. Rosser ordered his troopers to "come down on them," his favorite expression when attacking. The leaderless Federals quickly surrendered. Rosser's troopers took control of the garrison. The starving Confederates feasted before heading back to Swope's Depot. They plundered quartermaster supplies, dry goods, and commissary stores. They loaded the horses while the snow continued to fall and were in a jovial mood.[10]

During the plundering, a female Confederate sympathizer sent a note to the handsome cavalry commander inviting him to breakfast. Rosser accepted the invitation. The woman had a very attractive

Philadelphia Weekly Times, April 5, 1884; Thomas J. Arnold, "A Battle Fought in the Streets (Rosser's Beverly Raid of 1865);" *Magazine of History & Biography*, Randolph County Historical Society, Civil War Centennial Issue, vol. 12 (1961); Bushong, *Fightin Tom Rosser*, 157.
9. Ibid.
10. Myers, *The Comanches*, 335; William Lyne Wilson, *A Borderline Confederate*, 88.

daughter who engaged Rosser in enticing flirtation. Rumors circulated after the war that the charming Rosser had a tryst with the young woman upstairs in the mother's bedroom before leaving.[11]

The victorious Confederate horsemen marched out of town and went into camp just two miles from Beverly. The troopers were loaded down with plunder, had little ammunition, and many, including officers, were drunk. Their 600 prisoners exceeded the total number of Rosser's command. Trooper William L. Wilson, 12th Virginia, recalled Rosser and his staff "took possession of the largest store in town, loaded a four-horse ambulance with the spoils, while our wounded are left in Beverly." Wilson further stated, "I do not object to Gen. R's share—but to see the worthless Qm's [and] Commissaries take twenty [and] thirty times as much as the men who fought the Yankees, is enough to disgust any soldier."[12]

An amusing incident occurred when the expeditionary force stopped and encamped about 18 miles from Beverly, on the Huntersville Pike, at the farm of Hamilton Stalnaker. The troops and prisoners were freezing cold, and with many rail fences at hand, the troopers soon had blazing campfires. Stalnaker complained to Rosser, "I am a strong Confederate supporter, yet your men burn my fences. My brother, Warwick, across the way, is a strong Federal supporter and you have not touched his rails." Rosser looked at him and answered, "Never mind, Mr. Stalnaker, we will get to Warwick's rails after a while."[13]

On the return trip Rosser's troopers had to camp for two nights in the mountains, unprotected from the weather. The prisoners suffered unbearably without blankets, and had to stay up all night tending fires to keep themselves from freezing to death. Many prisoners suffered severe frostbite and could not walk, so they were left behind to a horrible fate. Private George Row of the 6th Virginia wrote his sister: "A great many of my company were frosted on the Beverly Raid of Rosser... Rosser has ruined our Brigade [and] we have not over 100 men in my regt." On January 18 Rosser's invaders reached their camp at Swope's Depot. Private William Wilson recalled, "Thank heavens we are in camp at last. I feel like an Arctic Explorer returning from a trip to the North Pole." The raid had succeeded in capturing 580 prisoners,

---

11. *Highland Recorder* (Monterey, Virginia), January 19, 1894. Allegedly, an unidentified Union captain was hiding under the bed during the tryst. The date reported in the newspaper as 1862 should read 1865. Rosser recalled in Riding with Rosser (pp. 59–60) that a surgeon dressed his wound in the upstairs bedroom, and he took a nap.
12. William Lyne Wilson, *A Borderline Confederate*, 90.
13. Kenneth L. Carvell, "Historic Beverly in the Tygart Valley," *West Virginia Magazine*, February, 2001, vol. 65, No. 2, Charleston, West Virginia.

100 horses, 600 arms and equipment, and 10,000 rations. The Federals lost six killed and 32 wounded. Those Federal officers who had been absent from their units were recommended for dismissal from the service "for disgraceful neglect of their commands."[14]

Rosser's exhausted troopers, finally back in the Shenandoah Valley, looked forward to plenty of rest before the weather improved and the spring campaign began. Fitz Lee moved Payne's and Munford's brigades east of the Blue Ridge Mountains, leaving only Rosser's Laurel Brigade in the Valley. Rosser detached some of his troopers, allowing them to go home to find enough supplies to survive the winter. The remaining troopers engaged in picket duty, which brought occasional skirmishes with the Federals.[15]

Rosser visited Betty on January 28 and again on February 11. Clinton Gallaher, a family friend, remembered that he accompanied Rosser from Richmond to Courtland on January 28. "I nearly fell in love with Sally Winston, Mrs. Rosser's younger sister. A lovely girl. She and I corresponded for a while even while I was at the University [of Virginia] later," he reminisced.[16]

Rosser attempted to maintain some kind of organization in his command, but he found it difficult with many absentees. His manpower continued to drain as troopers left for home after becoming increasingly concerned about their families, many of whom were facing starvation.[17]

West Pointer Tom Rosser was concerned about the breakdown of discipline during the remaining winter months. He attributed the breakdown to dysfunctional company organizations. Rosser knew there were some capable junior officers, but deplored the shortage of able lieutenants and captains who lacked the moral courage to properly carry out their duties, fearing unpopularity in their communities. Rosser wrote to Adjutant and Inspector General Samuel Cooper in Richmond:

> **It is useless to prefer charges against men or officers, especially if they are well connected, because the courts (the permanent ones)—being composed of politicians and men who have seen no service, or, if any, so little that**

14. George Row to his sister, January 29, 1865, *Row Family History,* http://spotsylvaniamemory.blogspot.com; *OR* 46/1:449; *Philadelphia Weekly Times,* April 5, 1884; William Lyne Wilson, *A Borderline Confederate,* 90; McDonald, *Laurel Brigade,* 338; *OR* 46/1:451.
15. Wilson, *A Borderline Confederate,* 90.
16. Diary of DeWitt Clinton Gallaher: 1864–1865, Valley Personal Papers, AD1000, UVA.
17. McDonald, *Laurel Brigade,* 358.

they have no conception of the relation between superior
and inferior officers and regard every act of firmness as
one of tyranny—always acquit the accused.[18]

Rosser requested of Cooper that at least one officer of the Regular
Army be assigned to each brigade to serve as drillmaster and provost
marshal.[19]

Despite waning discipline and sagging morale, some partisan raids
brought success. A Rosser-sanctioned raid sent Lt. Jesse C. McNeill of
Maj. John S. Mosby's command with 63 mounted troopers, including
about 15 from Rosser's 7th and 11th regiments of his brigade, to a
Union department headquarters where 7,000 Federal soldiers
garrisoned at Cumberland, Maryland. Scouts John B. Fay and C.
Ritchie Hallar had reconnoitered the area, gathering important details.
Entering the town at 3:00 a.m. on February 21, 1865, McNeill's
troopers overpowered the pickets and proceeded quickly to
headquarters, located in a hotel. They seized the guards. With Sgt.
Joseph L. Vandiver and Sgt. Joseph W. Kuykendall leading, two squads
quietly entered the rooms of Maj. Gen. George C. Crook and Brig.
Gen. Benjamin F. Kelly, without alarming anyone else. The surprised
generals, along with Kelly's adjutant, Maj. Martin Thayer Melvin, were
roused from their sleep, forced to quickly dress, and hustled down to
awaiting horses. Another squad of John H. Cunningham and Sgt. John
B. Fay destroyed the telegraph office. Although the Federals sounded
the alarm within ten minutes, McNeill's raiders escaped, and, along
with their distinguished prisoners, returned to Staunton within three
days. This event, though of minimal military significance, was a source
of pride for the Confederates in a time of falling fortunes.[20]

Meanwhile, on February 20 Grant ordered Maj. Gen. Philip
Sheridan to mount a cavalry assault on Lynchburg to destroy the
transportation facilities at that strategic locale. Sheridan left
Winchester on February 27 with a force of about 10,000 troopers and
additional artillery. He marched through Harrisonburg and along the
Valley Turnpike without opposition until he reached Mount
Crawford; there, Rosser's 500 hastily assembled troopers attempted to
block his way. Rosser had planned to stop Sheridan's cavalry until
Early's infantry could come up from Staunton. The North Fork of the
Shenandoah River was swollen; the fords were impassable. Rosser's
resistance slowed Sheridan's horsemen for a full 24 hours. The next day
the waters subsided just enough for Sheridan to send two cavalry
regiments across an upstream ford north of the bridge to assault

18. *OR*, Series 4, vol. 3:1080.
19. Ibid.
20. McDonald, *History of the Laurel Brigade*, 341–57.

Rosser's flank. Sheridan's troopers drove Rosser's horsemen pell-mell southward toward Staunton. Sheridan captured five commissioned officers, 37 enlisted men, and some wagons.[21]

Rosser fell back to Staunton, arriving on the evening of March 1, but Early had abandoned Staunton and proceeded to Waynesboro, where Sheridan, on the next day, routed his tiny army, capturing most. Early escaped, but it marked the last battle for him in the Confederate army. The Waynesboro defeat effectively ended the war in the Shenandoah Valley. Robert E. Lee ordered Rosser's cavalry to go east to replace the troopers sent south with Lt. Gen. Wade Hampton, who was busy fighting Maj. Gen. William T. Sherman. Sheridan marched toward Charlottesville after sending about 1,100 prisoners back to Winchester under a guard of about 1,200 cavalrymen. He soon joined Grant for the final campaigns of the war.[22]

Before leaving Waynesboro on the return march to join Sheridan, Brig. Gen. George A. Custer came up with a prank to play on Rosser and Early. Apparently, Custer's troopers found an issue of the local weekly paper. Custer obtained a printer and wrote out "reward posters" for "two able-bodied Negroes who had escaped." A die was found that exhibited a picture of a runaway slave, and the poster was created showing two runaways with height and weight descriptions. Custer printed Rosser's name beneath one slave and Early's name beneath the other. A number of these posters characterizing Rosser and Early as "fugitives" were printed and distributed among the townspeople. Rosser "knew of no other joke played during the war that was brighter or more cleverly designed." Indeed, when it came to Custer, Rosser enjoyed the master prankster's jokes.[23]

Meanwhile, after the defeat of Early's army at Waynesboro, Rosser witnessed the long train of Confederate prisoners heading for Winchester. He was determined to rescue as many as possible. He followed the marching column with about 300 troopers, awaiting an opportunity to strike. At night on March 4, Rosser attacked the Federal column near Harrisonburg. The Federals repulsed the attack, but some of the prisoners escaped in the chaos. Rosser sent detached troopers ahead to hold the fords, enabling his raiders and prisoners to escape. He passed through Meems Bottom at Mount Jackson where his troopers, aided by the swollen North River, had held the Federals at bay for two days.[24]

21. *OR* 46/1:127; *Philadelphia Weekly Times*, April 5, 1884.
22. McDonald, *Laurel Brigade*, 362.
23. Elizabeth Bacon Custer, Arlene Reynolds, eds., *The Civil War Diaries of Elizabeth Bacon Custer* (Austin, 1994), 33.
24. McDonald, *Laurel Brigade*, 362; *Thomas L. Rosser Scrapbook*, Thomas L. Rosser Papers, UVA, 1171a.b., Box 2, 70.

The evening of March 5, Rosser decided to employ a subterfuge in an effort to free more prisoners. He sent detachments against the flanks of the Union column with orders to move continuously over a hill in full view of the Federals, thus fooling them into thinking he had many more soldiers than he did. He sent spies to mingle among the prisoners, telling them to break for freedom when they saw him attacking.[25]

On the morning of March 6, Rosser charged the Union prisoner guards while the column crossed a river. The captives failed to revolt, even though Rosser attacked repeatedly. The prisoners, however, "were too much exhausted and dispirited to make any such attempt." Though thrown into great confusion, the Federals escaped across the river, forcing Rosser to give up his effort to rescue the men. Instead, he headed back to the upper Valley near Staunton.[26]

By now, Sheridan, including Custer's horsemen, had crossed the Blue Ridge Mountains and was on his way to join Grant in the Richmond-Petersburg area. Rosser's only recourse was to follow and harass Sheridan, not an easy task considering the size of his army. Sheridan's 10,000 men stripped the countryside bare, so Rosser's troopers and horses had no sustenance. The roads were almost impassable, broken up from the heavy traffic of Sheridan's column and the frequent rains. Rosser could only envision the destruction of large sections of the Virginia Central Railroad left in Sheridan's path. The brutality and totality of the destruction put revenge in the hearts of the Confederate horsemen, but they had little recourse. Sheridan pushed forward to the White House, on the Pamunkey River, arriving on March 19. He looked forward to joining with Grant for the final campaigns of the war.[27]

Trooper Daniel C. Snyder of the 11th Virginia recalled:

> **We are however all safe once more but after undergoing a terrible time through rain and mud. The waters were very high and in one case as the front wagon containing Gen'l Rosser's baggage was crossing a large stream near where it emptied into North river, the Bridge gave way and the Wagon and contents, 4 mules and driver (a white man) all went down the stream and have never been heard of since. The last that was seen of them, the man had gotten in the wagon and holding on to the bow and all was going**

25. McDonald, *Laurel Brigade*, 362.
26. Ibid., 362–63; August Forsberg transcript, Special Collections, Washington and Lee University.
27. McDonald, *Laurel Brigade*, 363.

down the rapid stream riding on the water as a boat until they arrived at the Falls (a frightful looking place indeed) when all went over and were never seen afterwards.[28]

After Early's defeat at Waynesboro, Rosser's division reorganized. Brigadier General James Dearing, Rosser's West Point friend and best man at his wedding, took command of the Laurel Brigade, consisting of the remnants of the 7th, 11th, and 12th Virginia, along with Lige White's Comanches. The other brigade in Rosser's division, Brig. Gen. John McCausland commanding, included remnants of the 16th, 17th, 21st, and 22nd Virginia. Losses and desertions had decimated the division, probably numbering no more than 1,200 troopers.[29]

On March 16 Rosser's division reached Hanover Court House. They found part of Lt. Gen. James Longstreet's corps on guard against Sheridan, who was near Mangohick Church on the north side of the Pamunkey River in King William County. Part of Longstreet's corps crossed the Pamunkey to position itself in front of Sheridan. The prearranged arrival of a pontoon train failing to arrive, along with a bridge of boats and rafts that was not completed until the 17th, foiled the crossing of the rest of Longstreet's troops. General Lee recalled Longstreet's men to Richmond after noticing they were not favorably executing the operation.[30]

Rosser's division was ordered to Petersburg and camped along Lee's extreme right near Spencer's Mill, on the Nottoway River. Lee strengthened his lines as best he could to protect the South Side Railroad, which connected City Point in Hopewell, on the James River, and extended westward through Petersburg, Burkeville, Farmville, Appomattox Station, and finally Lynchburg. Rosser moved his camp to Atlee's Station on March 25.[31]

On March 29, 1865, after arriving from the Shenandoah Valley, Sheridan's troopers started west on a flanking movement around the right of Lee's blockading Army of Northern Virginia. Lee extended his entrenched army lines 35 miles from northeast of Richmond to Hatcher's Run, west of Petersburg. Grant's objective remained unchanged from the previous summer: force the Confederates out of their fortifications, so he could strike them in the open with his entire army. Failing this, his secondary objective entailed destroying the South Side Rail-road to tighten the noose around the embattled Confederate forces, leaving them with no choice but to flee or die. The

28. D. C. Snyder to his wife, Rachel, March 15, 1865, The Valley of the
    Shadow, Valley Personal Papers, A1406, UVA, 2002.
29. McDonald, *Laurel Brigade*, 364–65.
30. Ibid., 362.
31. Ibid., 364–65.

Confederate soldiers manning Lee's lines faced a decreasing morale; sick-ness and limited supplies and rations were taking their toll. Atlanta and Savannah had fallen, and reports from soldiers' homes revealed hardships and gloom. Desertions from the Army of Northern Virginia numbered about 3,000 between February 15 and March 18.[32]

Grant ordered Sheridan's cavalry force of 9,000 troopers, well supported by infantry, to march to Dinwiddie Court House. Sheridan's horsemen came from three divisions: Maj. Gen. Wesley Merritt's 1st and 3rd Divisions of 5,700 men and Maj. Gen. George Crook's 2nd Division of 3,300 men. From scout reports, Lee concluded that the route the Federals would use to attempt to turn his right flank was by way of Dinwiddie Court House and Five Forks. Accordingly, the Southern commander decided the best way to oppose Grant's move was to put together a mobile force of infantry and cavalry to attack Sheridan at Dinwiddie Court House, 13 miles southwest of Petersburg, as he attempted to outmaneuver the Army of Northern Virginia. Lee sent a Confederate cavalry force of about 7,400 troopers to oppose Sheridan at the crossroads town.[33]

Per Grant's orders, Maj. Gen. George Meade ordered Maj. Gen. G. K. Warren's 15,000-man V Corps from their winter camps south of Petersburg to march north on the Quaker Road to secure the strategically important Boydton Plank Road. Once there, they pushed the Confederates back into their lines along the White Oak Road, taking control of the Boydton Plank Road. This position afforded access for an assault on the South Side Railroad, only three miles to the north. By the next day Warren's infantry had completed fortifying its position. Across from them, Confederate Lt. Gen. Richard H. Anderson's corps entrenched on White Oak Road.[34]

On March 30, after a nightlong forced march through a drenching rain, Rosser's command reached the vicinity of Five Forks, where the main body of the Confederate cavalry camped. The recent rains prevented Rosser from crossing Stony Creek, so he marched farther up river to Scott's Ford and crossed. His men got little rest before Fitz Lee sent the cavalry to face Sheridan at about noon on the 31st. Rosser's and Maj. Gen. Rooney Lee's divisions, followed by Maj. Gen. George Pickett's infantry division, marched via a concealed wooded road to attack Sheridan's left flank. Colonel Munford, now in command of Fitz Lee's former division, positioned his men in front of the Union horsemen. The Confederates already lost the element of surprise, as

32. Douglas Southall Freeman, *Lee's Lieutenants*, 3:624.
33. *OR* 46/1:1101.
34. *OR* 46/1:798, 1101–2.

Sheridan had anticipated their movements and placed his force across from the Confederates at Chamberlain's Bed. Nevertheless, Fitz Lee ordered an attack with his cavalry fighting on both sides of Pickett.

As the armies' moves and countermoves developed, Maj. Gen. Fitzhugh Lee was in command of all the cavalry of the Army of Northern Virginia. Hampton had left for South Carolina on January 20, 1865, to rally defenses. Fitz Lee had positioned at Five Forks, six miles northwest of Dinwiddie Court House, and had 2,500 troopers with him. Roughly 20 miles southeast of Five Forks, at the Stony Creek Depot on the Weldon Railroad, Rooney Lee had brigadier generals Rufus Barringer's, William P. Roberts's, and Richard T. Beale's brigades, totaling about 3,000 men. In addition, Major General Rosser's division of 1,200 troopers reinforced Rooney Lee. During the ensuing battle at Chamberlain's Bed (or Run), Munford's 700 troopers provided further reinforcements.[35]

As Sheridan moved into position at Dinwiddie Court House, his troopers became situated between Fitz Lee's and Rooney Lee's cavalrymen. After a lengthy detour around Sheridan's command, on March 31 the two Lees united at the intersection of Five Forks on the White Oak Road. Four miles to the southeast, a small, swampy tributary known as Chamberlain's Bed fed into nearby Stony Creek. This inconsequential stream separated the Confederates from Sheridan's 9,000-man force at Dinwiddie Court House; it was destined to be the scene of one of the final battles of the North-South conflict in Virginia.[36]

Chamberlain's Bed (Dinwiddie Court House): March 31, 1865

Robert E. Lee positioned the Confederate cavalry on the extreme right of his entrenched infantry. Approaching Chamberlain's Bed, northwest of Dinwiddie Court House, the Confederate horsemen discovered Maj. Gen. George Crook's troopers had already crossed the flooded stream at Fitzgerald Ford and were advancing to attack them. In response, at 10 a.m., Rooney Lee ordered Brig. Gen. Rufus Barringer to dismount his command to meet the onrushing Federal assault. Dismounted men from the 6th Ohio and 2nd New York had

35. Ed Bearss and Chris Calkins, *The Battle of Five Forks*, (Lynchburg, VA, 1985), 10; Wellman, *Giant In Gray*, 165. Note: Although recommended numerous times for promotion to brigadier general, Munford never officially received the rank.
36. Chris Calkins, "The Battle of Five Forks: Final Push for the South Side," *Blue and Gray Magazine*, Volume 9 (April 1992), Issue 4:17.

taken positions on the opposite bank. Barringer positioned the 5th North Carolina in front, supported by the 1st and 2nd North Carolina, with Brig. Gen Richard T. Beale's brigade in reserve and Capt. William McGregor's horse artillery battery in a position to support the 5th, which would take the brunt of the Federal attack. Barringer's troopers halted the attack on Bvt. Brig. Gen. Charles H. Smith's 1st Maine Brigade, forcing them to retreat to the east bank of the swollen stream. Rooney Lee ordered the 9th Virginia from Beale's brigade to make a mounted charge in pursuit of the staggering Union forces. However, because of a mistake in the order, only one squadron of the regiment made the charge, which Smith's brigade repulsed, inflicting terrible losses. At the same time, the Federals rallied and forced the North Carolina brigade back across the ford.[37]

Both sides began to fortify their lines up and down Chamberlain's Bed in preparation for the inevitable resumption of the conflict. Meanwhile, Pickett crossed Chamberlain's Bed at Danse's Ford, about a mile north of Fitzgerald's Ford. Rosser's and Munford's cavalries, which also crossed at Danse's Ford, supported Pickett in the afternoon fighting against Brig. Gen. Thomas Devin's cavalry division and Bvt. Brig. Gen. Henry E. Davies's 1st New Jersey, 10th New York, 24th New York, and 1st Pennsylvania. Pickett hoped to swing south and launch a surprise attack on the Union left flank.[38]

Finally, at about 3 p.m., with the rains finally stopped, Fitz Lee ordered Rooney Lee to drive the Federals from their front lines in preparation for another full attack on the Federal positions across Fitzgerald's Ford. Barringer's brigade was ordered to be the vanguard of the offensive, but because the 3rd North Carolina remained absent guarding the rear and after the terrible losses to his other regiments that morning, Barringer asked Rooney Lee to withdraw the order. If that was not possible, he requested that one of Rooney Lee's other brigades lead the movement. Rooney Lee wrote to Fitzhugh Lee, urging withdrawal of the possibly disastrous order, but his superior told him that "military necessity" required it carried out.[39]

Rain had filled Chamberlain Bed, more than 150 yards wide, and the mounted troops could cross at only one area, because dense foliage obstructed the banks. Barringer planned to position the 1st North Carolina on the left, dismounted in line, to attack and draw the fire of their adversaries. Then, at the proper moment, the 2nd North Carolina would charge across the ford and attack the Federal's main

37. Clark, NCR, 1:439, NCR, 3:637; *OR* 46/1:1102, 1110; Edward P. Tobie, *History of the First Maine Cavalry, 1861–1865* (Boston, MA, 1887), 397–98.
38. Clark, NCR, 1:439–40.
39. Ibid.

defenses. Barringer's remaining regiment would closely support the troops making this assault. Fitzhugh Lee promised active support from the other brigades.[40]

To succeed in surprising the Federals, the Confederates made every effort to shield the initial movements. When everything was ready, Lt. Col. William H. Cheek, 1st North Carolina, formed his line and entered the stream. At once the Federals concentrated a rapid fire upon Cheek and his men. When Cheek was about halfway across the stream, Barringer ordered the 2nd North Carolina, Maj. John P. Lockhart commanding, to make a charge in close column by sections of eight, with instructions to deploy right and left on crossing the stream, depending on what the circumstances required. With some mounted and others dismounted, the 5th North Carolina followed and adopted the same line of movement. Rooney Lee ordered Beale's brigade stationed between the 1st and 2nd North Carolina and to their rear to help either flank, if needed.[41]

The Confederate horsemen successfully executed the plan. Lockhart drove the Federals from their works opposite the ford, while Cheek swept the lines to his left, and Capt. John R. Erwin and the 5th North carried the right. Smith's brigade again defended the Confederate right, while Davies's troopers shielded the left. When the Confederates flanked and drove back Davies, Sheridan sent word to Smith of the situation, with instructions for him to "look out for his right." Left to right, Munford's, Rooney Lee's, and Rosser's divisions led Pickett toward Dinwiddie Court House.[42]

About this time, Sgt. James H. Hodam of the 17th Virginia saw Rosser "galloping through the pines on the right hurrahing and declaring we were driving them on the right ... then, Rosser and his horse went down. Rosser jumped up and called for a horse."[43]

As the situation deteriorated, Sheridan again sent word to Smith, stating, "Everything on your side is gone now—look out for yourself, and when you fall back, fall back to Dinwiddie." In ten minutes the whole Federal line was in full retreat with the Confederates pursuing. The pursuit of the Union forces continued for some distance, with further losses to the Federals. Then, night closed in, and a halt was ordered within two miles of Dinwiddie Court House.[44]

---

40. Ibid.
41. Ibid., 1: 441.
42. *OR* 46/1:1110; *OR Supplement*, 7:829–30.
43. *OR Supplement*, 7:830.
44. Clark, NCR, 1: 439–41, 476; Edward P. Tobie, *History of the First Maine Cavalry*, 397; *OR* 46/1:1110.

Sheridan's losses at Chamberlain's Bed included 40 killed, 254 wounded, and 60 missing. The Southern cavalry losses were estimated at 360 casualties out of the 7,400 engaged, while the infantry lost 400 out of 3,400.[45] Rosser had been wounded in the arm, staying on duty with his limb in a sling.[46]

Battle of Five Forks:
The Waterloo of the Confederacy

About 11:00 a.m. on March 31, a detachment of Maj. Gen. Bushrod Rust Johnson's infantry, from Lieutenant General Anderson's corps, attacked Major General Warren's infantrymen. The Confederates pushed the Federals back southwest to a branch of Gravelly Run. With Brig. Gen. Nelson Miles's division of the II Corps as reinforcement, Warren counterattacked. The Confederates were driven back to their works along the White Oak and Claiborne roads. The battle of White Oak Road effectively exposed most of Johnson's communication lines with Pickett, endangering the Confederate infantry.[47]

That same day Warren dispatched Maj. Gen. Joseph J. Bartlett's brigade to a position behind Pickett's left flank. Sensing the precariousness of his position, Pickett decided to withdraw toward Five Forks, retreating as far as Hatcher's Run. Soon Sheridan's cavalry and Warren's V Corps began pressing Pickett and his infantry as they retreated toward the Five Forks crossroads.[48]

Five Forks was an intersection of five roads: White Oak (two branches or lanes), Scotts, Fords (or Church), and Dinwiddie Court House roads. The intersection was located six miles northwest of Dinwiddie Court House and was crucial to controlling the South Side Railroad, Robert E. Lee's last supply link to Petersburg. To hold the vital intersection, General Lee's cavalrymen rendezvoused at Five Forks with Pickett's 5,000 infantrymen.[49]

Pickett's men dug in at Five Forks and strengthened their fortifications. Their works covered a three-quarter-mile expanse with artillery placed at strategic locations along their front. Robert E. Lee's instructions to Pickett reflected the importance of his defensive stand:

45. Suderow, "Confederate Strengths and Losses."
46. Frank Myers Diary, March 31, 1865.
47. Bearss and Calkins, *The Battle of Five Forks*, 62–63, 72; *OR* 46/1:1287–88.
48. Bearss and Calkins, *The Battle of Five Forks*, 75–76.
49. Bearss and Calkins, *The Battle of Five Forks*, 8; Louis H. Manarin, *North Carolina Troops, 1861–1865, A Roster* (Raleigh, 1989), 2:278. Wade Hampton had been sent south to fight Maj. Gen. William T. Sherman.

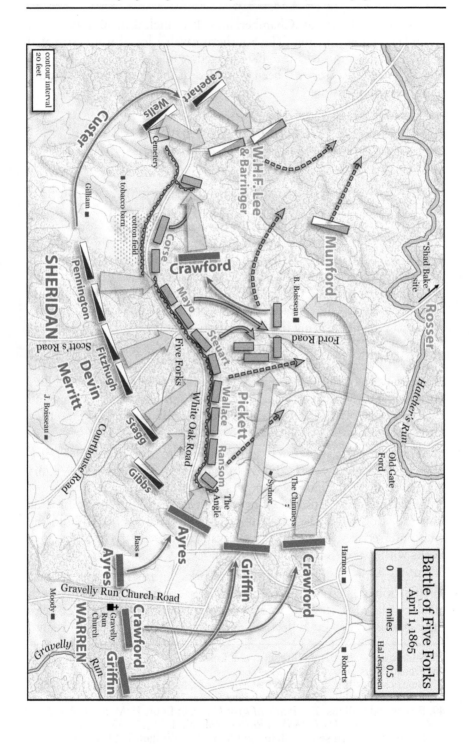

contour interval
20 feet

Capehart

Custer

Wells

Cemetery

W.H.F. Lee & Barringer

Munford

"Shad Bake" site

Rosser

Gilliam

tobacco barn

Corse

cotton field

Crawford

B. Boisseau

Hatcher's Run

SHERIDAN

Pennington

Mayo

Ford Road

Old Gate Ford

Scott's Road

Fitzhugh

Devin

Merritt

Stuart

Five Forks

Wallace

Pickett

J. Boisseau

Courthouse Road

Stagg

White Oak Road

Ransom

Sydnor

The Chimneys

Gibbs

The Angle

Ayres

Bass

Ayres

Griffin

Crawford

Harmon

Ayres

Gravelly Run Church Road

Moody

Crawford

WARREN

Gravelly Run Church

Griffin

Gravelly Run

Roberts

Battle of Five Forks
April 1, 1865

0   miles   0.5

Hal Jespersen

"Hold Five Forks at all hazards. Protect road to Ford's Depot and prevent Union forces from striking the South Side Railroad."[50]

At the outset of the climactic battle of Five Forks on April 1, Pickett placed his division of infantry in the line of battle, with Rooney Lee's and Munford's cavalries on his right and one regiment of Munford's on his left. Rosser's division was placed in reserve in the rear of the center, with Hatcher's Run between it and the others. Rosser wanted to rest his jaded horses as much as possible and feed the starving animals.[51]

A gap of several miles stood between Pickett's line and the extreme right of Robert E. Lee's position at Burgess's Mill, held by Anderson with Johnson's division. Brigadier General William P. Roberts's small cavalry brigade picketed the gap. Against the backdrop of the order for Pickett to "hold Five Forks," the infamous "shad bake" occurred. Rosser's brigade, by request, had been placed in reserve a few miles north of Hatcher's Run. Rosser, who commanded a division of Virginia cavalry, had spent March 29 ten miles southwest of Blackstone, once known as Blacks and Whites, Virginia, on the Nottoway River, catching a nice supply of shad. When Rosser moved north to Five Forks on March 30 and 31, he brought the shad with him. As soon as he moved his division north of Hatcher's Run, he arranged for the fish to be cleaned, split, and baked over fires of dry wood. Rosser, many years later, recalled:

> I had brought some excellent fresh shad from the Nottoway River with me, and I invited General Pickett to go back and lunch with me—he promised to be with me in an hour. He and Fitz Lee came back to me... Some time was spent over the lunch, during which no firing was heard. We concluded that the enemy was not in much of a hurry to find us at Five Forks.[52]

50. Freeman, *Lee's Lieutenants*, 3:661; La Salle Corbell (Mrs. George E. Pickett), *Pickett and His Men* (Atlanta, 1899), 386; Bearss and Calkins, *The Battle of Five Forks*, 76–77.
51. *OR* 46/1:1299, McDonald, *Laurel Brigade*, 366–67.
52. *Philadelphia Weekly Times*, April 5, 1895; *OR Supplement*, 8:404–5, 477; Michael J. McCarthy, *Confederate Waterloo: The Battle of Five Forks, April 1, 1865, and the Controversy that Brought Down a General* (El Dorado Hills, CA, 2016), 90; C. Irvine Walker, *The Life of Lieutenant General Richard Heron Anderson of the Confederate States Army,* (Charleston, SC, 1917), 229–30; Letter from Thomas L. Rosser to Joshua Lawrence Chamberlain, August 29, 1902, Joshua Lawrence Chamberlain Papers, Curtis Library, Bowdoin College, Pejepscot Historical Society, Brunswick, Maine; Thomas Munford to Joshua Lawrence Chamberlain, January 24, 1911, Joshua Lawrence Chamberlain Papers, Curtis Library, Bowdoin College, Pejepscot Historical Society, Brunswick, Maine; Joshua Lawrence Chamberlain, Passing of the Armies: An Account of the Final Campaign (Lincoln,

Feasting and probably enjoying whiskey or brandy, the men were approximately four miles from the front and perhaps in an "acoustic shadow," preventing any gunshot noise from reaching them. The lunch was kept secret; Pickett and Fitz Lee had slipped off to feast on the shad without telling anyone in their commands where they were going.[53]

While Rosser, Pickett, and Fitz Lee feasted, the Confederates waited for Sheridan's attack. Sheridan waited impatiently for Warren to come up and attack the left rear of the Confederate infantry. About 2:30 p.m. Sheridan's cavalry approached Mary Gilliam's house, less than a mile southwest of the Five Forks intersection. Mrs. Gilliam, a widow, owned 2,800 acres, including the critical Five Forks intersection. Pickett and Fitz Lee were away from their troops when the Federals attacked in the late afternoon of April 1. About 4:00 p.m. Sheridan drove a 9,000-man wedge of Warren's corps between the Confederate infantry and their cavalry on the left. The Federal column turned against the left flank of the Confederate infantry, which broke and retreated. When a courier finally warned about Warren's attack, Col. Ellis Spear's regiments of Brig. Gen. Henry Baxter's brigade prevented Rosser's troopers, along with Pickett and Lee, from crossing Hatcher's Run. Pickett managed to break through, but the defeat of his troops was assured.[54]

The battle of Five Forks sealed the fate of the Army of Northern Virginia. Barringer later recalled, "At Five Forks on April 1 the last hope of the Confederacy went down in darkness and despair." The Federals cut Robert E. Lee's last supply line to Petersburg the next day, April 2, at Sutherland's Station. Lee now knew Petersburg and Richmond were lost and ordered them evacuated. He realized he could not move directly south to join Gen. Joseph E. Johnston's Army of Tennessee in North Carolina with Grant blocking his path. Instead, Lee decided on a rapid westward move in hopes of escaping his pursuers, and then he would move south to join Johnston. Union losses in the climactic battle of Five Forks were about 630 killed,

Nebraska, 1998), 173; John B. Phillips to Thomas Munford, September 7, 1895, Munford Family Papers, DU; Anne Trice Thompson Akers, "Colonel Thomas T. Munford and the Last Cavalry Operations of the Civil War in Virginia," Master's Thesis, Virginia Tech, December, 1981, 60–61, 73, 76–78; Thomas L. Rosser to A. S. Perham, August 29, 1902, Perham Collection, LC.

53. Ibid.

54. Ibid. Sheridan relieved Warren of command and had him court-martialed for being late to arrive and attack. A Court of Inquiry posthumously exonerated Warren in December 1879.

wounded, or missing. Confederate losses were about 545 killed and wounded and between 2,000 and 2,400 captured.[55]

Rosser blamed Pickett for the loss at Five Forks: "It seems to have been a surprise to General Pickett, yet one would have supposed that he would have been on alert in the presence of the enemy he had so recently been fighting, but from all I could see on the occasion, I am satisfied that all the generalship and management was on the Federal side."[56]

That night Rosser's division remained north of Hatcher's Run, and the next morning it headed with difficulty toward Amelia Court House. On April 3 the Confederates abandoned Petersburg, and Sheridan pursued Fitz Lee's rear guard closely while pressing his flanks. Rosser's command acted as the rear guard at the beginning of the retreat. Sheridan continually pressed the Confederate horsemen; numerous skirmishes occurred with Fitz Lee's dismounted troopers.[57]

The pressing Federals constantly threatened the army's wagon trains, so Fitz Lee ordered Rosser to march down Cralle's Road to protect them. Upon reaching the wagons, Fitz Lee met up with Anderson's infantry; together they beat off the Federal attacks. The retreating Confederates had been promised provisions awaiting them at Amelia Court House, but they were soon disappointed.[58]

High Bridge

The anticipated rations were not at Amelia Court House on April 5, and Robert E. Lee's army lost an entire day of retreating while scouring the countryside for sustenance to feed their starving troops and animals. Grant pressed ahead, seeking to prevent Lee from moving southward to join Joseph E. Johnston in North Carolina. Grant wished to destroy High Bridge, which carried the South Side Railroad over the Appomattox River. He sent a large infantry force under his Chief of Staff, Bvt. Brig. Gen. Theodore Read, to Maj. Gen. Edward O. C. Ord, commander of the Army of the James, to accomplish the task. He also sent a squadron of Col. Francis Washburn's cavalry. The combined force numbered between 1,200 and 1,500 men.[59]

55. Clark, NCR, 1:442; Bearss and Calkins, *The Battle of Five Forks*, 113; Bryce Suderow, "Confederate Strengths and Losses."
56. *Thomas L. Rosser Scrapbook*, Thomas L. Rosser Papers, UVA; *Philadelphia Weekly Times*, April 5, 1895; Walker, *The Life of Lieutenant General Richard Heron Anderson*, 229–30.
57. *Thomas L. Rosser Scrapbook*, Thomas L. Rosser Papers, UVA, 1171a.b., Box 2, 17.
58. Bushong, *Fightin' Tom Rosser*, 177.
59. Ibid., 179.

On the morning of April 6, Fitz Lee ordered Rosser to take his command and report to Longstreet at Rice's Station on the South Side Railroad. Longstreet allowed Rosser to bring along parts of Rooney Lee's and Munford's divisions, totaling about 1,500 troopers, to attempt saving High Bridge. About 1:00 p.m. Rosser encountered Read's infantry posted behind a high fence at Watson's farm.[60]

Munford, in command of Fitz Lee's previous division, dismounted his troopers and approached the Federals in front, while the daring Brig. Gen. James Dearing led the Laurel Brigade against Read's flank. Washburn's force charged Dearing's troopers, bringing on a desperate hand-to-hand fight. Dearing, Washburn, and Read, all West Pointers, were killed or mortally wounded within a few minutes of each other in this fight. Dearing shot Read; shortly thereafter, Dearing was mortally wounded, perhaps the victim of friendly fire.[61]

The loss of Dearing left Lt. Col. Elijah White of the 35th Virginia Battalion in charge of the Laurel Brigade. White's Comanches continued the vigorous fight for High Bridge, charging the Union line time after time with sabers drawn. Finally, the Federal cavalry broke, and brigade commander McCausland, of Rosser's division, ordered Capt. Frank Myers to take a dismounted regiment, the 6th Virginia, and assault the Federal infantry. The attack was successful, with about 780 Yankees captured.[62]

The mortally wounded James Dearing, Rosser's good friend, was carried nearby to the Watson's farmhouse. After the fight at High Bridge ended, Rosser went to see his dying friend, and White came to pay his respects too. Dying, Dearing took Rosser's hand and pointed to his own brigadier's stars, saying in a barely audible voice, "I want these to be put on his [White's] coat." Dearing was signaling that Lieutenant Colonel White should be promoted in his stead. Dearing was taken to Lynchburg where he died on April 23, gaining the distinction of being the last Confederate general officer killed in the war. Rosser, wounded in an arm himself, later called the battle at High Bridge "a glorious victory, but dear was its cost! Gen. Dearing, with his musical voice and laughing eye, the bravest of the brave... and many others were killed there."[63]

60. McDonald, *Laurel Brigade*, 375.
61. Ibid., 366–67; William Miller Owen, *In Camp and Battle with the Washington Artillery of New Orleans* (Boston, 1885), 376. William Miller Owen reported that Rosser personally told him on the battlefield that Dearing killed Read in hand-to-hand fighting with sabers, and then Read's orderly shot Dearing.
62. McDonald, *Laurel Brigade*, 376; Myers, *The Comanches*, 377–79.
63. Myers, *The Comanches*, 286, 380; "The Cavalry, A.N.V.," *Address by General T. L. Rosser at the Seventh Annual Reunion of the Association of the*

Rosser remembered the loss of artilleryman Maj. James W. Thomson:

> Thomson and I rode out together on the field to watch the fight, for we were both wounded, but when Dearing fell, he drew my sword from its scabbard and dashed into the fight. . . . He rushed into the conflict with what seemed a spirit of deathless devotion. He could do little execution, but on he rode past the forefront right into the ranks of the enemy. The Federal line gave way, but still, broken into squads and retreating into the woods, they continued to fight, and it was in the midst of one of these squads that Major Thomson was last seen.[64]

Captain Jacob Engle witnessed Thomson shot off his horse, mortally wounded when leading a third charge.[65]

Rosser later stated it would have been better for the Federals to have burned the bridge and captured all of the Confederates. He believed the victory at High Bridge was not worth the losses of Dearing, Col. Reuben Boston, Thomson, and Maj. John L. Knott, as well as more than 300 enlisted men, especially since only three days remained until General Lee would surrender at Appomattox. Rosser stated the sacrifices of his men had been wasted.[66]

Rosser's command retired to Rice's Station, taking up a position on the right of Longstreet's infantry, which had positioned itself to confront advancing Federals. All night an attack was expected, yet it did not come. Still, the already exhausted troopers got little sleep. On the evening of April 6, the Confederates abandoned Rice's Station, and Fitz Lee's cavalry moved in the rear of Longstreet toward Farmville. The Federals attempted to prevent Fitz Lee from crossing the Appomattox River, but he managed to get over at Cumberland Court House Road bridge. Rosser had to cross two miles upstream. He then moved downstream to reunite with Fitz Lee. Near the Buckingham (or Maysville) Plank Road he found the Federals attacking Munford's division, and assisted Munford in driving off the Union force. White's Laurel Brigade struck the Federal flank, and McCausland's brigade also joined the fight. The engagement essentially ended in a draw. The

Maryland Line, Academy of Music, Baltimore, Maryland, February 22, 1889, 43.

64. SHSP, vol. 22, *The Confederate Dead in Stonewall Cemetery, Winchester, Virginia; Memorial Services, June 6, 1894, Eulogy of Major James W. Thomson by Captain Wm. N. McDonald;* SHSP, vol. 19:366.

65. Ibid.

66. *Thomas L. Rosser Scrapbook,* Thomas L. Rosser Papers, UVA.

Confederates then continued their retreat toward Appomattox. The Federals pursued, generally along the line of the railroad from Farmville to Appomattox.[67]

The evening of April 8, Rosser's division relinquished its rear-guard duties, and its commander rode into the village of Appomattox. Near the courthouse, Wilmer McLean, a longtime acquaintance of Rosser, had a home; the final surrender of Robert E. Lee's army occurred at McLean's house the next day. Rosser recalled that the two "spent the night talking over our war experiences." At about 2:00 a.m. on the 9th, they were interrupted by a knock on McLean's front door. Major General John B. Gordon and Fitz Lee entered with sorrowful expressions on their faces. According to Rosser, "[I saw] by the dim light of several tallow candles, which were burning in the room, that something terrible had happened and I at once demanded the news." Robert E. Lee had decided that come morning he would either surrender or disperse the army. Not willing to give up, Rosser jumped to his feet, avowing, "General Lee [will] not surrender me in the morning!" Scouts informed Rosser the Lynchburg Road was clear, and he made plans to move out shortly, but Gordon convinced him to wait for daylight before trying his escape.[68]

At daybreak on April 9 the Cavalry Corps of the Army of Northern Virginia, about 2,400 troopers, took a position on the right of Gordon's infantry on the Lynchburg Road, just a short distance from Appomattox Court House. Rosser's horsemen were positioned in the center of the cavalry line. Shortly after sunrise Rosser's troopers attacked the Federal cavalry, drove it back, and captured a number of prisoners and several guns. Rosser's division thus participated in the last cavalry charge of the war in Virginia. White flags soon began to pop up, and with the intermingling of blue and gray, it was apparent the war was over. Rosser bemoaned, "I for the first time became alarmed. Early that morning [April 9], a communication came in to me from the Yankees addressed to Gen. R. E. Lee... We all soon would be prisoners!"[69]

Rosser and Munford, however, rode westward along an open road with the remnants of their commands to Lynchburg, arriving about 9:00 p.m. White disbanded the Laurel Brigade, or rather the remnants of it, in Lynchburg. Rosser disbanded his men temporarily. He then

67. McDonald, *Laurel Brigade*, 378–80.
68. Keller, *Riding with Rosser*, 72–73; Longacre, *The Cavalry At Appomattox*, 183.
69. McDonald, *Laurel Brigade*, 381; Thomas Lafayette Rosser, "Memorandum, Report of Operations Around Richmond After Retreat to Appomattox Court House." [n.d.] New York Historical Society Manuscript Collection, Misc. Rosser.

proceeded to Danville, the Confederacy's third and final capital (the last meeting place of the Confederate Government), where he conferred with Confederate Secretary of War John C. Breckinridge. President Jefferson Davis had already left Danville, heading south. Breckinridge instructed Rosser to return to central Virginia, collect all soldiers who had not been paroled, and to report to Virginia Governor William Smith, if he could not contact Davis or the War Department.[70]

Rosser rode to Staunton, and on April 12 issued a stirring proclamation to his troopers:

I hereby call upon you in the name of Liberty, Honor, and all that is dear in life, to shoulder your muskets and return to the field to meet the arrogant invader who has insulted you, robbed you, murdered your dearest friends and relatives, outraged your fair women, despoiled your homes, and dishonored all that is dear and sacred. I will lead you against them, and will never abandon or surrender you until the purple curtain ceases to flow from my heart, or until you are a free, independent, and happy people! If we are true to ourselves and to honor, we can never abandon a cause we have so nobly sustained for the last four years, and for which we have made the heaviest sacrifices of blood and property—and above all as true men we can never "Kiss the rod that smites us," or bend our knees to our bitterest foe.[71]

Tom Rosser had the audacity to sign his proclamation as "Lieutenant General," because Secretary of War Breckinridge had ordered him to command all troops in Virginia that could be mustered. On the other hand, Rosser would publicly dispute Thomas Munford's right to be called "general" after Munford was recommended for promotion to the brigadier rank.[72]

Rosser assembled about 500 troopers at Swope's Depot, ten miles west of Staunton, on May 10. While Col. M. D. Ball tried to organize them, Rosser journeyed to Courtland to say goodbye to Betty. He planned to escape westward to join Gen. Edmund Kirby Smith in the Trans-Mississippi Department. While he was at Courtland on May 2, Federal cavalry surrounded his house, and Rosser realized he had no escape and gave himself up. He was taken to Richmond as a prisoner of war. He learned the charge against him was violating his parole, which,

70. *Bushong, Fightin' Tom Rosser*, 182.
71. *Betty W. Rosser Scrapbook*, Thomas L. Rosser Papers, UVA, 1171a.b., Box 2. Note: Rosser signed his proclamation as "Lieutenant General." Supposedly, Robert E. Lee recommended him for this promotion, but if so, the Confederate Senate never confirmed it.
72. Ibid., Bushong, *Fightin' Tom Rosser*, 182–83. Munford's "promotion" was never confirmed.

unbeknownst to him, Lee had obtained at Appomattox. He was released when Lee, who was in Richmond at the time, assured the Federal authorities Rosser was exempt from the terms of surrender due to his escape. Lee advised him to go to the Shenandoah Valley, disperse his troops, and obtain paroles for them. Accomplishing these tasks, the war ended for Thomas Rosser.[73]

Rosser was asked years after the war what he considered the greatest triumph of his military career. His answer:

> **I will say without hesitation or doubt, that the greatest triumph of my military career, and indeed I may say of my life, for it is the one which I shall always be the proudest of, was the successful charge which I made at Appomattox Courthouse on the 9th of April, 1865, when after General Robert E. Lee had decided to surrender the Army of Northern Virginia, to which I belonged, to General U. S. Grant, about 5 o'clock in the morning, at the head of my command, composed of my division (McClausland's and Dearing's brigades) and Fitz Lee's division (Wickham's and Payne's brigades) I took these hungry, wasted, and worn out brigades forward, lining on the right of General John B. Gordon, rode over a brigade or more of the enemy, captured the Lynchburg road and left that fatal field in triumph, refusing to surrender either myself or my command to the enemy.[74]**

For Tom Rosser the war was over. He began as an artilleryman, transferred to J.E.B. Stuart's cavalry, and participated in most of the battles in the Eastern Theater. He had performed well until the debacle at the battle of Tom's Brook in the 1864 Shenandoah Valley campaign. William T. Sherman accepted Joseph E. Johnston's surrender of the Confederate army at Bennett Place, near Durham Station, North Carolina, on April 26, 1865.

---

73. *Thomas L. Rosser Scrapbook*, Thomas L. Rosser Papers, UVA; OR 46/2:1117, 1123. War Department records indicate Rosser apparently signed a parole at Appomattox Court House, Virginia, on April 9, 1865. Whereas from other records on file, it appears that Rosser escaped from Lee's army on the day of its surrender, and on May 4 he surrendered himself to the United States authorities at Richmond, Virginia, where he evidently subscribed to the parole.
74. Thomas L. Rosser to William B. Dupree, April 27, 1895, Thomas L. Rosser Papers, UVA.

Chapter 9

Rosser Postwar: To the Northwest

"I can truly say now that I never met a more enterprising, gallant or dangerous enemy during those four years of terrible war, nor a more genial, wholesouled, chivalrous gentleman in peace than Major General George A. Custer."

Thomas Rosser on learning of George Custer's death at the Little Bighorn.

When the war ended Tom Rosser returned to Courtland, where his wife, Betty, had spent most of the war with her widowed mother. He had to decide what profession to undertake to provide a living for his family. Would he become a lawyer, farmer, business man, or a politician? As things unfolded, he first tried his hand as a business owner and co-owner, but these ventures failed. He ultimately found his calling in the railroad business in the great Northwest.

Even though Tom and Betty had been married almost two years, like so many others married during the war, they hardly knew each other. Nevertheless, Rosser began preparing for his new life as a civilian. His war wounds had healed, but he carried scars from a saber cut above his right eye and a bayonet gash on his forehead. He suffered no serious physical impairments; now 28 years old, he was in good health. He stood six feet, two inches tall, weighed about 220 pounds, and had a vigorous, muscular body. His strong physical presence commanded the respect of others.[1]

Like many, the war left the Rossers largely impoverished. President Abraham Lincoln envisioned Reconstruction as a period of healing and reconciliation, but with his assassination on April 14, 1865, that dream died with him. Congress imposed a far harsher policy in the Reconstruction Act of 1867. Rosser, however, favored Reconstruction, believing it would speed the reunification of a divided nation. He also approved of voting rights for freed slaves, but opposed permitting blacks to hold office or to have full social equality.[2]

---

1. Bushong, *Fightin' Tom Rosser*, 185.
2. Maslowski, Peter, "From Reconciliation to Reconstruction: Lincoln, Johnson, and Tennessee, Part I," *Tennessee Historical Quarterly* 43, no. 3 (Fall 1983), 281–98. Maslowski, Peter, "From Reconciliation to Reconstruction: Lincoln, Johnson, and Tennessee, Part II," *Tennessee Historical Quarterly* 43, no. 4 (Winter 1983), 343–61.

Post War Engraving of Thomas Lafayette Rosser. Rosser, like many others, was broke after the war.

Reproduced by permission of Eleanor Cochran and Douglass Cochran, Jr.

Rosser tried to figure out what sort of profession would best enable him to support his family. He decided not to move back to Texas, reasoning, "The State of Society is so bad in Texas ... it is not safe to go amongst the population that had flocked there since the war."[3]

Somehow, probably with loans from his mother-in-law, Rosser scraped together enough funds to enroll in Judge John W. Brockenbrough's law school in Lexington, Virginia, which later became Washington and Lee University. Nonetheless, Rosser did not take to studying in a classroom. He felt comfortable in the outdoors and had no real interest in the law, so he decided to find some other way to make a living.[4]

He next went to work for the National Express & Transportation Company. In May 1866, he found himself in Mobile, Alabama, as

3. Thomas L. Rosser to Maj. Holmes Conrad, October 19, 1865, Holmes Conrad Papers, 1840–1916, VHS.
4. W. G. McDowell to Betty W. Rosser, October 9, 1913, Thomas L. Rosser Papers, UVA.

superintendent of its Southern district. The new company had formed to provide a faster method of transportation for small parcels. While attempting to open a branch office in Mobile, Rosser looked forward to working with one of the company's officers—Joseph E. Johnston. The Mobile branch office idea failed, so he soon moved to New Orleans, Louisiana, where he wrote Betty:

> **The cholera is rapidly spreading and I am hurrying through my business that I may leave the City... I was very much alarmed this morning about myself—indeed felt that I had the fearful thing upon me. I ran off after the doctor and could not find him. I then took a strong drink of ginger of pepper mint & was soon relieved... If it were not for you [and] Daughter I would not want to live. There is so much suffering and cruelty in the world that there are no pleasures outside of a man's own family.**[5]

Rosser sensed the company's fortunes were on the demise, telling Betty, "I am much troubled now dearest about the offices of the Co. I think the whole thing is about to break up. I am almost sure of it... I know I can make a comfortable living in the Valley of Virginia area [as a farmer], where there I would have my darling wife and child always with me." Rosser's hopes were finally dashed when the new company soon went bankrupt.[6]

On June 20, 1866, while in New Orleans, Rosser decided to request amnesty and a pardon from President Andrew Johnson. He submitted a respectful request for a pardon, but without letters of recommendation, or more importantly, without endorsement of the governor of Texas, under the third (high-ranking Confederate military officers) and eighth (Confederate military personnel with West Point or Annapolis educations) exceptions permitting pardons, his bid failed. The provisional governor of Texas, Andrew Jackson Hamilton, refused to endorse applications from any soldiers who had attended West Point. Thus, Rosser's pardon was not forthcoming, but was later included under President Johnson's blanket pardon issued on Christmas Day of 1868.[7]

Rosser had put the war behind him, in some respects, but he continued to uphold Southern principles and was proud of his military

---

5. Thomas L. Rosser to Betty W. Rosser, August 9, 1866, Thomas L. Rosser Papers, UVA; *Mobile Evening Times*, May 12, 1866, Thomas L. Rosser Papers, UVA.
6. Ibid.
7. Rosser Papers, UVA, 1171g.h.j, Box 1; Brad R. Clampitt, "Two Degrees of Rebellion: Amnesty and Texans after the Civil War," *Civil War History*, September 2006, vol. 52, Number 3:266.

service until the end of his life. He subscribed to the Southern code of honor, including providing for one's family, maintaining one's pride, and fighting when necessary on what he believed to be a fair field. To many Southern military men, like Rosser, honor was a paramount element of the public's opinion of them. He was always on guard against what he perceived as attacks on his manliness. He often reacted in an overzealous manner to prove his manhood in the face of these assaults.[8]

Even old Jubal Early finally capitulated and sought a pardon. Early had written Rosser from Mexico, where he had fled after Robert E. Lee's surrender:

> **I shall never return to the states unless I can come back under the Confederate flag—of which I do not yet despair. My hatred of the infernal Yankees is increasing daily, if possible, and I do not speak to any of them that I meet. My motto is still "war to the death," and I yet hope to have another chance at them. Whenever war arises between the U. S. and any other power, I shall be in, and God forbid that I meet any Confederates on that side.[9]**

President Johnson pardoned him in 1868, and Early changed his mind about repatriating, returning to Lynchburg, Virginia, the next year to practice law.

Several months later Rosser traveled to Baltimore, Maryland, to solicit for a general commission business with the firm of Ferguson and Tyson. The company accepted consignments for every type of country produce, specializing in the sale of cattle, sheep, and hogs. The business failed, however.[10]

On January 30, 1867, the Virginia legislature passed an act incorporating the Southern Association for the Benefit of the Widows and Orphans of the Southern States. The purpose of the corporation was to dispose of certain personal property and real estate and direct the proceeds to relieve the sufferings of the widows and orphans who the Civil War left homeless, helpless, and penniless. Rosser became the managing director of the cause and moved to Richmond. Even this seemingly innocuous endeavor was not without controversy. John S. Mosby, still angry about the letter Rosser had written during the war concerning the partisans, found this an opportunity to attack Rosser in the press. Mosby essentially accused Rosser of being associated with "a

8. William Griffith Thomas, III, "Under Indictment: Tom Rosser and the New South," Master's Thesis, UVA, p.3.
9. Jubal A. Early to Thomas L. Rosser, May 10, 1866, Thomas L. Rosser Papers, UVA.
10. Bushong, Fightin' Tom Rosser, 186.

scheme once proposed to him, intended to swindle the people of the South." Rosser, exasperated anyone would attack his efforts in a humanitarian enterprise, wrote mutual friend Gen. William H. F. Payne, asking him what he could learn about Mosby's motives. Rosser told Payne that he had written Mosby concerning the printed attack, but had heard nothing back. Rosser pointed out he and Charles Purcell were each bonded "for the faithful discharge of our duties and each [was] superintended by an Executive Committee." Rosser perceived Mosby's actions as an unprovoked attack with no clear motive. A duel between Rosser and Mosby became a possibility. Rosser's friend met with Mosby who denied he had any purpose in offending Rosser. Yet, he did not answer Rosser's letter and refused to withdraw his criticisms in the press.[11]

Rosser wrote Betty of his woes:

> I cannot command language which will do justice or convey to you the slightest idea of my sufferings at this time. I am assailed by everybody and there seems to be no way to escape but to fight everybody—can I do this? Of course I can as long as I live, but a course of this charade would soon terminate my life. Then the question would still be left unsettled and my reputation lost... I know my dear wife that I am not a bad man—that I never intended to do a mean act and in this view of it would it not be better to go where I am not known... I can't leave here 'till I hear from Col. Mosby, whom I wrote to immediately upon my arrival here and I must settle with him before I leave... Where on Earth are we to get money from? I have not enough to take me back to you. I suppose I can borrow enough for that but I will have to go to work like a slave to support you.[12]

During these lean times, marked with her husband's infrequent trips home, Betty remained at Courtland. Rosser struggled elsewhere to hold jobs. With his financial troubles deepening, he set up as a business, Thomas L. Rosser & Starr, to broker wheat and farm animals. But it failed too. He then moved to Baltimore where he

---

11. Mosby did not learn of this letter until after the war; *Richmond Examiner*, February 8 and 16, 1867; Thomas L. Rosser to Gen. William Henry Fitzhugh Payne, February 12 and 23, 1867, William Henry Fitzhugh Payne Papers, Accession #21705, LVA. It is unclear how the situation between Rosser and Mosby was resolved, but they averted a duel. It appears Mosby's words to Payne settled the matter for Rosser.
12. Thomas L. Rosser to Betty W. Rosser, February 18, 1867, Thomas L. Rosser Papers, UVA.

worked with the city waterworks. Struggling, his failing work and fading prospects left Rosser disenchanted and destitute.[13]

In July 1867, Tom wrote Betty, "Oh where are the hopes we cherished? Today I received a letter from Col. Harman saying that he could do nothing for me, and now I am left alone without a single one to turn to. I am not desperate. I am not going to kill myself or do anything rash, but I am sorely troubled."[14]

Meanwhile, in 1868, Tom Rosser accepted a minor engineering position with the Pittsburgh & Connellsville Railroad. When this job failed to satisfy him, he sought work with the Cincinnati & Ohio Railroad, but the officers of the company, who were biased against former Confederates, rejected him.[15]

Rosser may have been discouraged, but he liked the railroad business. It afforded him the great outdoors, so he decided to try again, this time, out West. In the western part of the country there were more employment opportunities and less prejudice against Southerners. He also hoped for an escape from the sting of constant criticism after his performance in the fiasco of Tom's Brook. Borrowing money from his mother-in-law, in 1869 he ventured to St. Paul, Minnesota. He also tried to raise money by giving lectures, but even these efforts failed. Discouraged, on Christmas Eve he wrote Betty, "I failed utterly with my lecture [yesterday], the night was bitter cold, the thermometer stood 23 [degrees] below zero, and no one came out. . . . I now have only three cents to my name. But [I] am not in the least dismayed." Rosser was depressed and perhaps even despondent, but he was also irrepressible. He would pick himself up and go on about the business of securing a job—any job.[16]

Tom next had an interview with the president of the Lake Superior and Mississippi Railroad, which connected St. Paul with Lake Superior. Although impressed by Rosser's appearance and robustness, the president informed him all the leading positions in his engineering firm had been filled. He must have been even more impressed when Rosser told him he was not expecting a head position, but would take any job available. When the president offered him a post as an axe man at a salary of $40 per month, the ex-cavalry general accepted. Blessed with a strong body, Rosser took easily to the swinging of an axe and clearing trees from the railroad's right-of-way. Rosser's performance in

13. Hanson, 27; Rhyn, *Thesis*, 77.
14. Thomas L. Rosser to Betty W. Rosser, July 16, 1867, Thomas L. Rosser Papers, UVA.
15. Beane, *Thesis*, 56.
16. Thomas L. Rosser to Betty Rosser, December 24, 1869, Thomas L. Rosser Papers, UVA.

this menial job impressed his boss, and he was promoted quickly to survey crew supervisor. He was overjoyed to have a steady income to support his family in Courtland, but he also sought better opportunities. In 1870, he joined James J. Hill's Northern Pacific Railroad, and before long he became their assistant engineer of construction.[17]

In 1869, Jay Cooke, the country's leading banker, decided to finance the surveying and construction of the Northern Pacific Railroad (NPRR). The railroad would be a transcontinental track from Duluth, Minnesota, to Seattle, Washington. The NPRR pushed its line westward by 1870. In February, Rosser was offered an engineer position in charge of surveys and construction from Twin Lakes to the Red River in Minnesota, a distance of 250 miles. His salary would be $150 per month, including room and board. He excitedly wrote Betty, "If I secure a good place on the NPRR my fortune is made if the work is anything like it was on the Union Pacific Road." With his outlook improving, he realized he would have opportunities to invest in real estate close to the rail lines. Thrilled, he told Betty, "The excitement is great over the NPRR and I will invest some money in a good place I think." Thomas Rosser was on his way to becoming, among other things, a land speculator. His access to inside information would make investing in land a low risk venture.[18]

Life on the railroad frontier was lonely for the men, and some sought the company of women in nearby towns or at the camps. By February 1870, Betty had heard a rumor that her husband had an affair with a servant, and she confronted him in a letter. Rosser responded, "The vile report concerning that servant is a base slander. I don't even recollect the woman and before Heaven I am innocent. But if the report is out there, there is no remedy—yet you are all the world to me."[19]

The 1871 Yellowstone Expedition

One of Rosser's first assignments was to locate the place where the railroad would cross the Red River at Fargo, Dakota Territory. The Sioux Indians in the area were hostile, even though the government had negotiated treaties with Indians living in territories where the railroad would cross. Hostilities became so strong that the railroad requested government military protection. The federal authorities

17. Rhyn, *Thesis*, 78; Bushong, *Fightin' Tom Rosser*, 186.
18. Thomas L. Rosser to Betty Rosser, February 13, 19, 1870, Thomas L. Rosser Papers, UVA.
19. Thomas L. Rosser to Betty W. Rosser, March 1, 1870, Thomas L. Rosser Papers, UVA.

Left to Right: Sarah Ann Gregory Winston, Thomas Rosser, Jr., General Thomas Rosser, William Rosser, Barbara Winston Rosser, and Sally Rosser,

With permission from Elizabeth Bushong Potter,
Executor of the Milliard K. and Dean M. Bushong estates.

complied, realizing the importance of the Northwest railroad. Rosser's military experience proved he could lead men, and he became head of the engineering party that left Fort Rice, south of Bismarck, on September 9, 1871. The 500-man military escort, Gen. Joseph N. Whistler commanding, included 50 Indian scouts, two Gatling guns, and 100 wagons filled with supplies. Rosser led the expedition up the Heart River, across the Dakota Territory, through the Badlands of Little Missouri, and on to the Yellowstone River in Montana. He prepared preliminary engineering studies for construction of a rail line. This survey was the first practical route developed to the Yellowstone River. Surveying the railroad line took five weeks, after which the party returned to Fort Rice on October 14.[20]

With winter approaching, Rosser chose a location to encamp along Front Street in Fargo, Dakota Territory. He set up a camp, "Fargo on the Prairie," consisting of about 50 tents, which housed the railroad surveyors and engineers. His own tent had a wooden floor, six pieces of furniture, and about a dozen wall pictures.[21]

20. "1871 Yellowstone Expedition" (Thomas Rosser typewritten article), Rosser Papers, UVA; Louis Tuck Renz, *The History of the Northern Pacific Railroad* (Fairfield, WA, 1980), 37; Rhyn, Thesis, 84; Beane, *Thesis*, 58.
21. Bushong, *Fightin' Tom Rosser*, 188.

Thomas L. Rosser and three of his children (Sally, Will, and Thomas, Jr.) at a Northern Pacific Railroad Construction Camp, Fargo, North Dakota -Circa 1872. As Chief Construction Engineer, he used inside information to make speculative land purchases that made him a rich man.

Credit: *Minnesota Historical Society*

Once settled in for the winter, Rosser sent for his family, which now included four children: Sally Rosser, born August 17, 1864; Thomas L. Rosser Jr., born September 5, 1867; William Overton Rosser, born May 10, 1869; and John Pelham Rosser, born June 5, 1871. During the family's stay in the West, two more children were born: Elise Florence Rosser, born May 10, 1874, and Marguerite Rosser, born December 26, 1879.[22]

Not far from Rosser's "Fargo on the Prairie" was another camp called "Fargo in the Timbers," which housed about 600 construction workers, including rougher types and other less than desirable elements of society. Sometimes this crowd would steal food from the wagons headed for Rosser's camp. One such incident was reported in the local press:

22. Clayton Torrence, ed., *Winston of Virginia and Allied Families* (Richmond, 1927), 52–53; Bushong, *Fightin' Tom Rosser*, 188.

General Rosser and Staff in front of "Engineer's Office" at Fargo, North Dakota – Circa 1872. Rosser is third from the left.

Credit: Minnesota Historical Society

One day before Christmas, Fargo in the Timbers learned that a 4-horse wagon had gone east to get a supply of potatoes for Rosser's camp. Just after dark the wagons crossed the river and started to climb the bank on the Dakota side. The drivers were well muffled up and were cold from the long drive. They didn't notice that several men had taken out the rod which held the end board in place. The potatoes had been loosely packed. When the wagon reached the steepest part of the bank, the men raised the end board and fired their revolvers. This scared the horses and they ran off; so the potatoes which were strung out along the trail were picked up by the men, women, and children.[23]

Rosser, still in financial straits, made small, quick trade profits from land speculation, of which he had inside knowledge. He also aided his brothers-in-law, William and Fendall Winston, in setting up a construction company that built small bridges as an NPRR subcontractor.[24]

Rosser's job required long and frequent separations from his family. These absences took a toll on his marriage, but he dearly loved his wife and children. He wrote Betty:

---

23. Bushong, *Fightin' Tom Rosser*, 188; Beane, *Thesis*, 59–60.
24. M. John Lubetkin, *Jay Cooke's Gamble: The Northern Pacific Railroad, The Sioux, and The Panic of 1873* (Norman, Oklahoma, 2006), 72.

> **Little did I think when seven years ago as I offered my heart to you and asked in return your love that before we had lived in wedlock ten years it would become necessary for me to leave you and so desolately roam over the far west in search of a home for you and our precious offspring. But there is one thing which I did expect and which has been realized: that today I love you far better than the night of our wedding and I feel that that love will continue ... until eternally sealed by the hand of Heaven.[25]**

Rosser was always conflicted between his desire to be with his family and his intensely ambitious need to succeed. Money and ambition always triumphed, even after Betty and the children moved back to Virginia in 1883. He once wrote, "I can but be regarded in the East as a fossil of a period now past and to initiate myself with another would require either money or happy opportunity and I have not the first... Away off here in the west these unpleasant things will be forgotten and I will be a happy cheerful man." His confidence returned, and in June he wrote Betty promising his job would last 10 years, and "in that time I will make my dear Lizzy rich. You see if I don't." Rosser simply did not want to live in the East. He loved the outdoors and the challenges the West posed. Above all, it afforded him opportunities unavailable elsewhere to succeed in his search for wealth.[26]

The 1872 Surveying Expeditions

Two surveying expeditions started for Yellowstone in 1872, but both ended in failure, damaging banker Jay Cooke's fundraising efforts. The first expedition began from Fort Rice on July 26, with more than 600 military men and 100 wagons. Another surveying party started out from Helena, Montana, the next day. The parties were supposed to meet at the Powder River. Three months earlier, Col. David S. Stanley, commander of the army's military escort for Rosser's surveying party, had met with emissaries of Chief Sitting Bull prior to leaving Fort Rice. The Sioux, who had left the 1871 surveying parties alone to do their work, warned if the NPRR tried to build through Indian territory, they would tear up the railroad and kill its builders. Stanley wrote Rosser, "I had a long talk with Spotted Eagle... [He said]

---

25. Thomas L. Rosser to Betty W. Rosser, February 16, 1870, Thomas L. Rosser Papers, UVA.
26. Thomas L. Rosser to Betty W. Rosser, March 1, 1870, Thomas L. Rosser Papers, UVA.

he would destroy the road and attack any party that tried to build it... I tried to make him understand the fatal consequences. He said he did not care, 'it was life or death and he would fight it out.'"[27]

One purpose of the expedition was to determine if a more direct route to Yellowstone from that of the 1871 survey could be established. The military escort consisted of 33 officers and 553 enlisted men; they carried a twelve-pound Napoleon and three Gatling guns. Colonel Stanley's request for two cavalry companies was refused. The party included more than 100 teamsters, support personnel, and surveyors.[28]

Stanley had taken Spotted Eagle's threats seriously and had devised a good protection scheme. He assigned an infantry company to work with the surveyors daily. The rest of his soldiers acted as pickets, marching in formation around the wagons and beef herd. Gatling guns were placed in the front and rear, with the Napoleon and a Gatling gun in the center. At the end of the day, the wagons formed in a square, and the cattle, horses, and mules grazed nearby until dusk, when they were driven inside the formation. The soldiers slept just outside the wagons. One company kept guard each night.[29]

The first two weeks of the expedition were uneventful. The men marched 180 miles by July 31, following the Heart River to Antelope Creek. On August 13 Stanley's scouts reported seeing a score of hostile Indians. The first Indian attack, including about 20 raiders, came at dawn on August 16; the Hunkpapa band of Lakota war chief Gall led the charge. They made a lot of noise, fired a few volleys, and then fled. The march continued, and by day's end the expedition reached a spot only 10 miles from Yellowstone, which the convoy reached the following day. Unbeknownst to Rosser, a family tragedy was unfolding at home. Back in Fargo, Betty penned in her diary, "Poor little Pelham is not very well."[30]

Upon reaching the angle between the Yellowstone and Powder rivers, Rosser's party had completed their mission. They marked the spot by planting a large cottonwood post, penciling the date on it. Once again, Gall and his braves attacked the expedition party, but no one was hurt. Gall, a striking figure, was almost six feet and heavy boned with an erect posture; he was described as sensually handsome. Even Betty, when shown a photograph of Gall, proclaimed, "Painful as

---

27. Lubetkin, Jay Cook's Gamble, 114–15; "Indian War Brewing," *St. Paul Weekly Pioneer,* April 26, 1872.
28. Lubertkin, *Jay Cooke's Gamble,* 112–13, 118–19.
29. Ibid., 121.
30. Ibid., 123; Betty W. Rosser Diary, August 17, 1872, Thomas L. Rosser Papers, UVA.

it is for me to look upon the pictured face of an Indian, I never in my life dreamed there could be in all the tribes so fine a specimen of a warrior as Gall."[31]

John A. Haydon led the second surveying team, the Western Yellowstone Surveying Expedition, and Maj. Eugene M. Baker commanded its military escort. Its mission entailed crossing the Yellowstone River to the south and surveying downstream to the Powder River, where it would meet Rosser's surveyor team. Haydon's team got an unexplained late start on July 27 from Fort Ellis, and had to hurry to meet Rosser at the Powder River. A late snowmelt and unseasonable rain created high water levels on the Yellowstone River, making crossing impossible. In the unusually hot weather the marching pace slowed significantly. The men were forced to continue marching on the wrong side of the Yellowstone River, and thus they accomplished no surveying. Sitting Bull's warriors launched a surprise attack on August 18, but the military escort drove them back after a fierce fight. Finally, at Livingston, present-day Montana, Haydon's party crossed the Yellowstone River. Major Baker established a defensive camp position, and then refused to move farther. Each day the surveyors trekked out to their previous day's ending spot to do another day's surveying. Baker was fed up, refusing to move camp. Haydon finally gave up, asking Baker to lead them back to Fort Ellis. They abandoned the expedition—nixing the rendezvous with Rosser. When they reached Fort Ellis, Baker was placed under arrest, and Haydon's career was over.[32]

Back at Powder River, Colonel Stanley felt lucky his group had survived so far, but after Baker failed to meet them and under mounting pressure, he began drinking heavily. Rosser and Stanley decided to keep working between the Powder River and O'Fallon Creek. On August 20, however, Stanley, knowing Gall's Hunkpapas had reinforcements and were becoming more aggressive, decided not to wait for Baker any longer and to return to Fort Rice. In fact, Sitting Bull was on his way with reinforcements. In the narrow valley of O'Fallon Creek, about 150 of Sitting Bull's warriors, including Gall, attacked. Rosser remembered the Gatling gun was used to good effect. "I jumped off my horse, took a stand near the Gatling gun, and began using my rifle vigorously... The Indians came up within a hundred yards of us and a collision seemed inevitable, when suddenly, as one man, they broke by the flank and dashed up a ravine, and out of sight over the hills," Rosser exclaimed. "Oh, my! What a relief!" Rosser,

31. Betty W. Rosser Diary, August 1, 1872, Thomas L. Rosser Papers, UVA; Lubetkin, *Jay Cooke's Gamble*, 126.
32. Lubetkin, *Jay Cooke's Gamble*, 133, 140, 147.

noticing the troops had wavered and were forced to hold formation, believed if the Indians had come 25 feet closer, the soldiers would have fled. It was then he "realized the difference of an army fighting for patriotism and one fighting for a business or working for a living. A company of volunteers of '61 and '65 would have killed every Indian in that platoon under similar circumstances and these escaped without leaving a single one of their miserable carcasses behind."[33]

Sitting Bull, low on ammunition, abandoned the fight, and Stanley led the expedition out of Yellowstone. With Sitting Bull and Gall gone, the surveyors went back to work. Daniel C. Lindsay, Rosser's boss and an outstanding engineer, ordered Rosser to "find a short cut or else." Lindsay was a cold-hearted bureaucrat who threatened Rosser in his weak spot—fear of unemployment.[34]

Meanwhile, tension crept into Rosser's marriage. Sometime during the expedition Rosser responded to a letter from Betty, writing:

> **I can't see why we are not happy—please don't scold me anymore. You sour and provoke me by chiding such as charging me with not loving you—I know that my devotion is as deep as [the] Ocean when you are gentle—but when you quarrel and feel that I must resent it and then my heart sickens and my love dies... It is absolutely necessary that we be separated for a little while, and we never can live constantly together until we can do so without quarreling.**[35]

On August 24, now confident of reaching Fort Rice, Stanley sent back 37 empty wagons and two infantry companies, along with Lindsay and two other civilians, while Rosser began hunting for a viable shorter route for the railroad. He remained in the area almost three weeks, frantically trying to find a shortcut in eastern Montana. The Northern Pacific Journal highlighted the lack of progress and the likelihood that the "line would have to be abandoned." In the field, Rosser and his men had become exhausted, and the evening weather began to chill by mid-September.[36]

Tragedy struck the Rosser family on August 20, 1872, when their infant son, John Pelham Rosser, who had contracted cholera, died. Betty had to endure her grief alone at the tent city in Fargo. She wrote in her diary, "Anguish to bear it and say, 'Thy will be done.'" It was

33. Rosser, "Death of Adair," Thomas L. Rosser Papers, UVA; Lubetkin, *Jay Cooke's Gamble*, 150–51.
34. Rosser, "Death of Adair," 19; Lubetkin, *Jay Cooke's Gamble*, 151–52.
35. Thomas L. Rosser to Betty W. Rosser, unknown month, 27th day, 1872, Thomas L. Rosser Papers, UVA.
36. Lubetkin, *Jay Cooke's Gamble*, 152–53.

not until September 21, when 50 resupply wagons from Fort Rice reached Rosser, that he first learned the news of his son's death. He remained stoic, writing Betty, "It is hard to give him up, but these griefs are inevitable, and we must be prepared to meet them." The next evening, he wrote in his diary, "How I ... [miss] my dear wife and crave so much to be with her. She misses our dear little Pelham more than I do."[37] This tragedy, which greatly affected both parents, weakened the bond between them.[38]

Meanwhile, on October 2, the expedition crossed the divide between the Cannonball and Heart rivers. Stanley, at Rosser's suggestion, released Major K. E. A. Crofton and his 17th Infantry's 125 men to proceed to Fort Rice. The expedition party was unaware that Gall, with 100 Hunkpapas, shadowed their moves. Crofton camped 15 miles east of Stanley, close to the Heart River crossing. One of Crofton's officers, Lt. Eban Crosby, went out hunting on foot on October 3, spotted an antelope, and followed it. He proceeded too far from camp, and Gall and his Hunkpapas surrounded him. He was tortured, killed, and scalped.[39]

On several occasions during the Yellowstone expedition, Rosser barely escaped death. On a clear and warm October 4 morning, he and several companions rode ahead of their military escort to examine the line, but suddenly found themselves surrounded by about 80 hostile Indians. A member of the survey team wrote in his diary:

> **They did not rush on him [Rosser] as they evidently thought they had a sure thing of it—Lieut. Adair, who was out with the escort that day was a mile away from the command on foot hunting. Gen. Rosser saw him and motioned him to run. [Albert O.] Eckelson joined the Gen. just then and they turned back to help Adair whom they had not recognized but thought was a private soldier. When they reached him they found he had been wounded and had wounded one of the Indians. There were three Indians within five hundred feet of him when Rosser got there, and he killed the one that Adair had wounded and got all his trappings off him. The fight occurred six miles from camp. The ambulance and a company of soldiers were sent out to bring Adair in. Steve [Harris] [Stanley's servant cook] was caught by the Indians while out hunting and when found had three arrows in his body and five gunshot wounds in his head and neck. Adair, the**

37. Thomas Rosser Diary, Thomas L. Rosser Papers, UVA.
38. Betty W. Rosser Diary, August 21, 1872, UVA; Lubetkin, *Jay Cooke's Gamble*, 149; Bushong, *Fightin' Tom Rosser*, 189, 193; Rhyn, *Thesis*, 104.
39. Lubetkin, *Jay Cooke's Gamble*, 154–55.

first cousin of First Lady Julia Dent Grant, died the next day. Hearing gunfire, the military escort soon arrived and drove off the Indians. Rosser recalled it as "a narrow escape for me."[40]

Philip Sheridan's observer on the expedition released a positive report, but the press gave full coverage to the Indian fighting, negating any positive aspects of the enterprise. It was a public relations nightmare. Rosser had failed to meet Haydon, had not found a shorter route to eastern Montana, and had lost fine men like Adair and Crosby. Upon returning to Minnesota, Rosser and most of the surveyors were laid off. Jay Cook's financial health had declined markedly.[41]

When Tom Rosser returned from the expedition, he was still terribly shaken about the loss of his son; he had become very attached to the young lad named after his West Point roommate and good friend, John Pelham. The nearest doctor was 135 miles away in Brainerd, Minnesota, so Rosser decided to relocate his family to Minneapolis, where better medical care was available. The family took up residence in Minneapolis until Betty and the children moved back to Virginia, before Rosser "retired" from the railroad business in 1885.[42]

The 1873 Yellowstone Expedition

Officials of the NPRR wanted to complete the Yellowstone survey in order to establish a 2,000-mile continuous survey line from Duluth, Minnesota, to Tacoma, Washington. In the summer of 1873, the company sent out a 22-man surveying party to map out the uncompleted portion of the rail line from the Missouri River in the Dakota Territory to the interior of Montana west of Yellowstone. The expedition became known as the "Yellowstone Surveying Expedition."[43]

40. Lubetkin, M. John, "Thomas L. Rosser and The Yellowstone Surveying Expedition of 1873," *North Dakota History*, 2003, 2; Thomas Rosser Diary; *Jay Cooke's Gamble*, 153–54; John A. Phillips, III, Tell Tale Extra: Heart River; URL: www.employees.org/~davison/nprha/tteexpedition.html; Journal of N.P.R.R. surveying expedition from Missouri River to Powder River - two parties - A. O. Eckelson [and] W. E. Welch chiefs of party - accompanied by Gen. Rosser [and] Mr. Linsley [1872], February 22, 2001, University of Montana, Mike and Maureen Mansfield Library, K. Ross Toole Archives, Northern Pacific Collection 128, Box 218, Folder 12.
41. Lubetkin, *Jay Cooke's Gamble*, 168–69.
42. Bushong, *Fightin' Tom Rosser*, 189, 193; Rhyn, *Thesis*, 104.
43. Lubetkin, "Thomas L. Rosser and The Yellowstone Surveying Expedition of 1873," *North Dakota History*, 2003, 3.

Major General George Armstrong Custer

Thomas Rosser was Custer's best friend at West Point. This photograph was taken by Mathew Brady at the close of the Civil War. Rosser and Custer reunited in the Northwest.

With a reputation as a great motivator, leader, and improviser, Rosser led the surveying party. Yet, his managerial and organizational skills were modest, at best. According to Montgomery Meigs Jr., son of the army's wartime quartermaster general, "Rosser muddles things up so awfully. He hasn't the slightest method in him, and rushes engineers off their own work into somebody else's and makes confusion all the time."[44]

A force of 1,350 soldiers, including cavalry, infantry, a battery of artillery, and a detachment of 40 Indian scouts, escorted the party. Three hundred fifty teamsters and their wagons accompanied the

---

44. Rhyn, *Thesis*, 90; Montgomery Meigs Jr. to his parents, July 11, 1872; Elizabeth Atwater, "The Letters of Montgomery Meigs," Master's Thesis, State University of Montana, 1937, Montana Historical Society, microfilm #140; Lubetkin, "Thomas L. Rosser and The Yellowstone Surveying Expedition of 1873," 3.

expedition. Colonel Stanley, already known as a heavy drinker, commanded the force, which included Lt. Col. George Armstrong Custer's Seventh United States Cavalry.[45]

Rosser remembered a day from June 1873 when Custer, resting in his tent, heard the unmistakable voice of his West Point pal outside. Custer called out, "Haloo, old fellow! I haven't heard that voice in thirteen years, but I know it. Come in and welcome!" The former West Point classmates greatly rejoiced when Rosser entered the tent. No longer enemies at war, they could now resume their close friendship and enjoy each other's company. For hours they lay on a buffalo robe and reminisced about the war. They recalled the times they had fought each other, along with their victories and defeats, and even the captures of each other's uniforms and personal effects.[46]

Rosser confided the worst defeat he ever experienced was at the battle of Tom's Brook, in October 1864, when Custer's horsemen captured his headquarters wagon containing his uniform and other belongings. Rosser told Custer that on the morning of the fight, while looking through his field glasses, he had recognized Custer leading his column of troopers. He had pointed to Custer, calling to his staff, "You see that officer down there? That's General Custer, the Yanks are so proud of, and I intend to give him the best whipping today that he ever got. See if I don't." Rosser continued, "And so, we would have done had you attacked us as we thought you intended to; but, instead of that you slipped another column away around us, and so my men began calling out, 'We are flanked! We're flanked!' and then broke out and ran, and nothing could stop them."[47]

The two famous cavalrymen could not have looked much different from their war days. A contemporary described Rosser: "Rosser is a man about six feet two inches in height, broad and erect, with a well-knit frame, and weighing about 220 pounds. His face is round and full, his hair black, his complexion fair, and with a ruddy tinge." William E. Phelps, president of Winona (Minnesota) College, described Rosser and Custer:

> He impresses you in his physical presence as a man of great strength and endurance. In conversation his voice is never pitched on a high key, but is deliberate without being slow, energetic without being demonstrative. He is one who is eminently fitted to exert great influence over men and to retain a hold on their confidence... He enjoys

45. Bushong, *Fightin' Tom Rosser*, 189; Fargo Forum, June 4, 1950.
46. Bushong, *Fightin' Tom Rosser*, 189; Beane, *Thesis*, 60.
47. Bushong, *Fightin' Tom Rosser*, 190.

in a high degree the confidence of the company [Northern Pacific], and it is safe to affirm that this confidence is in no respect likely to be misplaced. Custer, on the other hand, was less than six feet tall, lean at 165 pounds, well proportioned, lithe, agile, with deep-set piercing blue eyes, tawny mustache, wavy golden hair, and a face that habitually wore a thoughtful expression. He was personable and fun-loving, with a penchant for practical jokes. He spoke rapidly, often as if his words ran ahead of his thoughts, and he moved about rapidly.[48]

Throughout the Yellowstone expedition, the Sioux Indians, with Sitting Bull as their leader, continued looking for opportunities to kill anyone that became separated from the military escort. Rosser left for Bismarck on June 13 to begin the survey. On June 17, Rosser, his engineers, and one company of infantry left camp, located about a mile from Fort Lincoln. Though a squad of about 50 "hooting" Indians assaulted them, they "escaped without injury, ran 3 miles and walked 5 miles to camp."[49]

Rosser and his team found themselves caught in a horrific hailstorm on June 24. One cavalryman wrote, "Suddenly, about sunset the sky became overcast with thick clouds which assumed a greenish hue and caused all surrounding objects to have the most ghastly appearance." Balls of ice the size of marbles, or larger, suddenly hammered down on the surveying party. One soldier had to be hospitalized and some 30 mules and a few horses had to be destroyed after the 10-minute storm. As the horses tried desperately to escape the pounding hail, Rosser was the only rider not thrown from his mount. Rosser's hands were cut, and like the other men, he was badly bruised. His body looked as if it had been "beaten with a tact hammer." A nearby creek was renamed "Hailstone Creek." It took almost a week to repair the wagons.[50]

Rosser was anxious to press ahead, but Stanley, often drunk, was bringing up the rear of the protecting army, then 15 miles behind Rosser and Custer. Stanley had insisted they not move farther until he could join the rest of the soldiers. Stanley did not trust Custer, but Rosser managed to keep them at peace for a while. Custer had a

48. Thomas L. Rosser Papers, UVA, 1171a.b., Box 1, quoted from the Richmond Whig, August 12, 1873; Lubetkin, *Jay Cooke's Gamble*, 193–94.
49. Thomas Rosser Diary, Thomas L. Rosser Papers, UVA; Lubetkin, "Thomas L. Rosser and The Yellowstone Surveying Expedition of 1873," 5.
50. Lubetkin, "Thomas L. Rosser and The Yellowstone Surveying Expedition of 1873," 5–6; Frost, *Custer's 7th Cavalry*, 43–44; Thomas L. Rosser to Betty W. Rosser, June 28, 1873, Thomas L. Rosser Papers, UVA.

reputation for quarreling with weak superiors. He had threatened to arrest Stanley during one mutinous fracas. Finally, Stanley arrived and the surveyors moved on, connecting with the 1871 surveyors at Heart River on July 7.[51]

Custer, Rosser, and a squadron of cavalry reached Yellowstone on July 15. On July 21, Rosser wrote, "Stanley is very drunk and I fear Custer will arrest him and assume command." Custer vented his feelings to Rosser, but decided not to arrest Stanley. The surveying work was completed on July 28, and Rosser started for his camp in Fargo. He made it to Bismarck by July 31, and on August 11 he took a train for New York to meet with NPRR management. He arrived a couple days later, presenting a report to management the next day. Rosser's optimistic report resulted in the NPRR issuing invitations for bids for construction of the railroad portion between the Missouri and Yellowstone rivers, a distance of 205 miles, 23 miles shorter than the 1871 survey had projected.[52]

While Rosser was in New York, two brisk fights between the military escort of his surveying crew and the Indians broke out on August 4 and 11, 1873, along the Yellowstone River, near the mouth of the Tongue River. The Indians suffered greater losses than Custer's troopers in the fights near the town of Big Horn in present-day Montana. The press picked up the story, and though Custer's heroics thrilled the citizenry, the financial community became nervous.[53]

Jay Cooke's investment firm set off the financial Panic of 1873 when it declared bankruptcy on September 18. The boom in railroad reconstruction in the South, coupled with successful westward expansion projects like the Union Pacific Railroad, had enticed investors and speculators to invest heavily on new transportation projects (such as the Second Transcontinental Railroad and the NPRR). Cooke's firm financially overextended itself in rail investments and could not meet its debt obligations. Cooke had to declare bankruptcy. Fearing more defaults, banks around the country began calling in loans, causing more firms and investors to default, which inevitably severed the rail industry's cash flow. A major financial depression resulted; the New York Stock Exchange closed for 10 days. Between 1873 and 1879, unemployment reached a record high

51. Lubetkin, "Thomas L. Rosser and The Yellowstone Surveying Expedition of 1873," 9.
52. Thomas Rosser Diary, Thomas L. Rosser Papers, July 21, 1873, UVA; Lubetkin, "Thomas L. Rosser and The Yellowstone Surveying Expedition of 1873," 13.
53. Lubetkin, "Thomas L. Rosser and The Yellowstone Surveying Expedition of 1873," 14.

of 14 percent. Out of the nation's 364 railroads, 89 went under, and 18,000 businesses failed along with them. In the meantime, the depression spread to Europe with the international fall in demand for silver, which followed Germany's decision to abandon the silver standard in the wake of the Franco-Prussian War. Rosser, already underway with pre-construction work, had to lay off his contractors and conduct an auction sale of the company's property and supplies.[54]

Rosser left New York on August 16, stayed overnight in Chicago, and arrived in St. Paul on August 21, 1873. Next, he travelled west to clear up a few last details, returning to Bismarck and then Fargo. While in Fargo he visited his son John Pelham's grave, remarking, "Rank weeds have grown over him but he sleeps undisturbed." Now unemployed, Rosser joined his family in Minneapolis, where he was fortunate to land a job as the city engineer.[55]

Almost three years later, on June 25, 1876, Custer and 225 of his men attacked the Sioux Indians along the Little Bighorn River; Custer and his men were killed. Rosser, wishing to take revenge for his courageous friend's death, wrote, "I should like to be commissioned by my country to avenge the death of my gallant friend and old enemy and return to old Virginia and get my division, who once so fiercely fought him, and who, like myself have learned to respect, honor, and appreciate his high soldierly qualities and exalted manhood of Gen. Custer."[56]

Rosser eulogized his friend in a letter to the Minneapolis Pioneer Press and Tribune, penning, "I can truly say now that I never met a more enterprising, gallant or dangerous enemy during those four years of terrible war, nor a more genial, wholesouled, chivalrous gentleman in peace than Major General George A. Custer." Rosser continued pouring out his praise of Custer in the Chicago Tribune: "As a soldier I would sooner today lie in the grave of Gen. Custer and his gallant comrades alone in that distant wilderness, that when the last trumpets sound I could rise to judgment from my post of duty, than to live in place of the survivors [Frederick W. Benteen and Marcus Reno] of the siege on the hills."[57]

After Custer's death, many people whom he had offended spoke up to assail his character. As might be expected, his lifelong friend Rosser came to his defense often and did so outspokenly. He blamed

---

54. Ibid.
55. Ibid.
56. *Raleigh Sentinel*, July 18, 1876. Authority figures, such as Philp Sheridan, never seriously considered Rosser's proposal.
57. Bushong, *Fightin' Tom Rosser*, 192; Graham, *The Custer Myth: A Source Book of Custeriana*, 225.

Custer's subordinates for failing to carry out orders. He had particular criticism for Maj. Marcus A. Reno, second-in-command of the 7th Cavalry, for failing to follow Custer's orders by retreating to the hills and by abandoning his commander to his fate. Rosser wrote a letter to the editor of the St. Paul and Minneapolis *Pioneer-Press and Tribune*, which was printed on July 8, 1876, and reprinted in the *New York Herald* on July 11, 1876. He concluded his public statement with the following emotional outburst, reiterating what he had penned for the *Pioneer Express and Tribune*:

> It was expected that when the expedition was sent out that Custer and the Seventh Cavalry were to do all the fighting, and superbly did a portion of them do it... I knew Gen. Custer well; have known him intimately from boyhood; and being on opposite sides during the late war we often met and measured strength on the fields of Virginia, and I can truly say now that I never met a more enterprising, gallant or dangerous enemy during those four years of terrible war, or a more genial, wholesouled, chivalrous gentleman and friend in peace than Major General George A. Custer.[58]

Major Reno wasted no time in defending himself, writing a letter to Rosser printed in the *New York Herald* on August 12. In part, Reno's letter stated:

> My thought was that your motive had only the object of a defense of a personal friend [and] a gallant soldier, against whom you had fought, but after reading all of it, I could no longer look upon it as the tribute of a generous enemy, since through me you had attacked as brave officers [and] men, as ever served the government, [and] with the same recklessness and ignorance of circumstances as Custer is charged with in the attack upon the hostile Indians, both charges, the one against him [and] the one made by you against us, are equally untrue.[59]

Reno went on to explain in detail the fight at Little Bighorn and his part in it. After finally reading the official reports of the engagement, Rosser subsequently retracted his imputations of Reno's

58. Bruce A. Rosenberg, "Custer and the Epic of Defeat," *The Journal of American Folklore*, Vol. 88, No. 348:167; *The Chicago Tribune*, July 8, 1876.
59. W. A. Graham, *The Custer Myth: A source Book of Custeriana* (Harrisburg, PA, 1953), 226–27; Major Marcus A. Reno to Thomas L. Rosser, July 31, 1876, Thomas L. Rosser Papers, UVA.

and the other officers' courage. He stuck to his belief, however, that the surviving soldiers' tactical errors caused Custer's demise.[60]

Rosser found himself in trouble again in an 1878 altercation with Louisiana Congressman Joseph H. Acklen at the Welcker's fashionable restaurant in Washington, D.C. Acklen was a rich, eccentric bachelor who owned sugar plantations and courted many ladies. One evening after an opera, Rosser and a lady friend arrived ahead of their dinner party. Rosser's companion told him she had heard a loud commotion in the next room. Rushing to help after hearing what he thought was a lady's cries of distress, Rosser became convinced that Acklen was assaulting a widow named Lilly Godfrey. According to one version of the events, the big and powerful Rosser ejected the diminutive Acklen from the restaurant. Many observers expected a duel to result from the disturbance. A duel, however, was not in the offing, and Acklen later emphatically denied the incident ever happened. He threatened to find out how the malicious rumor had started and to punish the offender. Acklen was reportedly an excellent pistol shooter and swordsman. The story was confusing; Rosser supposedly told Acklen he was not the source of the rumor, and Acklen published Rosser's denial in the newspapers. Restaurant officials, hoping to limit the damage to the establishment's reputation, denied the event ever occurred. Whatever the exact circumstances surrounding the scandal, Rosser returned to Minneapolis to start on a survey trip.[61]

By 1878 the Northern Pacific's financial situation had improved, the company had been reorganized, and construction had resumed. Rosser left Minneapolis and headed west, where he became engaged in surveying the line across the Missouri River in the Dakota Territory. He located the site for Mandon, North Dakota.[62]

During the winter of 1878 and 1879, Rosser used daring ingenuity to solve a complex engineering problem involving the laying of rail during the winter months. At Bismarck, in present-day North Dakota, the rail had to cross the Missouri River, but the railroad executives decided to postpone construction of a bridge until spring. Rosser, who hated to waste four or five months, came up with an idea to continue working through the winter. He proposed waiting until the river froze to a depth of at least three feet, then to lay rails across the ice, and to transport the locomotives on the rails across the "ice bridge."

60. Ibid. Rosser was probably also concerned over a possible lawsuit by Reno.
61. *San Francisco Chronicle*, June 28, 1878, *New York Times*, June 23, 25, 26, and 29, 1878, July 5 and 6, 1878; *San Francisco Daily* Alta California, November 10, 1886. Perhaps Rosser wanted to avoid a duel at the time, so he assured Acklen he was not the source of the newspaper story.
62. *Thomas L. Rosser Scrapbook*, Thomas L. Rosser Papers, UVA.

Somehow, he convinced management to approve the risky venture. On March 15, 1879, Rosser rode on the last locomotive over the ice, which had a foot of water on top of the ice due to warmer than expected conditions. This ingenious technique worked. The railroaders laid 25 miles of track until the spring thaw enabled them to construct a permanent bridge.[63]

In March 1879, under authority of vice president George Stark of the Northern Pacific Railroad, Rosser began to issue permits to those desiring to buy and occupy lots in Mandon. This upset claim jumpers who were anxious to keep the railroad company from "occupying the town." These armed jumpers attempted to take control of the company's town site and to order off its workmen. Rosser was sent to settle the dispute and to command the rioters to disperse. He was unarmed, but the authority conveyed in his manner and voice had the desired effect. He told his men to keep working and warned the raiders not to shoot. One raider told Rosser "[t]he General would have to walk over his dead body before the company got his lot." Rosser quipped "he had walked over many a carcass in his time." The jumpers reluctantly decided to retire.[64]

Before Rosser completed his work with the NPRR, a disturbing incident involving his wife occurred when she visited Fort Lincoln, a military post about seven miles south of Mandon. It seems that an Italian-born soldier named Giovanni made Betty very uncomfortable by his advances toward her while she was a guest of Maj. John Scroggs Poland. Betty formally complained to Poland, in whose quarters she was apparently staying. Poland had been one of Rosser's tent mates at the plebe summer camp at West Point. Poland wrote Betty, expressing his deep regret regarding the matter, which had happened when he was absent from the fort. Poland petitioned Col. Elwell S. Otis of the 22nd Infantry to arrest the "impertinent" Giovanni if he ever visited his quarters again. He also asked Giovanni's commander, Lt. W. S. Edgerly of the 7th Cavalry, to ensure that from hence forward the "insolent" Giovanni remained in his barracks after tattoo.[65]

When the railroad was extended to Glendive, Montana, in 1880, Rosser completed his work with the NPRR. He then moved to Winnipeg, Canada, where he became the chief engineer of the Canadian Pacific Railroad (CPR). There, he left a lasting tribute to his legacy: the station just west of Winnipeg bears the name Rosser Station.[66]

---

63. *Chicago Tribune*, March 21, 1879.
64. Ibid.
65. John S. Poland to Betty W. Rosser, August 20, 1879, Thomas L. Rosser Papers, UVA.
66. Beane, *Thesis*, 64, Bushong, *Fightin' Tom Rosser*, 193.

Rosser surveyed a new route for the CPR from Portage la Prairie to Grand Valley, on the Assiniboine River, and then through the Brandon Hills to Flat Creek (Oak Lake). Near the crossing of the Assiniboine at Flat Creek, the first of the CPR towns, Brandon, would be built. Rosser's approach to obtaining land along the survey routes involved establishing new CPR communities, instead of adding to existing ones. In 1881, rumors began to spread of a new city to be built west of Winnipeg. Everyone speculated the CPR would build a town at the intermediate point of the rail line between Portage la Prairie and Flat Creek. This would place it about 130 miles west of Winnipeg, near Grand Valley. Surveyors had driven the stakes, and land speculators quickly arrived. The new town would be built on pioneer residents John and Dugald McVicars' land. In April 1881, Rosser visited John McVicar and made him an offer for his property. McVicar, already prodded by the land speculators, demanded double Rosser's offering price. Angered, Rosser reportedly retorted, "I'll be damned if a town of any kind is ever built here." The CPR simply moved the site of its station a couple miles farther west. The CPR would repeat this pattern when land speculators tried to gouge the company for excess profits.[67]

Rosser chose the location for a major divisional point of the Canadian Pacific Railway in May 1881; he named the new town "Brandon" for the nearby Brandon Hills. Hundreds flocked to the area to gain a foothold in the new development and to reap the benefits of the abundant local farmland. Before they could put up permanent structures, new inhabitants arrived and pitched their tents. Brandon grew so rapidly that it never attained the status of a village or a town, but almost overnight became a city, which it was officially incorporated as on May 30, 1882. Its main street was named "Rosser Avenue."[68]

Land around the site where Brandon would be built was purchased for a fraction of the money McVicar had demanded. Unknown at the time, Rosser and his immediate supervisor, Alpheus B. Stickney, general superintendent of the western division of the CPR, had speculated in real estate using insider information that their positions had afforded them. According to the *Toronto Globe*, Rosser and Stickney made $130,000 on land speculating.[69]

---

67. Pierre Berton, *The National Dream: The Last Spike* (Toronto, 1974), 254–55.
68. Martin Kavanagh, *The Assiniboine Basin: A Social Study of Discovery, Exploration and Settlement* (Manitoba: Canada, 2007), 111, 150, 166.
69. Ibid., 255; C. J. Cochrane, "General Rosser and The Canadian Pacific Railroad," *The Cannoneer,* Newsletter of the John Pelham Historical Association, September 1990, vol. 9, No. 2:5–7.

Rosser became deeply involved in land speculation. As the speculation boom peaked in Winnipeg, the CPR brought in a new general manager, William Cornelius Van Horne. Van Horne moved immediately against the land speculators. He discovered a letter in which Rosser revealed to a railroad contractor the future location of the terminus of the CPR's Pembina Mountain Branch. Van Horne warned the general public against purchasing lots, and then set his sights on Rosser. In February 1882, he fired Rosser for "shamelessly colluding with town builders and land speculators along the route." Rosser rushed to St. Paul to meet Van Horne to try to save his job, but the general manager remained adamant. He allowed Rosser to resign, effective February 13, 1882, rather than suffer the humiliation of being fired.[70]

Rosser's resignation did not take effect without complications. Apparently, Rosser obtained the railroad company's newest plans for the railroad's western route before he left the company. After a subsequent investigation, the engineering staff was fired, while Rosser was arrested and charged with fraudulently obtaining the plans. Determined to avenge the insult to his pride and reputation, Rosser filed a $20,000 lawsuit against the railway company for "malicious prosecution, and its managers and others for libel." He predicted a Canadian jury would "redress my wrongs and punish those who have so maliciously and wantonly slandered me." Rosser won an award of only $2,600 for malicious prosecution.[71]

Seemingly, Rosser's posturing worked, because the criminal charges against him were dropped when the CPR lawyers failed to appear in court. That should have been the end of the affair, but Rosser and Van Horne ran into each other at the Manitoba Club in Winnipeg that July. They argued, each brandished a pistol, and a gunfight almost ensued, but bystanders broke them up. It was typical Rosser—hot-tempered, vain, prideful, fearless, and inflexible. He would resort to violence whenever he deemed it necessary to correct a perceived wrong.[72]

Rosser finally decided it was time to return home to Virginia in 1884. He loved the beauty, people, and adventure of the Northwest, but at 48 years old it was time to retire to a simpler life. Fortunately, while chief engineer of the Canadian Pacific, he had saved enough money from his land transactions to buy a 200-acre farm near Charlottesville with a large Victorian house called "Rugby Hall." Betty

70. Rhyn, *Thesis*, 101–2; Berton, *The Last Spike*, 290.
71. Ibid.; *New York Times*, June 2 and 14, 1882.
72. Berton, *The Last Spike*, 291, 298; Rhyn, *Thesis*, 102; *Sacramento Daily Record Union*, June 7, 1882.

and the children had returned to Virginia a year earlier. Rosser liked the area, which offered educational opportunities for his children. He did not want his sons to attend West Point, where they would be exposed to the violence and rigors of military life and feel the pangs of regret he had experienced.[73] Tom Rosser would soon embark on another chapter in his life.

73. Bushong, *Fightin' Tom Rosser*, 193.

"Rugby Hall"

Home of the Thomas L. Rosser Family, Charlottesville, Virginia. Built in 1850 and named after the Boys' School in England.

Photo reproduced by permission of Eleanor Cochran and Douglass Cochran, Jr.

Chapter 10

Retirement Years: Land Speculation, Feuding, and Politics

"Incompetency is not a crime, and that you failed in the Valley is not due to your neglect or carelessness, but I know you were assiduous, but God did not make you a general, and it was Gen. R. E. Lee's mistake in trusting so important a command as you had to you before you had been more fully tried."

Thomas Rosser on General Jubal Early.

For Tom Rosser, now a gentleman farmer, the last adventurous phase of his life was about to unfold. It would involve more financial hardship, losing his wealth in the same manner he obtained it: speculative land ventures. He became nearly destitute, going on the road again seeking affluence, while leaving Betty at home to run a dairy business and rent out cottages in order to keep their Charlottesville, Virginia, home. He found work in Cuba, hoping to make a fortune in land deals. Failing, he returned to Charlottesville broke again, but determined to overcome his troubles. He tried his hand in the political arena, falling short there also. Finally, President Theodore Roosevelt named him postmaster of Charlottesville, thereby securing a steady, reliable income for his family.

With wealth accumulated from the sales of his speculative properties along the routes of the Northern Pacific Railroad and Canadian Pacific Railroad, Rosser purchased an $8,000 estate in Charlottesville. In 1850, Andrew Brown had built "Rugby Hall," named after the famous all-boys school in England. For a while it too had served as a boys' school. Rosser planned to farm the 200-acre estate to supplement his income from his investments. When a friend asked what crops he would raise, he replied, "Grow grapes, make brandy, and raise Hell."[1]

The Rossers enjoyed returning to life in Virginia, but they did not sever their ties with the Northwest entirely. Rosser had purchased a cottage on Lake Minnetonka in Minnesota. His family vacationed

---

1. Betty Smith, "Major General Thomas Lafayette Rosser, My Great Grandfather," 16, Thomas L. Rosser Papers, UVA; Rhyn, *Thesis*, 104.

there during summers to escape the heat of Charlottesville, until financial hardship forced them to sell the cottage.[2]

Tragedy struck the family in 1884 when the Rosser's youngest surviving son, William Overton Rosser, died. The 15-year-old, a youngster of promise, died of blood poisoning after cutting his ankle. Only two years later tragedy struck again; another child, 12-year-old Elise Florence Rosser, died of tuberculosis on June 10, 1886. Elise had been very much concerned about her father's drinking, and at one time had written him: "I is so 'fraid you is drunken." Rosser, yet again, made a promise to his family, vowing to his dying daughter that, henceforth, he would abstain from alcohol. It appears, for the most part, he kept his pledge.[3]

Meanwhile, Rosser's oldest son, Tom Jr., enrolled at Hanover Academy, a Virginia boarding school. Rosser wrote his son often, and when Tom Jr. experienced trouble with the school's headmaster, he advised his son:

> **Now, Tom, Colonel Jones is a gentleman, so, are you... Colonel Jones is my friend, but Tom you are my child... Read this over two or three times before you act, but in any event son, your father is with you in all quarrels, and I don't care with whom they are, my confidence in you is such that I know you can do no cowardly act, but I wish to say that the bravest of men are cool, and go slowly and I am an old and an experienced man, loving you better than I do my life, you had better consult me in all questions of honor... But Tom, my dear son, fight on the spot if you are insulted, even if it costs you your life. Dead a brave man is better than live a coward and life is too short that all we can do is to give our name and reputation to the world and generation after generation will hang on your portrait in their parlor and in pride say, "that is my relative who died as he lived, a Brave and Honest man."[4]**

Rosser attempted to teach his son the code of honor by which he lived: manliness depended upon honor, courage, and reputation.

Between 1885 and 1895, Rosser became involved in several new business ventures, most of which involved land speculation. He partnered with other like-minded individuals, investing in farmland, town sites, and railroads across the upper South. The partners determined, as

---

2. Bushong, *Fightin' Tom Rosser*, 194.
3. Ibid. Rosser surely partook of some brandy from his homegrown winery.
4. Thomas L. Rosser to Tom Rosser Jr., March 12, 1886, Thomas L. Rosser Papers, UVA.

best they could, the routes of new rail lines, purchasing the lands or conveyances on these routes before anyone else learned about the ventures. They would then plan a town site, terminal, depot, or other facility. When the rail lines went through these areas, Rosser and his partners would sell the town lots, splitting the profits with the original investors. The profitable scheme appeared foolproof.[5]

Some of Rosser's partners and investors included Virginia Senator John W. Daniel, generals James T. Wilder, M. C. Butler, and wealthy New York financier, A. B. Harris. Rosser and his partners created the New South Mining and Improvement Company to buy lands along the proposed route of the Charleston, Cincinnati, and Chicago Railroad. Rosser also worked as a consulting engineer, once again obtaining inside information about the routes. Conspiring with the railroad's board of directors, he expected to make huge profits off the land speculations.[6]

Rosser repeated the land speculating scheme by creating the Minneapolis Improvement Company. He purchased land in Russell County, Virginia, to start a new town. He offered the North and West Railroad a right-of-way and financial assistance to run a rail line into the area. The board of directors for both improvement companies was composed of the same group of individuals who often invested with Rosser, thereby profiting from insider information. The set up was "legal," if not ethical, and seemed assured of success. Investment money poured in.[7]

The purchase of lands increased, including acreage in Catlettsburg, along the Clinch River in Russell County, Virginia, as well as in Kentucky. As purchases accumulated Rosser organized new companies to manage them. He also sold the Minnesota Improvement Company to the New South Mining and Improvement Company, consolidating his holdings. When the Clinch River properties opened for sale, he created the St. Paul Improvement Company, in which he heavily invested. In 1890, the Marion Manufacturing and Improvement Company was created with Rosser as a one-sixth partner. He transferred the properties of the New South Mining and Improvement Company to the new firm. The properties lay along the Charleston, Cincinnati, and Chicago rail line, which ran to the city of Marion, Indiana.[8]

Rosser made substantial money for his services and investments. For example, he received $38,000 during a two-month period in 1892.

5. Rhyn, *Thesis*, 105.
6. Ibid.
7. Ibid.
8. Ibid., 108.

Rosser's financial bliss, however, would soon change. The improvement companies were totally dependent upon the completion of the rail lines to make the investors their fortunes. As the 1890s progressed, delays in railroad construction tied up Rosser's money in the lands he had purchased. Becoming overextended, he sold his Minnesota "vacation" properties for $50,000. In 1891, the Marion Manufacturing and Improvement Company went bankrupt. When financier A. B. Harris died in February 1892, his estate "froze," and his heirs withdrew their support. The end seemed near for Rosser's improvement companies, and his financial cushion depleted. The depression of 1893 ultimately ended his land speculation business.[9]

Rosser had gone from being almost destitute just after the war, to wealthy, and back to nearly insolvent, with the exception of his only asset, Rugby Hall. He tried to rebound, planning to bid on various public works projects, but could not bring himself to actually submit bids. Finally, in 1894, he re-entered the land business by purchasing options on large tracts of land in New Kent and James City counties in Virginia. This venture also failed. He and his family were reduced to surviving on proceeds from their farm and a $1,000 annual rental fee for the post office building in Charlottesville.[10]

In 1895, hoping to alleviate financial stress, Betty had published a popular cookbook and household manual, in which she noted:

> **With a good cookery book and manual all housewives have the power within their grasp of ... perfecting themselves in various accomplishments and arts far more potent in a majority of household than those acquired at fashionable and expensive boarding-schools. In acquiring this knowledge, she is abundantly able to train and instruct all servants in her employ so there will be little friction in the domestic machinery.[11]**

The proceeds from the book did contribute some much-needed funds to the family.[12]

Tom Rosser hit bottom in 1897. He mortgaged Rugby Hall to his in-laws for $6,500, and his remaining properties were placed in trust under his son Tom Jr., who paid the back taxes and liens. Most of his holdings were in Betty's name. Rosser borrowed money from his brothers-in-law, who had become contractors in Minneapolis.[13]

---

9. Ibid.
10. Ibid., 109–10.
11. Elizabeth Winston Rosser, *Housekeeper's and Mother's Manual* (Richmond, 1895).
12. Ibid.
13. Ibid., 110.

Tom Rosser, 61 years old, decided on another gamble to escape his financial burdens. He wanted to go to the gold fields of the Yukon and asked his mother-in-law, Sarah Winston, for a $5,000 loan to finance the project. He explained to her: "The tide is now against me and I must make one more hard heavy pull to get up again, and I feel that I am strong enough to make it if I only had a little help." Again, he felt opportunity lie in the West. "There is now a great rush to the newfound gold fields in Alaska, and there is a great deal of money there. If I could get there, with my knowledge of Western life, I could find profitable employment and could make a lot of money." His mother-in-law promptly turned him down, refusing to gamble her money away. Her rejection shocked Thomas Rosser back into reality, and he apologized to her for suggesting such a risky venture.[14]

Post War Photo of Thomas Lafayette Rosser

Rosser was in demand as a speaker after the war.

Reproduced by permission of Eleanor Cochran and Douglass Cochran, Jr.

The staff at Rugby Hall, including a coachman, butler, maid, cook, housekeeper, teacher, and washerwoman, drew a combined $100 per month salary. To pay the expenses, the Rossers rented out cottages at Rugby Hall. Betty set up a dairy farm and ran it alone, selling butter, milk, and cream to the locals. The dairy brought in several hundred dollars a month, enough to pay the bills, yet General Rosser would not stoop to the level of helping her with the dairy business or taking a regular paying job. He felt entitled to a higher-paying job—not just any job, but one speculating in land schemes or public speaking.[15]

---

14. Thomas L. Rosser to "Mother," August 5, 1897, Thomas L. Rosser Papers, UVA: Rhyn, *Thesis*, 110; Thomas, "Under Indictment," 66.
15. Thomas, "Under Indictment," 43, 56–58.

Rosser, clearly feeling the financial pressure, travelled to Minnesota to visit William Overton and Fendall Gregory Winston, his in-laws. He wrote Betty, "F. G. and W. O. will do something for me if they can, but I am prepared for the worst and shall return home with my mind fully made up and all I ask for, is that you may cheerfully stand by me, bear with me, and help me."[16]

While his financial troubles mounted, he continued his career in public speaking. An effective orator, he was in great demand to speak before many functions in the postwar era.

One of his earliest speeches was at an agricultural fair in Staunton, Virginia. Rosser touched on many themes of the emerging "New South." He stated:

> There is no life with lessons. All life is a school. For the past twenty-five years I have been a close student of life. I have ridden on its peaceful tides, and I have been lashed and beaten in its angry storms. I have experienced the stern reversals of hope, and my feet have been bruised and blistered in traversing the pathless wastes of experiment and adventure, of promise and expectation. The dearly bought experience which I have acquired teaches me that the sooner we abandon the formulae and delusions which guided our ancestors, the better it will be for us. We must realize that all systems progress, and that every age is one of revolution.[17]

Rosser extolled the virtues of agriculture, calling it "the basis of civilization, the foundation upon which rests American liberty." He felt that husbandry enabled one to obtain associations more elevated than other pursuits. Despite his experience in the Northwest, he discouraged anyone wishing to relocate, warning that the large corporations had acquired the best land and that the presence of great monopolies made it difficult for the common man to make a living. Rosser noted that many who had gone west had returned, disenchanted. He reminded his audience there was no state in the union that suited Virginians so well as Virginia itself; they should remain at home, where needed.[18]

Rosser advised attracting immigrants to Virginia. He gave a standard "New South" response when asked about the postwar plight of blacks: "If the white man of the South prospers, the black man will

---

16. Thomas L. Rosser to Betty W. Rosser, April 15, 1893, Thomas L. Rosser Papers, UVA.
17. Thomas L. Rosser Papers, 1171g., Box 5 clippings; Thomas, "Under Indictment," 16.
18. Newspaper clipping from the Staunton Spectator, October 20, 1886, *Thomas L. Rosser Scrapbook*, Thomas L. Rosser Papers, UVA, 1171a.b., Box 2, 42.

also, and under no possible circumstances can one prosper in combating the other... It is not true that his presence in the South dwarfs its growth, and he is not objectionable to the emigrant." For Rosser, granting blacks political equality did not equate to granting them social equality. In another speech, he asserted that the black man was "the best laborer in the world—but he needs a leader ... he works well and faithfully for low wages, but the moment he is done, he sits down and waits for somebody to come along and give him a new job."[19]

Years after the gunshots of the Civil War ceased, Tom Rosser still seemed to be fighting the war, unrepentant and unreconstructed. On one speaking occasion, he vigorously expressed:

> I chuckle over the results of socialism anarchism in the North, from which we are free. It has been said that we are the same people, but that was a long time ago. Now evolution or some other process has made us different creatures, and soon capital and oppressed manhood will flee to the South where honest men can protect them. The world will see that Rebels are the only true patriots and supporters of constitutional liberty... I approve all the Southern Confederacy did. It destroyed evil forces and established good ones. Its monuments are to truth, patriotism and glory, not brazen images resulting from blemished hearts and conduct.[20]

At Baltimore in 1889, Rosser gave a speech at the annual reunion for the workers of the Maryland Railroad. They enthusiastically supported him when he stated:

> I am tired of Gettysburg insincere reunions and "Blue and Gray" love feasts which politicians are holding, while old Sherman threatens in his "Old Shady stories" and others dare to call the loyal citizens of the South "traitors." I feel that I am, and I believe that every brave Confederate soldier living today is more loyal to the constitutional government of the New United States than are the rank and file of the Grand Army of the Republic (so called) and I believe that we have more affection for, and are more loyal to the flag of the New Union than they.[21]

19. Ibid.; Interview in New Orleans, April 25, 1887, Thomas L. Rosser Papers, UVA; Thomas, "Under Indictment," 29.
20. *Thomas L. Rosser Scrapbook*, Thomas L. Rosser Papers, UVA, 1171a.b., Box 2, 85.
21. Ibid., Box 2, 69.

General Rosser's undying loyalty to the Southern cause did not blind him to the good in some Federal veterans. For example, when Ulysses S. Grant fell seriously ill in 1885, Rosser visited him, carrying a basket of flowers. When Grant died Rosser gave a stirring eulogy for his former adversary at a memorial service held in Minneapolis.[22]

On rare occasions, Rosser appeared pragmatic. In an interview with a newspaper reporter, he stated that there was no man, North or South, who was more in perfect harmony with and better satisfied with the adjustment of the political differences between the North and South than he. Even if he could, he emphasized he would not re-establish slavery nor would he countenance secession. He went so far as to express his belief that the new order of things was far better than the old. He thought in good time all Southerners would agree.[23] Later, he would even acknowledge slavery as a catalyst for the war:

> **The Southern states legalized African slavery, and although it was also recognized and protected under the Constitution of the general government, the northern states were repugnant to it, and its geographical division of sentiment developed a political antipathy which destroyed the political amity between the states North and South.**

Rosser reportedly stated that "slavery was a stain on the South."[24]

Years after the war, attending a banquet in Boston, Rosser was asked to say a few words about some of his war experiences. He told the story of how he had received a sword that was still in his family. He told of how, after one battle in which he had captured a number of Union prisoners, a young Federal officer requested to see him. The officer asked for his sword to be returned, as it was a gift from his sweetheart. Now in tears, the officer said he wanted to destroy the sword, because he had disgraced it. This display of weakness thoroughly irritated Rosser, so he decided to keep the sword for himself. The fact that the Confederate government did not have an abundance of metal for swords, and Rosser badly needed one himself, influenced his decision to keep the sword. He admitted that upon reflection he should have given the sword back, but the soldier's

22. Bushong, *Fightin' Tom Rosser*, 197; *Thomas L. Rosser Scrapbook*, Thomas L. Rosser Papers, UVA.

23. *Thomas L. Rosser Scrapbook*, Thomas L. Rosser Papers, UVA, 1171a.b., Box 2, 52.

24. Thomas L. Rosser, 1901 Speech, Papers of Thomas L. Rosser Jr., Rosser and Gordon Family Papers, Special Collections Library, UVA; John Y. Simon, Michael E. Stevens, eds., *New Perspectives on the Civil War: Myths and Realities of the National Conflict* (New York, 1998), 110; Jubal Early to William H. Payne, August 27, 1885, Jubal Early Papers, LC.

behavior had so angered him that he did not. Incredibly, that very soldier was in the audience listening to Rosser's remarks and rose to speak: "General Rosser, I am the man and you needn't give the matter another thought, because when I got back from the war, my girl had married another fellow."[25]

Rosser, when not on speaking tours, supplemented income by establishing a vineyard at Rugby Hall. He planted 3,500 grapevines on a five-acre tract. By 1891, he was selling at least 10 tons of grapes at harvest to the Monticello Wine Company, while keeping enough to produce 40 barrels of his homemade brandy.[26]

Though reconciled to the results of the war, Rosser spent much of his retired life at Rugby Hall involved in disputes with former war associates, either Confederate or Union. Many veterans of the war wrote him about their experiences, and it was inevitable that old disagreements and wounds reopened. The disagreements served no useful purpose, but only embittered the adversaries. Rosser responded to criticisms with going on the attack, verbally assaulting and belittling opponents while undermining their credibility. [27]

One of Rosser's most persistent critics was his former Shenandoah Valley commander Jubal Early, the man who had recommended him for promotion to major general. Early had a biting tongue, a harsh temperament, and a tendency to make sarcastic attacks in his disputes with Rosser and many others. Rosser wrote a series of articles for the *Philadelphia Weekly Times* about the Valley campaign of 1864. He criticized Early in the articles, blaming him for failing to group cavalry in the Valley under Lunsford Lomax (the senior cavalry commander), instead of making two division commanders report individually to Early himself. He was also critical of Early for sending him 25 miles ahead of the infantry at the battle of Tom's Brook to engage Philip Sheridan, when the army commander knew Sheridan had far superior numbers. Infuriating Rosser further, Early asserted that William H. Payne, not Rosser, deserved most of the credit for the successes of the New Creek and Lacey Springs engagements. Trying to deflect blame, Rosser concluded his remarks with a stinging attack on Early:

> **Incompetency is not a crime, and that you failed in the Valley is not due to your neglect or carelessness, but I know you were assiduous, but God did not make you a**

25. Bushong, *Fightin' Tom Rosser*, 197.
26. Thomas, "Under Indictment," 37.
27. Bushong, *Fightin' Tom Rosser*, 197–98.

general, and it was Gen. R. E. Lee's mistake in trusting so important a command as you had to you before you had been more fully tried.[28]

Adversaries, such as Early and Thomas T. Munford, responded to Rosser's series of articles published in the *Philadelphia Weekly Times*. They attacked the accuracy of his accounts of the war point by point. Munford protested, "General Rosser gallops over his campaigns as though he held a kaleidoscope in his hand, but only turns it sufficiently to exhibit his own surprising ability and tactics." Munford's criticisms seemed more accurate than Early's. To widen the dispute, Mottrom Dulany Ball, who had led the 11th Virginia under Rosser, criticized Early's and Munford's accounts and supported Rosser's claims. Louis E. Fisher of the Minneapolis *Pioneer Press* thanked Munford for his reply to Rosser's articles, stating, "For years the locals had to endure Rosser's stories about his service, taking it on faith, despite the fact that many things seemed implausible."[29]

Rosser, incensed about Munford's reply to the *Philadelphia Weekly Times*, issued a challenge of satisfaction (a duel) through an intermediary. Munford wrote a friend that his reply made Rosser so "indignant with me and he knew it was true; so to ease himself he sent me a challenge to 'relieve my wrath.' It tickled me to see what a fool he was, and amused me because instead of answering it in a square manly way in the paper, he sent a challenge to me through another medium—who neither the cause nor the facts had appeared." Munford also wrote that Rosser suppressed his reports on the fighting in the 1864 Valley campaign in order to more easily cast blame on Early.[30]

Rosser's feud with Munford stemmed, in part, from Rosser's recommendation of Payne, junior in service to Munford, for promotion to brigadier general. Munford felt aggrieved, and his ill will toward Rosser continued until Rosser's death in 1910. Rosser claimed Munford did not get promoted because he was not a man of sufficient coolness and judgment to command troops in battle. In a series of articles about the 1864 Shenandoah Valley campaign, published in the *Southern Historical Society Papers*, Munford criticized Rosser's handling

---

28. Bushong, *Fightin' Tom Rosser*, 198; *Rosser Scrapbook*, Thomas L. Rosser Papers, UVA.
29. *Philadelphia Weekly Times*, May 17, July 12, 1884; Louis E. Fisher to Thomas T. Munford, May 7, 1884, Munford-Ellis Papers, DU.
30. Thomas T. Munford to Senator John W. Daniel, July 20, 1905, Munford-Ellis Family Papers, Perkins Library, DU; Akers, "Colonel Thomas T. Munford," Master's Thesis, Virginia Tech, 122. In 1890, the General Assembly of Virginia passed an act to "remove the political difficulties of Gen. T. L. Rosser and others for dueling," *Journal of the Senate of Virginia* (Richmond, 1899), 367. This is probably in relation to Rosser's challenge to Munford.

of the cavalry at Tom's Brook. Munford stated Rosser's troopers were mortified by their commander's ego, and he did not give them proper credit for their accomplishments. Munford had been recommended for promotion to brigadier general in November 1864, although the commission was never officially confirmed. He took command of Fitzhugh Lee's cavalry division late in the war, fighting at Five Forks, High Bridge, and Sailor's Creek. Following the war, some Confederate soldiers referred to Munford as "general." Rosser publicly denied Munford made brigadier general rank, boasting, "I am in a position to state positively that T. T. Munford served under me as Colonel, and was never commissioned as brigadier general." Robert E. Lee had favored Munford's promotion, so Richmond would have confirmed the rank had the war lasted longer.[31]

In 1887, Rosser became embroiled in a feud with Sheridan. Rosser learned Sheridan was planning a visit to the Shenandoah Valley to see how much it had recovered from the ravages of the war—ravages Sheridan had inflicted. Rosser let his quick temper and impulsiveness get the best of him. He foolishly fired off letters to newspapers, penning, "I had hoped that our beautiful valley would never again be desecrated by his [Sheridan's] footprints. Cold, cruel, and brutal must be the character of this soldier who fondly cherishes memories of the wild wanton waste and desolation which his barbarous torch spread through the valley."[32]

During an interview at Charleston, West Virginia, Rosser continued to hammer at Sheridan, opining that in 1864 it had not been necessary for Sheridan to resort to the extreme and inhumane way he had treated the Valley. He said Sheridan had falsely justified his actions by claiming he had merely carried out Grant's order. Rosser further said Grant's order was cruel and severe, and Grant had not intended for Sheridan to go to such extremes in obeying it. Rosser also claimed after the war he had met many of Sheridan's soldiers, all expressing regret about the destruction.[33]

Rosser's attacks on Sheridan gave the former Union commander an opportunity to ridicule him about the Tom's Brook debacle in newspapers throughout the East. Sheridan remarked the Federal cavalry had given Rosser such a thrashing it was no wonder he wrote so bitterly about the campaign. He called the fight at Tom's Brook

31. Bushong, *Fightin' Tom Rosser*, 198–99; Thomas L. Rosser to A. S. Perham, August 29, 1902, Perham Papers, LC; *Richmond Times Dispatch*, September 25, 1904. Munford let it be known to everyone that he preferred to be called "general."
32. Beane, *Thesis*, 68: Newspaper Clipping, May 2, 1887, Thomas L. Rosser Papers, UVA–no heading.
33. *Thomas L. Rosser Scrapbook*, Thomas L. Rosser Papers, UVA.

doubly humiliating for the "Savior of the Valley." Sheridan and his cavalry subordinates had referred to Rosser's moniker facetiously. Sheridan regretted nothing, and suggested Rosser had made an issue of it in order to enhance his chances of being elected to Congress. Although the general public willingly forgot the emotionally charged accusations, Sheridan and Rosser spoke bitingly of each other's role in the incident for the remainder of their lives. After Sheridan's death in 1888, Rosser's animosity for his foe remained: "but as I disliked him very much, I fear I failed to see any high military virtues in him. To me he always appeared vulgar and coarse. I often met him while I was connected with the Northern Pacific Railroad, and saw that he was very intemperate, and barbarously profane, and was neither great nor good."[34]

Rosser's strong views also characterized his political activities during this phase of his life. He tried to convince friends not to support independent candidates for office. He was a Democrat who deplored third parties entering the political arena. In October 1886, he wrote an open letter to newspapers asking his associates and friends not to vote for independent candidate Gen. John E. Roller for Congress. He denounced Roller's candidacy as dangerous to the South's and Virginia's interests. Instead, he urged support of the Democratic candidate, Charles T. O'Ferrall, explaining:

> As you well know there are really but two political parties in the United States, the Republican and Democratic... The drift of the Republican Party is, as you well know, towards centralization, aristocracy, and monopolies. The aim of the Democratic Party is, as you well know, to adhere to the Constitution of the United States in treating all national affairs, giving "Home Rule" to the individual states. In supporting Gen. Roller, you strengthen the Republican Party, the natural and hereditary enemy of Virginia, and you weaken the hands of our friends who are struggling for the rights of Virginia and the South, and defending those principles of government for which so many of our comrades fell on the field of battle.[35]

Rosser's friends urged him to become a candidate for the Virginia House of Delegates in 1891, but he had reservations about running for office. He felt others were more qualified, urging his friends to support

34. Ibid., *The Daily Argus News*, May 7, 1887, Crawfordsville, Indiana; Thomas L. Rosser to Edward F. Gladwin, September 3, 1888, Thomas L. Rosser Papers, UVA; Sergent, *They Lie Forgotten*, 179.
35. *Thomas L. Rosser Scrapbook*, Thomas L. Rosser Papers, UVA, 1171a.b., Box 2, 43.

the Democratic nominee, whomever it was. During this period, rumors circulated that Rosser might be appointed marshal of the western district of Virginia or internal revenue collector of the second Virginia district. However, these appointments never came to pass.[36]

In the fall election season of 1891, Rosser attacked the Republican Party for its political association with African Americans. He rejected Republicans' assertions that their party redeemed the South from its rebellious past and reestablished authority of the United States. Rosser preached the South was not disloyal, for it had seceded in defense of constitutional states' rights. In Rosser's opinion, the "bankrupts, reinforced scalawags and adventurers" trained the blacks to vote only for the Republican Party, and he claimed, "All the respectable principles of the great political parties to which their fathers belonged, were forced into an alliance defensive and offensive for the preservation of law and order."[37]

The Democratic Party had the serious issue of how to incorporate blacks into society. The United States government threatened to pass the Henry Cabot Lodge Bill in Congress, which would authorize the federal government to oversee federal elections and protect voters in the South from violence and intimidation. Before a courthouse audience, Rosser deplored the implications of the proposed bill: "If we were to come to you and tell you that a party of men, outlaws were interfering with my right to vote and your right to vote as we like or that they were attempting to force to put 'niggers' in charge of all the offices of the county. You would all arm yourselves and go with me to arrest or kill the last one of them. Is that not what the Lodge Bill proposes?"[38]

A year later Rosser changed his mind, deciding he qualified for office. He sought the Democratic nomination for Congress from Virginia's seventh district. Incumbent Charles T. O'Ferrall defeated him; O'Ferrall had been expected to step aside and run for governor. Rosser's opportunity for a prestigious seat in Congress—and a badly needed salary—disappeared with O'Ferrall's victory. Greatly disappointed about falling short, Rosser, in his typical fashion, immediately displayed a strong distaste for O'Ferrall, blasting him in the press.[39]

36. Ibid.; *Richmond Dispatch*, December 13, 1891; *Newport News Daily Press*, February 4, 1895.
37. Thomas L. Rosser Papers, UVA, 1171g., Box 5; Thomas, "Under Indictment," 46.
38. Thomas L. Rosser Papers, UVA, 1171g., Box 5; Thomas, "Under Indictment," 47.
39. Beane, *Thesis*, 71–72; Thomas, "Under Indictment," 49; *Charlottesville Daily Progress*, September 2, 1893.

After entering politics enthusiastically, Rosser would not give up his quest so easily. When the 1893 elections were held at Albemarle County for delegates in the state Democratic convention, Rosser played an active role. The convention had been called to nominate a candidate for governor, and the leading candidate was Rosser's nemesis and incumbent congressman, Charles T. O'Ferrall.[40]

When Democratic officials met to select delegates for the state convention, a fight developed between a pro-O'Ferrall group and an anti-O'Ferrall faction, which Rosser led. When the pro-O'Ferrall contingent succeeded in electing the convention's chairman, the opponents revolted and met outside on the lawn. According to the *Charlottesville Daily Progress*, the upshot was "the most inharmonious meeting that has taken place in Albemarle County in years." The pro-O'Ferrall group elected John R. Moon and J. N. Lawhorn as their delegates to Richmond. The other faction chose Rosser and Morris Walker as their delegates. Albemarle County was entitled to only two delegates, so the credentials committee would decide which delegates to send to the capital. They finally decided to seat Moon and Lawhorn, an outcome that infuriated Rosser. When the convention subsequently nominated O'Ferrall for governor, Rosser compulsively and foolishly exploded in anger, essentially severing his association with the Democratic Party. The newspapers castigated Rosser for his overly harsh words, and his political fortunes virtually disappeared. [41]

Rosser's friends were concerned about his behavior and self-serving fidelity to the Democratic Party. When Fitz Lee, preparing for a Senate race, heard of Rosser's withdrawal from the party, he wrote him:

> **I hate to put you under arrest and issue the orders for a court martial, but I'll swear, if you have any fighting to do, you must do it inside party ranks... I hope I am unduly alarmed. Great Jerusalem! Old fellow, you would make a mistake from which you would never recover... You were too good a soldier and have got too much snap and vim and all that, to throw somersaults in a china shop ... we must fall into line when the bugle blows.[42]**

Rosser would not listen to reason. Perceiving a threat to his manliness, he burned bridges, throwing everything he had into an attempt to defeat O'Ferrall in the 1893 gubernatorial election. Though he had hated third parties until this point, Rosser backed a newly

40. Bushong, *Fightin' Tom Rosser*, 201.
41. *Daily Progress* (Charlottesville), August 7, 1893; Beane, *Thesis*, 72–74, Thomas, "Under Indictment," 50.
42. Fitzhugh Lee to Thomas L. Rosser, September 27, 1893, Thomas L. Rosser Papers, UVA: Thomas, "Under Indictment," 52.

organized Populist Party and its nominee, Edmund Randolph Cooke. He ventured forth on a statewide speaking tour in support of the Cooke, yet his speeches reflected more of a hatred for O'Ferrall than an ideological commitment to the principles of the Populist Party. Rosser explained to the public his switch in loyalties, saying he had "abandoned the Democratic Party because it had deserted the creed of Jefferson." He further asserted he left the Democratic ranks with a "sad heart" and in "bitter grief," like a captain who leaves a sinking ship. Rosser felt the Democratic Party "has degenerated into mere spod's [talker's] association and that under machine management it has lost its character and cohesiveness, and is rapidly disintegrating and wasting away. It is being eaten up by parasites and losing its vital powers in a dry rot, and it is no longer possible to cleanse, purify, or redeem it." In subsequent elections he continued to vote Democratic, but without enthusiasm. As he mentioned, he was a Jeffersonian and Jacksonian Democrat, not a Grover Cleveland or Charles T. O'Ferrall Democrat. Following the 1893 elections, when the Populist Party was swept away in defeat at the polls, Rosser's political ambitions cooled, and he returned to the Democratic Party. Rosser, sometimes called the "Prince of Albemarle," declared, "I am entirely out of politics. I have never been anything but an old fashion Jeffersonian Democrat."[43]

"Out of politics" or not, in May of 1894, Rosser attended the unveiling of the Soldiers and Sailors Monument in Richmond. He managed to enrage many listeners with an impromptu speech at the event. He repeated his old assertion: "the blue and gray cannot blend." He emphasized what he called the Republican Party's "abuse of power" in supporting federal pensions for Union soldiers of the Civil War, while the Southern states had to pension their own veterans from the war. He declared if he was in Congress, he would vote against all pensions in a civil war. He relayed to Tom Jr. that he "was called on to make a speech and as usual made everybody mad—and got mad myself—I shall not go to another gathering of the kind ever."[44] On June 13, he told Tom Jr., "People of the South are whipped and afraid to applaud me, yet they approve of what I said. I shall keep out of politics and make no more speeches."[45]

Abandoning politics for the moment, Rosser's finances continued to unravel. Desperate for money, he agreed to raise funds for the Battle Abbey in Richmond by travelling and lecturing throughout the South.

43. Beane, *Thesis*, 76; *Atlanta Constitution*, October 9, 1895; Thomas, "Under Indictment,", 53–54; *The Landmark* (Statesville, NC), June 3, 1898.
44. Thomas L. Rosser to Thomas Rosser Jr., June 6, 1894, Thomas L. Rosser Papers, UVA; Thomas, "Under Indictment," 58–59.
45. Thomas L. Rosser to Thomas Rosser Jr., June 13, 1894, Thomas L. Rosser Papers, UVA; Thomas, "Under Indictment," 59.

He agreed to take 10 percent of his gross receipts from the lecture tour and to pay his own expenses. From early 1895 to late 1896, Rosser lectured on the great Civil War. Sometimes he enjoyed advanced bookings, but often he had to advertise upon arriving at a lecture venue. He visited at least 32 towns and grossed about $1,500, but his expenses came to more than $900. He sent his entire income home to Betty to pay debts. Along with proceeds from her dairy business, they remained solvent.[46]

The 1896 presidential race began to heat up when Rosser started his lecture tour of the South. Still asked by reporters about political matters, he occasionally gave interviews. He called for a Republican victory to correct the Democrat's imposed tariff and financial affairs. Rosser claimed Democrat Grover Cleveland had no support from his party in the South, and asserted, "No man is connected with or supported by Cleveland can receive any kind of support from Democrats in the South. No, we are looking for relief from the Republicans."[47]

While on the lecture circuit Rosser wrote Betty every day, sending her whatever money he had accumulated. Life on the road took its toll on the 60-year-old Rosser; his voice often became strained, and at some venues he made insignificant profits. Finally, in June 1896, Rosser decided it was time to return to Charlottesville.[48]

In 1898, the United States became embroiled in the Spanish-American War. Rosser spoke of it warily: "If we really have a war with Spain, young men for officers, soldiers, and seamen are what we shall need, and not rheumatic, deaf, and blind Major Generals who know nothing of modern tactics or modern weapons, who cannot drill a squad without a prompter or mount a horse without a ladder." Rosser changed his mind, however, perceiving an opportunity to show his patriotism while also earning income. He sought a commission, writing Senator John W. Daniel several times about obtaining an appointment as a brigadier general. In an arrogant tone, he pressed Daniel to push the recommendation on to President William McKinley. He sent follow-up letters, rudely increasing the pressure on Daniel. Rosser played to Daniel's desire to have his son receive a safe position on Rosser's staff. Rosser assured Daniel that his son "would be kindly cared for as if he were my own son." He even encouraged the senator to lie about his son's appointment, and say it was Rosser's idea

46. The Battle Abbey, a shrine built to honor the Confederate dead and house war records, would become the Southern Historical Society's repository; Thomas, "Under Indictment," 61–62.
47. *Scrapbook*, Thomas L. Rosser Papers, UVA, 1171a.b., Box 2; Thomas, "Under Indictment," 62.
48. Thomas, "Under Indictment," 62.

if anyone suggested favoritism. Finally, on June 10, 1898, President McKinley appointed Rosser a brigadier general of Volunteers of the United States Army. Rosser became one of four previous Confederate generals to win high rank, along with Fitzhugh Lee, Joseph Wheeler, and Matthew C. Butler.[49]

Tom Rosser, still financially troubled, had to furnish his own uniforms and horse. A newly appointed officer asked Rosser where he was going to buy his uniforms (nice ones cost more than $100 each). Rosser replied, "I will only need a flannel shirt ... a pair

Brigadier General Thomas Lafayette Rosser – 1898, United States Volunteers, Spanish-American War.

Albert and Shirley Small Special Collections Library, University of Virginia.

of shoulder straps and a string or piece of braid around my hat to designate that I am an officer." When asked where he would obtain a good horse, he answered, "I have some good stock down on my farm; but from what I learn a horse will not be the suitable thing in Cuba; I think a mule will be best, and it is my expectation to ride a mule."[50]

Rosser's health was not optimal at this stage of life, and, consequently, he did not see service in Cuba. In fact, he caught pneumonia in camp and almost died. Upon recovering, he was assigned to the camp at Chickamauga Park, Georgia, where he was responsible for training the soldiers of the Third Brigade, Second Division, First

49. *New York Times*, April 22, 1898; Thomas L. Rosser to John W. Daniel, June 11, 1898, John W. Daniel Papers, Rare Book Room, DU; Bushong, *Fightin' Tom Rosser*, 202.

50. (Shreveport, LA) *The Progress*, December 10, 1898.

Army Corps. Ironically, he trained mostly men from Northern states in the operation of the infantry, rather than in cavalry tactics. Some observers found Rosser's appointment controversial: a Southerner in a command position. Rosser's methods of training his regiments drew criticism from army officers, who may have wanted him to fail. "It is perfectly evident," he wrote, "that the regular Army officers intend to keep such men as myself and Fitz Lee down if possible, and they may succeed." Senator John W. Daniel reported to Rosser, based on rumor, that he would be last to go to Cuba, and confirmed Rosser's suspicion that resistance against him was rooted in his "rebel" past. Demonstrating their animosity toward Rosser, the Regulars assigned black regiments to him for training. Rosser did not take the bait; he trained all his men alike.[51]

Rosser's chief surgeon at Chickamauga, Maj. R. Stansbury Button, described Rosser:

> **General Rosser is a man who has been educated in the art of war, from West Point through all the wars of the last and present generation. He is kind and resolute, companionable, and pure in his daily conduct, indefatigable in the pursuit of his duties despite poor health. Not a drop of spirituous liquors of any kind was ever seen at his headquarters, and, as we stood about our mess table with its plain and simple food, frequently in the rain without cover, General Rosser, with all heads uncovered, never failed to invoke the blessing of God upon that table and its participants. But General Rosser, like all old generals of the Army, was physically impaired. Their livers are bad, their digestive organs generally are permanently deranged, and the dynamo in every one of them has begun to fail.[52]**

Rosser spent the summer obtaining supplies and preparing his troops for battle, but the shortness of the war prevented them from seeing action. The primary issue of the war regarded Cuban independence, but the ten-week war was fought in the Caribbean and the Pacific. A series of one-sided American naval and military victories followed on all fronts, owing to the United States's numerical superiority in most of the battles. The 1898 Treaty of Paris resulted from the war's ending, which was favorable to the United States. Temporary American control of Cuba followed, as well as indefinite

51. Thomas L. Rosser to Betty W. Rosser, July 28, 1898, Thomas L. Rosser Papers, UVA; Thomas, "Under Indictment," 69; Congressional Serial Set, U.S. Government Printing Office, DOC 5295, 263.

52. John B. Hamilton, ed., *The Journal of the American Medical Association* (Chicago, 1898), 31:651.

colonial authority of Puerto Rico, Guam, and the Philippines. Wishing the war had lasted longer for financial reasons, he wrote Betty, "If I could have been retained 'till the spring we would have gotten out of the woods and been comfortable." Rosser was discharged on October 7, 1898.[53]

During the summer, while preparing for war, Rosser had become very ill. He wrote Senator Daniel after the war. "This illness left me in a weak physical condition, and I am rapidly growing worse as I grow older, and have become so disabled that my physician and friends have suggested that I am entitled to, and should apply for a pension." Rosser continued, "Such a thing is most revolting to my patriotism and pride." Rosser needed money desperately at this time in his life. He even suggested to Senator Daniel that if the pension amount was too small, then the senator should help pass a special bill, which would fix the pension for him at a higher amount.[54]

Rosser had continued to send money home to Betty during the war. His military income had helped to mend their financial situation, but Rosser worried about another matter: his relationship with Tom Jr. His son had grown increasingly frustrated with his parents' financial struggles. Animosity developed between Tom Jr. and his mother. Rosser wrote Betty, "I am not surprised at Tom's behavior towards you, after all he has made me suffer—Poor boy, he has wrung my heart until it was very sore." On another occasion, he wrote, "Tom's behavior has almost killed me." And in yet another instance, Rosser penned to Betty, "I don't like Tom's letters. He evidently has cut loose from us and doesn't want us to encumber him. I shall not, may God prosper him, he was once very dear to me."[55]

In January 1899, with his health somewhat improved, Rosser set off for Cuba in hopes of landing an engineering job during postwar reconstruction of the island. Once again, he fled to a "frontier land" to find a solution to his financial woes. He wanted to set up a construction company to pave the streets of Havana and to build sewer lines and water mains, while Betty remained at home paying bills with proceeds from her dairy farm and boarding cottages. Rosser hoped the company would appoint him superintendent at a good salary. Unfortunately, Rosser had trouble attracting any potential investors,

53. Thomas L. Rosser to Betty W. Rosser, October 7, 1898, Thomas L. Rosser Papers, UVA.
54. Thomas L. Rosser to John W. Daniel, November 14, 1904, John W. Daniel Papers, Rare Book Room, DU; There is no record of any Senate action ever occurring.
55. Thomas L. Rosser to Betty W. Rosser, February 4, 1899, Thomas L. Rosser Papers, UVA.

except for Fitzhugh Lee.[56]

Rosser saw this venture as a test of his manliness. He corresponded to Betty, "I am going to make the fight of my life right here. If I win you shall have all the fruits of the victory. If I fail I shall go down gloriously and honorably. I feel that my manhood made this demand on me." He gave himself until April 1 to land a well-paying position, or he would go home.[57]

Betty remained very busy at Rugby Hall. The frequency which she wrote letters to her husband dropped to once a week. Her husband begged her to write more often, saying he needed to hear from her to maintain his sanity. "I wake up at night and think about you and how you are getting on, and my brain seems to be oppressed and a strange feeling comes over me as if I were losing my mind. I never had the sensation before," he proclaimed. "I shall give all my strength to the great effort I am now making, realizing that this is my last chance. Please bear up and be brave and give me all the encouragement you can, for I need it." Whether he admitted it or not, his inability to provide for his family terrified him; he viewed this insufficiency as a threat to his manhood.[58]

The construction company venture in Cuba failed to develop, so Rosser resorted to land speculation again, hoping to build a railroad, lay out a town site, and develop tobacco and sugar cane industries east of Havana. He hoped to buy a town, make minimal improvements, build docks, wharves, and warehouses, then charge rents for them once the "big boom" came, as he believed would happen by the following winter. Rosser felt "big money" would come "from the sale of lots and the growth of the city." To Betty he revealed modest expectations. "I don't lust for wealth, I only want enough to be comfortable and I like to help others who are needy, so if I succeed, I shall do great good by helping others," he stated. "If I can provide for all your wants, settle my children in life on a competency, and make a few of our poor kin comfortable [his sister Florence's family, in Texas, was very poor, for example], I will be satisfied." Rosser was convinced American colonization of Cuba would be the best solution to the island's many problems. He declared, "Not only will my city be a glorious success, but the colonization scheme will be just the thing to attract the young men of the South."[59]

56. Bushong, *Fightin' Tom Rosser*, 203–4.
57. Thomas L. Rosser to Betty W. Rosser, February 4, 1899, Thomas L. Rosser Papers, UVA.
58. Thomas L. Rosser to Betty W. Rosser, February 1, 1899, Thomas L. Rosser Papers, UVA; Thomas, "Under Indictment," 71.
59. Thomas L. Rosser to Betty W. Rosser, February 16, March 3, 1899, Thomas L. Rosser Papers, UVA.

Meanwhile, back home debts were accumulating. Rosser encouraged Betty to sell the dairy and the estate itself, if she had to. He again wrote the Winston brothers for additional loans, but they turned a deaf ear. He also needed money to cover his expenses in Cuba. "I have a good stock of manhood in store yet, and until that is exhausted and the infirmities of age or ill health strike me down, I propose and intend to stand up and battle and when I go down, provided fate decrees it, I shall go down under fire, with colors flying. I shall never surrender," he declared to Betty.[60]

Rosser succeeded in securing promises for options on most of the land surrounding the harbor in Bahia Honda, Cuba, but the investors grew nervous, refusing to sign unless he put up $2,000 as partial payment, something he found impossible to do. At the last minute, potential investors from New York considered the plan and sent representative Hugh Kelly to inspect the property. Rosser took Kelly on a tour of the site, discussing his plans in detail. He came away from the meeting with a favorable impression that he might succeed. But just like the times before, Rosser failed at yet another commercial venture. In June, the investors backed off, forcing Rosser to abandon the project and return home to Virginia.[61]

Back home, Tom Rosser's disillusionment with the Democratic Party and his amiable association with Republicans during the Spanish-American War, persuaded him to change his political affiliation. He switched to the Republican Party, following the examples of James Longstreet, John S. Mosby, Williams C. Wickham, Rufus Barringer, and others. He admired William McKinley as president, promising to support him when he ran for reelection in 1900, stating:

> **I am now what politicians call an expansionist, and am in full accord with the President of the United States on all leading political questions of the day. I am, therefore, unalterably and emphatically opposed to changing our present chief executive at this time for any unknown or untried man. Our President now has on his hands a great work, and he is performing it well, but it is unfinished, and he should be allowed to complete it.[62]**

60. Ibid. The Rugby Hall estate was inherited by Thomas Rosser Jr. at the time of Betty Winston Rosser's death in 1915. When Thomas Rosser Jr. died in 1940, the estate was willed to Harriet G. Rosser, after being extensively subdivided. Rugby Hall was willed to Barbara Winston Rosser upon Harriet's death in 1962. In 1967, Nathan Poole purchased it (Reference: Charlottesville Deed Books), and it has been sold and subdivided since then.
61. Thomas L. Rosser to Betty W. Rosser, March 6, 1899, Thomas L. Rosser Papers, UVA; Thomas, "Under Indictment," 73.
62. Thomas, "Under Indictment," 74–75.

Rosser had great respect for vice-presidential nominee Theodore Roosevelt, who had served bravely in Cuba as lieutenant colonel of the famed "Rough Riders." Explaining his switch of political allegiance, Rosser wrote Roosevelt, "When war was declared against Spain in 1898, the fear that my country was in danger passed through me like an electric spark, clearing my vision and revealing the follies behind which I had been sulking... If the North can prosper, as it does, under Republican administration, the South should blush to admit she cannot do the same, for she has equal opportunities." Roosevelt responded to Rosser, thanking him for his support. "I know your record in the army from A to Z, and so you can appreciate it means a good deal to me to have you treat me as a fellow-soldier," Roosevelt commended.[63]

In his typical style, Rosser laid out his reasons for abandoning the Democratic Party and joining the Republicans, who many saw as an anathema to the South:

> **No one can deny that the North has prospered under Republicanism, nor is there any denying the fact that the South has not prospered under Democracy. Nature has blessed the South with soil and climate superior to that of the North. Then, shall we be expected to admit that, under like conditions, the South is not equal to the North in a fair field of business competition. My experience, which has been extensive, will not allow me to admit it, but on the contrary, I can deny it... I regard the Republican Party as the only national party in the field. It is interesting, aggressive, and patriotic; it has on hand and unfinished a great work of clearing off the debris left in the fields by Spain after the war was over, which both Democrats and Republicans put us into. The work is being done satisfactorily, and there should be no change in the Chief Executive as long as this important work is going on.**[64]

Rosser expanded on his reasons for supporting the Republicans in a Charlottesville speech. Referring to the Democratic Party in the South, he said:

> **It is founded wholly on the old secession war grudge, and is the greatest obstacle in the way of Southern prosperity... The North grows and prospers, while the South lags behind, looking backward and brooding over events which have transpired and cannot be recalled...**

---

63. *The Tazewell (Virginia) Republican*, July 5, 1900.
64. Thomas, "Under Indictment," 78; *The Richmond Times*, June 30, 1900.

> The war of secession is over, and the sooner you turn
> away from those old issues the better for you and for the
> South.[65]

Not surprisingly, Democrat officials criticized Rosser, pushing
"white supremacy" as an issue. Rosser responded with his views on the
subject: "We have in our midst a race inferior to our own ... whatever
those circumstances may have been, the fact is only to be considered
and the problem given us is to be just to them considering their
circumstances and at the same time preserve the integrity of our own
race. That the Northern European Anglo-Saxon race which is our own
is superior to all others we cannot doubt." Later, Rosser would state,
"The material of the mental as well as the moral construction of the
negro cannot be refined or perfected. It may be improved, but it
cannot be refined, highly tempered and elegantly furnished, and ... no
degree of cultivation will or can make the negro a gentleman."
Elaborating on his racial views, Rosser warned, "If the white and black
race remain together in the South, or anywhere else in the United
States, the white race will sooner or later enslave or exterminate the
black one, and while the negro will never again be a chattel as in the
days of slavery, he will become a peasant of low degree, and will again
obey and serve the white lord of the manor."[66]

Republicans happily welcomed Rosser to the fold, and in 1901,
political allies in Charlottesville, noting his prominence and
reputation, urged him to run for governor. Thrilled at the possibility
of attaining the highest office in the Commonwealth, he promised to
do all in his power to make Virginia, once more, an important factor
in promoting the pride and power of the nation. Rosser, unfortunately,
mishandled the preparations for the upcoming Charlottesville
summertime Republican convention, which would have provided him
with a favorable venue for obtaining the nomination for governor. The
State Republican Committee, including Chairman Park Agnew,
worried about the lack of preparations, including making
accommodations for the delegates and the tardiness of obtaining a
reserved hall for the actual convention. They confronted Rosser before
ultimately moving the convention to Roanoke. Infuriated, Rosser
viewed it as a conspiracy against him.[67]

Political victory proved elusive, as Rosser failed in his bid for the
Republican nomination. Colonel J. Hampton Hoge defeated him, but

65. *Thomas L. Rosser Scrapbook*, Thomas L. Rosser Papers, UVA. 1171a.b.,
　　Box 2, 105.
66. *Richmond Times*, September 4, 1900; Thomas, "Under Indictment," 80; *The
　　Richmond Times*, September 12, 1893.
67. Ibid., Bushong, *Fightin' Tom Rosser*, 204–5.

Thomas Lafayette Rosser was unsuccessful in attaining political office until President Theodore Roosevelt appointed him Postmaster of Charlottesville in 1905.

Reproduced by permission of Eleanor Cochran and Douglass Cochran, Jr.

the party, badly split and with its power eroding, lost the gubernatorial election by a wide margin. In 1903, Rosser ran for the nomination to the House of Delegates, but Democrats W. R. Duke and H. W. Boaz soundly defeated him.[68]

In one sense, Rosser's political fortunes finally succeeded in 1905 when then-President Teddy Roosevelt appointed him postmaster of Charlottesville. The appointment came with controversy, an everlasting predicament for Rosser. During a meeting of the McKinley-Roosevelt Club at the Rosser Post Office, J. Henry Rives, the first announced candidate for the postmaster appointment, lashed out at Rosser, who was chairing the meeting. Rosser pronounced him "out of order," but Rives paid no attention. He accused Rosser of "parading the name of Roosevelt throughout the state to the exclusion of those far better representatives of the party." He also made disparaging remarks about Rosser's Civil War service. With that, Rosser forcibly ejected Rives from the room. In the corridor, the confrontation continued before friends interceded. Rives left the premises.

Rosser was duly appointed postmaster, serving in this capacity until his death. At last, he had landed a rather prestigious position with a regular salary, which solved many of his financial problems. That

68. *Richmond Daily Dispatch*, August 4, 1901.

Mrs. Thomas L. Rosser

*Holsinger Collection,
Albert and Shirley Small
Special Collections Library,
University of Virginia.*

same year, 1905, he suffered a stroke that left him speechless, but his hearing remained unimpaired, his sight still normal, no facial paralysis existed, and any mental impairment soon declined. With the aid of Betty, capable clerks, and assistants, he was able to continue his service as postmaster.[69]

On March 18, 1910, Rosser was taken with chills and retreated to his room. The chills continued, and the family physician, Dr. E. E. Magruder, was summoned. The doctor found Rosser's temperature to be 105 degrees, his pulse rapid and irregular, and he had a cough. The symptoms indicated bronchial pneumonia, a condition complicated by an irregular heartbeat and the return of an old kidney ailment. He suffered another stroke. Rosser was not in pain, but his breathing was labored, and soon he was barely conscious. On March 29, 1910, Thomas Lafayette Rosser's heart gave out.[70]

He was survived by his devoted wife, Betty, a son, Thomas L. Rosser Jr., and two daughters, Marguerite (Elliott) and Sally (Cochran).

69. Thomas, "Under Indictment," 84; Cox-McPherson Papers, UVA, clippings. No-5; Mrs. Thomas Rosser to Thomas Rosser Jr., August 18, 1905, Thomas L. Rosser Papers, UVA; *Los Angeles Herald*, Vol.32, Number 174, March 24, 1905; *Richmond Daily Dispatch*, November 29, 1900; *Washington Times*, November 29, 1900.
70. Bushong, *Fightin' Tom Rosser*, 205; *Thomas Rosser Scrapbook*, Thomas Rosser Papers, UVA.

He lies buried in Riverview Cemetery, Charlottesville, Virginia. His tombstone reads: "Major General C.S.A., followed Lee from Manassas to Appomattox, Brigadier General of Volunteers, Spanish-American War, Engineer and Locator of the Northern Pacific Railroad, 1870–1880, Chief Engineer of the Canadian Pacific Railroad 1880–1882." Mrs. Betty Winston Rosser died February 2, 1915, and is buried in the family plot with her husband.[71]

Thomas Rosser was seemingly larger than life. He was an important figure in the Civil War and in the expansion of the Northern Pacific and Canadian Pacific Railroads. Like his friend George Custer, Rosser was an imposing and fearless warrior who loved the glory of battle, ostensibly oblivious to danger. A compulsive soul, he often reacted foolishly to criticism, immediately attacking his antagonists in an effort to demean them, thereby undermining their credibility—often without facts on his side. Life to Tom Rosser was a series of contests or fights, which he fought with everything he had—sometimes knocked down, but always rising to resume the battle.

71. Bushong, *Fightin' Tom Rosser*, 205–6.

BIBLIOGRAPHY

PRIMARY SOURCES

Manuscripts and Special Collections:

College of William and Mary, Williamsburg, Virginia.

Mark Alexander Papers, Mss. 86sA12, Special Collections, Earl Gregg Swem Library.

Duke University, Durham, North Carolina.

Jacob Click Papers
Munford-Ellis Family Papers
Presley Carter Person Papers
W. A. Curtis, "Reminiscences of the War."

Emory University, Atlanta Georgia.

J.E.B. Stuart Letters, Special Collections Department, Robert W. Woodruff Library.

Library of Congress, Washington.

Willard Family Papers. #1029. MSS5836, Jeb Stuart Correspondence, 1861-1862.
Jedediah Hotchkiss Papers.
Louis T. Wigfall Family Papers.
Aurestus S. Perham Papers.

Library of Virginia, Richmond, Virginia.

Common Law Order Book 5, Campbell County, Virginia
Chancery Records of Campbell County, Virginia

Proceedings of the General Court Martial in the case of Lieut. Col. H. Clay Pate, 5th Virginia Cavalry, Confederate Imprints, 1861-1865, No. 2535, Reel 82, Film 3556.

Diary of James W. Wood, Accession 25506.

Diary of Charles William McVicar.

National Archives, Washington, D.C.

Compiled Service Records of Confederate Soldiers Who Served in Organizations From the State of Virginia, Record Group M324.

Compiled Service Records of Confederate Generals and Staff Officers, and Nonregimental Enlisted Men, Record Group 94, M331.

Confederate States Army Inspection Reports.

Letters Received by the Confederate Adjutant and Inspector General, 1861-1865, Record Group 94.

United States Federal Census of 1850 – Slave Schedules, John Rosser, Panola, Texas.

United States Federal Census of 1850 – Panola, Texas, Roll M432, e.d. 913, P. 162.

Southern Historical Collection, Wilson Library, University of North Carolina, Chapel Hill, North Carolina

Rufus Barringer Papers.

Peter W. Hairston Papers #00299.

University of Michigan

George W. Hunt Memoir

University of Nebraska, Lincoln, Nebraska.

Mark Van Rhyn. "An American Warrior: Thomas Lafayette Rosser, 1836-1910."   1998 Master's Thesis. Smith College, Northampton, Massachusetts.

Garrison Family Papers, Sophia Smith Collection. Tulane University, New Orleans, Louisiana.

Frank Labrano Diary, Sept. 17, 1862, Special Collections Division of the Howard Tilton Library, as part of the collection of Memorial Hall Museum.

University of Virginia, Manuscripts and Special Collections, Alderman Library, Charlottesville, Virginia.

Thomas Lafayette Rosser Papers

William Griffith Thomas III. "Under Indictment: Tom Rosser and the New South." 1991 Master's Thesis.

Thomas O. Beane. "Thomas L. Rosser: Soldier, Railroad Builder, Politician, Businessman (1836-1910)." 1957 Master's Thesis.

Diary of DeWitt Clinton Gallaher: 1864-1865, Valley Personal Papers, AD1000.

United States Military Academy at West Point, New York

Official Register, Officers and Cadets.

United States Military History Institute, Carlisle, PA.

Frank M. Myers Papers.
August V. Kautz Papers.

Virginia Historical Society, Richmond, Virginia

J.E.B. Stuart Letters.
Henry B. McClellan Papers.
Conrad Holmes Papers.
William Clark Corson Papers.

Virginia Military Institute Archives, Lexington, Virginia.

Andrew C. L. Gatewood Papers.

Virginia Polytechnic Institute and State University, Blacksburg, Virginia.

Anne Trice Thompson Akers. "Colonel Thomas T. Munford and the Last Cavalry
Operations of the Civil War in Virginia." Master's Thesis, 1981.

Newspapers

Alexandria (VA) Gazette.

Baltimore Clipper.

Charleston (SC) Daily Courier.

Charleston Mercury.

Chicago Tribune.

(Charlottesville, VA) Daily Progress.

Fargo (ND) Diamond Jubilee Edition, Sunday, June 4, 1950, Thomas Rosser Papers,

UVA, Clippings, 1171, 1849-1950, Box 2.

Jacksonville Republican

New York Herald.

New York Times.

Philadelphia Weekly Times.

Richmond (VA) Dispatch.

Richmond (VA) Enquirer.

San Francisco Chronicle.

St. Paul and Minneapolis Pioneer-Press and Tribune.

St. Paul Weekly Pioneer.

Washington (D. C.) Evening Star.

Washington Post.

PUBLISHED SOURCES:

Andrew, Rod. Wade Hampton: Confederate Warrior to Southern Redeemer. Chapel Hill: University of North Carolina Press, 2008.

Armstrong, Richard L. 11th Virginia Cavalry. Lynchburg, Virginia: H. E. Howard, 1989.

_____ 7th Virginia Cavalry. Lynchburg, Virginia: H. E. Howard, 1992.

Arnold, Thomas J. "A Battle Fought in the Streets (Rosser's Beverly Raid of 1865)," Magazine of History & Biography, Randolph County Historical Society, Civil War Centennial Issue, Vol. 12 (1961).

Ashby, Thomas Almond. The Valley Campaigns: Being the Reminiscences of a Non-Combatant While Between the Lines in the Shenandoah Valley During the War of

The States. New York: The Neale Publishing Company, 1914.

Ayers, Edward L. The Promise of the New South: Life After Reconstruction. New York: Oxford University Press, 1982.

Barnett, Louise. Touched by Fire: The Life, Death, and Mythic Afterlife of George Armstrong Custer. Lincoln: University of Nebraska Press, 1996.

Baylor, George Baylor, From Bull Run to Bull Run: or Four Years in the Army of Northern Virginia. Richmond: B. F. Johnson Publishing Company, 1900.

Beale, G. W. A Lieutenant in Lee's Army. Boston: The Gorham Press, 1918.

Beale, Richard L.T. History of the Ninth Virginia Cavalry, in the War Between the States. Cornell University Library: BiblioLife, 2009 Reprint.

Bearss, ed, and Chris Calkins. The Battle of Five Forks. Lynchburg, Virginia: H. E. Howard, 1985.

Benedict, George G. Vermont in the Civil War, A History of the Part Taken By the Vermont Soldiers in the War for the Union,1861-65. Burlington, Vermont: The Free Press Association, 1888.

Benz, Louis Tuck. The History of the Northern Pacific Railroad. Fairfield: Washington: Ye Galleon Press, 1980.

Berton, Pierre. Toronto: The National Dream:The Last Spike, Toronto: McClellan and Stewart, Ltd., 1974.

Blackford, William W. War Years With Jeb Stuart. New York: Charles Scribner's Sons, 1946.

Booth, George Wilson. Maryland Boy in Lee's Army:Personal Reminiscences of a Maryland Soldier in the War Between the States,

1861-1865.Lincoln, Nebraska: University of Nebraska Press, 2000.

Borcke, Heros von. Memoirs of the Confederate War of Independence. Philadelphia: J. B. Lippincott & Company, 1867.

_____Memoirs of the Confederate War of Independence. Volume II. Dayton, Ohio:
Morningside Books, 1985 Reprint.

Botkin, Benjamin Albert. Ed. A Civil War Treasury of Tales, Legends, and Folklore. Lincoln, Nebraska: University of Nebraska Press, 1960.

Boykin, Edward. Beefsteak Raid. New York: Funk and Wagnalls, 1960.

Bridges, Hal. Lee's Maverick General. Lincoln, Nebraska and London: University of Nebraska Press, 1991 Reprint.

Brock, R. A., ed. "Brook Church Fight: Death of James B. Gordon." Richmond, Virginia: Southern Historical Papers, 1901. Vol 29. Reprinted in the Charlotte Observer, January 3, 1902.

_____"Wade Hampton's Strategy: An Attack on Richmond Foiled." Richmond, Virginia: Southern Historical Papers, 1896. Vol 24. Reprinted in the Charlotte Observer, April 7, 1895.

Brooks, U. R. Butler and His Cavalry in the War of Secession,1861-1865. Columbia, South Carolina: The State Company, 1909.

_____ Stories of the Confederacy. Columbia, S.C.: The State Company, 1912.

Burton, Brian K. Extraordinary Circumstances:The Seven Days Battles. Bloomington, Indiana: Indiana University Press, 2001.

Bushong, Millard K and Dean M. Bushong. Fightin' Tom Rosser. Shippensburg, Pennsylvania: Beidel Printing House, Inc., 1983.

_____ General Turner Ashby and Stonewall's Valley Campaign. Verona, VA: McClure Print Company, 1980.

Calkins, Chris M. The Appomattox Campaign, March 29-April 5, 1865. Conshohocken, Pennsylvania: Combined Books, Inc., 1997.

_____"The Battle of Weldon Railroad (or Globe Tavern), August 18-19 & 21, 1864." Blue and Gray Magazine. (Winter 2007).

Cardwell, David. "The Battle of Five Forks." Nashville, Tennessee: Confederate Veteran Magazine, vol. 22.

Cardwell, Colonel D. A Brilliant Coup. (Charleston, South Carolina: News and Courier), October 10, 1864. Reprinted in the Southern Historical Society Papers, vol. 22. Reprinted in the Confederate Veteran Magazine, vol. 26, 474-76.

Carman, Ezra Ayers and Joseph Pierro, The Maryland Campaign of September 1862: Ezra A. Carman's Definitive Study of the Union and Confederate Armies at Antietam. New York: Taylor and Francis Group, 2008.

Carvell, Kenneth L. "Historic Beverly in the Tygart Valley." Wonderful West Virginia Magazine, February, 2001, Vol. 65, No. 2, Charleston, West Virginia.

Casdorph, Paul D. Prince John Magruder: His Life and Campaigns. New York, New York: John Wiley and Sons, 1996.

Chamberlain, Joshua Lawrence. Passing of the Armies: An Account of the Final Campaign Of the Army of the Potomac. Lincoln, Nebraska: The University of Nebraska Press, 1998.

Clark, Walter. ed. Histories of the Several Regiments and Battalions in the Great War, 1861 1865. 5 Vols. Raleigh, North Carolina: E. M. Uzell, Printer and Binder, 1901.

Commager, Henry Steele. The Blue and The Gray. Two Vols. New York: The Fairfax Press, 1991.

Conrad, Captain Thomas Nelson. The Rebel Scout. Washington City: Big Byte Books, 1904.

Cooke, John Esten. Wearing of the Gray: Personal Portraits. Scenes and Adventures of the War. New York: E. B. Treat & Co., 1867.

Corbell, La Salle (Mrs. George E. Pickett). Pickett and His Men. Atlanta: Foote and Davies, 1899.

Cornwall, James Marshall. Grant as Military Commander. New York: Barnes and Noble, 1995.

Corson, Blake W. Corson, Jr. ed., My Dear Jennie. Richmond: Dietz Press, 1982.

Cozzens, Peter and Robert I. Girardi, eds., John Pope, The Military Memoirs of General John Pope. Chapel Hill: The University of North Carolina Press, 1998.

Cozzens, Peter. General John Pope: A Life for the Nation. Chicago: University of Illinois Press, 2000.

Crist, Lynda Lasswell, Mary Seaton Dix, and Kenneth H. Williams, eds. The Papers of Jefferson Davis: January-September 1863. Baton Rouge: LSU Press, 1997.

Crowley, Robert, ed. With My Face to the Enemy:Perspectives on the Civil War. New York: Berkley Books, 2001.

Cunningham, S. A. Confederate Veteran. Serial, 40 Vols. Nashville, Tennessee: 1893-1932.

Cullen, Joseph P. Cullen. The Peninsula Campaign,1862. Crown Publishers, Inc., 1973.

Current, Richard N, (Editor in Chief). Encyclopedia of the Confederacy. New York: Simon and Schuster, 1993.

Custer, Elizabeth B. Boots and Saddles. Norman, Oklahoma and London: University of Oklahoma Press, 1897.

_____ Arlene Reynolds, ed. The Civil War Diaries of Elizabeth Bacon Custer. Austin: University of Texas Press, 1994.

Daughtry, Mary Bandy. Gray Cavalier: The Life and Wars of General W. H. F. "Rooney" Lee. Cambridge, Massachusetts: Da Capo Press, 2002.

David, William C. and Meredith L. Swentor, eds. Bluegrass Confederate: The Headquarters Diary of Edward O. Guerrant. Baton Rouge: LSU Press, 1999.

Davis, Burke. The Last Cavalier: J.E.B. Stuart. New York: Fairfax Press, 1988.

Davis, William C. Confederate Generals. Volume 1. Harrisburg, Pa: National Historical Society.

_____ The Civil War: Strange & Fascinating Facts. New York: Fairfax Press, 1982.

Dawes, Rufus Robinson, Memoir of Rufus Dawes, in Service with the Sixth Wisconsin Volunteers. Marietta, Ohio: E.R. Alderman & Sons, 1890.

Dawson, Francis Warrington. Reminiscences of Confederate Service, 1861-1865. Baton Rouge: LSU Press, 1980.

Dowdey, Clifford and Louis H. Manarin, eds., The Wartime Papers Of Robert E. Lee. Originally Published - Boston: Little, Brown, 1961, Republished - New York: Da Capo, 1991.

Downey, Fairfax. The Clash of Cavalry:The Battle of Brandy Station. New York: David McKay Company, Inc., 1959. Reprinted in 1987 by Olde Soldier Books, Inc., Gaithersburg, Maryland.

Driver, Robert J. 5th Virginia Cavalry. Virginia Regimental Series. Lynchburg, Virginia: H. E. Howard, Inc., 1997.

Early, Jubal A. Narrative of the War Between the States. New York: Da Capo Press, 1989.

Early, Ruth Hairston. Campbell Chronicles and Family Sketches: Embracing the History of Campbell County, Virginia, 1782-1926. Baltimore: Regional Publishing Company, 1978.

Ellis, Thomas T. Leaves from the Diary of an Army Surgeon. New York: John Bradburn Publishing, 1863.

Evans, General Clement A., ed. Confederate Military History. 12 vols. New York: Thomas Yoseloff, 1992.

Faeder, Gustav S. "Jeb Stuart and Hid Reluctant Cavalryman." Blue and Gray Magazine, October, 1992.

Faust, Patricia L. Historical Times Illustrated Encyclopedia of the Civil War. New York: Harper Perennial, 1991.

Fleming, Thomas J. West Point: The Men and Times of the United States Military Academy. New York: William Morrow and Company, 1969.

Foard, Noah P. "An Attack on Richmond Foiled." Southern Historical Society Papers, vol. 24.

Foote, Shelby. The Civil War: A Narrative. 3 Vols. New York: Random House, 1974.

Foner, Eric. Reconstruction: America's Unfinished Revolution, 1863-1877. New York: Harper & Row, 1993.

Frank, Lisa Tendrich, ed. An Encyclopedia of American Women at War: From the Home Front to the Battlefields. Santa Barbara, CA: ABC-CLIO. LLC, 2013.

Freeman, Douglas Southall. Lee's Lieutenants. 3 vols. New York: Scribner's Sons, 1942.

_____ ed. Lee's Dispatches: Unpublished Letters of General Robert E. Lee to Jefferson Davis and the War Department of The Confederate States of America, 1862-1865. New York: G. P. Putnam's sons, 1957.

Frye, Dennis E. 12th Virginia Cavalry. Lynchburg, Virginia: H. E. Howard, 1988.

Furgurson, Ernest B. Freedom Rising: Washington in the Civil War. New York: Vintage Books, a Division of Random House, 2005.

Gallaher, DeWitt Clinton. A Diary Depicting the Experiences of Dewitt Clinton Gallaher in the War Between the States While Serving in the Confederate Army. 1961.

Gallagher, Gary W., ed. Struggle for the Shenandoah: Essays on the 1864 Valley Campaign. Kent, Ohio: Kent State University Press, 1991.

_____ The Shenandoah Valley Campaign of 1864. Chapel Hill, North Carolina: UNC Press, 2006.

_____ The Wilderness Campaign. Chapel Hill, North Carolina: UNC Press, 1997.

Garnett, Theodore Stanford. Riding With Stuart: Reminiscenses of an Aide-de-Camp

Robert J. Trout, ed., Shippensburg, Pennsylvania: White Mane Publishing Company, 1994.

Gilmor, Harry. Four Years in the Saddle. New York: Harper & Brothers, 1866.

Glatthaar, Joseph T. General Lee's Army: From Victory to Collapse. New York: Free Press, Simon and Shuster, 2008.

Gordon, John Brown. Reminiscences of the Civil War. New York: Charles Scribmer's Sons, 1904.

Graham, W. A. The Custer Myth: A source Book of Custeriana. Harrisburg, PA: Stackpole, 1953.

Greene, A. Wilson. The Second Battle of Manassas. National Park Service Civil War Series. Eastern National, 2006.

Grimsley, Daniel Amon. Battles in Culpeper County, Virginia, 1861-1865: And other Articles. Culpeper, Virginia: Raleigh Travers Green, 1900. vol. 21.

Gwin, Mimrose C., ed. A Woman's Civil War: A Diary with Reminiscences of the War, From March 1862 by Cornelia Peake McDonald (Author). Wisconsin Studies in Autobiography.

Haden, B. J. Reminiscences of J. E. B. Stuart's Cavalry. Palmyra, Virginia: Progress Publishing Company, 1993.

Hall, Clark B. "The Battle of Brandy Station." Civil War Times Illustrated. (May/June 1990).

Hamilton, John B., ed. The Journal of the American Medical Association. Chicago, 1898.

Hanson, Joseph Mills. Cavalry Journal, vol. XLIII:182, 1934.

_____ Dictionary of American Biography, Dumas Malone, ed. 20 vols. New York: Scribner & Sons, 1935.

Harrell, Roger H. The 2nd North Carolina Cavalry. Jefferson, North Carolina: McFarland and Company Publishers, 2004.

Harris, Samuel. Personal Reminiscences of Samuel Harris. (1897). Elk Grove Village, Illinois: Kessinger Publishing Company, 2008.

Hartley, Chris J. Stuart's Tarheels: James B. Gordon and His North Carolina Cavalry. Baltimore: Butternut and Blue, 1996.

Haselberger, Frances. "General Rosser's Raid on the New Creek Depot," West Virginia History: a Quarterly Magazine, XXVI, No. 2, January, 1956.

Hatch, Thom. The Custer Companion: A Comprehensive Guide to the Life of George Armstrong Custer and the Plains Indian Wars. Mechanicsburg, Pennsylvania: Stackpole Books, 2002.

Hatch, Tom. Clashes of Cavalry. Mechanicsburg, PA: Stackpole Books, 2001.

Hattaway, Herman and Archer Jones. How the North Won. Chicago: University of Illinois Press, 1991.

Heatwole, John L. The Burning: Sheridan in the Shenandoah Valley. Charlottesville, Virginia: Rockbridge Publishing, 1998.

Heitman, Francis B. Historical Register and Dictionary of the United States Army vol.1. Washington, D. C.: Washington, Government Printing Office, 1903.

Henderson, William D. The Road To Bristoe Station. Lynchburg, Va: H. E. Howard, Inc., 1987.

Hennessy, John J. Return to Bull Run: The Campaign and Battle of Second Manassas. Norman, Oklahoma: University of Oklahoma Press, 1993.

Herbert, Walter H. Fighting Joe Hooker. Lincoln, NE: University of Nebraska Press, 1999.

Higginson, Henry Lee and Bliss Perry. Life and Letters of Henry Lee Higginson. Boston: The Atlantic Monthly Press, 1921.

Hopkins, Luther W. From Bull Run to Appomattox: A Boy's View (Baltimore: Fleet-McGinley Company, 1908.

Horn, John. The Petersburg Campaign; The Destruction of the Weldon Railroad; Deep Bottom, Globe Tavern and Reams Station; August 14 25, 1864. Lynchburg, Virginia: H. E. Howard, Inc., 1991.

Hubart, Lt. Robert T., Jr., Thomas P. Nanzig, ed. The Civil War Memoirs of a Virginia Cavalryman. Tuscaloosa: The University of Alabama Press, 2007.

Hubbell, Jay B., ed. "The War Diary of John Esten Cooke." The Journal of Southern History, vol. 7, No. 4.

Humphreys, Andrew A. The Virginia Campaign of 1864 and 1865: The Army of the Potomac and the Army of the James. Reprint. New York: Da Capo Press, 1995.

Hunter, Alexander. Johnny Reb and Billy Yank. New York: The Neale Publishing Company, 1905.

Hutton, Paul Andrew, ed. The Custer Reader. Lincoln, Nebraska: The University of Nebraska Press, 1992.

Johnson, John Lipscomb, ed., The University Memorial; Biographical Sketches of Alumni Who Fell in the Confederate War, Pate biography by Robert S. Morgan, Baltimore: Turnbull Brothers,1871.

Johnston, Frontis W., The Papers of Zebulon Baird Vance. Vol 1. Raleigh, North Carolina: State Department of Archives and History, 1963.

Jones, J. William. Personal Reminiscences, Anecdotes, and Letters of Gen. Robert E. Lee. New York: D. Appleton and Company, 1875.

Jones, William, et al, eds. Southern Historical Society Papers.. volumes 1-52. Richmond, Virginia: Southern Historical Society, 1876-1959.

Jones, Wilmer L. Generals in Blue and Gray: Davis's generals. Westport, CT: Praeger Publishers, 2004.

Kavanagh, Martin. The Assiniborne Basin: A Social Study of Discovery, Exploration and Settlement. Manitoba: Canada: Manitoba Historical Society, 2007.

Keller, S. Roger. Riding with Rosser. Shippensburg, Pennsylvania: Burd Street Press, 1997.

Kennedy, Frances H., ed. The Civil War Battlefield Guide, Second Edition. New York: Houghton-Mifflin Company, 1998.

Keys, Thomas Bland. Tarheel Cossack: W. P. Roberts, Youngest Confederate General. Orlando, Florida. 1983.

Kidd, J. H. Personal Recollections of a Cavalryman Riding with Custer's Michigan Cavalry Brigade. Ionia, Michigan: Sentinel Printing Company, 1908.

Kirshner, Ralph. The Class of 1861: Custer, Ames, and Their Classmates after West Point. Carbondale and Edwardsville, Illinois: Southern Illinois University Press, 1999.

Krick, Robert K. Lee's Colonels: A Biographical Register of the Field Officers of the Army of Northern Virginia. Dayton, Ohio: Morningside Press, 1992.

_____ The American Civil War: The War in the East 1863-1865. Great Britain: Osprey Publishing, 2001.

_____ The Smoothbore Volley That Doomed the Confederacy. Baton Rouge, Louisiana: LSU Press, 2002.

Labree, Ben, ed., Campfires of the Confederacy. General Thomas L. Rosser, "Capture of Cattle."Louisville, Kentucky: Courier Journal Job Printing Co., 1898.

LaFantasie, Glenn W. Twilight at Little Round Top: July 2, 1863--The Tide Turns at Gettysburg. New York: Wiley, 2007.

John Lamb, "The Confederate Cavalry," Southern Historical Society Papers (SHSP).

Lepa, Jack H. The Shenandoah Valley Campaign of 1864. Jefferson, North Carolina: McFarland, 2003.

Longacre, Edward G. The Cavalry at Gettysburg. Lincoln: The University of Nebraska Press, 1993.

_____ Mounted Raids of the Civil War. Lincoln, Nebraska and London: University of Nebraska Press, 1994.

_____ Lincoln's Cavalrymen: A History of the Mounted Forces of the Army of the Potomac. Mechanicsville, Pa: Stackpole Books, 2000.

_____Lee's Cavalrymen, Mechanicsburg, Pennsylvania: Stackpole Books, 2002.

_____ The Cavalry at Appomattox: A Tactical Study of Mounted Operations during the Civil War's Climatic Campaign,March 27-April 9, 1865. Mechanicsville, Pennsylvania: Stackpole Books, 2003.

_____ Fitz Lee: A Military Biography of Major General Fitzhugh Lee, C.S.A. Cambridge, Massachusetts: Da Capo Press, 2005.

_____ Pickett: Leader of the Charge. Shippensburg, Pennsylvania: White Mane Publishing Company, 1995.

_____ Gentleman and Soldier: A Biography of Wade Hampton III. Lincoln, NE: University of Nebraska Press, 2003.

Longstreet, Helen D. Lee and Longstreet At High Tide: Gettysburg in the Light of the Official Records. Gainesville, Georgia: Published by Helen D. Longstreet, 1904.

Lubetkin, M. John. Jay Cooke's Gamble: The Northern Pacific Railroad, The Sioux, and The Panic of 1873. Norman, Oklahoma: University of Oklahoma Press, 2006.

_____ "Thomas L. Rosser and The Yellowstone Surveying Expedition of 1873." North Dakota History Magazine: A Journal of the Northern Plains. Volume 70, No. 3, 2003.

Monaghan, Jay. Custer: The Life of George Armstrong Custer (Lincoln: University of Nebraska Press, 1971).

Manarin, Louis H., North Carolina Troops, 1861-1865, A Roster. Raleigh, North Carolina: State Division of Archives and History, 1989.

Martin, David G. The Peninsula Campaign. Conshohocken, PA: Combined Books, 1992.

Maxwell, Jerry H. The Perfect Lion: The Life and Death of Confederate Artillerist John Pelham. Tuscaloosa, Alabama: University of Alabama Press, 2011.

McCarthy, Michael J. Confederate Waterloo: The Battle of Five Forks, April 1, 1865, and the Controversy that Brought Down a General. El Dorado Hills CA: Savas Beatie, 2017.

McClellan, Major Henry Brainerd. I Rode With Jeb Stuart: The Life and Campaigns of Major General J.E.B. Stuart. Bloomington, Indiana: Indiana University Press, 1981.

McDonald, Cornelia Peake. Mimrose C. Gwin, eds. Woman's Civil War: A Diary with Reminiscences of the War, from March 1862. Madison: University of Wisconsin Press, 1992.

McDonald, William N. A History of the Laurel Brigade. Baltimore and London: The Johns Hopkins University Press, 2002.

McEnany, Brian R. For Brotherhood and Duty: The Civil War History of the West Point Class of 1862. Lexington: The University Press of Kentucky, 2015.

McKim, Randolph Harrison. A Soldier's Recollections. Norwood, Massachusetts: The Plimpton Press, 1921.

McMullen, Glenn L. ed., The Civil War Letters of Dr. Harvey Black. Baltimore: Butternut And Blue, 1995.

Mewborn, Horace. "Herding the Yankee Cattle: The Beefstake Raid, September 14-17, 1864." Blue and Gray Magazine. (Summer 2005).

Miller, William J. Decision at Tom's Brook: George Custer, Thomas Rosser and the Joy of the Fight. El dorado Hills, CA: Savas Beatie, 2016.

Mitchell, Adele H., ed. The Letters of Major General James E. B. Stuart, Stuart-Mosby Historical Society, 1990.

_____ The Letters of John S. Mosby, Stuart-Mosby Historical Society, 1986.

Monaghan, Jay. Custer: The Life of George Armstrong Custer. Lincoln, NE: University of Nebraska Press, 1959.

Moon, George Edward. Wagon Tracks. Bloomington, IN: Trafford Publishing, 2014.

Moore, Frank, ed. The Rebellion Record: A Diary of American Events. New York: D. Van Nostrand, 1865.

Myers, Frank M. The Comanches: A History of White's Battalion, Virginia Cavalry.

Marietta, Georgia: Continental Book Company, 1956.

Nanzig, Thomas P. Lt. Robert T. Hubart, Jr.,The Civil War Memoirs of a Virginia Cavalryman. Tuscaloosa, Alabama: The University of Alabama Press, 2007.

_____ 3rd Virginia Cavalry. Lynchburg, Virginia: H. E. Howard, Inc., 1989.

Neese, George M. Three Years in the Confederate Horse Artillery (New York: The Neale Publishing Company, 1911.

Nichols, James L. General Fitzhugh Lee: A Biography. Virginia Battles and Leadership Series. Lynchburg, Virginia: H. E. Howard, Inc., 1989.

Nofi, Albert A. The Civil War Treasury. Boston: Da Capo Press,1992.

Noyalas, Jonathan A. The Battle of Cedar Creek: Victory from the Jaws of Defeat. Charleston, S. C.: History Press, 2009.

Owen, William Miller. In Camp and Battle with the Washington Artillery of New Orleans. Baton Rouge: Louisiana State University Press, 1999.

Palmer, Oscar C. "Father Rode with Sheridan; Reminiscences of Oscar C. Palmer As A Cavalryman in Company B, 8th N. Y. Volunteer Cavalry." Petersburg, Virginia.: Petersburg National Battlefield, n.d.

Parker, William L. General James Dearing, CSA. Lynchburg, VA: H. E. Howard, 1990.

Pfanz, Donald C. The Petersburg Campaign: Abraham Lincoln at City Point, March 20 April 9, 1865. Lynchburg, Va: H. E. Howard, Inc., 1989.

Phillips, Larissa. Women Civil War Spies of the Confederacy. New York: Rosen Publishing Group, Inc., 2004.

Piatt,Donn. General George H. Thomas: A Critical Biography. Cincinnati: Ohio: Robert Clarke & Company, 1893.

Pickett, La Salle Corbell (Mrs. George E.). Pickett and His Men. Atlanta: Foote and Davies, 1899.

Poland, Charles Preston, Jr. The Glories of War: Small Battles and Early Heroes of 1861. Bloomington, Indiana: Author House, 2006.

Power, J. Tracy. Lee's Miserables: Life in the Army of Northern Virginia from the Wilderness to Appomattox. Chapel Hill: University of North Carolina Press, 1998.

Rafuse, Ethan S. Rafuse. McClellan's War: The Failure of Moderation in the Struggle for the Union, Bloomington and Indianapolis, Indiana: Indiana University Press 2005.

Ramage, James A. Gray Ghost. Lexington, Kentucky: University of Kentucky Press, 1999.

Rawle, William Brook, William E. Miller, James W. McCorkell, Andrew J. Speese, and John C. Hunterson (Regimental History Committee). History of the Third Pennsylvania Cavalry (Sixtieth Regiment Pennsylvania Volunteers) in the American Civil War, 1861-1865. Philadelphia: Franklin Publishing Company, 1905.

Rea, D. B. "Cavalry Incidents of the Maryland Campaign." The Maine Bugle. Campaign II. Rockland, Maine, April, 1895.

Renz, Louis Tuck. The History of the Northern Pacific Railroad. Fairfield, Washington: Ye Galleon Press, 1980.

Rhea, Gordon C. To The North Anna River: Grant and Lee, May 13-24, 1864. Baton Rouge, Louisiana: LSU Press, 2000.

_____ The Battle of the Wilderness, May 5-6. Baton Rouge, Louisiana: LSU Press, 2004.

Rhodes, Robert Hunt. All For The Union: Diary of Elisha Hunt Rhodes. New York: Orion Books, 1991.

Robertson, James I., Jr., Stonewall Jackson: The Man, The Soldier, The Legend. New York: Simon and Schuster McMillan, 1997.

Rosenberg, Bruce A. "Custer and the Epic of Defeat." The Journal of American Folklore, vol. 88, No. 348.

Rosser, General Thomas L. Addresses of Gen'l T. L. Rosser at the Seventh Annual Reunion, Association of the Maryland Line, Baltimore, February 22, 1889 & Staunton, Virginia, June 3, 1889. New York: L. A. Williams Printing Company, 1889.

_____ Reminiscences, Rosser Papers, Special Collections Library, UVA, Charlottesville, VA.

_____ Autobiographical Sketch, Rosser Papers, Special Collections Library, UVA, Charlottesville, VA.

Rosser, Elizabeth Winston Rosser. Housekeeper's and Mother's Manual. Richmond: Everett Waddey Company, 1895.

Savage, Douglas. The Last Years of Robert E. Lee: From Gettysburg to Lexington. New York: Rowman and Littlefield, 2016.

Schaff, Morris. "The Spirit of Old West Point, 1858-1862," Boston: Houghton, Mifflin, 1907.

Sears, Stephen W. To The Gates of Richmond: The Peninsula Campaign. New York: Ticknor & Fields, 1992.

_____ Landscape Turned Red: The Battle of Antietam. New York: Houghton Mifflin, 1983.

_____ The Civil War Papers of George B. McClellan: Selected Correspondence1860-1865. New York, New York: Da Capo Press, 1992.

_____ Gettysburg. New York: Houghton Mifflin Company, 2003.

Sergent, Mary Elizabeth. "Classmates Divided." American Heritage Magazine, February, 1958, vol. 9, Issue 2.

_____They Lie Forgotten: The United States Military Academy, 1856-1861. Middletown, New York: The Prior King Press, 1986.

Sheridan, Phil. Personal Memoirs. 2 Vols. New York: Charles L. Webster and Company, 1888.

Simon, John Y., ed. The Papers of Ulysses S. Grant. Carbondale and Edwardsville: Southern Illinois University Press, 1967.

_____ John Y. Simon, Michael E. Stevens, eds., New Perspectives on the Civil War: Myths and Realities of the National Conflict. New York: Roman and Littlefield, 1998.

Simpson, Brooks D. The Civil War in the East: Struggle, Stalemate, and Victory. Santa Barbara, CA: Praeger Publishing, 2011.

Sommers, Richard J. Richmond Redeemed: The Siege at Petersburg. Garden City, New York: Doubleday & Company, Inc., 1981.

Starr, Stephen Z. The Union Cavalry in the Civil War. 3 Vols. Baton Rouge, La: LSU Press, 1979-1985.

Stedman, Charles M. "Battle at Ream's Station," R. A, Brock, ed. Richmond, Virginia: Southern Historical Society Papers, 1891. Vol. 19.

Steer, Edward. The Wilderness Campaign. New York: Bonanza Books, 1960.

Stiles, Robert. Four Years Under Marse Robert. New York: The Neale Publishing Company, 1904.

Suderow, Bryce A. "Confederate Strengths & Losses from March 25-April 9, 1865," May, 1987; revised September 29, 1991, Washington, D.C.

Swank, Walbrook D. Ed. Battle of Trevilian Station: The Civil War's Greatest and Bloodiest All Cavalry Battle, with Eyewitness Memoirs. Civil War Heritage, vol. 4. Shippensburg, Pennsylvania: White Mane Publishing Company, 2007.

The War of the Rebellion: A Compilation of the Official Records of the Union and Confederate Armies. 70 Volumes. 128 Parts and Atlas. Washington, D.C.: Government Printing Office, 1880-1901.

Thomas, Emory M. Bold Dragoon: Life of J.E.B. Stuart. New York: Vintage Books, 1988.

_____ Robert E. Lee: A Biography. London: W. W. Norton and Company, 1995.

Thomason, John William. Jeb Stuart. New York: Charles Scribner's Sons, 1929.

Thomsen, Brian M., ed. The Civil War Memoirs of Ulysses S. Grant. New York: Tom Doherty Associates, 2002.

Tobie, Edward P. History of the First Maine Cavalry, 1861-1865. Boston: Press of Emery & Hughes, 1887.

Torrence, Clayton, ed., Winston of Virginia and Allied Families. Richmond: Whittet & Shepperson, 1927.

Trout, Robert J. Galloping Thunder: The Story of the Stuart Horse Artillery Battalion. Mechanicsville, Pennsylvania: Stackpole Books, 2002.

_____ With Pen and Saber: The Letters and Diaries of J.E.B. Stuart's Staff Officers (Mechanicsburg, PA: Stackpole Books, 1995), 182-83.

Trudeau, Noah Andre. The Last Citadel: Petersburg, Virginia, June 1864-April 1865. New York: Little, Brown & Company, 1991.

Tucker, Glenn. Lee and Longstreet At Gettysburg. New York: The Bobbs-Merrill Company, 1868.

Tucker, Spencer C. ed., American Civil War: The Definitive Encyclopedia and Document Collection. Santa Barbara, CA: ABC-CLIO, LLC, 2013.

Tyler, Lyon G. Editor-in-Chief. Men of Mark in Virginia: A Collection of Biographies of The Leading Men of the State. Volume I. Washington, D. C.: Men of Mark Publishing Company, 1906.

Urwin, Gregory J. W. Custer Victorious: The Civil War Battles of General George Armstrong Custer. Lincoln, Nebraska: University of Nebraska Press, 1990.

Venter, Bruce M. "Hancock the (Not So) Superb: The Second Battle of Reams' Station, August 25, 1864." Blue and Gray Magazine. (Winter 2007).

Vogtsberger, Margaret Ann. The Dulany's of Welbourne. Berryville, Virginia: Rockbridge Publishing, 1195.

Walker, C. Irvine Walker. The Life of Lieutenant General Richard Heron Anderson of the   Confederate States Army. Charleston, South Carolina: Art Publishing Company,1917.

Warner, Ezra J. Generals in Blue. Generals in Blue: Lives of the Union Commanders. Baton Rouge: LSU Press, 1995.

Watkins, Raymond W. The Hicksford Raid. The Greensville Historical Society, April 1978.

Welsh, Jack Walsh, M. D. Confederate Generals Medical Histories. Kent, Ohio: Kent State University Press, 1995.

Wellman, Manly Wade. Giant in Gray:A Biography of Wade Hampton. New York: Charles Scribner's Sons, Inc., 1949.

Wells, Charles. The Memoirs of Colonel John S. Mosby. Boston: Little, Brown, and Company, 1917.

Wells, Edward L. Hampton and His Cavalry in '64. Richmond, Va.: B. F. Johnston Publishing Company, 1899.

Wert, Jeffrey D. General James Longstreet: The Confederacy's Most Controversial Soldier. New York: Simon & Schuster, 1993.

_____ From Winchester to Cedar Creek: The Shenandoah Campaign of 1864. New York: Simon & Schuster, 1997.

_____ Cavalryman of the Lost Cause: A Biography of J.E.B. Stuart. New York: Simon & Schuster, 2008.

_____ The Sword of Lincoln: The Army of the Potomac. New York: Simon and Schuster, 2005.

Wilson, James Harrison. Under The Old Flag. New York: D. Appleton and Company, 1912.

Wilson, William Lyne. A Borderline Confederate. Pittsburg: University of Pittsburgh Press, 1962. Edited by Festus P. Summers.

Wise, Jennings Cropper, The Long Arm of Lee: Bull Run to Fredricksburg. Lynchburg: J. P. Bell Company, 1915.

Wise, John. End of An Era. New York: Houghton, Mifflin and Company, 1902.

Wittenberg, Eric J. The Union Cavalry Comes of Age: Hartwood Church to Brandy Station, 1863. Washington, D.C.: Potomac Books, 2003.

_____ Glory Enough For All: Sheridan's Second Raid and The Battle of Trevilian Station. Washington, D. C.: Brassey's, Inc., 2002.

_____ The Battle of Brandy Station: North America's Largest Cavalry Battle. Charleston, SC: The History Press, 2010.

Index

About the Author

Sheridan R. Barringer retired from NASA where he worked as a mechanical engineer and project manager at Langley Research Center for 37 years. He graduated from Virginia Tech in mechanical engineering in 1965. He is the author of Fighting for General Lee: General Rufus Barringer and The North Carolina Cavalry Brigade about his ancestor for which he won the Douglas Southall Freeman Best Southern History Book Award and the North Carolina Society of Historians History Book Award in 2016. Future projects include biographies of noted cavalry figures Thomas Taylor Munford and Williams C. Wickham. He and his wife Pam have two grown children and reside in Virginia.

CPSIA information can be obtained
at www.ICGtesting.com
Printed in the USA
BVHW050132090919

557747BV00002B/2/P